MW00773878

INDUSTRIAL RELATIONS RESEARCH

ASSOCIATION SERIES

Going Public
The Role of Labor-Management Relations in Delivering Quality Government Services

EDITED BY

Jonathan Brock and David B. Lipsky

First Edition

ISBN 0-913447-86-2

Price: $29.95

INDUSTRIAL RELATIONS RESEARCH ASSOCIATION SERIES:
Proceedings of the Annual Meeting
Annual Research Volume
IRRA 2002 Membership Directory (published every four years)
IRRA Newsletter (published quarterly)
Perspectives on Work (published biannually)

Inquiries and other communications regarding membership, meetings, publications, and general affairs of the Association, as well as notice of address changes, should be addressed to the IRRA National Office.

INDUSTRIAL RELATIONS RESEARCH ASSOCIATION
University of Illinois at Urbana-Champaign
121 Labor & Industrial Relations Bldg.
504 East Armory Ave.
Champaign, IL 61820
Telephone: 217/333-0072   Fax: 217/265-5130
Internet: www.irra.uiuc.edu   E-mail: irra@uiuc.edu

To Terry Thomason
1950–2002

CONTENTS

v

Public Sector Collective Bargaining and the Imperative for Service Delivery: An Overview

JONATHAN BROCK
University of Washington

DAVID B. LIPSKY
Cornell University

In the last 15 years, significant forces have affected public sector labor-management relations in the United States. The primary forces have pressed for increased efficiency and improved services—in terms of both quality and delivery. Other forces, however, have pressed for a smaller government presence and for privatization of many government responsibilities. Similar forces have affected other industrialized countries.

Lorenzo Bordogna examines this comparison with regard to non-U.S. industrialized countries in the first chapter of this volume, noting that most other industrialized countries started out with a larger public sector and more state-run enterprises, greater union density, more-pervasive use of participative models, and broader labor rights. He describes efforts in many of those countries to reduce the influence and independence of collective bargaining, often by shifting wage-setting authority to the employer or by increasing the role of centralized settlements. His basic conclusion is that pressures on governments are becoming similar to pressures in the private sector: to provide better services, reduce employment, improve applications of information technology, and "privatize" or subcontract work.

Privatization is usually viewed in the United States as a serious threat to public sector unions. Yet even though there was considerable interest in privatization during the 1990s, public sector employment actually grew overall during that period. Marick Masters and Robert Albright

1

inform us in their chapter that there was a decline in federal employment, but that it was not specifically the result of privatization. Bipartisan support for a smaller federal government during the Clinton administration led to the federal decrease, but it was outweighed by state and local sector growth.

Terry Thomason and John Burton's research indicates that widespread interest in privatization did not on balance affect U.S. public sector employment growth and union density during the past two decades. In their chapter they show that both public sector employment and public sector union membership grew by 25 percent over the period 1983–2002 and that, consequently, union density (the proportion of employees who are union members) remained relatively stable over this period, within the range of 36–39 percent. They also show, however, that privatization has had some significant effects in several important public sector functions, including health care and education. In the hospital industry, for example, the public share of employment declined from about 25 percent to about 13 percent over the past 20 years. The public share of employment in education also declined, by about six percentage points. Privatization apparently led to lower union density in hospitals, but in education it did not. Because in the private sector union density steadily declined over the past 20 years, the importance of public sector unions as a segment of organized labor has steadily increased. In 2002 public sector union membership constituted over 46 percent of total union membership in the United States.

These pressures and patterns have created some responses that are unique to the United States. One has been the formation of collaborative, service-oriented relationships, which have shown substantial evidence of reducing costs, improving service, improving the quality of work life, and markedly changing the nature of the bargaining relationship. Collaboration represents a potential answer to pressures for increased efficiency and improved service quality, even though it does not significantly address the more political or ideological calls for less government and more privatization. Although still very much the exception, service-focused, cooperative relationships show promise for improving labor-management relations and the climate surrounding the role of unions in the public workplace. They thus represent a significant and useful response to the pressures on government and on unions of public employees. Such relationships are still new enough, however, that it is difficult to judge their efficacy or to predict the factors that might sustain them and help them succeed.

The basic premise of such relationships is not new. Effective labor-management interaction requires a relationship that goes beyond contract negotiation and grievance handling and allows the parties to solve problems of mutual importance that occur between bargaining rounds. Even early works such as Slichter, Healy, and Livernash recognized the importance of informal dealings in oiling the labor-management relationship and promoting problem solving (Slichter, Healy, and Livernash 1960:841–78). Many of the more-traditional relationships that have led to respectful and productive interaction and have produced effective service and work-life improvements have done so without moving to an explicitly cooperative model, however. Both explicit and implicit cooperative relationships appear to require quality leadership, mutual trust and respect, stability over time, recognition of common interests, and an atmosphere that acknowledges the legitimacy of differing opinions.

Given the nearly universal pressures on public employees and public employee unions to improve the efficiency and quality of public services, this volume focuses principally on the growing and promising practice of cooperative relationships. It is part of an ongoing IRRA series on public sector employment relations.[1] Our volume seeks to explore the prospects, ingredients, and key issues surrounding this nontraditional approach to labor-management relations. It also explores other important issues related to the state of public sector labor relations, such as union density and the inclusion of supervisors in bargaining units—the latter being a long-standing topic of debate in the field.

Most of the authors in this volume share the view that the expanded use of more-collaborative, service-oriented approaches to public sector labor-management relations would be valuable. As the practice expands and matures, additional research will be required to help determine its specific value and effects. The parties will need to learn to understand the ingredients associated with successful collaborative relationships, the effects of political and economic pressure on them, the prospects for such relationships to weather changes in leadership, and the effect of collaboration on their roles as advocates. We hope this volume serves to stimulate research on this important phenomenon.

For now, it appears that, while cooperative relationships are difficult to initiate, they do indeed both contribute to the quality of services received by the public and enhance employee satisfaction. Evidence in this volume also suggests that cooperation enhances the value of the union to employees and makes the jobs of union leaders more interesting. Cooperation also leads to increased flexibility, usually benefiting all parties, and reduces the cost per unit of service. It can also help to avert layoffs, even as productivity and quality improve, and under the right circumstances it can confer political benefits to both management and union leaders. But, as several authors in this volume note, cooperation entails risk and risk taking by both parties.

Public Sector Labor-Management Relations

Collective bargaining in the public sector grew dramatically in the 1960s and early 1970s. During that period many states passed statutes supporting the right of public sector employees to join unions and engage in collective bargaining. These statutes significantly mirrored statutes governing the private sector, but strikes were generally prohibited and impasse procedures differed across jurisdictions. From the start it was widely recognized that labor-management relations in the public sector existed in an environment that was inherently political. As Wellington and Winter wrote, "Collective bargaining by public employees and the political process cannot be separated. The costs of such bargaining, therefore, cannot be fully measured without taking into account the impact on the allocation of political power in the typical [jurisdiction]" (Wellington and Winter 1971:31). Although private sector unions and employers are certainly involved in the political process (they are often active participants in lobbying and election campaigns, for example), their involvement is vastly different from that of public sector unions and employers. In the public sector, unions not only engage in lobbying activities and campaigns for elected officials, they typically deal with these officials across the bargaining table as well.

The politics of public sector bargaining significantly affected the nature of the rights granted to unions, the character of union organizing, the strategies of contract negotiation, and other factors. The difference between the bargaining dynamic in the public sector and the private sector is more significant than those who created most public sector bargaining statutes generally contemplated (Kheel 1999:105–06).

Public sector bargaining statutes reflect one major difference between the public and private sectors. Public sector statutes in most jurisdictions established boards or commissions that have responsibility for four basic activities: resolving representation issues, deciding improper practices, managing conciliation and dispute resolution procedures, and handling other regulatory matters. In most segments of the private sector, however—those governed by the Taft-Hartley Act—the responsibility for representation issues and improper practices is separated from dispute resolution and conciliation procedures: the former resides in the National Labor Relations Board (NLRB), while the latter resides largely in the Federal Mediation and Conciliation Service (FMCS).

Regrettably, because little attention has been paid to state boards and commissions in the recent research literature, we know relatively little about their current status and effectiveness or their influence on the practice of labor-management relations within and beyond their jurisdictions. It is ironic that so little is known because, collectively, state boards and commissions monitor the rights of almost as many represented workers as does the NLRB. Leaders of boards and commissions have reported that they have been burdened by both increases in workload and reductions in resources and constrained by political factors that influence the appointment of their members. Board and commission representatives tell a story of significant staff turnover and great difficulty in performing their functions effectively.[2]

Martin Malin points out, in his chapter on public sector labor law and labor-management cooperation, that labor relations in the public sector has a tradition of being highly litigious and process oriented. In a typical relationship, the parties devote significant amounts of time to arguments over alleged violations of their respective rights and disputes over the scope of bargaining. The dominant activities in many (but certainly not all) traditional relationships are arguments between the parties over issues that ultimately need to be resolved in legal forums (boards, commissions, and courts) or in other settings (arbitration hearings, regulatory agencies) that rely on lawyers and other specialists who are not involved in service delivery and do not have to live with the outcomes of these proceedings.

Malin, Masters and Albright, and Charles Kerchner all say that persistent arguments over substantive and procedural rights are clearly not productive. (By implication, other contributors to this volume make the same point.) They suggest that expanding the scope of the parties' ongoing discussions and focusing greater attention on the quality of work life would help foster both constructive relationships and better public services. Malin notes that in authentic collaborative relationships most of the interactions between the parties are devoted to improving the quality of service delivery, reducing the costs of delivery, and improving the quality of work life.

Requirements of a Collaborative Relationship

The key to an effective collaborative relationship is that both parties become aware of, and assume responsibility for, issues that are traditionally the responsibility of only one of them. In these relationships public sector employers focus more on the quality of their employees' work life and public sector unions focus more on improving the quality of public services. If the parties are willing to move in these directions, then even within the current restrictive statutory framework they can overcome wasteful legal disputes that sour their relationships. In fact, even in traditional relationships that are free of such wasteful disputes, the evidence presented by the authors in this volume suggests that a collaborative, service-oriented approach can enhance the parties' relationships and assist in carrying out their respective responsibilities.

Malin makes a modest proposal: he suggests that requiring consultation between the parties on issues normally considered to be beyond the scope of bargaining would help solve service-delivery and workplace problems and reduce the number of disputes ending up in legal forums. Kerchner and Malin believe that expanding the scope of the discussions between the parties would have desirable effects. Nearly all current cooperative relationships—in which the scope of discussions is by definition broad—exist under preexisting statutory frameworks in which the formal scope of bargaining is narrow. A legal regime that is more encouraging and protective of cooperation—such as that proposed by Malin or Kerchner—might foster the acceptance, diffusion, and sustainability of these relationships.[3]

If the parties confine their interactions to those required by statute, they are unlikely to be able to deal jointly and effectively with issues affecting either the delivery of services or the quality of work life. They are more likely to become entrapped in the arcane and often absurd disputes Malin documents. In traditional relationships in which the parties are able to develop informal channels of communication based on mutual trust, they have a better chance of dealing with more fundamental issues. They would seem to have an even greater chance in a more complete form of cooperative relations. When teachers are precluded from participating in curriculum discussions, Kerchner would argue, the result is bound to be substandard and impractical. When sanitation truck drivers and mechanics are not consulted about mechanization and new equipment purchases, the result will likewise be inadequate. When social workers cannot offer advice to agency managers about new policy issues or a new information system, the treatment of families in crisis and the flow of information within the agency are likely to be weakened. When well-trained professionals are not consulted by their managers, they are likely to feel that they are not respected and to have their dignity undermined.

The lack of consultation and cooperation will lead to increasing levels of frustration as governments become increasingly dependent on "knowledge workers" (to use Peter Drucker's well-known term).

If the parties want to broaden the scope of their discussions beyond strict statutory requirements, they must be willing to take risks and do the difficult work of building and maintaining trust. Only when each party is willing to learn about the other's internal culture and leadership pressures can ways be found to expand their interactions. Both public sector managers and union leaders are often risk-averse, however, and either unable or unwilling to broaden their perspectives beyond a traditional definition of their roles and responsibilities. Perhaps it is not surprising, then, that developing cooperative and trusting relationships is such a difficult undertaking. Moreover, even when management and union leaders are able to overcome the barriers to developing cooperative relationships, turnover in the leadership ranks can obliterate the gains they have made. Union and management officials sometimes become champions of innovations in labor-management relations, but in these cases, when the champion leaves the organization, the innovation often dies. When union and management leaders successfully reach agreements that incorporate innovative practices, their successors may abandon those agreements.[4] Thus, adopting labor-management cooperation is a difficult challenge, but institutionalizing the practice is even more so.

What can unions and employers do to institutionalize the practice of labor-management cooperation? The chapters in this volume, as well as our own professional experiences, suggest that several steps can be taken. Institutionalization usually requires a concerted effort to change the culture of the relationship. It may help, for example, if a new program is embedded in the collective bargaining contract. Also useful is the commitment of the parties to invest in joint education and training programs. The more fully employees and managers understand the process of collaboration, including the risks involved, the greater the likelihood of success. Institutionalization ultimately depends on acceptance of the new approach by all stakeholders: rank and file union members, first-line supervisors, middle managers, and elected officials. Efforts must be made during transitions to show new leaders, on both sides of the table, the benefits of a collaborative system. Moreover, a communication strategy designed to keep key internal and external stakeholders fully informed is a valuable component of any effort to institutionalize innovative practices.

Labor and management representatives will likely change their attitudes about cooperation if they observe that cooperative relationships
produce positive results, including not only improvements in service
delivery and the quality of work life but also in their own relationships
with one another. Mayors and governors appear to be swayed by service
results that help them do their jobs and maintain political capital. Positive results will then probably lead to greater commitment to cooperative
systems. Sonia Ospina and Allon Yaroni, in their chapter on the changing
role of labor and management leaders, describe the skills leaders need to
sustain an effective relationship in this new mode. They note that union
leaders who seem to be successful have more involvement with budgets
and systems, and management leaders who seem to be successful deal
more effectively with human and emotional issues in the workplace.
Developing the reciprocal responsibilities required in cooperative relationships results from a conscious effort to implement a joint decision-
making structure and to avoid the legalistic approach Malin decries.

Government Support versus Government Barriers

Although the steps just described may help sustain an innovation, it is
less clear how a successful collaborative system can be diffused from one
location to others. Statutory changes of the type proposed by Malin
might help, but it is clearly difficult to achieve the passage of new public
sector bargaining laws. Only a couple of states have done so recently. In
March 2003, New Mexico passed a law reinstating collective bargaining
rights for teachers and other public employees; the previous public
employee bargaining law had expired under a sunset provision in 1999.[5]
Also in 2003, the State of Washington passed a law that allows state employees to bargain over wages, hours, and other terms and conditions of
employment but at the same time liberalizes the possibilities for contracting out.[6]

At the federal level, though, recent history has been different. The
Clinton administration adopted the concept of labor-management cooperation and the president issued Executive Order 12871 in 1993, establishing the National Partnership Council (NPC) and "mandating that
federal agency and department heads partner with their unions to improve government service and performance" (Clinton 1993). Masters
and Albright observe that this initiative was arguably successful, or at
the very least promising. Immediately after taking office in 2001, however, President Bush revoked Executive Order 12871 and dissolved the
NPC. The new administration steered federal sector labor relations in a

different direction—away from cooperation and toward the restoration of traditional adversarial approaches. Most noteworthy was the Bush administration's insistence that employees of the two new agencies created in the wake of September 11, 2001—the Department of Homeland Security and the Transportation Security Administration—should not have the right to engage in collective bargaining. Many national unions reacted to the Bush administration's new approach by even further reducing the priority they attach to labor-management cooperation in their strategic plans.[7]

The Stance of Umbrella Organizations

How do union and management organizations and government boards and commissions—at the national or state or regional level—view collaboration? Traditional functions in public sector collective bargaining, such as contract negotiations, dispute resolution, and grievance handling, have by-and-large been standardized across many jurisdictions and, accordingly, have become predictable and familiar. Institutions and practices that support these functions have grown up around them. Collaborative practices seem to be more idiosyncratic, at least for now. They are rarely taught or encouraged in venues where most advocates, negotiators, and practitioners receive formal or informal training. As a task force appointed by the Secretary of Labor noted in 1996, law schools, schools of public administration, and other professional graduate institutions seldom teach about the cooperative approach or, indeed, about public sector practices more generally (U.S. Department of Labor 1996). Likewise, cooperation is not usually included as a substantial portion of the agenda of public sector unions or professional association meetings. Fostering cooperative relationships is not generally a part of the responsibilities of state boards and commissions. The budgets for these boards and commissions almost never include funds to foster collaborative relationships even though these bodies are in a prime position to recognize parties that are in need of help in developing new approaches. There are some important exceptions, however—some state boards and, notably, the FMCS will help parties seeking assistance to develop cooperative approaches.

The ranks of both labor and management leaders at the national level typically do not place collaborative relationships high on their agendas. In fact, there is some evidence at the national level of wariness of cooperative approaches. The perceptions and attitudes of the leaders of these umbrella organizations affect the willingness and preparation of local labor and management leaders to attempt a cooperative approach.

The national and international unions in the United States that have significant public sector representation showed some interest in promoting the collaborative approach during the mid-1990s, but most have omitted it from their strategic priorities since then. Although there are important exceptions, many local and national leaders on both sides do not even consider it a viable choice for dealing with the pressures and changes they are experiencing. A strong lore exists that labor-management cooperation frequently results in betrayal or embarrassment (in the form of layoffs, for example, or changes in authority relationships). Mutual trust is a necessary ingredient for sustaining cooperative relationships, but trust is much harder to achieve and sustain than such traditional practices as the periodic renegotiation of new contracts and the arbitration of unresolved grievances. As a result most national unions in the United States give priority to sustaining current membership levels, organizing nonmembers, and engaging in political activity as methods of advancing the status of their unions and attach a much lower priority to the promotion of labor-management cooperation. The major national-level management associations have also not expressed strong support for labor-management cooperation. Although there is serious interest at the top levels of the International Personnel Management Association and some support among the staff of several other management organizations, there is no evidence that the senior leaders of most management organizations are champions of cooperation. Is there hope for labor-management cooperation if the leaders of the national unions and management associations do not attach a high priority to it?

Evidence in this volume, as well as in the 1996 report of the Secretary of Labor's Task Force (U.S. DOL 1996), shows that adopting labor-management cooperation is almost always a local decision. Such a move is generally made only after the occurrence of a crisis, often accompanied by a change in local leadership, when a non-confrontational approach has more immediate appeal. The key decision makers are the chief executives and elected officials of schools, cities, counties, and other jurisdictions, on the one hand, and local union leaders and their constituents, on the other. So the support of national-level organizations might be helpful with the diffusion of such relationships, but it does not appear to be essential to their establishment or effectiveness.

There have been instances, however, when a national union, such as the American Federation of State, County and Municipal Employees or the Service Employees International Union, has provided assistance to local affiliates seeking to reform their relationship with their management counterparts. These interventions by the national unions have usually had beneficial effects on local relationships. At the federal level, the National Treasury Employees' Union (NTEU) and the American Federation of Government Employees have also encouraged cooperative approaches. Masters and Albright describe how the major unions representing federal employees actively embraced labor-management cooperation during the Clinton administration.

Likewise, in those cases where public employee relations commissions and boards or public sector management associations have encouraged collaborative relationships, their support appears to have made a difference, particularly in relationships characterized by frequent disputes and impasses. The role these activist boards and the FMCS have played in encouraging cooperative relationships demonstrates the value of intervention and support services by a neutral agency.

In the field of education, both major teacher unions—the American Federation of Teachers (AFT) and the National Education Association (NEA)— have advocated teachers' playing a greater role in guaranteeing and improving the quality of education. As Kerchner states, "Increasingly unions are realizing that their role is to negotiate on behalf of *teaching* as well as teachers." The NEA grew out of efforts by teachers in the early part of the twentieth century to form a professional association. Until the 1960s, most members of the NEA did not regard their organization as a union and did not believe it should formally endorse collective bargaining. The AFT, by contrast, was clearly a union from its inception and promoted the use of collective bargaining. When collective bargaining took root in public education in the 1960s, the rivalry between the NEA and the AFT was often manifested in a debate about whether teachers' interests were best promoted by a professional association or a union. Eventually, of course, the NEA did increasingly behave like a union and begin to be aggressive about pursuing members' rights. But the debate over the most effective form of teacher representation continues today. Are teachers professionals in the same sense as doctors, lawyers, and accountants? Or are they more like other employees in public sector bureaucracies? If one assumes the former, then a teacher union should be more like a professional association; if one assumes the latter, then a teacher union should be more like an industrial union.

Meanwhile, while teachers were debating their most effective form of representation, the public became increasingly concerned about the quality of education provided by the nation's schools. Particularly after the 1983 publication of *A Nation at Risk* (U.S. Department of Education

1983), a study sponsored by the Reagan administration, alarm about the deteriorating quality of public education increased dramatically. In response to the public's concern, both the NEA and the AFT "officially put themselves in the quality education business," as Kerchner says. Pursuing this theme even further, if teacher unions are going to play a significant role in improving the quality of education, should they define their role as more analogous to professional associations or to industrial unions? Kerchner believes neither is appropriate and proposes a different approach. He believes that the more deeply teacher unions become involved in the delivery and quality of educational services, the more they begin to resemble the guilds of the Middle Ages—organizations of skilled craftsmen that were formed to enhance and protect the standards of the products their members produced. The collaborative approach, with a focus on service delivery, appears to allow attention to both the quality of work life and the quality of the educational product.

Conceiving of teacher organizations as either professional or industrial unions is not sufficient, Kerchner argues, because both forms of unionism focus on improving teachers' compensation and other terms and conditions of employment and relegate the quality of education to a lower priority. Kerchner also notes that in most school districts union leaders and the teachers they represent are a more stable group in the local system than the superintendents and principals who manage the schools and that the turnover of elected union leaders is usually lower than that of elected school board members. Both these factors serve to enhance the value of the guild approach. Furthermore, as teacher unions have increasingly focused on improving the quality of education, they have become more like the medieval guilds, even if most teachers are unaware of it. One measure Kerchner believes would encourage guildlike behavior of teacher unions would be to make educational quality a mandatory subject of bargaining.

The Benefits of a Collaborative Approach

The former president of the NTEU, Robert Tobias, suggests in his contribution to this volume that the collaborative approach has been crucial to attracting and engaging union membership in recent times. NTEU's membership consists not only of federal employees in more traditional "pink-collar" occupations but also of doctors, lawyers, accountants and auditors, and other professionals employed by federal agencies. He discusses the success the NTEU has had in gaining new members in spite of the absence of such union security provisions as the union shop or the agency shop. Between 1982 and 2000 the NTEU grew from 55,000 to 71,000 members, an increase of 29 percent, while most other federal sector unions suffered declines in their memberships. Tobias believes his union's impressive gains are a consequence of its emphasis on cooperative, service-oriented relationships.

In another chapter, Stephen Goldsmith, a former mayor of Indianapolis, describes how efforts in his city to promote labor-management cooperation resulted in lower tax rates, better public services, and improvements in his city's budget. The Indianapolis story, Goldsmith maintains, is not about privatization—for which he is incorrectly credited or pilloried in the popular literature on public labor relations—but about a carefully developed labor-management partnership that resulted in benefits for all parties: higher wages, reduced costs, better service, better jobs, improved job security, and gain-sharing bonuses. Goldsmith tells of entering office with the idea of privatizing the city's services but soon coming to realize that collaboration was a more effective strategy. He was strongly opposed by most of the local unions at the beginning, but by the end of his first term in office he received their support in his bid for reelection. Although most observers note the risks to politicians of promoting collaboration, Goldsmith's story illustrates the potential political gains of service-oriented partnerships.

Goldsmith suggests that the path to a cooperative relationship depends on local circumstances. Union and management officials need to tailor their relationship so that it fits the environment in which they operate and serves each party's goals. Generally, successful collaboration requires the formation of better and broader forums for discussion, an ongoing commitment to training, a chief executive who has compassion for the welfare of his employees, and union leaders who have a genuine interest in improving the quality and lowering the costs of the services their members deliver. Goldsmith describes how he exercised leadership in establishing goals and defining standards used to judge improvement in his city's financial health. He worked diligently with union leaders to develop a relationship in which both the City of Indianapolis and its unions could contribute to achieving mutually beneficial results. As a consequence of this collaboration between the city's officials and its unions, taxes were reduced, gain-sharing bonuses were regularly distributed, and layoffs were minimized. Goldsmith's chapter offers valuable insights into how elected officials can establish and maintain the kind of labor-management relationships that serve the purposes of both municipalities and unions.

Risks of Collaboration

Several contributors to this volume note the risks union leaders assume when they foster cooperative relationships with management. For example, Jeffrey Keefe recalls that a major corporation laid off a very large number of employees in the late 1990s following cooperative efforts by their union leaders to accommodate management's needs. Both Keefe, and Masters and Albright, writing separately about public sector labor relations at the local and federal level, respectively, note the sense of betrayal felt by many union leaders when cooperation is followed by significant layoffs or other negative consequences for workers and their unions. Masters and Albright remind us that the establishment of the NPC during the Clinton administration was followed by major reductions in force of federal employees and ultimately by President Bush's decision to abolish the NPC. These cases certainly do not prove causality, but they illustrate that the levels of instability and uncertainty of the cooperative model usually exceed the levels associated with more-conventional labor-management relations. Even when cooperation appears to fail in other relationships, and not in one's own backyard, Keefe argues, such failures dampen enthusiasm for undertaking the risks involved in collaboration.

The forces impeding collaboration in the public sector are real and powerful. In the 1996 IRRA research volume, Richard Freeman (1996: 76–78) reported on a survey about public and private sector employee attitudes toward cooperation. On the one hand, he found that a majority of union members in both sectors believed that their unions could only be effective if management cooperated with them. On the other hand, he found that "public sector union members were almost twice as likely (40% vs. 23%) as private sector union members to prefer an organization with power that management opposed [over an organization without power that management cooperated with] and considerably less certain (60% vs. 75%) that management cooperation was the *sine qua non* of effective employee organizations." What accounts for this difference? Freeman wrote, "One plausible explanation consonant with the way in which the two sectors operate, rests on the fact that public sector employees have greater power outside collective bargaining to affect management decisions than do private sector employees. They have this power through the political process: They are voters and, through unions, a force in electing public sector leaders; whereas in the private sector, workers rarely are shareholders who can vote and appoint management" (Freeman 1996:78).

The recent peak in the cyclical interest in privatization may serve to motivate public sector unions and their members to undertake the risks associated with cooperation. Ironically, labor's reluctance to risk collaboration and management's unwillingness to expand discussions with unions beyond the formal scope of bargaining decrease the opportunities the parties have to improve the quality and reduce the costs of public services. There is ample evidence in this volume and elsewhere that union reluctance to engage in cooperation ultimately diminishes the public's perception (and perhaps the reality) of the value of unions in the public workplace. By the same token, management's reluctance leads to missing the advantages that Goldsmith and others have noted.

An issue that was widely discussed in the early years of public sector bargaining has been thought to carry with it a special risk of collaboration. That is the issue of including supervisors in the same bargaining units with rank-and-file employees, which is the topic of a chapter by Adrienne Eaton and Paula Voos in this volume. The core risk question is whether this creates a conflict of interest for supervisors by pitting their loyalty to their union against their obligation to maintain discipline.

Public sector supervisors are commonly entitled to join unions and engage in collective bargaining, in contrast to supervisors and managers in the private sector. In some jurisdictions supervisors have separate bargaining units but in others they are included in the same unit as their subordinates. A number of observers have feared that including supervisors and their subordinates in the same bargaining unit would hamper effective supervision and make collective bargaining more complicated. The research done by Eaton and Voos suggests, however, that in the units included in their sample there was little practical difficulty in having supervisors in broader bargaining units. Their research showed that "if problems arose, they did so in the highly unusual context of a work stoppage or around the nonroutine issue of discipline." They found that the problems encountered could be accommodated and concluded that, "People can wear two hats. People can be loyal to the mission of the agency (and act as supervisors to further that mission), while they are also union members."

There are several other potential risks to both management and union officials in adopting a cooperative approach: the dangers of leaving familiar turf and being stuck out on a limb, of misjudging the opponent and losing face, or of failing to deliver on promises and being faced with dire choices. The most incendiary risk is probably privatization. While privatization seems to be a real threat to unions and has been a major factor in other industrial democracies with larger public sectors and more state enterprise, its impact in the United States has actually been remarkably small. The Bush administration, however, has specifically called for greater privatization of federal services (as have others before it). It is too soon to tell now what the effect of President Bush's push for privatization will be, but previous initiatives have had limited results.

The Secretary of Labor's Task Force reported that almost every instance of labor-management cooperation resulted in significant cost savings, even with stable employment levels, and thus blunted the call for privatization. Some evidence shows that few jurisdictions, other than newly incorporated cities, have, in fact, embarked on wholesale privatization (U.S. DOL 1996:13–25). In public education, some school districts are experimenting with various forms of privatization, but the major teacher unions are clearly betting that schools and education will be better off in public hands.

Other factors make it difficult for local labor leaders to engage in cooperative relationships. Keefe points out that they face a triple threat. First, they may lose member support if the members feel they are too close to management and too involved in collaborative efforts. Second, they can seldom expect to get support for cooperative efforts from their national or regional bodies. Third, they face the possibility that their commitment to cooperation will be followed by management decisions, such as layoffs and reductions in force, that leave them looking like dupes. Goldsmith notes that *managers* in the public sector face a parallel set of risks, but Tobias suggests that the risks to the parties of not working together may exceed the risks of cooperation, particularly in the face of falling public confidence in government.

Public sector managers and union leaders are always engaged in a balancing act, weighing the risk of cooperation failing against their obligation to serve the best interests of their constituents. In truth, on a long-term basis, continuing conventional labor-management relationships may prove to be as risky as attempting to move to cooperation. The conventional approach can result in arcane and wasteful conflicts, and, as Malin notes, it necessarily limits employee involvement and motivation to improve the delivery of public services. Accordingly, it reduces the potential contribution public employees can make to their communities. Arthur Hamilton, former president of the National Conference of State Legislatures and a member of the Secretary of Labor's Task Force, was fond of saying that in bringing about change in the labor-management relationship, "Someone has to risk first." Union leaders and managers may want to keep that statement as the fulcrum of their balancing act.

Summary

When public sector officials and union leaders are willing to enter into cooperative arrangements, the evidence in this volume and elsewhere suggests they usually find that cooperation results in improvements in both the delivery of public services and the quality of work life. Certainly there have been instances when cooperation has failed to produce desirable results, but this volume includes ample testimony to its potential beneficial effects and depicts successful experiences with cooperation at the federal government level, in a number of state governments, in Indianapolis, and elsewhere. Also, we know that in places such as Los Angeles; Phoenix; Portland, Maine; Toledo, Ohio; Cincinnati, Ohio; and numerous other locales the cooperative approach has achieved positive results (U.S. DOL 1996). Yet cooperation in the public sector remains the exception rather than the rule.

Why is this? Entering into cooperative relationships requires a willingness by the parties to engage in risk-taking behavior. Public sector unions and managers are usually reluctant to undertake the risks necessary to establish cooperative relationships and prefer the comfort of traditional and familiar approaches. Both management and union bureaucracies tend to be conservative in the sense that they ordinarily prefer the status quo. Moreover, public sector bargaining statutes, which were mostly enacted in the turbulent 1960s—and the practices that emerged around them—serve to enshrine the traditional, adversarial approach to labor-management relations rather than to promote cooperation. At the national level both unions and management organizations usually place a higher priority on other objectives (organizing and engaging in lobbying and political activity, for example) and consider cooperation to be a less-significant priority. The pursuit of cooperation is also affected by political and ideological factors. The election of a new mayor or a new union leader sometimes destroys efforts by previous leaders to establish cooperative relations.

Nevertheless, there are union and public officials who have been willing to undertake the risks necessary to embark on a cooperative path. Often cooperation between the parties has arisen as the consequence of a crisis—one that may be related to fiscal distress, for example. Occasionally cooperation follows a disappointing effort to privatize public services. Cooperation may also occur when union leaders and public officials come to believe that it serves their respective political interests. And there are instances when enlightened public sector managers and union leaders turn to cooperation out of sincere conviction that doing so serves the best interests of both their employees and their communities.

Cooperation is almost always the result of local-level initiatives by union and management decision makers. It ordinarily occurs below the radar screen of national-level organizations. When cooperation occurs, however, it requires that the parties develop structures that will help ensure its success. Training and education programs for representatives on both sides of the table are one example. The parties must also be prepared to create new mechanisms of support, such as nontraditional approaches to conflict resolution like grievance mediation, joint committees to handle topics like the quality of work life and the improvement of service delivery, and forums that encourage employee participation in decision making.

Taken together, the chapters in this volume suggest the following conclusions about labor-management cooperation in the public sector:

- The vast majority of statutes that provide collective bargaining rights for public sector employees do not promote or support cooperative labor-management relationships that potentially would benefit both the parties and their communities.

- Where a common desire exists, however, parties have been able to work around the statutory framework to participate in a regularized regime of collaborative problem solving.

- Politics can significantly affect the context and the specific relationship, creating instability and uncertainty that interfere with establishing and operating collaborative relationships—or even productive traditional relationships.

- National union leaders, who must juggle many forces affecting their unions' growth and influence, in general respect the cooperative approach but remain wary of the risks associated with it.

- With the possible exception of some federal sector unions, teacher unions, and school board associations, active support for collaboration occurs primarily at the local level, spurred by a local crisis, new leadership, or dissatisfaction with bargaining outcomes. The use of cooperation, although still limited to a minority of relationships, appears to be growing at the local level and has proved to be highly valuable to the parties on both sides of the table and to the citizens who, as a consequence, receive improved public services.

- Some state boards and the entire FMCS encourage and support cooperative efforts, but other boards take a conservative approach, emphasizing in their mission the legal adjudication of rights rather than improvement in the quality of the relationship. Members of these boards, and many union and management representatives, believe they do not receive sufficient resources to support their core functions, let alone to promote labor-management cooperation.

- In specific localities, however, legislators and local executives have found that cooperative relationships have not only resulted in improved public services but have also helped them fulfill their other responsibilities to their constituents.

- Trends in union membership, largely the consequence of changes in the economy and the workforce, have resulted in public sector union membership now constituting nearly half of the total number of union members in the United States. Public sector union members tend to have more education and to occupy more-highly skilled and more-professional jobs than their private sector counterparts. The demographics of public sector membership, accordingly, make the use of traditional union-management relationships even more problematic there than in the private sector. As the number of knowledge workers in the public sector grows, the need to explore new approaches to union-management relations will be even more pressing.

- Workers rather than managers are often the constant figures in schools, firehouses, social service agencies, and other public sector organizations. Given this characteristic of some spheres of public sector employment, unions may want to consider adopting more of a "guild" role, focusing as much on guaranteeing and improving the quality of public services as on the improvement of their members' terms and conditions of employment.

- The inclusion of supervisors in public sector unions and bargaining units may result in fewer difficulties than some experts had previously expected.

- The pressure to privatize, which is strongly advocated by the current presidential administration—along with limits on taxes—will continue to create cost and quality pressures. Under traditional relationships, conflict and resistance to service improvement are the typical response. Cooperative, service-oriented models, perhaps in combination with appropriate political strategies, offer a way to counter that response to these pressures.

We hope that this volume contributes to both the knowledge of, and debate about, the value of cooperative service-oriented relationships and the barriers to their use. We also hope that this model will be more fully explored in the future, against the backdrop of major changes affecting labor union membership and the rights and reasonable expectations of citizens, workers, and managers in the public sector.

Acknowledgements

In addition to the excellent authors who have contributed to this volume, we owe many thanks to those who have helped inspire our work. Most especially to John Dunlop and Theodore Kheel, we extend our thanks not only for their pioneering work in the development of public sector labor-management relations but also for their continuing leadership and mentorship of many of us in the field. We also thank Leslie Redd, who first suggested to us that we organize a volume on this topic, Alice Ostdiek, who assisted in recruiting the authors, and Kasha Roseta, who managed the process of assembling the papers. We are sincerely grateful for their constant focus on action and implementation. We are indebted to Henry H. Perrit, Jr., and Martin Malin of the Chicago-Kent College of Law, who joined with us as cosponsors of a conference, held in Chicago in April 2000, that proved to be the genesis of this volume. We thank Chris Colosi of the Institute on Conflict Resolution at Cornell for his assistance on the project. We are especially grateful to Paula Voos, who, along with other members of the IRRA Editorial Committee, made many helpful suggestions in developing this volume. We offer special thanks to Elaine F. Goldberg and Paula D. Wells, who managed the editorial process and ensured that the volume would meet the high standards traditionally maintained by the IRRA. To Missy Harrington, who has been a constant friend and colleague, we offer our deepest thanks for coordinating all aspects of this project and making sure that the editors kept their noses to the grindstone. Portions of this project were funded by The Ford Foundation, and we express our appreciation for the foundation's support. Most especially, without the support of the foundation's Michael Lipsky (no relation to the co-editor of this volume), who has been dedicated to exploring the role of labor relations in the quality of community life, this project could not have begun or been completed.

Notes

[1] The most recent IRRA research volume devoted to public sector employment relations was edited by Belman, Gunderson, and Hyatt (1996). Earlier volumes included two editions of the volume edited by Aaron, Najita, and Stern, one published in 1979 and the other in 1988.

[2] In this paragraph we have summarized comments made by Parker Denaco, Pauline Kinsella, and Linda Hanson, each of whom is or was a member or senior staff of a state board or commission, at a conference, "The Future of Public Sector Labor-Management Relations: Working Together to Achieve Excellence for the Twenty-First Century," held on April 13–15, 2000, at the Chicago-Kent College of Law. The editors of this volume were the organizers of that conference.

[3] Some scholars, particularly economists, are skeptical about the degree to which any legal regime can significantly influence behavior. Many of them believe that although the law may have its intended desirable effects, those effects are often outweighed by the unintended, and often undesirable, consequences of statutory regulation. This ongoing debate about the efficacy of government regulation is the focus of an earlier IRRA research volume (Kaufman 1997).

[4] For a discussion of the role of champions in introducing change in an organization, see Lipsky, Seeber, and Fincher (2003, especially pp. 135–37) and Ulrich (1997).

[5] The text of the New Mexico law can be found on the New Mexico Legislature's website at <http://legis.state.nm.us/>. See also, "New Mexico Governor Signs Measure Reinstating Public Employee Bargaining" (2003: A-6).

[6] The act is known as the Personnel System Reform Act of 2002. See State of Washington, House Bill 1268 (2001). For the provisions pertaining to subcontracting, see Section 208. See also, "State Labor and Employment Laws Enacted in 2002" (2003: S-51–52).

[7] Richard Hurd reported on this development in his presentation on January 5, 2003, at the 55th Annual Meeting of the Industrial Relations Research Association held in Washington, D.C.

References

Aaron, Benjamin, Joyce Najita, and James Stern, eds. 1988. *Public Sector Bargaining.* 2d ed. Washington, DC: Bureau of National Affairs.

Belman, Dale, Morley Gunderson, and Douglas Hyatt, eds. 1996. *Public Sector Employment in a Time of Transition.* Madison, WI: Industrial Relations Research Association.

Clinton, William J. 1993. "Labor-Management Partnerships." Executive Order 12871. *Federal Register,* Vol. 58, no. 192 (October 6).

Freeman, Richard B. 1996. "Through Public Sector Eyes: Employee Attitudes Toward Public Sector Labor Relations in the U.S." In Dale Belman, Morley Gunderson, and Douglas Hyatt, eds., *Public Sector Employment in a Time of Transition.* Madison, WI: Industrial Relations Research Association, pp. 59–83.

Kaufman, Bruce E., ed. 1997. *Government Regulation of the Employment Relationship.* Madison, WI: Industrial Relations Research Association.

Kheel, Theodore W. 1999. *Keys to Conflict Resolution: Proven Methods of Resolving Disputes Voluntarily.* New York: Four Walls Eight Windows.

Lipsky, David B., Ronald L. Seeber, and Richard D. Fincher. 2003. *Emerging Systems for Managing Workplace Conflict: Lessons from American Corporations for Managers and Dispute Resolution Professionals.* San Francisco: Jossey-Bass.

"New Mexico Governor Signs Measure Reinstating Public Employee Bargaining." 2003. *Daily Labor Report* (Bureau of National Affairs), no. 46 (March 10), p. A-6.

Slichter, Sumner H., James J. Healy, and E. Robert Livernash. 1960. *The Impact of Collective Bargaining on Management.* Washington, DC: Brookings Institution.

"State Labor and Employment Laws Enacted in 2002." 2003. *Daily Labor Report (Special Report)* (Bureau of National Affairs), no. 43 (March 5), pp. S-51–52.

Ulrich, Dave. 1997. *Human Resource Champions: The Next Agenda for Adding Value and Delivering Results.* Boston: Harvard Business School Press.

U.S. Department of Education. National Commission on Excellence in Education. 1983. *A Nation at Risk: The Imperative for Educational Reform.* Washington, DC: GPO.

U.S. Department of Labor. 1996. *Working Together for Public Service.* Report of the U.S. Secretary of Labor's Task Force on Excellence in State and Local Government Through Labor-Management Cooperation. Washington, DC: GPO.

Wellington, Harry, and Ralph K. Winter, Jr. 1971. *The Unions and the Cities.* Washington, DC: Brookings Institution.

CHAPTER 1

The Reform of Public Sector Employment Relations in Industrialized Democracies

LORENZO BORDOGNA
University of Milan

Introduction

The aim of this chapter is to present an overview of the main features and problems of public sector employment relations in a group of industrialized countries, so as to allow comparisons with the U.S. system (Brock 2001).[1] The countries considered are mostly European, although references are also made to Japan, Australia, New Zealand, and Canada.

In all these countries, as in almost all industrialized democracies, there have been several attempts in the last two decades to reform public sector labor relations. These attempts have been prompted primarily by two conflicting pressures. First, the governments have been pressed to contain public expenditures, of which the wages and salaries of public service employees are a major component. Second, they have been pressed to improve the quality of the services delivered to their consumers and citizens at large to satisfy their increasingly differentiated and sophisticated demands, which are in sharp contrast to the uniform and bureaucratic forms of provision that prevailed in the past.

In Europe the macroeconomic constraints underlying the cost-efficiency pressures increased after 1992, in connection with the process leading to the European Monetary Union, and even more after the provisions of the Pact on Stability and Growth were approved by the 1997 Amsterdam summit of the European Union. But the increasing internationalization of the economy has made fiscal severity an economic imperative for all governments in order to control inflation, sustain investments and employment, contain or reduce the burden on taxpayers, and improve the overall competitiveness of their economies.

To deal with these problems, a series of proposals were formulated during the 1980s and 1990s suggesting a structural reform of the organization and financing of public services, often summarized under the label of New Public Management. They found support in several OECD Public Management Service publications, in which the need was stressed for the public sector to borrow the model of governance and employment relations typical of the private sector, to the extent possible (OECD 1995, 1996a and 1996b; see also Pollitt and Bouckaert 2000). The main lines of reform included the following: (1) redrawing the boundaries between the private and public sectors both by transferring services from public ownership to private hands and by subcontracting or outsourcing processes; (2) various forms of organizational restructuring aimed at subdividing large, bureaucratic structures into smaller, independent units with devolved managerial authority, in order to make them closer to citizens' demands and more transparent in costs and results; (3) a shift from management-by-hierarchy to management-by-contract by the introduction of market, or marketlike, mechanisms of governance into the financing and provision of public services—such as compulsory competitive tendering, market testing, and internal markets; (4) the strengthening of the powers and prerogatives of managers, subject to tighter financial controls, and the promotion of management techniques typical of private sector firms; and (5) the reform of personnel policies and labor relations (Dell'Aringa 2001; Bach and Della Rocca 2001; Bordogna and Winchester 2001). With reference to the last feature, pressure has often been exerted for a weakening of the special status of civil servants and public employees in general; for an extension of "free" collective bargaining (that is, on a voluntary basis) as the main method of regulating the employment relationship; for a decentralization of the bargaining structure to the local level; and, to some extent, for an individualization of pay. These measures have been proposed as a means to make pay and conditions of employment more responsive to variations in local market conditions, organizational requirements, and individual employee performance.

Although the term "privatization" is not entirely accurate to describe these interconnected proposals for reform (many of them do not imply a transfer of services or administrative units to private owners), it is indicative of the broad meaning underlying this picture of the ideal process of change. That is, the reform aims profoundly to modify the system of constraints and opportunities, of incentives and controls governing the entire functioning of the public services; to reduce the differences between the public and private sectors by importing the private sector's methods of management and "best practices" into the public sector; and to promote a logic of behavior and a governance of labor transactions in the public services significantly closer to those prevailing in the private sector.

Despite the appeal of this reform approach in public debate, not all industrialized democracies seem to have followed that sequence of changes. The impression is that strong national variations persist in employment practices and regulations, rooted in country-specific legal and institutional traditions, which are less easily modifiable in the public sector than in the private sector.

In the following pages I will present a comparative overview of recent trends in state policies to reform the public sector and control labor costs, the changing role of managers and the introduction of new management practices, the structure and role of trade unions, and the reform of labor relations and collective bargaining.

Size and Legal Regulation of Public Sector Employment

Assessing the size of public sector employment in the countries under examination is difficult, partially due to differences in the definition of the aggregates to be included in the public sector. Although the data are not always strictly comparable among countries and over time, the OECD data presented in Table 1 give an idea of the share of public employees in a representative group of industrialized countries' total labor forces between 1991 and 2001. Denmark's highest share, well above 20 percent, was (and is) typical of the Nordic countries, in connection with the strength of the welfare state, and was also common to Finland and Sweden. Although Sweden was not included in the OECD table, it had (and has) an even higher proportion—about one third. At the end of the decade, this group was followed by France, while in the majority of the other countries public employment weight varied from about 11 to 15 percent. (In Japan, the public employment share in the mid-1990s was below 10 percent, although it had been about 14 percent in 1967 [Koshiro 2001.157–58]).

In sharp contrast with the rapid growth of the 1950s, 1960s, and 1970s, the last decade or two have often witnessed a decrease in public sector employment in absolute terms. As Table 2 shows, between 1990 and 2001 (the last year for which data are available), total public sector employment decreased strongly in Australia (–15 percent), under both the Labor and the new (1996) Liberal National Party Coalition government;

TABLE 1

Share of Public Employment in Total Labor Force (percentages)

Nation	1991	1995	1999	2000	2001
Australia[a]	20.5	17.9	15.6	15.2	15.2
Austria	12.3	12.0	11.3	11.2	n.a.
Canada[b]	18.9	18.0	16.0	15.8	15.7
Denmark[c]	n.a.	n.a.	22.6	22.6	23.1
Finland	22.7	20.9	21.0	20.8	20.8
France	n.a.	n.a.	18.3	n.a.	n.a.
Germany	13.3	12.2	11.0	10.7	n.a.
Ireland	15.2	15.0	13.9	14.1	n.a.
Italy	n.a.	n.a.	13.2	n.a.	n.a.
Netherlands	n.a.	n.a.	10.4	10.5	n.a.
New Zealand	14.6	12.6	12.2	11.6	11.8
Spain	11.4	11.8	12.1	11.2	12.0
United States	14.1	14.0	13.9	14.1	n.a.

Source: OECD-PUMA/HRM 2002: Table 5.
[a] Public employment excludes permanent defense forces.
[b] Public employment excludes government business enterprises.
[c] Public employment data are in full-time equivalents.
Note: For cells marked n.a., no data were available.

in Germany (–18 percent after unification with the former German Dem-ocratic Republic; see also Keller 1999:85–88); in Sweden (–11 percent since 1995 in the central administration) and more moderately in Finland (–7 percent); New Zealand (–5 percent, but much more if the late 1980s privatization of government business enterprises were included); and Canada (–4 percent), while it increased considerably in Spain, the United States, and the Netherlands. This trend is due mainly to two factors. One is privatization processes, especially of state-owned enterprises and such public monopolies as telecommunications, postal service, and railways. The second factor is restructuring: major restructuring decisions in several countries (Denmark, Spain, Sweden, Australia, Canada, and the United States) led to notable reductions of central-government employees, al-though at times these created increases in regional and local government employees. In some cases, this process was accompanied by a shrinking of the scope and perhaps the number of public employees with special legal status, whose employment relationship is regulated by administrative law rather than by the ordinary law of the private sector.

In the mid-1980s and early 1990s in Italy, for instance, the state railways and postal service, previously strictly integrated in the ministries of transport and telecommunications, were transformed into joint stock

TABLE 2

Total Public Employment

Nation	1990	1995	1999	2000	2001
Australia[a]	1,746,100	1,603,000	1,464,200	1,466,000	1,485,800
Canada[b]	2,662,563	2,648,908	2,513,016	2,524,790	2,552,613
Finland[b]	580,487	518,291	536,632	539,334	542,078
France	n.a.	n.a.	4,704,087	n.a.	n.a.
Germany	5,275,300[c]	4,801,300	4,433,600	4,347,300	n.a.
Italy	n.a.	n.a.	3,108,803	n.a.	n.a.
Netherlands	n.a.	785,075[d]	828,033	846,257	n.a.
New Zealand	238,810[e]	224,020	230,090	220,170	227,220
Spain	1,801,006	1,926,551	2,101,724	2,009,206	2,136,788
Sweden[f]	n.a.	241,000	227,000	222,000	215,000
United States	17,766,044	18,586,615	19,424,607	19,869,558	n.a.

Source: OECD-PUMA/HRM 2002: Table 1.
[a] Public employment excludes permanent defense forces.
[b] Public employment excludes government business enterprises.
[c] 1991.
[d] 1996.
[e] 1991.
[f] This includes central administration only.
Note: For cells marked n.a., no data were available.

companies, with the state as the only shareholder. Consequently, their employees lost the special employment status and job security they had shared with other public employees. This transformation was a precondition for the downsizing and massive redundancies (lay-offs) pursued after the privatization, especially in the railways (Bordogna, Dell'Aringa, and Della Rocca 1999). Moreover, in 1993 a law reforming the organizational principles of public administration as a whole was approved under the pressures of the 1992 financial crisis and the need to meet the Maastricht criteria for joining the European monetary union. This law weakened the special status and almost entirely "contractualized" the employment relationship of most public employees, the exceptions being the armed forces and military corps and other small groups like judges, university professors, diplomats, and prefects. In Spain the 1990s saw both the privatization of state-owned enterprises and the elimination of legal monopolies in telecommunications, television, air transport, and cigarettes, with the loss of the special civil servant status for their employees. Moreover, in the same period there was a significant increase in the proportion of public personnel hired as ordinary employees, up to

about 27 percent in 1997 (state-owned enterprises excluded). This increase
of ordinary employees occurred mainly in the autonomous governments
and local authorities, not in the central government; despite this change,
however, public employees with civil servant status remained the large
majority of total public employment in Spain (Jódar, Jordana, and Alós
1999:168–70).

Wide programs of contracting out and of privatization of national-
ized industries—in sectors like telecommunications, gas, air transport,
electricity, railways, and coal mining—were very important in the
United Kingdom in the 1980s and early 1990s, contributing to both the
decline in aggregate public sector employees and the decrease of about
25 percent in civil service employment (Winchester and Bach 1999:
23–24). Moreover, although civil servants are not endowed with a special legal status in the United Kingdom as they are in many European
countries (Germany, France, Spain, and Denmark, for example), the job
security of even senior staff has diminished in the last decade as a result
of new competitive recruitment methods that weakened the previous
importance of the internal labor market.

Similar processes of privatization occurred in Denmark, although
they were restricted to large-scale public services like telecommunications, postal service, railways, and the Copenhagen airport. They were
accompanied by a decrease in the number of central-government
employees, from the transfer of functions to regional and local government, and by a decline in the share of employees with civil servant
status: new staff were recruited predominantly with agreement-covered
status (Andersen, Due, and Masden 1999:200, 214, 219). In Sweden the
distinctions among civil servants and white-collar and blue-collar
employees no longer exist and employees in central-government posts
no longer enjoy a lifelong employment guarantee, with a few exceptions
(like judges). In Australia important government business enterprises
(like the Australian Post), where employment conditions were similar to
those of public servants, became more like private corporations in the
1990s, leading to a change in the employment conditions of their
employees. But the basic concept of job security there, which once
characterized many areas of public sector employment, has been eroded
beyond government business enterprises, especially for senior staff,
weakening the traditional differences between the public and private
sectors (Lansbury and Macdonald 2001:221).

Since the mid-1980s New Zealand has been the site (along with the
United Kingdom) of probably the most-radical restructuring program in

OECD countries, causing dramatic changes in the size and structure of the state and its role in society. This resulted in a rapid decrease in the number of central-government employees, where more than three quarters of total public employment has traditionally been concentrated, mainly due to the incorporation and privatization of state-owned enterprises that began in 1988 and to the restructuring of the public service. This restructuring has been guided by the desire for smaller, single-purpose departments. Meanwhile, though, the health and education sectors (which are part of the central government in New Zealand) have remained relatively stable. Local government employment also declined strongly over the decade, by more than 20 percent, with a slight recovery in 2000 and 2001. In local government, workers do not hold the legal status of state employees, and industrial relations and personnel management are run, by and large, under the legislative regime prevailing in the private sector (Walsh, Harbridge, and Crawford 2001).

National government personnel have been decreasing in Japan from the early 1960s through the late 1990s, due to a strict limitation on the number of employees allowed since 1967 and the privatization of public corporations and national public utilities (Nippon Telegraph and Telephone, Japan Tobacco and Salt Monopoly, and Japan National Railways) that took place between 1985 and the early 1990s. The employees of these companies, previously covered by a special labor relations law, were covered only by trade union law following privatization (Koshiro 2001:156–57). Finally, since the mid-1980s the goal of cutting public expenditures in Canada has been pursued, at both the federal and provincial levels, through the control of employee compensation and the reduction of the size of the state. Public enterprises in telecommunications, railways, and airports have been transferred to the private sector or to a quasi-governmental agency and contracting out has increased for tasks like solid-waste management in many municipalities (Thompson 2001).

Two important European countries—France and Germany—present a somewhat different picture, however. There, either privatization and subcontracting processes have been less relevant or they have hit the special employment status of the employees involved to a limited degree. In France, where the public-enterprise subsector was very large at the beginning of the 1980s (more than 10 percent of the total French workforce), with employment conditions lying somewhere in between the private sector and civil service, a movement toward privatization began to take place in the late 1980s; it involved industrial firms like Renault, banks and insurance companies, railways, and utilities industries. But in some important cases that were no longer directly governed by the public service regulations, like the reformed postal and telecommunications services, most staff retained their civil service status (in 1995, 400,000 out of a total of 460,000; Mossé and Tchobanian 1999).

Similarly, in Germany, railway and postal service employees with civil servant status (*Beamte*), who constituted more than 50 percent of total employment in those organizations, maintained their special status rights even after the transformation of these services into joint-stock companies, which brought about a shift in labor relations toward private sector patterns (Keller 1999:63–64). Privatization processes also took place in the airport and airways sector (Lufthansa) and in some services at the federal-state and local or municipal level (garbage collection and street cleaning).

In these countries, employees with special legal status (*Fonctionnaires titulaires* in France and *Beamte* in Germany) and limitations on their collective bargaining or strike rights still make up a large part of total public sector employment (about 40 percent in Germany and a majority in France). The same is true in Spain and Japan. In Spain the civil service staff still makes up between two thirds and three quarters of all public employees. This group is appointed with tenure, is regulated by administrative law, and has only a limited right to collective bargaining, despite its recognition in the mid-1980s.[2] In Japan the right to strike is denied to all public employees (more than 4 million) and the right to bargain collectively to all nonindustrial national and local public employees. On the contrary, in other countries special legal status (with limitations in some cases on the right to strike or to bargain collectively) is restricted to a minority of public employees, namely the armed forces, police, judges, and a few other groups.

Organizational Structure and Public Sector Labor Market

The distribution of public sector activities (excluding from here on the sector of former government business enterprises and public utilities that have been more or less privatized) across levels of government, and the relative weight of central versus regional and local government, are strongly influenced by the administrative structure of the state. Particularly relevant is the distinction between federal states—like Germany, Canada, Australia, and the United States—and unitary states. In some cases in the last two decades some decentralization has taken place, at least in administrative terms: in Spain the creation of autonomous regions had wide effects on the distribution of employees, and in France the 1982 law on decentralization codified a three-tier local government structure (22 regions, 96 districts, and thousands of communes). Denmark abandoned centralized models of governance and planning, and devolved several public sector functions to the local level; for example, it switched its primary and lower secondary schools to the municipal level in 1992. Similarly, in Italy a series of responsibilities were transferred to the regional level during the 1990s, especially in the health sector, and in 2001 a "regionalistic" constitutional reform was approved, with the prospect of wide-range effects on labor relations in the public sector. The content of these effects, however, is still highly uncertain.

Defense functions (armed forces and military corps) are usually concentrated in the central or federal government, where they are often one of the larger components, as in Germany. This is also true for police in most countries; exceptions include Japan, where the police function is managed by local authorities, and France, where it is divided between state and local government (OECD-PUMA/HRM 2002). Education, which is generally among the largest components of the public sector, is highly centralized under the national government in Italy and France, whereas it is managed at the state, regional, provincial, or municipal level in other countries (the United Kingdom, Germany, Denmark, Spain, Canada, Australia, Japan, and the United States). The other large sectors, health and social services, are usually covered by state or regional and local government (as in the United States), with some exceptions, as in Spain.

In several European countries attempts to introduce competition and marketlike mechanisms have bred changes in the organizational structures and organization of work of the health services sector. The creation of internal markets in the National Health Service in the United Kingdom, the *aziendalizzazione* (hospitals operating like companies) in Italy after 1992–93, and the *contractualization* of the financial relations between the single hospital and the regional health authorities established in 1996 in France are cases in point (Keller, Due, and Andersen 2001). In Japan most hospitals are private, although financially supported by national health insurance schemes, but there are a number of public hospitals that are owned and managed by local governments. Overall, fewer changes have been made in the education sector.

In most countries, the public sector labor market has peculiar characteristics. The main one, probably, is that a segmentation exists between employees with special civil servant status—usually recruited through open public competition based on objective and universalistic criteria, appointed with tenure, and regulated by administrative law in quite rigid internal labor markets—and other employees, who are subject to ordinary law. Where the special group is large, as in Germany and Spain, this dualism is rather important, although recent government policies have tried to attenuate the difference. One of these policies is the U.K.'s introduction of competitive tendering and market testing, which have encouraged convergence of private and public sector employment conditions, especially those covering low-skilled manual workers and clerical staff (Winchester and Bach 1999:26). Another policy recently activated has been the increasing use of fixed-term and temporary workers instead of full-time permanent employees, which usually allows quicker, less costly, and more flexible procedures of recruitment. These kinds of employment contracts have twice the presence in the United Kingdom public sector as in the private sector and are found in varying degrees in many other countries: Spain (a high of 16 percent in late 1990s, which is less than half of that in the private sector, however), New Zealand (about 10 percent), Canada (about 18 percent, with notable differences across provinces), and Denmark, in such services as kindergartens, nursing homes, care institutions, and postal services. A much more limited use of such employment contracts is observed in other countries: in Italy, where the possibility of utilizing temporary agency workers in the public sector—as a limited proportion of those in permanent positions—was introduced only by a framework agreement in the summer of 2000; in Germany, although this type of worker is increasing in hospitals, education, postal service, and social services; and in France, where an agreement between the government and the main unions in 1996 aimed to avoid the use of atypical or contingent workers (Mossé and Tchobanian 1999:140).

A second characteristic feature of public sector labor markets is a higher proportion of white-collar and professional occupations. A third feature is the higher rate of female employees, due to the importance of activities, such as education, health, and social services, in which female employment has traditionally prevailed. The proportion of women in total public sector employment increased markedly in most countries in the 1990s, reaching peaks of 60 percent or even higher in New Zealand and the United Kingdom, around 55 percent in Canada, and slightly less in Italy, Germany, Spain, and Australia. This proportion is usually lower in central government and much higher in education and health (teachers and nurses).

Part-time work also increased rapidly in the public sector in the last decades, especially among women in hospitals and education, and is usually more diffused there than in the private sector. In Germany, where part-time employment increased from 6 percent in the late 1960s to about 20 percent in the mid-1990s and spread from salaried employees and wage earners to *Beamte,* women make up about one out of three full-time employees, but almost 90 percent of part-time employees (Keller 1999:61). Likewise, in the United Kingdom, among the part-time employees who make up about 33 percent of total public sector employment, 90 percent are women (Winchester and Bach 1999:25); in New Zealand part-time workers almost doubled in a decade, to about 26 percent in 1998. Clear exceptions are Spain and Italy, where the proportion of part-time employees is no higher than 5 percent, significantly lower than that in the private sector.

In sum, the public sector labor market in industrialized democracies is often characterized by a segmentation between employees with civil servant status, in many countries subject to special (administrative) law, and employees on ordinary contract; by lengthy and cumbersome recruitment processes for the first group, but often for the second one as well; by high levels of job security; and by uniformity of conditions within rigid and rather protected internal labor markets, where seniority traditionally plays an important role in pay and career systems. In the last decades various attempts have been made to attenuate some of these features: (1) increasing the proportion of fixed-term and temporary workers subject to leaner recruitment and dismissal procedures in order to achieve a greater numerical flexibility, (2) reforming the job-classification systems toward a lower number of grades with broader job descriptions (as in Italy or in Australia) to allow greater functional flexibility, and (3) increasing managerial discretion on organizational issues as well as in pay and career decisions about employees. But wide differences across countries still persist.

Employers and Employers' Associations

Status and Role of Public Managers

Apart from (but often in connection with) the processes of privatization, marketization, and contracting out that have characterized public sector reform in the last decades, the internal organization of public administration and the role of managers have also been transformed as a means of containing public expenditures and improving the effectiveness of government policies and the quality of public services (Pollitt and

Bouckaert 2000). In some cases, changes in the complex system of
incentives and controls, powers and responsibilities to which public
managers are exposed have been made as a means of achieving overall
improvement in the performance of public administration, one of the
intended cornerstones of the effort of reforming the public sector. The
aim of this new managerialism has been to move public administration
from a Weberian model—based on hierarchical and highly centralized
organizations operated according to uniform rules in order to grant
equal treatment to all citizens—where process is emphasized, rather
than results, toward a more performance-oriented system, where efficiency and effectiveness are taken as the main objectives rather than the
observance of formal rules (Dell'Aringa 2001:10; Bach and Della Rocca
2001; OECD 1995).

From this new managerialism, important effects on human resource
management practices derive. First there is an impact on managers
themselves with respect to their relationship with political power and
their recruitment procedures, career systems, and pay schemes. In
Europe, public service management has probably been most radically
reformed in the United Kingdom, strengthening the management
function and developing chief-executive roles accountable for their
performance. To this aim, private sector managers have been appointed
to high-profile positions; recruitment procedures have been increasingly
based on open competition and delegated to departments and agencies;
schemes of individual performance-related pay have been introduced
and age-related incremental pay scales abolished, especially in the civil
service; and managers have been empowered to rationalize the labor
process, changing the work organization, designing new roles, and
recruiting, promoting, and motivating their staff. One goal of the new
management role has been to curb the power of interest groups, not
only trade unions but also professionals, such as doctors and school-
teachers (Bach and Della Rocca 2001:32–33).

Similar reforms have been pursued in several other countries, albeit
not always as radical as those in the United Kingdom. In Italy, for instance, laws approved in 1993, 1998, and 2002 strengthened the responsibilities of managers in pursuing the general objectives defined by
politicians and introduced temporary assignments (at most, five years
long), individually (and in part collectively) bargained with the administration, at the end of which managers can be removed from their
positions if the results achieved are evaluated as unsatisfactory. Managers
can even be dismissed from the public service itself in extreme cases.

The managerial role in personnel matters has been strengthened by eliminating or reducing the mandatory participation of unions in such issues as recruitment, internal mobility, career development, and training. These laws also introduced a sort of spoils system for (mainly) central-government managers (which was widened in 2002);[3] enlarged the possibility of recruiting managers from the private sector on fixed-term contracts; changed their pay scheme to a three-tier system (base salary, salary connected to the position assigned, and performance-related pay), in which the last two components can be quite important; and strengthened their discretionary powers on organizational and personnel matters, on the grounds that these powers are instrumental in the achievement of the results on which the managers themselves are evaluated. Despite such efforts to import personnel management practices typical of the private sector, however, a significant proportion of Italian administrations, especially smaller ones, still lack specialized human resource management functions or departments for both managers and lower-level employees (Bordogna 2002).

In New Zealand the 1988 State Sector Act extended to managers of the noncommercial activities of the public service powers comparable to their private sector counterparts (Walsh, Harbridge, and Crawford 2001:194). Tenured permanent department heads were replaced by chief executives employed on fixed-term contracts of up to five years, renewable for up to another three years, whose salaries were individually negotiated with the State Service Commission. They and, by delegation, lower levels of management were given broader autonomy in managing the resources allocated to their departments, including personnel and labor relations matters, with corresponding accountability for departmental performance. The process for appointing chief executives was also changed, raising the specter of political appointments.

In Australia the 1984 Public Service Reform Act introduced a major step toward increasing efficiency in the public sector based on new-managerialism principles and on the adoption of private sector practices. Greater emphasis was put on results over conformity, management over administration, flexibility over tenure, and performance measures over traditional command-and-control mechanisms (Lansbury and Macdonald 2001:223). The concepts of program budgeting, performance indicator use, and corporate planning were introduced, as well as a type of cost-benefit approach to be used in place of absolute compliance with formal rules. With the creation of the Senior Executive Service, the concept of career service—according to which the majority of government employees could expect to progress along extended career paths—was challenged, layers of middle management disappeared as the principle of devolution was implemented, performance payment systems were introduced, and reclassification and redeployment of staff were freed from previous statutory constraints (Lansbury and Macdonald 2001:224). According to the 1992 Public Service Act, the top-level managers, secretaries of departments under the minister, and agency heads, increasingly referred to as CEOs, no longer enjoy tenure in their positions, nor in the public service itself. This move toward the new managerialism was further intensified in the late 1990s under the Liberal National Party Coalition government.

Other countries, however, have followed different paths. In France, Germany, and Spain, in particular, changes in the role of managers have not been the main focus of reform. Some strengthening of the managerial roles has been pursued, as in the French hospitals, for instance, and some management techniques similar to those in the private sector have been introduced (for example, total quality management). But job security of civil servants is not considered an impediment to reform, access to top executive positions is governed by public selection procedures, direct recruitment from the private sector is limited, management prerogatives are regulated within a dense network of administrative and legal rules (including rights regarding employees' codetermination in Germany), and performance-related pay has not been introduced on a large scale. The internal labor market in these countries for managerial positions is still based on a hierarchical system of different grades for different groups or professional corps, with their own career paths, mostly based on seniority rather than on individual performance (Bach and Della Rocca 2001: 34–35).

In Denmark, signs of the emergence of a more prominent managerial role are associated with strong elements of continuity, and most senior managers are usually given civil servant status. Political appointments, spoils systems, and performance-related pay are also little diffused in Canada, where they are limited to the most-senior levels of government (Thompson 2001:137).

The Representation of Employers' Interests and Employers' Associations

The representation of employers' interests is somehow more complicated in public sector labor relations than in the private sector. The complications come from the complex diffusion of managerial responsibilities in the public sector, related to the constitutional structure and political system of nation states, which sometimes makes it difficult to identify exactly who the public employer is. Another complicating feature is the higher potential role of political parties in the representation of employers' interests and in some cases even in collective negotiations. A third complicating feature is the dual role played by the state in labor relations—usually as the actual employer of public workers and direct counterpart of trade unions, but also as the key actor that sets the rules of the game (Keller, Due, and Andersen 2001).

Within this framework, public sector employers' associations present some common features and some differences across countries. In some countries they hardly exist or at most play a rather modest role in labor relations (France, Spain, and Japan). Where they do exist, the main common feature is their high density rate. This is obviously the case where the representation of public employers' interests is somehow compulsory, but even where membership is voluntary, density ratios are usually higher than those in private industry. On the other hand, differences in structures and functions exist. Regarding functions, in some countries these associations combine the representation of employers' interests with the power to negotiate on their behalf with trade unions. This is the case of the Local Government Association in the United Kingdom, for instance, which reached a single-status national agreement covering 1.5 million manual and nonmanual staff in 1997, and of the U.K.'s National Health Service Confederation; in Denmark, of KL, the private voluntary association of municipalities, and of ARF, which conducts negotiation on behalf of the counties and is the dominant partner in the hospital sector; in Germany, of the Federation of Local Government Associations (VkA) and of the Bargaining Associations of German States (TdL), both founded in 1949.

In other cases the right to negotiate with trade unions is exercised not by employers' associations, but either directly by the national government (as in France, although it is not collective bargaining in its full sense) or by special agencies, as in Italy and partly in the Swedish central government. In Italy a public agency, Aran, which was created by law in 1993 and reformed in 1997, is a technical or professional organization that has been given the role of compulsory representation of all public administrations in national-level negotiations and, on request, also at the local level. Given the fragmentation of the Italian political system and the presence of large coalition governments, it was designed to depoliticize public sector labor relations, preventing the direct political interference in negotiations that had frequently occurred in the 1980s and early 1990s. After the 1997 amendment, Aran became somehow responsive to employers' associations, such as the associations of regional and local governments and the association of (about 70) state universities, receiving their inputs before negotiations start, keeping them informed of the negotiation process, and submitting draft agreements to them for their approval; these associations do not participate directly at the bargaining tables for national collective agreements, however. Not even the government (since 1993) takes part directly in negotiations concerning ministries' employees, schoolteachers, and other employees it more-or-less directly controls, although it must approve draft agreements reached by Aran concerning its employees. The role of the government (and of the parliament) is crucial, however, since it fixes the overall amount of resources available for contract renewals in the budget laws of the State, and the Treasury exerts tight control on the financial costs of both national and local-level agreements.

A partly similar system has been present in Sweden since 1965, when, along with recognition of the right for all central-government employees to negotiate and to take industrial action, the authority to conclude collective agreements on behalf of the State was delegated to the Swedish Agency for Government Employers (Arbetsgivar Verket or AgV). The agency may delegate this authority to other government agencies, but membership in the agency is compulsory for all (about 270) central-government agencies.

Associations can organize employers' interests either at different levels of administration (central or federal, regional or state, or local government) or according to different tasks (education, health, and so forth). An important issue regarding organizational structure is the degree of centralization or decentralization related to personnel and labor relations matters. Generally speaking, even where there have been moves toward decentralization of organizational structures and devolvement of managerial authority—as in the United Kingdom, New Zealand, Australia, Canada, and partly in Denmark—we have not witnessed processes of radical fragmentation of employers' interests. Forms of coordination, if not centralization, in labor relations matters still persist, mostly for fiscal discipline and cost-control reasons. In New Zealand and Australia, for instance, there are no associations at the federal or national government level to represent employers' interests and negotiate on their behalf with trade unions, and departmental or agency chief executives are the employers of their staff. However, some central bodies—such as the State Service Commission in New Zealand or the Public Service and Merit Protection Commission and the Department of

Workplace Relations in Australia—have retained an important supervisory role in negotiations, setting constraints on the outcomes chief executives can negotiate. Central governments can also mantain control on management autonomy through the use of fiscal restraints and of contractual agreements between ministries and departmental chief executives or boards (Lansbury and Macdonald 2001:225–26; Walsh, Harbridge, and Crawford 2001:195). Tensions of this type between decentralized responsibilities and centralized control are also frequent in other countries, as in the United Kingdom (between the Treasury on the one hand and the more than a hundred central-government executive agencies on the other, or for the National Health Service Confederation, created in 1997 to represent both purchasers and providers of services), and in Canada (between provincial governments and local employers), and partly in Italy (between central government and regions and municipalities).

Coordination of employers' interests is obviously even stronger where either a single agency is in charge of carrying out negotiations for the entire public sector, like Aran in Italy, or where the central government itself takes the lead among and above employers' associations— through the role of the ministry of the interior (in Germany) or of finance (in Denmark) or of public services (in Spain).

Trade Unions

In most of the countries considered in this chapter, the right of association is recognized for all public sector employees, although in some cases it has been more recently conceded or implemented than in the private sector, as in Spain, for example.[4] Even those with civil servant status, like German *Beamte* (about 40 percent of total public employment), who are deprived of the right to strike and to negotiate their employment relationship collectively, enjoy the right to organize and have their own union (or association). Frequent exceptions are a few groups of employees like the armed forces and military corps, police, judges, and at times firefighters and prison officers, although in some countries, like Spain and Italy, even some of these groups have the right to set up and join professional associations, if not trade unions in the strict sense.

On the whole, the trade union structure often resembles that prevailing in the private sector, replicating traditional divisions based on ideological and political orientations (Keller, Due, and Andersen 2001). There are some characteristically different features, however.

The first one is the extension of trade unions to all areas of the public sector, with virtually no union-free zone, combined with the presence of density rates usually higher and more stable than those of private sector unions. In some cases this difference can be of a few percentage points, but in others, perhaps the majority, it can reach double (or even more) that of private sector density—like in France, Germany, the United Kingdom, Canada, Japan, the Netherlands, Australia, New Zealand, and the United States (Ozaki 1993:21–22). In Australia, for instance, union density was 60 percent for the public sector and 24 percent for the private sector in 1996 (Lansbury and Macdonald 2001:230), while in New Zealand a survey at the end of the 1990s showed that over 90 percent of public sector workplaces were unionized, compared with just 13 percent of private sector workplaces, always with a much higher union density in public sector workplaces (Walsh, Harbridge, and Crawford 2001:203). The reasons for this feature had been suggested by Clegg more than 30 years ago: the smaller number of public administration units and their larger size; the fact that once a public policy to recognize unions is adopted, individual authorities cannot easily oppose it (and in some instances they are required by statute to recognize trade unions); the circumstance that only by collective action can employees have a reasonable chance of changing the bureaucratic rules that govern public administration; and the fact that public managers may be less resistant to trade unions than their private sector counterparts, because they themselves are highly unionized (Clegg 1976:23–25). Moreover, in many countries, trade unions are, or have been until recently, quite involved in the management of the public sector internal labor market (hiring, promotion, mobility, and organization of work), thus providing additional incentives for membership (Keller, Due, and Andersen 2001). A synthetic view of the differences in union density in the private and public sector is offered in Table 3, although it covers a group of countries only partially overlapping with those analyzed in this chapter. These data show that in the last two decades unions in most countries have been much better able to preserve, and in a few cases even to improve, their position in the public sector than in the private sector.

A second characteristic feature of trade union structure in the public sector is the large and durable presence of occupational unions, in several cases derived from former professional associations. Unions representing nurses and teachers, and in some countries medical doctors, with their concern about professional issues, are probably the most typical examples (Ozaki 1993). These professions and occupations are

TABLE 3
Union Density Ratios in Private and Public Sectors (percentages)

Nation	Year	Private	Public	Year	Private	Public
France	1981	18	44	1993	4	25
Germany[a]	1980	29	67	1997	22	56
Italy[b]	1980	48	60	1997	36	43
Spain	1991	14	26	1997	15	32
UK[c]	1980	45	69	1999	19	60
Sweden	1980	n.a.	n.a.	1995	77	93
Norway	1980	47	74	1994	44	79
Finland	1980	n.a.	n.a.	1989	65	86
Netherlands	1980	26	60	1997	19	45
Ireland	1980	n.a.	n.a.	1994	43	68
Austria	1980	40	68	1998	30	69
Switzerland	1980	24	71	1987	22	71

Source: Boeri, Brugiavini, and Calmfors 2001.
[a] In 1980 this refers to Western Germany.
[b] Excluded are independent unions not affiliated with the three largest confederations.
[c] In 1999 this refers to Great Britain.
Notes: Public sector includes central and local government, public education, public health, railways, postal service, and telecommunications (before privatization). For cells marked n.a., no data were available.

frequently organized into trade unions separated from the largest confederations or labor centrals of the country, like teachers into SNALS (the national autonomous union of school workers) in Italy, GEW (the union for education and science) in Germany, and FEN (*Fédération de l'éducation nationale*) and FSU (*Fédération syndicale unitaire*) in France (Keller, Due, and Andersen 2001). Similar examples can be found in Spain (ANPE for teachers and CEMSATSE for nurses), in Canada (for teachers, nurses, police, and other professional employees), and other countries as well.

Another feature is the frequent co-existence of different organizational principles (craft, occupational, professional, and industrial, for example), often combined with a greater organizational fragmentation and harsher forms of interunion rivalry than in the private sector. This fragmentation is facilitated by the organizational structures of the public services, characterized by the diffusion of positions with very high disruptive power, that is, positions that allow forms of industrial action that have a disproportionate effect on the services' customers and the general public in comparison with the cost of the action itself (Accornero 1985; Bordogna, Dell'Aringa, and Della Rocca 1999). Italy is a clear example in point, with its high proliferation of so-called autonomous or independent unions (among teachers, medical doctors, nurses, pilots, air traffic controllers, railway engine drivers, and so forth), many of them very small but endowed with strong disruptive power. This feature can multiply free-riding behaviors based on fragmented forms of labor conflicts, as happened dramatically in the late 1980s and early 1990s in Italy.[5] In France unionism in the public sector was even more divided than in the private sector (Mossé and Tchobanian 1999:152), while in other countries some institutional features of the labor relations system kept this phenomenon under control: in Germany, for example, the general rules governing collective bargaining and the denial of the right to strike to all *Beamte* (Bordogna 1993).

Despite this greater fragmentation, mergers between public sector unions took place in several countries in the 1990s, often prompted by financial pressures (and perhaps also by the challenges coming from smaller and more aggressive unions); these mergers contributed a certain degree of centralization of trade union activities (Keller, Due, and Andersen 2001). Of particular prominence are UNISON, the largest trade union in the United Kingdom, the outcome of a merger of three unions in 1993, and Ver.di, the outcome of a merger of five unions in 2001 and presently, with 2.8 million members, the largest union in Germany. But mergers and amalgamations have also been observed in other countries: in Italy, among central government, local government, and health sector unions and in the transport sector; in France, FEN, which had split the previous year into two separate unions, merged with other autonomous civil servant federations in 1993 to form UNSA, the sixth largest (and representative) French union confederation; in Australia, CPSU, the largest union covering government employees; and in New Zealand, initially set in motion by the requirements of the 1987 Labor Relations Act but then driven by the imperative of organizational survival (Walsh, Harbridge, and Crawford 2001:202). In a somewhat similar vein, cartel-like coalitions that group unions in both the state and local government sector play a crucial role in the centralization of the bargaining system in Denmark.

Union Attitudes toward Reform

The attitudes of trade unions toward public sector reform have varied significantly across and within countries, from hostility to benign neutrality to positive, but cautious, cooperation (Dell'Aringa 2001). These distinctions may be due to the varying intensity and speed of the process of reform in the different countries and also to the various cultural and ideological traditions of trade unions.

In countries like the United Kingdom and New Zealand, public sector reform was an integral part of government policies to reduce the power of trade unions. Several features of the reform, as for instance the 1991 Employment Contracts Act in New Zealand, were hostile to collective bargaining and unionism in the workplace and favored a sort of individualization of the employment relationship. In both the United Kingdom and New Zealand the unions opposed the process of reform. The same happened in Australia, although the process of change there was less radical, at least until 1996 when the Liberal National Party Coalition came to office with a more pronounced anti-union and anticollectivist stance (Lansbury and Macdonald 2001). On the opposite side, in Italy, Denmark, and Sweden the trade unions took a more-or-less active part in the reform of the public sector, although trying to preserve their positions and the interests of employees within a renewed system of employment relationships. In Denmark, for instance, trade unions reached an agreement in 1997 to replace the traditional automatic, seniority-based pay increments by a system in which pay reflects qualifications and performance of each employee or group of employees (Keller, Due, and Andersen 2001:88). In Italy, the 1993 reform that "privatized" public employment and strengthened managerial prerogatives was in part supported by the public sector unions belonging to the three largest confederations of the country, although it was opposed by some autonomous unions and by the so-called *Cobas* (rank-and-file committees; Bordogna, Dell'Aringa, and Della Rocca 1999). In Japan there have also been divisions between different public sector trade unions, with those affiliated to Rengo moderately supporting the process of reform proposed by the government in the late 1990s while those affiliated with the leftist Federation of National Public Service, Kokko Ronen, strongly opposing it (Koshiro 2001:177).

Somewhere in between are the German and French cases. In Germany, the main public sector trade union of the 1980s and 1990s (ÖTV-DGB) argued in favor of the need to modernize the public sector beginning in the late 1980s; after 1995 it started a dialogue with the association of German cities and municipalities (KGSt) about the implementation of new steering concepts, inspired by more private sector–oriented principles of organization. In France, unions like the Confédération française du travail (CFDT) and the union of teachers (FEN) have shown openness to negotiating on the need for modernization, although this issue gave rise to severe internal conflicts that eventually led to splits and to the formation of two new, more-radical organizations, SUD and FSU (Keller, Due, and Andersen 2001:89). However, major reforms have not been pursued in these countries, perhaps in part because of the dense legal regulation that characterizes public sector employment relations there. The cases of Spanish and Canadian unions are somewhat similar, although the regulation of public sector employment relations in Spain has undergone important transformations since the reintroduction of democracy, while Canada has experienced only evolutionary and incremental change in public sector industrial relations, the main parameters of the system having remained intact (Thompson 2001).

Public Sector Labor Relations

Unilateral versus Joint Regulation

In many countries, since the early 1960s there has been a move from unilateral regulation, although often assisted by various types of consultation practices, to collective bargaining as the preferred method of determining public sector pay and conditions of employment and regulating the relationships between employers and trade unions (Treu 1987; Ozaki 1993; Andersen, Due, and Masden 1997). In the 1980s and 1990s this redrawing of the boundaries between joint regulation and unilateral decisions of the public employer has been strengthened by the processes of privatization and reform inspired by the new managerialism.

This is is not a universal rule, however. Some occupations or services are excluded from collective bargaining almost everywhere (the armed forces, judges, and a few other minor groups, for example), and in a significant group of countries unilateral employer decision making, or procedures other than free collective bargaining, are still important methods of regulating terms and conditions of employment.

In Japan, national and local nonindustrial public employees do not enjoy the formal right of collective bargaining nor the right to go on strike—in addition to police, firefighters, and prison officers, who do not even have the right to organize. Registered employee organizations are entitled to ask proper authorities to "negotiate" (or confer) on legally defined matters, but this does not include the right of collective agreement (collective bargaining is instead available to the employees of national and local public utilities). Pay increases of national public service employees covered by the National Public Service Remuneration Law are decided yearly by the Cabinet and the Diet, on recommendations of the National Personnel Authority. This authority is an independent administrative commission of three members (appointed by the Cabinet), established in 1948, which undertakes comprehensive comparisons with private sector pay. The pay of local government employees is also unilaterally determined (Koshiro 2001).

In Germany, public sector employees are divided into two main groups: that of *Beamte,* who do not have the right to strike or to bargain collectively, and that of *Angestellte* and *Arbeiter,* who have those rights. Such a distinction occurs in other countries, too, as in Denmark and in Spain. But what is unusual in the German case is that the *Beamte* include a wide variety of functions and public employees, well beyond central government—teachers, medical doctors, and the majority of state railway and postal employees (even after privatization)—up to about 40 percent of total public employment, or even more. The area covered by *Beamte* is now decreasing slightly because of the processes of privatization and of a government policy restricting the offering of the status of *Beamte* to new entrants. The legal distinction between the two groups has also weakened over time, so that its practical consequences on the pay movements has usually been of little importance in recent decades (Keller 1999). A distinction still remains, however, which in emergency conditions—by reversing the usual sequence of pay determination between *Beamte* and the other groups of public employees— makes it possible for the government to influence wage increases in the entire public sector and, indirectly, even in the private sector (Bordogna and Winchester 2001). This distinction also affects other labor relations issues, especially the control of conflict (see Bordogna 1993, for instance, for a sharp contrast with the Italian case).

In France, collective bargaining has an uncertain legal status, which does not rule out the ultimate power of the government unilaterally to determine the pay and working conditions of the *fonctionnaires titulaires* (the great majority of the 4.4 million public employees), who are still regulated by administrative law. The July 1983 law offers public employees and their organizations the right to a *négociation préalable* (usually every year) with government before government makes its decisions over pay increases, but it does not make the outcomes of these negotiations (called *relevé de conclusions*) legally binding on the government itself. Thus, government is free to decide whether to start a negotiation, whether to reach an agreement, and whether or not to observe the agreement even after it has been reached—all situations that actually occurred at least once after the approval of the law (Mossé and Tchobanian 1999; Bordogna and Winchester 2001).[6]

In Denmark, the 1969 Civil Servants Act formally gave to civil servants—about 20 percent of total public employees, located both in the state and in the regional and local authorities' sectors—the right to negotiate collectively over pay increases and other issues. At the same time, however, it denied them the right to strike and established that if the renewal of the current collective agreement ended in a deadlock, then pay and working conditions for the ensuing period could be determined by an act of the *Folketing* (Andersen, Due, and Marsden 1999).

Several pieces of legislation since the mid-1980s in Spain (1984, 1985, and 1987, as amended in 1990) and agreements between the public administration and trade unions (1990, 1991, 1994, and 1998) had a similar effect. The right to collective bargaining, along with trade union freedom, was recognized for civil servants, who are still the large majority of public employees, replacing the former statutory relationship. However, negotiating arrangements still have an ambiguous status compared with those in the private sector, and government ultimately reserves the right to establish the employment conditions (Jódar, Jordana, and Alós 1999).

Britain is a somewhat different case. There, the determination of pay for 1.3 million public service employees (more than 25 percent of total employment) is currently based on the recommendations of independent review bodies rather than on the results of collective bargaining (Winchester and Bach 1999; Elliott and Bender 1997). Until the 1980s, this system covered a relatively small group of employees whose status more or less precluded conventional collective bargaining: senior state officials (the highest grades in the civil service, military, and judiciary), doctors and dentists, and the armed forces. But it was extended to a half million nurses, midwives, and other health service professional staff members in 1982 and to a similar number of school-teachers in 1991, following a long history of difficult and inconclusive collective bargaining. The formal exclusion of these groups from collective bargaining coverage does not mean, however, that pay determination is simply a matter of unilateral government decision making. In a sense, the process can be viewed as a form of arm's-length bargaining, given that the review bodies receive detailed written and oral evidence from trade unions, employers, and government ministers and that their recommendations are usually adopted by the government, despite its nominal power to reject them. At the same time, it is not a perfect equivalent to collective bargaining, not only in formal terms: the means by which

unions and employers try to influence the independent review bodies
are different from negotiating directly with each other, and it can be
argued that sometimes the pay outcomes have been different from what
might have emerged from direct negotiations.[7]

In other countries the move toward collective bargaining for most
public employees is more clearly detectable. This is the case for Italy
after the reforms of 1983 and 1993. The first enlarged a trend started in
the late 1960s, and the latter privatized the employment relationship,
moving it away from the framework of administrative law, fully contractualized the terms and conditions of employment of all public employees—except for a few groups (mainly the armed forces, judges, and
university professors), and extended the scope of collective bargaining
to issues previously reserved to the law (Bordogna, Dell'Aringa, and
Della Rocca 1999). This contractualization was accompanied by measures to produce a more "voluntaristic" framework than in the past,
tighter financial constraints on collective negotiations, stronger managerial prerogatives in personnel policies, and a weakening of other
sources of regulation of the employment relationship in general and of
pay issues in particular (i.e., through parliament, administrative law,
and, at times, the constitutional court).

A similar weakening of unilateral regulation took place in Sweden
after the reforms of 1965, which recognized the right to collective
bargaining for central government employees, although until the 1980s
all collective agreements were signed under the condition of government approval (Schager and Andersson 1996; Elliott and Bender 1997).
Similarly, in the Netherlands, the reforms of the mid-1980s gave all
public employees the right to strike and to bargain collectively and
legally ended the previous procedure according to which public sector
pay was determined centrally by the minister of the interior, after
consultation with trade unions, on the basis of private sector pay trends
(Visser and Hemerijck 1997: ch. 5). In Canada, legislation that established collective bargaining as the preferred method for determining
terms and conditions for federal employees was enacted by the federal
government in 1967, and in subsequent years by most provinces, replacing consultation with negotiation at all levels of the public sector
(Thompson 2001:141).

Thus, while since the mid-1960s there has been a move from government unilateralism to collective bargaining as the main method of
regulating the terms and conditions of employment, different mechanisms often co-exist in the same country; in some cases large groups of

employees are still subject to methods other than free collective bargaining (as in Germany), and in a few cases (as in France) the right to engage in collective bargaining still has at best an uncertain status for all public employees.

Collective Bargaining: Centralization versus Decentralization

Collective bargaining in the public sector is characterized by some distinctive institutional features that differentiate it from the private sector, mainly due to the (variable) role of the state (Bordogna and Winchester 2001; Dell'Aringa 2001).

A first feature, stressed many years ago by Kochan (1974), is that, given the dispersion of power that characterizes the employers' side (among government ministries, politicians, state officials, and managers), negotiations in the public sector often take the form of multilateral bargaining. This invites political pressure from trade unions and professional associations, especially in electorally sensitive circumstances, and exposes public sector bargaining to the need to resolve internal conflicts within the employers' side, often with more troublesome consequences than in the private sector.

Other features have to do with the form of government, the administrative structure of the state, and the financing of public administrations. In particular, a critical point is whether the constitutional law recognizes—even at the lower levels of government—some degree of autonomy in determining pay and employment conditions for employees and, connected to this, the degree of devolution of authority and responsibilities within each level of government (for instance, to individual ministries or agencies). These features are important because they affect more or less directly the crucial issue of the centralization versus decentralization of bargaining.

As is well illustrated in the economics and industrial relations literature, the level at which negotiations mainly take place (that is, the degree of centralization or decentralization of the bargaining structure) is often considered one of the most important factors that influence other aspects of the collective bargaining structure (depth and scope), features of union behavior and labor relations in general (union density, type of union government, distribution of power, and strike behavior; see Clegg 1976), and national macroeconomic performance (Olson 1982; Calmfors and Driffill 1988; Soskice 1990; Calmfors 1993, among others).

In particular, the Calmfors and Driffill hypothesis that the best performers would be countries with very centralized or highly decentralized bargaining systems—since in both cases (although for different reasons) the trade unions have incentives to internalize the costs of their wage demands in real terms[8]—requires significant qualification when applied to the public sector. In effect, the idea of "responsible" trade union behavior in decentralized systems is based on the assumption that individual employers are financially accountable for their firms and for their capacity to compete with others, giving rise to a more or less direct trade-off between real wage increases and employment levels where bargaining takes place. Thus, trade unions have an incentive to adopt "responsible" behavior in order not to run the risk of seeing the potential area of their representation gradually eroded, up to a point that threatens their very existence.

But the assumption of a financially responsible employer, on which this chain of incentives is grounded, cannot be taken for granted in the public sector. Whether and how tightly each unit is responsible for its own budget depend on the form of government in each country, the administrative structure of the state, and the system of financing of public administrations.

This partly helps explain why, in the countries considered in this chapter, the decentralization of collective bargaining in the public sector has been less frequent and more limited than is often suggested, even where it has been openly pursued. Governments eager to contain public expenditures have often found that they could control public sector wage costs more easily through a centralized system, even if tight budget control is not incompatible, in principle, with decentralized bargaining.

With some simplification, three groups of countries can be identified. The first one consists of countries where the decentralization of the bargaining structure has been very limited and a rather strong centralization or coordination of the process of determining pay and conditions of employment still persists. This group includes France, Germany, Spain, and Japan (where nonindustrial public employees do not have the right of collective bargaining).

France probably has the most-centralized pay-determination system in Europe. Since the 1983 reforms, annual negotiations over pay increases (not binding on the government) take place at the national level, between government (with the Ministry of Public Service serving a pivotal role) and the representative trade union confederations, simultaneously covering all three subsectors of the *Fonction Publique* (central government, local authorities, and public hospitals). Thus, a single decision made at a central level is applied to the common pay scale and job-classification system, directly regulating the pay increases of about 4.5 million public employees and indirectly affecting a million others. The recent pressures toward greater pay flexibility, individualization, and performance-related pay found in many other countries have been very limited in France, although some attempts to allow greater diversity in the wage and job-classification system occurred after the 1990 Durafour Agreement (Mossé and Tchobanian 1999:142–44, 156).

The German bargaining system is a little less centralized, if only because of the separation between *Beamte* and other public employees and the federalist constitutional structure of the state, which gives the three levels of government autonomous rights in different policy areas. This potentially greater fragmentation is compensated for, however, by tight coordination between and within the bargaining parties and by the pivotal role played by the minister of the interior. At the federal level, the minister has been responsible for safeguarding the public interest and formally approving collective agreements since 1960. He not only leads the employers' bargaining committee in collective negotiations for wage earners and salaried employees (*Angestellte* and *Arbeiter*), but also prepares legislation on remuneration and working conditions for *Beamte*. Thus he is in a focal position in the negotiation and determination of income for all public employees. On the workers' side (wage earners and salaried employees), the Ver.di (the largest German public sector union with its 2.8 million membership, affiliated to the main German confederation DGB) is the pattern setter for the whole public sector, so that wages and working conditions are settled in one annual round of negotiations for all public employees at the national, federal-state, and local levels (Keller 1999:71, 79). Finally, as in Italy and France, this high degree of centralization of the bargaining structure and the regulation of employment relations is associated with a rather inflexible pay system, based on a purely collective, uniform character that leaves little room for links with individual performance.

While France and Germany have moved very little from their traditional bargaining structures, Spain has known several changes since the mid-1980s, when collective bargaining rights for civil servants (who are still the large majority of public employees) were first recognized— although with an uncertain status. The Spanish negotiating model is based on a two- or three-tier system. At the first level there are general joint bargaining councils (or tables) for each territorial administration (one for government, one for each autonomous region, and one for each local authority); at the second tier there are sectoral joint councils, while at the third level, which is more decentralized, the possibility of ad hoc tables exists, if the employer and the unions so decide. The entire system is fairly centralized and hierarchically structured, however, restricting the powers of the autonomous governments and local authorities (Jódar, Jordana, and Alós 1999:186).

In Japan (where nonindustrial national and local public employees[9] do not have the right to bargain collectively), the system of the determination of pay and employment conditions has been highly centralized for the entire postwar period, under the control of the Prime Minister's Office, the Minister of Finance, and the National Personnel Authority for national public employees and of the Minister of Home Affairs for local government employees. However, some steps toward decentralization have been taken in recent years in the central administration, envisaging a devolution of authority to specialized agencies.

The second group includes countries like Italy and Denmark in which the bargaining system has recently undergone a process that could be defined as organized or centralized or coordinated decentralization (Traxler 1995; Due, Masden, Jensen, and Peterson 1994; Bordogna, Dell'Aringa, and Della Rocca 1999). In these cases, in order to pursue greater flexibility and adaptability to the needs of individual administrative units and local labor market conditions, a new emphasis has been put on "enterprise bargaining," requiring public employers to take part in negotiations at the decentralized levels. But this decentralization has taken place under national-level control.

In Denmark, where the minister of finance plays a strong coordinating role on the employers' side by negotiating with a coalition of four trade union federations, part of the pay-determination process occurs at the local level, since the government sets aside a certain percentage of the pay bill to be distributed locally among workers or groups of workers.

A similar system has worked in Italy since the late 1990s. The core of the system comprises two pillars of bargaining. The first, and more important, pillar consists of national negotiations, held every four years for normative issues and every two years for pay issues. These negotiations, which cover about 2.9 million contractualized employees, are divided into bargaining units corresponding to the main subsectors of public service (central government, local government, public education, national health system, and so forth). The 1993 reforms gave managers separate bargaining units. Occasionally, there can be framework agreements at the national level that cover matters of general interest in all the subsectors, or part of them. On the employer side, all national negotiations are conducted by Aran, following the guidelines defined by the employers' associations and within the overall financial constraints set by the central government in accordance with the planned rate of inflation set in the state budget laws.

The second pillar consists of decentralized or integrative agreements at the local and individual-unit level. Bargaining on pay issues at this level must be restricted to the financial limits fixed at the higher, national level, with little possibility to negotiate additional resources. This possibility has been enlarged, though, to some extent by a 1997 amendment to the 1993 law (but protections, and tight controls of the Treasury, have been included to prevent inflationary effects of decentralization over the total public sector pay bill). Despite these changes, the percentage of total pay that is determined centrally remains very high in some functional subsectors (up to 90 percent, or even more, in education), although it is somewhat lower in other sectors, like health and local government. Job-classification systems and pay scales are determined in national agreements and so are rather similar in all the subsectors, with low wage differentials between grades (especially in education). The national collective agreements reached since the 1993 reforms have tried to change this situation. They have frozen pay linked to the length of service, encouraged more selective incentives for collective productivity, and—for the first time—allowed managers partially to differentiate the wages and salaries of their employees on an individual basis. Managers can do so by assigning additional allowances to positions with special responsibilities (usually, but not exclusively, of employees of the higher grades), according to criteria agreed upon with trade unions. Parts of these allowances are linked to results. Despite these changes, the amount of differentiation and individualization of pay is still rather limited, and the new pay system has met several difficulties in implementation. There have been greater changes in national collective agreements for managers, however, linking their pay scales more closely to performance, although at the local level these agreements have not always been implemented in an innovative way.

A two-tier collective bargaining system also applies to Swedish central-government employees. Since the late 1980s the concrete determination of pay has been decentralized to individual administrative units, and forms of individualization and performance-related pay have been introduced. These have replaced the previous system, which was based on very centralized pay and grading schemes. But these decentralized negotiations occur within central framework agreements between the government agency for negotiations (AgV) and trade unions, which identify the scope for pay increases. These changes, moreover, have been accompanied by a structural reform in the financing of services, based on the principle of cash limits: under this reform the (about 270) central-government agencies receive frame grants for their total administrative costs, with no restrictions on how they can use the grants. Thus, the devolution of managerial responsibilities in personnel matters has been combined with strong centralized control of the agencies' running costs (Bordogna and Winchester 2001). The decentralization of bargaining is higher in Sweden than in Italy and Denmark, however, making the Swedish case more similar to the third group of countries.

The third group consists of countries with the most-decentralized bargaining systems, like Britain, Canada, Australia, New Zealand, and the United States. Some of them are characterized by a federal adminis-trative structure that grants a substantial degree of administrative auton-omy to the lower levels of government, like the Australian states or the Canadian provinces. The most-radical decentralization has probably taken place in New Zealand, however, and in the British civil service. In Britain, the traditional centralized and bureaucratic pay-determination system and the unified salary structure covering almost half a million staff members have been replaced since the early 1990s by delegated bargaining in more than one hundred executive agencies, which are expected to develop their own grading, promotion, and performance-related pay schemes (Bordogna and Winchester 2001:59). Since the 1988 State Sector Act, the New Zealand central government—which, with about two hundred thousand employees, covers the largest part of total public employment—has moved in the same direction. The Act made chief executives of departments (or agencies) employers of their staff and replaced servicewide occupational determinations of pay with departmental agreements as the primary means of pay fixing (Walsh, Harbridge, and Crawford 2001:195). Even in these cases, however, rather strong elements of centralization in decisions over pay persisted as a means of reducing inefficiencies and controlling costs. Examples are the frequent use of strict cash limits on expenditures in Britain; the persisting role of the State Services Commission in negotiations over pay and employment conditions in New Zealand, despite the delegation of responsibilities on personnel matters to departmental chief executives; and the increased intervention of provincial governments in bargaining during the 1990s in Canada, especially in education and the health

sector, despite the legal rights of local employers to make industrial
relations decisions (Winchester and Bach 1999:44, 46; Walsh, Harbridge,
and Crawford 2001:195; Thompson 2001:136, 145; Dell'Aringa 2001:16).
In Canada the federal government also suspended bargaining rights for
all its employees for seven years after 1991, imposing a wage freeze or
severe layoffs in order to reduce public sector payroll costs; this move
was followed by all provinces' imposing restrictions on public service
wage increases and benefits.

In addition to these differences across countries, collective bargaining structures may vary widely within countries, among different subsectors. In Britain, for instance, the decentralization process mainly
affected the civil service; outside this sector national systems of pay
determination remain important, while nurses and teachers are subject
to the system of pay-review bodies. In Italy the education sector (the
largest in the whole public sector) has so far been almost entirely excluded from the decentralization of bargaining, although some limited
change in this direction is expected in the near future. The same is true
in Australia, where, despite the diffusion of enterprise bargaining all
over the public sector and especially in the public service that was
prompted by the 1996 Workplace Relations Act, collective bargaining
remains rather centralized in education.

In sum, although the need for greater decentralization of bargaining
is strongly stressed in the New Public Management approach, there
does not appear to be a general trend in this direction. Significant
differences across countries and within countries remain in place, and in
many cases a resilience of centralized systems for determining pay and
working conditions can be observed. By and large, the decentralization
of decision making has been higher and more diffused on nonpay
conditions of employment, while various forms of centralized control
have persisted on pay issues in order to contain or reduce the proportion of labor costs in total public expenditure. Finally, where the bargaining structure is more decentralized, pay-determination systems are
usually less rigid and pay differentials are wider (Dell'Aringa 2001:17).

Relations outside Collective Bargaining

In many countries, collective bargaining procedures are supplemented
by a dense network of information and consultation rights on a wide set of
work organization and personnel matters. These rights may be determined
by legislation or by collective agreements, are sometimes linked to specific
employee representation bodies, according to the so-called dual channel

system of representation, and are often also applied to personnel whose employment conditions are unilaterally regulated by their employer. The best-known example of a legally regulated, dual-channel system is probably that of staff councils in Germany, the quasi-equivalent of works councils (*Betriebsräte*) in the private sector. The staff councils are established by law at federal-state, and local or municipal levels; composed of the three groups of public employees (*Beamte* included), following proportional representation principles; and elected by all employees. They are not union bodies, although many elected representatives are also union members. They enjoy statutory rights of codetermination covering a wide range of powers (from information to veto) in social and personnel affairs, but not economic matters. They do not have collective bargaining rights and are not allowed to call a strike, being an element of cooperation with management. If conflicts of rights arise that cannot be solved by voluntary agreement, these are settled by an arbitration committee. Unlike private sector employee representation systems, however, employees in the public sector do not have the right of representation on company boards—either the management or the supervisory board (Keller 1999:75).

In France public employees also have representation rights, established by law, on several joint committees in which employees and employers have equal representation. These institutions have only consultative character, but their impact can be very significant, defining general, well-publicized rules that limit managerial prerogatives and establish co-management procedures. The most influential ones are probably the joint administrative boards (*commissions administrative paritaires*), one for each professional *corps*, which have the right to examine decisions regarding any civil servant career (recruitment, promotion, mobility, training, or discipline), with the effect of standardizing staff management rules and limiting managerial autonomy, even if the ultimate power to decide belongs to the employers. Representatives in these committees are elected from union lists, which is a reason why such elections provide a means to assess the relative influence of different unions. Other committees include the joint technical boards (*comités techniques paritaires*), health and safety committees, and the *Conseil supérieur de la fonction publique de l'Etat* at the national level. The important role played by these institutions in personnel management could help explain why collective bargaining was and is slow to evolve in French public services (Mossé and Tchobanian 1999:157–58).

Another case with a legally regulated, dual system of employee representation is Spain, where staff councils (*juntas de personal*) and workers' delegates (*delegados de personal*) are established by law (since 1987) and elected every four years by all statutory employees.

Unlike these cases, the measures to promote worker participation in Denmark are not based on legislation, but on collective agreements between the employers (the minister of finance and the employers' associations) and the cartels of state and local government trade unions. The works councils, or *cooperation committees*, both at the workplace and at higher levels, have the right to be consulted on many personnel matters subject to managerial prerogatives and even on strategic decisions, but they are not empowered to conclude agreements, even though employee representatives are often the shop stewards. Health and safety committees, however, are based on legislation.

Information and consultation practices seem less developed in Australia and in Canada. After a long tradition, dating from 1945, and a diffusion of formal consultative committees in government departments promoted by the Australian Labor Cabinet in the 1980s, the emphasis in the 1990s was focused on the strengthening of managerial prerogatives, although without automatically abandoning employee-participation practices. After the arrival of collective bargaining in the public sector in Canada at the end of the 1960s, labor-management consultation practices and institutions lost much of their importance, because many topics assigned to participatory bodies at the workplace level in other countries are included in collective negotiations. Consultation occurs on such topics as technological change, training, and pensions, but only when the employer so decides (Thompson 2001:149).

Italy, Japan, and Britain are countries in which a single-channel system of employee representation prevails. In Italy and Japan, however, this does not mean that information and consultation practices are neglected. In fact, in Italy, information and consultation rights are given to the same institutions that are empowered to participate in collective negotiations at the local level—the *unitary personnel representation bodies* that were created by the 1993 legislation (amended in 1997) and are elected every three years by all the employees. Thus, Italy's system is a single channel with double functions, which may explain why the boundaries between negotiable and nonnegotiable issues in its public administrations are often rather unclear, generating a sort of hyper-regulation of employment conditions at the local level in never-ending negotiations. In Britain, on the contrary, not only do trade unions offer the only channel for collective representation in the absence of legally regulated procedures for consultation and negotiation, but such practices are less diffused than in other European countries, and the relationships between the parties maintain a rather adversarial character.

Labor Disputes and Regulation of Strikes

In absolute terms, the evidence suggests that total days not worked due to labor disputes in the public service have declined in many industrialized democracies over the last 20 years or so, following the general trend of aggregate strike activity. This observation can be misleading, however, since in many cases the relative weight of public sector disputes on total labor conflicts has increased. In addition, and perhaps more important, it may be inappropriate to measure conflict in the public services with the traditional indicators most commonly utilized in the industrial sector: number of workers involved and number of days lost. Public sector workers—especially those employed in so-called essential public services—have a much higher disruptive power than their industrial sector counterparts. Their strike action can be very effective without involving a large number of workers and without lasting a prolonged period of time. This type of conflict does not need to be quantitatively relevant to be socially disruptive: the number of disputes may be much more important than the number of workers involved or days lost. Moreover, especially in cases of essential public services, this conflict notoriously impacts on subjects other than the parties directly in dispute, with possible threats on rights that, in several countries, are subject to the same constitutional protection as the right (or freedom) to strike. From a legal point of view, this raises the delicate problem of how to reconcile the two sets of rights. From the perspective of large, encompassing unions, this raises an equally delicate problem: how to safeguard their organizational cohesion, when those whose rights are wounded by public service strikes can be members of the same trade union confederations as the strikers (Bordogna and Cella 2002).

That is why strikes in the public service are often subject to some kind of special regulation (with different characteristics across countries), sometimes with a simple denial of the right to strike. It is also why large, encompassing unions can support this special regulation. In some cases, however, no special regulation exists, and the problem of managing these types of conflicts may be carried out by other institutional features of the labor relations system as a whole.

In Denmark, agreement-covered public sector employees are subject to a general peace obligation provision that prevents conflicts during the lifetime of a collective agreement. It is only in connection with the renewal of existing agreements that it is possible to resort to industrial action. Such action must be approved, however, by a qualified majority of the competent assemblies and is subject to a 30-day advance notice, double that required in the private sector. Almost half of state employees, moreover, have no right to strike.[10] In addition, as already mentioned, if the parties fail to reach an agreement for this group, their pay and working conditions are unilaterally determined by an Act of the *Folketing*. The same rules apply to the municipal and regional subsectors, where a more important role in conflict regulation is played by the Public Conciliator's Institution. (In these subsectors, the number of agreement-covered employees is notably higher than in the state sector; Andersen, Due, and Masden 1999:228–29).

Labor disputes in the public sector have been quite rare in Germany over the entire post–World War II period. The two major episodes of conflict took place in 1974 and 1992, and the risk of a third one was avoided in January 2003. There are no formal mechanisms of conflict resolution in Germany, although a mediation agreement voluntarily concluded by the social partners after the 1974 strike has been used several times afterward. The fact is, however, that other general features of the labor relations system help to prevent and control the outburst of open conflict: the special legislation of *Beamte*, who do not have the right to strike; the legislation on collective bargaining, which establishes a general peace-obligation clause and discourages union fragmentation; and the principle of *sozialadäquanz* for resorting to strike action.

Quite different is the situation in Italy, where very intense labor disputes have increased in the public services over the last 20 years, especially during the second half of the 1980s. No special legislation existed at that time, nor was there (nor is there) any legally binding peace-obligation clause in the Italian system during the lifetime of collective agreements. Codes of self-regulation of strike action were adopted by the larger trade unions, as they were a requisite to participate in public sector collective negotiations under the 1983 framework law on public employment. These codes were rather weak, however, systematically challenged by new unions and special-interest organizations (the so-called *Cobas,* which of course did not subscribe to them), and not infrequently ignored by local-level unions and rank-and-file members belonging to the largest confederations. Special legislation to discipline strikes in essential public services was adopted in 1990, supported by the largest confederations; it provides rules for advance notice and a guarantee of the delivery of a certain minimum standard of services (or indispensable services), to be agreed upon between the parties, in case of a strike. It also established the Guarantee Commission to supervise the implementation of the law and gave it some powers of control and sanction. This legislation has been reasonably successful in containing disputes in some parts of the public sector, like education and health, but much less so in others, especially transportation. It was amended and strengthened in 2000, giving the Guarantee Commission more powers in the conciliation and mediation of disputes, but the effects of this reform are still uncertain.

In France, as in Italy, no peace obligation exists between the signatories to a collective agreement. The right to strike is an individual constitutional right and collective agreements can never deprive employees of this right. While union self-regulation of strike action is little used, some special regulations apply in the public services: advance notice (five days), restriction of the right to initiate strike action to the representative unions, and prohibition of rotating strikes. The capacity of these rules to manage conflict in the public services is rather weak, however.

In Britain strikes in the public sector contributed significantly to the overall pattern of industrial conflict during the 1970s and early 1980s. The Conservative governments introduced several legal restrictions on strikes, covering both the private and public sectors, like compulsory strike ballots, a wider definition of unlawful "political" disputes, and an increasing liability of union officials and vulnerability of union funds to employers' litigation. The impact of these measures has been much greater in the public sector, which may explain why legislation specifically targeting disputes in the public services has not been introduced, except for one dealing with prison officers (Winchester and Bach 1999).

Outside Europe, in Japan, nonindustrial national and local public employees do not have the right to strike, although they did for a short while after the end of World War II (with few exceptions); at that time they were also the core of a revolutionary labor movement. Despite the prohibition of industrial action, public employees, especially postal workers, frequently resorted to illegal industrial action until 1975. The purpose of this action was to demand the restoration of their right to strike. Public sector strikes declined after 1975, partly as a consequence of a severe 1977 Supreme Court decision against work stoppages by postal workers (who were potentially subject to being criminally punished) and,

10 years later, of the privatization of the Japanese National Railways (Koshiro 2001).

In Canada, beginning in the mid-1960s, collective bargaining with the possibility of a strike was accepted by policy makers as the preferable technique for resolving labor disputes. With few exceptions (police and firefighters) municipal employees, federal employees, and employees in 7 of the 10 provinces can strike legally. Thus, about 75 percent of public sector employees have the right to strike. There are several alternate dispute settlement mechanisms not normally available (or less frequently used) in the private sector that are available in some Canadian provinces, like interest arbitration, back-to-work legislation, and the designation of essential service workers who must continue to provide essential services during a strike action. Furthermore, when, after a decline in the 1980s, several large strikes occurred in the late 1990s to regain some of the economic losses suffered earlier in the decade, the governments passed or threatened to pass legislation ordering the workers to end their strikes. This legislation was generally respected by trade unions, with the exception of the nurses' unions in two provinces (Thompson 2001:148).

In New Zealand, where labor militancy in the public sector was quite intense in the 1990s, the reforms intent on making public sector labor relations closer to those in the private sector focused heavily on the mechanisms regulating industrial action. By the early 1990s the system of tribunal arbitration (with the power to issue binding orders) was abolished, the right of public employees to strike and the countervailing right of employers to lock out were recognized, and the traditional procedures for resolving disputes of interest were cancelled by the Employment Contracts Act. This left the parties reliant on their own bargaining power to secure a favorable agreement and implied the end of specific means for resolving bargaining impasses and of the traditional reliance on ministerial interventions, since one of the reforms' goals was to remove the ministers entirely from the bargaining arena (Walsh, Harbridge, and Crawford 2001).

Conclusions and Discussion

In most industrialized democracies a process of reform of public sector employment relations has taken place in the last 10 to 15 years, as a part of governments' attempt to pursue the double goal of reducing or containing public expenditures while improving the quality of the services delivered. Not all the countries seem to have followed the guidelines suggested by the New Public Management mainstream as the preferred way to achieve a lasting reconciliation between these conflicting needs, however. The impression is that the reform process has been uneven across countries (and subsectors) and that strong national variations persist in employment practices and regulations, deeply rooted in country-specific legal and institutional traditions not easily modifiable in the public sector.

Three groups of countries have been described here, two with clearly opposite characteristics and a third somewhere in between.

The first group includes countries where the reform path more closely resembles the New Public Management recipe. The governments and public employers in this group have strategically taken the lead in the process of change, overseeing the privatization of services, introduction of marketlike mechanisms, strengthening and devolution of managerial authority, weakening of public employees' special prerogatives, increasing use of fixed-term and nonstandard employment contracts (for managers as well as employees), contractualization of the employment relationship, decentralization of bargaining, and (partial) individualization of pay. In these countries the single-channel system of employee representation prevails, and participatory institutions at the workplace or higher level either do not exist or are weak. In some cases, the importation of market or marketlike mechanisms into the public sector has been combined with the abolition of the special regulation of public service labor disputes. The attitude of the unions toward the reform process in these countries has usually been rather adversarial, partly because the reform had an anticollectivist character and often explicitly aimed at curtailing trade union influence. Britain, New Zealand, and Australia belong to this group, although not all of them share all these features entirely (it will be recalled, for instance, that in Britain teachers and nurses have their pay determined nationally by the pay-review bodies system).

At the opposite side we find countries that have changed their traditional system of employment relations only to a limited extent and in a very incremental way. Privatization and contracting out processes have been more restrained, the introduction of marketlike mechanisms have been shier, reductions in the proportion of employees with civil servant status have been quite small if not totally absent, the use of fixed-term contracts is very restricted, and collective bargaining is not universal or has an uncertain status and is highly centralized (as is the pay-determination system where collective bargaining is not allowed). In addition, employees receive rather uniform treatment with little flexibility, and schemes of performance-related pay are little diffused. To this group belong France and Germany, where the public administration is oriented

by a strong bureaucratic tradition focused on legality and on a tight respect for formal rules (Pollitt and Bouckaert 2000). Spain and also Japan
share several of these features, and all these countries are characterized
by well-developed and legally regulated participatory institutions at the
workplace level, in some cases (as in Germany and Spain) based on a
dual-channel system of employee representation. These countries differ
in other features, however, such as the regulation of strikes in public
services.

Italy and Denmark can be allocated to a less-coherent category,
sharing some features of both the preceding groups. Privatization processes, contracting out, and the introduction of marketlike mechanisms
(as in the Italian health sector) have been implemented but certainly to a
lesser degree than in Britain and New Zealand. The diffusion of nonstandard types of employment contract is somewhat limited, especially in
Italy, and conditions of employment are rather uniform and rigid. Unlike
in Germany and France, however, few public service employees have
their pay set by unilateral regulation; collective bargaining is the prevailing method of determining pay and working conditions and, despite a
still rather centralized bargaining system, recent reforms have facilitated
a controlled or coordinated decentralization. There have also been
modest attempts to link pay to measures of performance, and in Italy a
reform of the prerogatives and employment conditions of managerial
personnel has made them less distant from those of the private sector. In
these countries the largest trade unions have generally supported, and at
times negotiated, the process of change.

Sweden also has an uncertain allocation, characterized as it is by a
very narrow proportion of civil servants with special status, employment
relations essentially regulated by the same rules as in the private sector,
and, in the central government, strong managerial prerogatives, a high
decentralization of collective bargaining to the agency level, and a rather
diffused individualization of pay ever since the century-old system based
on nationwide pay scales related to job titles was ended in 1989–90.
Decentralized bargaining takes place within higher-level framework
agreements, however, and trade unions have not opposed these changes,
maintaining a rather collaborative attitude.

Additional considerations are necessary. First, the differences within
countries, among subsectors, can also be important. By and large, the
education sector has been most resistant to change, with the persistence
of a rather centralized system for the determination of pay and employment conditions. Second, even where bargaining has been decentralized,

governments have often maintained strong, centralized, financial controls in order to contain public expenditures and avoid inflationary consequences of the decentralization process.

Finally, as for the convergence-divergence debate, it is a shared observation (Bach 1999) that while the differences between public and private sector employment practices and regulations within countries have been fading away in many (but not all) cases under common cost-efficiency and quality-enhancement pressures, those across countries have been more resistant to change, deeply rooted as they are in country-specific legal and institutional traditions, which are less easily modifiable in the public than the private sector.

Notes

[1] The analysis that follows is generally based on two sources—Bach, Bordogna, Della Rocca, and Winchester (1999) and Dell'Aringa, Della Rocca, and Keller (2001)—although it updates and enlarges them in several points. These sources, in turn, are the research results of a network of scholars, initially European but later including non-European experts as well. Since the mid-1990s this network has studied the reform of public sector employment relations extensively in a rather wide group of industrialized countries.

[2] A Constitutional Court ruling in 1987 upheld the need to maintain civil service employment as the main form of employment in the public sector (Jódar, Jordana, and Alós 1999:172).

[3] A 1998 law allowed the government to appoint a certain number of top-level state managers within 90 days after the vote of confidence, possibly removing those already in charge before the expiration of their appointment period. This power has been widened in the 2002 amendment of the law, allowing the government to appoint managers even for a very short duration.

[4] During the period of Franco's rule, civil servants were forbidden from joining even the mandatory, official trade unions. From 1976 the formation of civil service associations was permitted, but civil servants were not yet allowed to join trade unions. In 1977 the government allowed trade union membership among civil servants, but it was only in 1984 and 1985 that two pieces of legislation came down clearly in favor of a trade union model of representation among civil servants. However, the first union election in the civil service (to elect staff councils) took place only in 1987, ten years later than in the private sector (Jódar, Jordana, and Alós 1999:181).

[5] In the second half of the 1980s Italy was the theater of a wide proliferation of strikes in the public sector, especially in transportation (railway engine drivers, pilots, air traffic controllers, and ground personnel in airports), schools, and hospitals (nurses and partly doctors). These struggles were due largely to small craft or occupational unions (many of them new: the so-called *Cobas*), independent or out of the control of the largest confederations and able to take advantage of the disruptive power of *tertiary* conflict and of the very weak system of conflict regulation in public services. A law regulating strikes in essential public services was approved in the

summer of 1990 and public sector reform was approved in 1993. Among the other features (see this chapter's section on labor disputes), these reforms made it more difficult to resort to industrial action, set more severe financial constraints on public administrations while strengthening the role of public managers in labor relations matters. As a consequence of these changes, strikes and union power dispersion in public services decreased in the 1990s, with the notable exception of the transport sector (Bordogna 1993; Bordogna and Cella 2002).

[6] Due to these features, in a study on public service pay determination in a selected group of countries, Marsden (1997:64) classifies France as a case of "free collective bargaining, but subject to unilateral veto by the government."

[7] In the already-mentioned Marsden (1997) scheme, the system based on recommendations of independent pay bodies is classified at the opposite pole of collective bargaining on the axis representing the employees' influence on pay fixing. Perhaps this overestimates the difference between the two systems and assigns the first one too closely to unilateral government regulation, obscuring the possibility of influence on the part of the unions. By the way, in recent decades pay outcomes have often been more favorable to employees subject to pay-review bodies than to those with collective bargaining rights (Winchester and Bach 1999).

[8] In an equally well-known article, Soskice (1990) stressed that what is most important is the degree of coordination of the process of pay determination, regardless of the specific level at which negotiations "technically" take place. But from the point of view that interests us here, the substance does not change very much, since the incentives that influence the behavior of the bargaining agents (especially unions) remain substantially the same. In a subsequent article, by the way, reviewing the evidence produced after the 1988 Calmfors and Driffill article, Calmfors (1993) suggested that the relationship between centralization or decentralization of the bargaining structure and macroeconomic performance might be more complicated than originally hypothesized.

[9] That is, public employees not belonging to public corporations.

[10] A reform of the Arbitration Court in 1981, establishing a state civil service court and a municipal civil service court, was an indirect recognition of the right to strike for civil servants, however (Andersen, Due, and Masden 1999:230).

References

Accornero, Aris. 1985. "La 'Terziarizzazione' del Conflitto e i Suoi Effetti." In Gian Primo Cella and Marino Regini, eds., Il Conflitto Industriale in Italia. Bologna: Il Mulino, pp. 275–313.

Andersen, Søren Kaj, Jesper Due, and Jørgen Steen Masden. 1997. "Multi-track Approach to Public Sector Restructuring in Europe: Impact on Employment Relations, Role of Trade Unions," Transfer, Vol. 3, no. 1 (May), pp. 34–61.

———. 1999. "Denmark: Negotiating the Restructuring of Public Service Employment Relations." In Stephen Bach, Lorenzo Bordogna, Giuseppe Della Rocca, and David Winchester, eds., Public Service Employment Relations in Europe. Transformation, Modernization or Inertia? London: Routledge, pp. 198–235.

Bach, Stephen. 1999. "Changing Public Service Employment Relations." In Stephen Bach, Lorenzo Bordogna, Giuseppe Della Rocca, and David Winchester, eds., *Public Service Employment Relations in Europe. Transformation, Modernization or Inertia?* London: Routledge, pp. 1–21.

Bach, Stephen, Lorenzo Bordogna, Giuseppe Della Rocca, and David Winchester, eds. 1999. *Public Service Employment Relations in Europe. Transformation, Modernization or Inertia?* London: Routledge.

Bach, Stephen, and Giuseppe Della Rocca. 2001. "The New Public Management in Europe." In Carlo Dell'Aringa, Giuseppe Della Rocca, and Berndt Keller, eds., *Strategic Choices in Reforming Public Service Employment. An International Handbook.* New York: Palgrave, pp. 24–47.

Boeri, Tito, Agar Brugiavini, and Lars Calmfors, eds. 2001. *The Role of Unions in the Twenty-First Century.* Oxford: Oxford University Press.

Bordogna, Lorenzo. 1993. "Public Sector Labor Relations between Macro-Economic Constraints and Union Fragmentation: The Italian Experience in Comparative Perspective." In International Industrial Relations Association, *Economic and Political Changes in Europe: Implications on Industrial Relations.* Bari: Cacucci, pp. 865–80.

———, ed. 2002. *Contrattazione Integrativa e Gestione del Personale nelle Pubbliche Amministrazioni (1998–2001).* Milano: Angeli Editore.

Bordogna, Lorenzo, and Gian Primo Cella. 2002. "Decline or Transformation? Change in Industrial Conflict and Its Challenges." *Transfer,* Vol. 8, no. 4 (Winter), pp. 585–607.

Bordogna, Lorenzo, Carlo Dell'Aringa, and Giuseppe Della Rocca. 1999. "Italy. A Case of Co-ordinated Decentralization." In Stephen Bach, Lorenzo Bordogna, Giuseppe Della Rocca, and David Winchester, eds., *Public Service Employment Relations in Europe. Transformation, Modernization or Inertia?* London: Routledge, pp. 94–129.

Bordogna, Lorenzo, and David Winchester. 2001. "Collective Bargaining in Western Europe." In Carlo Dell'Aringa, Giuseppe Della Rocca, and Berndt Keller, eds., *Strategic Choices in Reforming Public Service Employment. An International Handbook.* New York: Palgrave, pp. 48–70.

Brock, Jonathan. 2001. "United States Public Sector Employment." In Carlo Dell'Aringa, Giuseppe Della Rocca, and Berndt Keller, eds., *Strategic Choices in Reforming Public Service Employment. An International Handbook.* New York: Palgrave, pp. 97–126.

Calmfors, Lars. 1993. "Centralization of Wage Bargaining and Macro-economic Performance: A Survey." OECD, *Economic Studies,* no. 21 (Winter), pp. 161–91.

Calmfors, Lars, and John Driffill. 1988. "Bargaining Structure, Corporatism and Macro-Economic Performance." In *Economic Policy,* no. 6 (April), pp. 13–47.

Clegg, Hugh. 1976. *Trade Unionism under Collective Bargaining.* Oxford: Basil Blackwell.

Dell'Aringa, Carlo. 2001. "Reforming Public Sector Labor Relations." In Carlo Dell'Aringa, Giuseppe Della Rocca, and Berndt Keller, eds., *Strategic Choices in Reforming Public Service Employment. An International Handbook.* New York: Palgrave, pp. 1–23.

Dell'Aringa, Carlo, Giuseppe Della Rocca, and Berndt Keller, eds. 2001. *Strategic Choices in Reforming Public Service Employment. An International Handbook.* New York: Palgrave.

66   GOING PUBLIC

Due, Jesper, Jørgen Steen Masden, Carsten Strøby Jensen, and Lars Kjerulf Peterson. 1994. *The Survival of the Danish Model*. Copenhagen: DJØF.

Elliott, Robert F., and Keith A. Bender. 1997. "Decentralization and Pay Reform in Central Government: A Study of Three Countries." *British Journal of Industrial Relations*, Vol. 35, no. 3 (September), pp. 447–75.

Jódar, Pere, Jacint Jordana, and Ramón Alós. 1999. "Spain: Public Service Employment Relations since the Transition to Democracy." In Stephen Bach, Lorenzo Bordogna, Giuseppe Della Rocca, and David Winchester, eds., *Public Service Employment Relations in Europe. Transformation, Modernization or Inertia?* London: Routledge, pp. 164–97.

Keller, Berndt. 1999. "Germany: Negotiated Change, Modernization and the Challenge of Unification." In Stephen Bach, Lorenzo Bordogna, Giuseppe Della Rocca, and David Winchester, eds., *Public Service Employment Relations in Europe. Transformation, Modernization or Inertia?* London: Routledge, pp. 56–93.

Keller, Berndt, Jesper Due, and Soren Kaj Andersen. 2001. "Employer Associations and Unions in the Public Sector." In Carlo Dell'Aringa, Giuseppe Della Rocca, and Berndt Keller, eds., *Strategic Choices in Reforming Public Service Employment: An International Handbook*. New York: Palgrave, pp. 71–96.

Kochan, Thomas A. 1974. "A Theory of Multilateral Bargaining in City Governments." *Industrial and Labor Relations Review*, Vol. 27, no. 4 (July), pp. 525–42.

Koshiro, Kazutoshi. 2001. "Japanese Public Sector Employment." In Carlo Dell'Aringa, Giuseppe Della Rocca, and Berndt Keller, eds., *Strategic Choices in Reforming Public Service Employment. An International Handbook*. New York: Palgrave, pp. 155–84.

Lansbury, Russell D., and Duncan K. Macdonald. 2001. "Employment Relations in the Australian Public Sector." In Carlo Dell'Aringa, Giuseppe Della Rocca, and Berndt Keller, eds., *Strategic Choices in Reforming Public Service Employment. An International Handbook*. New York: Palgrave, pp. 216–42.

Marsden, David. 1997. "Public Service Pay Reforms in European Countries." *Transfer*, Vol. 3, no. 1 (May), pp. 62–85.

Mossé, Philippe, and Robert Tchobanian. 1999. "France. The Restructuring of Employment Relations in the Public Services." In Stephen Bach, Lorenzo Bordogna, Giuseppe Della Rocca, and David Winchester, eds., *Public Service Employment Relations in Europe. Transformation, Modernization or Inertia?* London: Routledge, pp. 130–63.

OECD. 1995. *Governance in Transition: Public Management Reforms in OECD Countries*. Paris: OECD.

———. 1996a. *Performance Auditing and the Modernization of Government*. Paris: OECD.

———. 1996b. *Performance Management in Government: Contemporary Illustrations*. Paris: OECD.

OECD-PUMA/HRM. 2002. *Highlights of Public Sector Pay and Employment Trends: 2002 Update*. October 3. Paris: OECD.

Olson, Mancur. 1982. *The Rise and Decline of Nations*. New Haven: Yale University Press.

Ozaki, Muneto. 1993. "Labour Relations in the Public Sector." In Roger Blainpain and Chris Engels, eds., *Comparative Labour Law and Industrial Relations in Industrialized Market Economies*. Deventer: Kluwer, pp. 501–21.

Pollitt, Cristopher, and Geert Bouckaert. 2000. *Public Management Reform*. Oxford: Oxford University Press.

Schager, Nils-Henrik, and Patrik Andersson. 1996. "Recent Reforms within the Central Government Sector in Sweden with Respect to Employment and Pay Policies." Paper prepared for Aran Conference, Rome, January 25–28.

Soskice, David. 1990. "Wage Determination: The Changing Role of Institutions in Advanced Industrialized Countries." *Oxford Review of Economic Policy*, Vol. 6, no. 4, pp. 36–61.

Thompson, Mark. 2001. "Canadian Public Sector Employment." In Carlo Dell'Aringa, Giuseppe Della Rocca, and Berndt Keller, eds., *Strategic Choices in Reforming Public Service Employment. An International Handbook*. New York: Palgrave, pp. 127–54.

Traxler, Franz. 1995. "Farewell to Labor Market Associations? Organized versus Disorganized Decentralization as a Map for Industrial Relations." In Colin Crouch and Franz Traxler, eds., *Organized Industrial Relations in Europe: What Future?* Avebury: Aldershot, pp. 3–19.

Treu, Tiziano, ed. 1987. *Public Service Labor Relations: Recent Trends and Future Prospects*. Geneva: ILO.

Visser, Jelle, and Anton Hemerijck. 1997. *A Dutch Miracle*. Amsterdam: Amsterdam University Press.

Walsh, Pat, Raymond Harbridge, and Aaron Crawford. 2001. "Public Sector Industrial Relations in New Zealand." In Carlo Dell'Aringa, Giuseppe Della Rocca, and Berndt Keller, eds., *Strategic Choices in Reforming Public Service Employment. An International Handbook*. New York: Palgrave, pp. 185–215.

Winchester, David, and Stephen Bach. 1999. "Britain. The Transformation of Public Service Employment Relations." In Stephen Bach, Lorenzo Bordogna, Giuseppe Della Rocca, and David Winchester, eds., *Public Service Employment Relations in Europe. Transformation, Modernization or Inertia?* London: Routledge, pp. 22–55.

CHAPTER 2

Unionization Trends and Labor-Management Cooperation in the Public Sector

TERRY THOMASON
University of Rhode Island

JOHN F. BURTON, JR.
Rutgers University

One major purpose of this chapter is to examine unionization trends in the public sector. The extent of unionization is an important topic because higher density is associated with greater union influence over wages and working conditions for both union members and other workers.[1] Higher rates of unionization are especially important in the public sector because greater membership augments the political influence of workers.

The percentage of workers who are organized in the public sector has been stable in recent decades, in sharp contract to the private sector, where union density has declined substantially. One possible explanation of changes in union density—different growth rates in the components of the workforce when separated along such dimensions as occupation or gender—provides little assistance in explaining recent developments in either the private or public sectors.

A second purpose of the chapter is to examine a topic relevant to the general theme of this volume, namely, the promotion of union-management cooperation in the public sector in order to improve the effectiveness and efficiency of government. We discuss several studies indicating that when unions organize public sector entities, they tend to increase employment as well as wages. We also provide evidence that privatization of government activities has expanded in several important functions since the early 1980s. The tendency for unions to inflate employment and the growing importance of privatization increase the difficulties of achieving, as well as the potential payoffs from, enhanced labor-management cooperation within the public sector.

Union Density from the 1950s to the 1980s

Burton and Thomason (1988) identified three distinct periods in the history of public sector bargaining between the 1950s and the mid-1980s: an initial period during which unions in the public sector were virtually nonexistent, a period of rapid growth in public sector unionization beginning in the early 1960s, and a period from the mid-1970s to the mid-1980s when (depending on the measure used) public sector union density ceased to grow or declined. These developments are illustrated in Figure 1, which shows union density rates for the public and private sectors, separately and combined, for selected years between 1956 and 1984. The term *union density* refers to the percentage of employees who are members of a union in the entire workforce or in specified components of the workforce, such as the public sector.

The rapid growth of public sector unionism in the 1960s and early 1970s and the stagnation during the latter half of the 1970s and first half of the 1980s were largely unexpected developments that have not been fully explained. Possible explanations for the rapid growth phase discussed in Burton (1979) include (1) changes in the attitudes of public sector workers toward unionization, (2) a more aggressive stance by many organizations representing public sector workers, and (3) changes in public policy favoring collective bargaining. Burton asserted, however, that the favorable legislation was as much a result as a cause of the increasing strength of public sector bargaining organizations.

The stagnation that began in the mid-1970s and lasted through the mid-1980s was attributed in part by Burton and Thomason (1988) to growing hostility among voters toward government expenditures and increasing resistance to unions by public sector management. They also indicated that the decline in unionization of state and local government employees might possibly be explained by structural changes in the distribution of employment in the public sector. For example, teachers, who represented the second most highly organized function in 1972, decreased as a proportion of total state and local employment between 1972 and 1982.[2]

Union Density Trends since 1983

Public and Private Sectors

Union densities in the total workforce, as well as the public and private sectors, for the period 1983 through 2002 are presented in Table 1 and Figure 2. The data for these decades are taken from the Current Population Survey (CPS) (U.S.Department of Labor 1983–2002).[3]

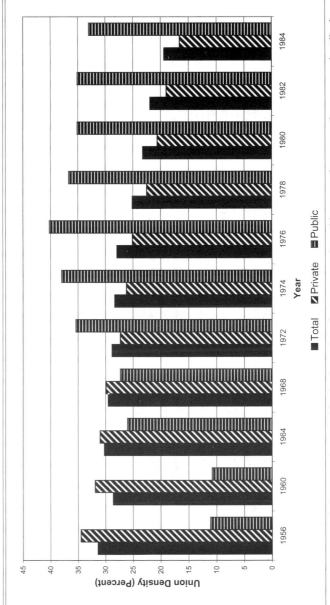

FIGURE 1
Union Density, by Sector, 1956-84

Source: Burton and Thomason (1988, Table 1). The 1956 and 1960 entries for public sector density are for unions only. All other entries are for all bargaining organizations.

TABLE 1

Employment, Union Membership, and Union Density
Private and Public Sectors, 1983–2002

Year	Total economy			Private sector			Public sector		
	Employment	Union membership	Union density (percent)	Employment	Union membership	Union density (percent)	Employment	Union membership	Union density (percent)
1983	87,972	17,660	20.1	72,480	11,976	16.5	15,492	5,684	36.7
1984	91,853	17,286	18.8	76,181	11,675	15.3	15,673	5,611	35.8
1985	94,198	16,942	18.0	78,292	11,257	14.4	15,906	5,685	35.7
1986	96,647	16,944	17.5	80,427	11,111	13.8	16,220	5,833	36.0
1987	99,071	16,878	17.0	82,348	10,881	13.2	16,723	5,997	35.9
1988	101,129	16,958	16.8	84,099	10,711	12.7	17,030	6,247	36.7
1989	103,480	16,960	16.4	85,989	10,536	12.3	17,491	6,424	36.7
1990	103,905	16,740	16.1	86,122	10,255	11.9	17,782	6,485	36.5
1991	102,786	16,568	16.1	84,793	9,936	11.7	17,993	6,632	36.9
1992	103,688	16,390	15.8	85,525	9,737	11.4	18,163	6,653	36.6
1993	105,067	16,598	15.8	86,438	9,580	11.1	18,630	7,018	37.7
1994	107,988	16,740	15.5	89,649	9,649	10.8	18,339	7,091	38.7
1995	110,038	16,360	14.9	91,681	9,432	10.3	18,358	6,927	37.7
1996	111,960	16,269	14.5	93,750	9,415	10.0	18,210	6,854	37.6
1997	114,533	16,110	14.1	96,386	9,363	9.7	18,147	6,747	37.2
1998	116,730	16,211	13.9	98,329	9,306	9.5	18,401	6,905	37.5
1999	118,963	16,477	13.9	100,025	9,419	9.4	18,938	7,058	37.3
2000	120,786	16,258	13.5	101,810	9,148	9.0	18,976	7,110	37.5
2001	120,708	16,289	13.5	101,577	9,141	9.0	19,130	7,148	37.4
2002P	120,016	15,964	13.3	100,585	8,605	8.6	19,431	7,359	37.9

Source: U.S. Department of Labor (1983–2002).
Note: Employment and union membership are in thousands of persons.
2002P are preliminary data for 11 months.

FIGURE 2
Union Density, by Sector, 1983–2002

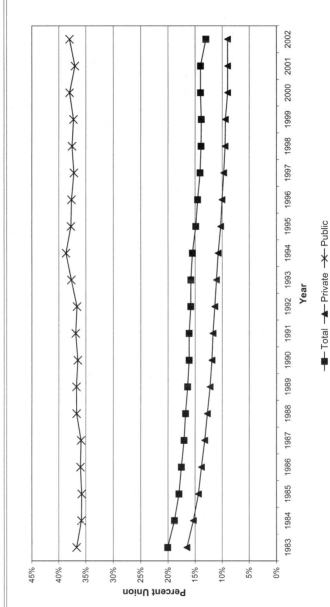

Source: Table 1.

Union density of the total workforce declined from 20.1 percent to 13.3 percent during these years. The reduction in total union density was largely attributable to developments in the private sector, where union density dropped by almost half over this period, falling from 16.5 to 8.6 percent. In contrast, public sector density remained stable, fluctuating only slightly—between roughly 36 and 39 percent—during the period.

Changes in union density can result from changes in the number of union members or in the total number of employees, or both. We present the data necessary to separate these effects in Table 1. The 7 percent decline in union density for the total economy between 1983 and 2001 resulted from an increase in total employment of 36 percent coupled with a 10 percent drop in union members.

When disaggregated by sector, the data reveal disparate developments. The number of union members in the private sector declined substantially by 2002, to about 72 percent of the number of members in 1983. In sharp contrast, the number of public sector union members grew by 29 percent. Table 1 reveals substantial differences in employment growth between the public and private sectors as well. Between 1983 and 2002, employment grew by 39 percent in the private sector, far faster than the 25 percent growth of employment in the public sector. Thus, in the private sector, union density declined because employment grew and union membership dropped, while in the public sector, employment and union membership grew at about the same pace. The faster growth of employment in the less-organized private sector also explains part of the decline of union density in the total economy.

Level of Government

The overall union density in the public sector masks important variations within the sector. Data by level of government for the period 1983 through 2002 show that union density at the local level (e.g., municipalities, counties, and school districts) was almost 50 percent greater than at either the federal or state levels (see Table 2). Over this 20-year period, the unionization rate among local government employees varied between 41 and 45 percent, while the corresponding rates for state and federal employees averaged around 30 percent (generally slightly higher in the federal government and slightly lower among state employees).

Once again, it is possible to gain additional insights by examining the numerator and denominator of the unionization percentages separately. Table 2 shows union membership and employment growth over the study period by level of government. The growth in both variables was

TABLE 2

Employment, Union Membership, and Union Density,
by Level of Government, 1983–2002

Year	Federal			State			Local		
	Employment	Union membership	Union density (percent)	Employment	Union membership	Union density (percent)	Employment	Union membership	Union density (percent)
1983	3,081	974	31.6	3,776	1,062	28.1	8,636	3,648	42.2
1984	3,117	930	29.8	3,839	1,076	28.0	8,717	3,605	41.4
1985	3,210	931	29.0	3,961	1,081	27.3	8,735	3,672	42.0
1986	3,285	976	29.7	4,051	1,135	28.0	8,884	3,722	41.9
1987	3,362	1,026	30.5	4,218	1,191	28.2	9,143	3,780	41.3
1988	3,378	1,071	31.7	4,247	1,223	28.8	9,406	3,953	42.0
1989	3,407	1,036	30.4	4,476	1,305	29.1	9,608	4,083	42.5
1990	3,439	1,057	30.7	4,568	1,289	28.2	9,775	4,138	42.3
1991	3,435	1,044	30.4	4,625	1,377	29.8	9,934	4,211	42.4
1992	3,346	1,033	30.9	4,820	1,403	29.1	9,997	4,217	42.2
1993	3,450	1,047	30.4	4,962	1,536	30.9	10,217	4,435	43.4
1994	3,518	1,181	33.6	5,174	1,596	30.8	9,647	4,314	44.7
1995	3,447	1,117	32.4	5,171	1,531	29.6	9,739	4,280	43.9
1996	3,284	1,040	31.7	5,132	1,566	30.5	9,795	4,249	43.4
1997	3,217	1,030	32.0	5,031	1,485	29.5	9,899	4,232	42.7
1998	3,269	1,105	33.8	5,150	1,431	27.8	9,982	4,370	43.8
1999	3,264	1,047	32.1	5,233	1,527	29.2	10,440	4,484	42.9
2000	3,233	1,033	32.0	5,464	1,641	30.0	10,278	4,436	43.2
2001	3,280	1,035	31.5	5,662	1,724	30.5	10,188	4,389	43.1
2002P	3,246	1,059	32.6	5,702	1,786	31.3	10,484	4,515	43.1

Source: U.S. Department of Labor (1983–2002).

Note: Employment and union membership are in thousands of persons.
2002P are preliminary data for 11 months.

greatest for state governments, where employment grew by 51 percent after 1983, while union membership grew by 68 percent, resulting in the 3 percent increase in union density. Employment in local government grew steadily from 1983 through 1993, declined substantially in 1994, and then increased again for the rest of the period. Union membership more or less tracked these changes so that density remained relatively unchanged throughout the period. Finally, federal government employment grew by 9 percent from 1983 through 1992 (during the Reagan and part of the Bush I presidencies) before increasing briefly during the first few years of the Clinton presidency. Then, beginning in 1995, the number of federal employees declined substantially so that by 2002, federal employment was only 5 percent higher than it had been in 1983. Union membership grew somewhat more rapidly than federal employment over the 20 years, so that density averaged about 30 percent in 1983–85 and about 32 percent in 2000–02.

Membership and Representation

Our primary focus is on union membership, but unions often represent workers who are not union members but who are covered by collective bargaining agreements. In the private sector (see Table 3), unions represented 9.7 percent of workers in 2001, in comparison to 9.0 percent of workers who were members.[4] In the total government sector (federal plus state and local governments), the spread was proportionately somewhat greater: in 2001, unions represented about 41.7 percent of workers, but only about 37.4 percent of workers were members. The greatest difference between extent of representation and union density was in the federal sector, where unions represented 4.9 percent of the workforce who were not union members.

Geographic Dispersion

Union density rates for the public and private sectors in 2001, disaggregated by state, are shown in Figure 3 and Table 4. The entries in the figure are arrayed according to the states' public sector density, which is represented by the gray bars; the black bars represent private sector density. One striking result is that a higher proportion of the public sector workforce was organized than that of the private sector in every state but Mississippi. Another significant finding is the substantial differences in union density across states, particularly in the public sector. The public sector unionization rates ranged from a high of 74.4 percent in New York to a low of 5.1 percent in Mississippi, representing a nearly 15-fold

TABLE 3
Union Membership and Union Representation, 2000–2001

	2000					2001				
		Members of unions		Represented by union			Members of unions		Represented by union	
Sector	Total employment	Total	Percent of employment	Total	Percent of employment	Total employment	Total	Percent of employment	Total	Percent of employment
Private Sector	101,810	9,148	9.0	9,969	9.8	101,577	9,141	9.0	9,903	9.7
Government Sector	18,976	7,110	37.5	7,976	42.0	19,130	7,148	37.4	7,975	41.7
Federal	3,233	1,033	32.0	1,186	36.7	3,280	1,035	31.6	1,198	36.5
State	5,464	1,641	30.0	1,867	34.2	5,662	1,724	30.4	1,949	34.4
Local	10,278	4,436	43.2	4,923	47.9	10,188	4,389	43.1	4,829	47.4

Source: U.S. Department of Labor (2000–2001).
Note: Total employment and members of unions are in thousands.

FIGURE 3

Union Density, by State and Sector, 2001

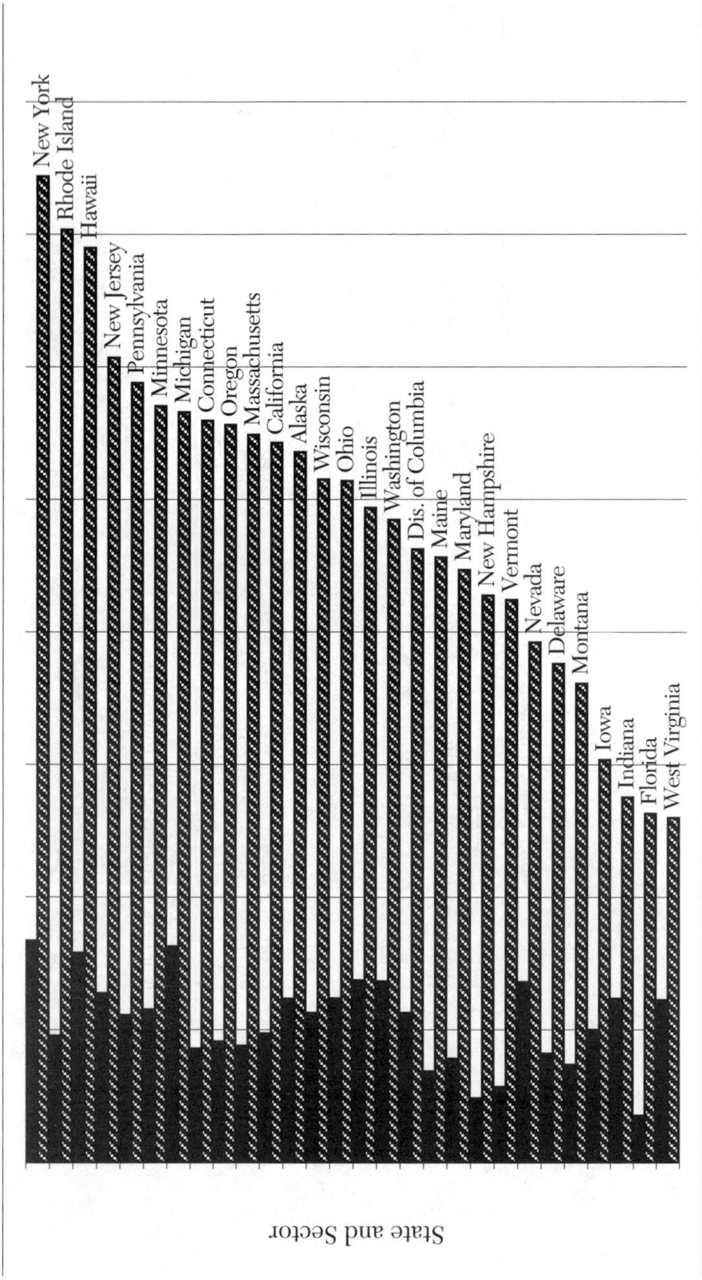

State and Sector

New York
Rhode Island
Hawaii
New Jersey
Pennsylvania
Minnesota
Michigan
Connecticut
Oregon
Massachusetts
California
Alaska
Wisconsin
Ohio
Illinois
Washington
Dis. of Columbia
Maine
Maryland
New Hampshire
Vermont
Nevada
Delaware
Montana
Iowa
Indiana
Florida
West Virginia

FIGURE 3 (Continued)

Union Density, by State and Sector, 2001

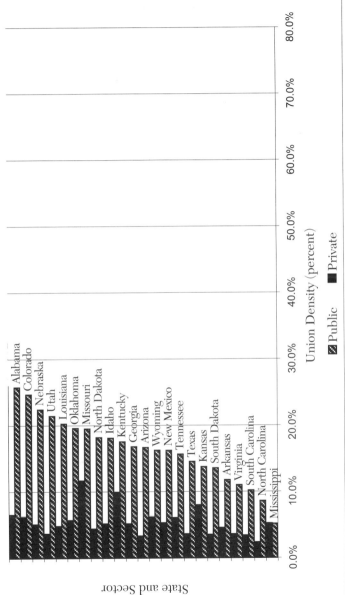

Source: Table 4.

TABLE 4
Employment, Union Membership, and Union Density
Private and Public Sectors, by State, 2001

State	Private sector			Public sector		
	Employment	Union membership	Union density (percent)	Employment	Union membership	Union density (percent)
Alabama	1,530,181	99,867	6.5	246,334	63,424	25.7
Alaska	191,485	23,598	12.3	57,198	30,641	53.6
Arizona	1,679,985	55,459	3.3	307,061	51,083	16.6
Arkansas	827,407	37,462	4.5	171,939	20,193	11.7
California	12,218,918	1,185,086	9.7	1,998,888	1,084,879	54.3
Colorado	1,647,298	101,929	6.2	229,878	56,688	24.7
Connecticut	1,277,172	108,975	8.5	194,066	108,564	55.9
Delaware	318,846	26,018	8.2	45,838	17,224	37.6
Dis. of Columbia	174,703	19,660	11.3	24,252	11,213	46.2
Florida	5,605,679	194,921	3.5	735,975	193,315	26.3
Georgia	3,096,043	159,108	5.1	414,734	69,483	16.8
Hawaii	411,574	64,923	15.8	68,037	46,924	69.0
Idaho	450,045	23,145	5.1	82,978	14,984	18.1
Illinois	4,744,048	650,110	13.7	617,792	304,910	49.4
Indiana	2,326,361	286,716	12.3	296,549	81,562	27.5
Iowa	1,132,660	113,040	10.0	190,763	57,890	30.3
Kansas	943,447	75,086	8.0	191,324	26,249	13.7
Kentucky	1,397,118	138,360	9.9	237,954	41,651	17.5
Louisiana	1,418,295	68,072	4.8	277,469	56,181	20.2
Maine	473,875	32,308	6.8	75,972	34,656	45.6
Maryland	1,856,402	144,310	7.8	300,270	134,133	44.7
Massachusetts	2,438,385	213,190	8.7	331,928	182,141	54.9
Michigan	3,832,345	622,819	16.3	559,442	316,510	56.6
Minnesota	2,018,946	232,311	11.5	285,747	162,975	57.0
Mississippi	897,284	46,591	5.2	185,702	9,510	5.1
Missouri	2,184,258	254,508	11.7	308,004	60,042	19.5
Montana	286,832	20,992	7.3	60,723	21,912	36.1
Nebraska	631,121	31,979	5.1	108,498	24,292	22.4
Nevada	759,327	103,046	13.6	97,568	38,236	39.2
New Hampshire	521,911	25,041	4.8	60,142	25,711	42.8
New Jersey	3,114,793	396,603	12.7	441,695	268,002	60.7
New Mexico	537,987	28,399	5.3	122,493	19,828	16.2
New York	6,208,118	1,035,675	16.7	1,217,691	905,732	74.4
North Carolina	2,879,474	67,106	2.3	449,516	38,464	8.6
North Dakota	225,649	9,894	4.4	47,838	8,681	18.1
Ohio	4,357,283	538,189	12.4	619,387	318,377	51.4
Oklahoma	1,117,134	63,372	5.7	197,704	38,689	19.6
Oregon	1,218,710	110,480	9.1	185,461	103,169	55.6
Pennsylvania	4,542,201	503,300	11.1	569,438	334,686	58.8

TABLE 4—(Continued)
Employment, Union Membership, and Union Density
Private and Public Sectors, by State, 2001

	Private sector			Public sector		
State	Employ-ment	Union member ship	Union density (percent)	Employ-ment	Union member-ship	Union density (percent)
Rhode Island	378,734	36,046	9.5	47,177	33,186	70.3
South Carolina	1,316,883	44,446	3.4	285,498	29,040	10.2
South Dakota	267,208	9,368	3.5	52,756	7,139	13.5
Tennessee	2,023,662	122,253	6.0	289,545	45,230	15.6
Texas	7,434,775	267,640	3.6	1,218,464	176,860	14.5
Utah	775,269	28,294	3.6	128,030	27,416	21.4
Vermont	235,518	13,308	5.7	35,154	14,912	42.4
Virginia	2,600,504	92,836	3.6	387,621	42,551	11.0
Washington	2,081,859	283,682	13.6	341,306	165,358	48.4
West Virginia	598,898	73,166	12.2	107,638	27,936	26.0
Wisconsin	2,207,096	248,522	11.3	297,317	153,160	51.5
Wyoming	163,581	10,058	6.1	45,346	7,351	16.2

Source: U.S. Department of Labor (2001).
Note: Employment and union membership are in thousands of persons.
    Public sector includes only state and local government employees.

difference. Private sector density ranged from 16.7 percent in New York to 2.3 percent in North Carolina, a "mere" 7-fold difference.

There is a high correlation (0.741) between density levels in the two sectors. That is, generally speaking, states with high levels of private sector unionization tended to have high public sector rates. There are some notable exceptions, however. For example, 12.2 percent of private sector workers were organized in West Virginia but only 3.5 percent in Florida were, even though the two states had almost exactly the same percent of their public sector workers organized. Obviously, the factors that determine the level of union density in the public and private sectors are not entirely congruent.

Government Function

Table 5 reports data for selected government functions, by level of government, on union density, union membership, and employment for 2001. The functions are three-digit industry classifications, with the exceptions of (1) the teacher and other subcategories for education and (2) the police, fire, and other subcategories for justice, public order, and safety, which are based on three-digit occupational classes.[5] There is

TABLE 5
Union Density, Union Membership, and Employment, by Level of Government, 2001

	Federal			State			Local		
	Employment	Union membership	Union density (percent)	Employment	Union membership	Union density (percent)	Employment	Union membership	Union density (percent)
Construction	38,153	4,865	12.8	148,087	46,846	31.6	275,219	93,475	34.0
Ship and Boat Building	18,350	7,448	40.6	1,062	584	55.0	2,238	—	0.0
Bus Service and Urban Transit	6,480	3,293	50.8	29,044	20,210	69.6	159,123	99,481	62.5
U.S. Postal Service	870,695	591,351	67.9						
Water Supply and Irrigation	967	—	0.0	16,736	6,932	41.4	144,705	51,058	35.3
Sanitary Services	3,321	1,644	49.5	7,911	3,173	40.1	128,577	52,372	40.7
Real Estate	13,188	3,846	29.2	1,880		0.0	72,295	19,509	27.0
Hospitals	164,662	28,220	17.1	297,627	82,356	27.7	201,583	57,315	28.4
Nursing and Personal Care Facilities	11,043	3,816	34.6	54,303	29,535	54.4	50,331	17,692	35.2
Health Services, n.e.c.	8,952	1,703	19.0	83,755	20,693	24.7	221,107	51,525	23.3
Elementary and Secondary Education Teachers	39,572	16,726	42.3	571,127	287,717	50.4	2,794,863	1,710,058	61.2
Other	28,822	9,780	33.9	429,796	127,402	29.6	2,455,032	925,965	37.7
Higher Education Teachers	8,162	1,630	20.0	512,087	105,561	20.6	84,528	32,244	38.1
Others	27,377	6,162	22.5	972,261	154,486	15.9	149,976	37,309	24.9
Libraries	6,215	2,480	39.9	7,689	3,142	40.9	122,434	21,086	17.2
Social Services, n.e.c.	14,396	2,717	18.9	66,660	14,367	21.6	235,430	78,501	33.3

TABLE 5 (*Continued*)

Union Density, Union Membership, and Employment, by Level of Government, 2001

	Federal			State			Local		
	Employment	Union membership	Union density (percent)	Employment	Union membership	Union density (percent)	Employment	Union membership	Union density (percent)
Executive and Legislative Offices	14,545	—	0.0	42,000	5,004	11.9	89,520	8,467	9.5
General Government, n.e.c.	104,325	15,705	15.1	132,012	37,920	28.7	497,600	121,205	24.4
Justice, Public Order, and Safety									
Police	36,430	11,993	32.9	97,429	56,354	57.8	586,895	326,458	55.6
Fire	4,839	2,486	51.4	9,801	6,277	64.0	221,364	164,456	74.3
Other	155,147	33,040	21.3	638,507	267,331	41.9	772,326	264,392	34.2
Public Finance, Taxation & Monetary Policy	158,418	52,102	32.9	109,993	44,942	40.9	102,705	24,681	4.0
Admin. of Human Resource Programs	185,881	34,152	18.4	607,335	173,155	28.5	64,130	29,255	45.6
Admin. of Environmental Quality & Housing	121,646	12,514	10.3	110,115	41,377	37.6	31,617	13,582	3.0
Admin. of Economic Programs	279,645	51,173	18.3	254,436	71,162	28.0	59,830	19,009	31.8
National Security & International Affairs	556,844	64,918	11.7	35,234	6,528	18.5	1,221	—	0.0

Source: U.S. Department of Labor (2001).

Note: Employment and union membership are in thousands of persons.

substantial variation in the level of union density by function, which ranges from nil for federal employees in executive and legislative offices to 74.3 percent for local firefighters.[6]

Structure of Employment and Union Density

An extensive literature examines the determinants of unionization.[7] We limit our discussion to relationships between the structure of employment and union density, in part because the CPS data facilitate such an examination.

Structural-Change Hypothesis

The structural-change hypothesis postulates that the propensity to unionize varies by demographic, industrial, and occupational characteristics and that overall union density changes over time as the composition of the workforce with respect to these characteristics changes. The decline in private sector union density since the 1950s has been attributed to a variety of such changes, including the rise in white-collar relative to blue-collar employment, the expansion of the service sector at the expense of the manufacturing, the shift in employment from northern and midwestern states (the "rust belt") to southern and western states (the "sun belt"), and the increased labor-force participation of women.[8] And, as previously noted, Burton and Thomason (1988) attributed part of the decline in public sector union density between the 1970s and the 1980s to a declining share of employment accounted for by teachers, who make up a highly organized occupation.

The structural-change explanation is nonetheless problematic for a number of reasons. The major limitation is that the hypothesis assumes that the propensity to organize among various components of the workforce remains relatively constant over time. In fact, there are periods during which certain sectors, such as the public sector during the 1960s, experienced substantial growth in unionization with no apparent change in employment composition that would explain the higher density.

The structural-change hypothesis suggests that the divergence in union density trends in the private and public sector since 1983 are attributable to differential changes in employment structure. The hypothesis can be analyzed in two ways: by examining union densities in the public and private sectors for different demographic and occupational groups to see if these densities were stable over time, and by comparing changes in the employment structures in the two sectors.

Structural-Change Data

We examine this hypothesis using CPS data on union density, employment share, and employment growth trends in the public and private sectors with respect to four types of structural change.

Occupations. One important structural change thought to affect union density in the private sector is the shift in employment from blue- to white-collar work. The data in Table 6 show that this shift, which began well before 1983, continued throughout our study period in the private sector. Employment growth in blue-collar jobs from 1983 to 2001 ranks next to last among occupational groups in the private sector. And blue-collar employment was by far the most highly unionized occupation in the private sector in 1983, further confirming this element of the structural-change hypothesis.

However, the data also reveal that union density within the blue-collar workforce decreased significantly after 1983 in the private sector. Indeed, union densities for all occupation groups in the private sector declined significantly between 1983 and 2001. Moreover, the shift in occupational composition would seem to explain only a small portion of the private sector decline, as the share of all jobs accounted for by blue-collar workers in the sector dropped by less than 7 percent.

The most highly organized group in the public sector is professionals (including teachers), not blue-collar workers, and so the declining share of blue-collar workers in the pubic sector did not have a material impact on overall density. Moreover, there was less variation in union density among public sector occupational groups than among private sector occupations. Blue-collar workers in 2001 were only about twice as likely to be organized as were managers in the public sector. In contrast, private sector managers were five times less likely to be organized than blue-collar employees—a difference that is probably due in part to private sector public policy, which discourages organization among managers.

Overall, these findings suggest that this element of structural change is a poor candidate to explain the divergence of union density trends in the public and private sectors in the recent past. Union density actually increased in four of the five occupational groups in the public sector, while density declined in all occupational groups in the private sector. In essence, the shifting shares of the workforce in various occupational groups in the public and private sectors had much less impact on densities in the sectors than did the changes in densities within the occupations.

TABLE 6

Union Density and Employment, by Occupational Group and Sector
(All figures in percentages)

Variable	Year	Managers	Professional	Technical	Adm. support and clerical	Blue collar	Total workforce
			Panel A: Public Sector				
Union Density	1983	25.3	42.2	21.1	33.3	37.9	36.7
	2001	22.8	42.3	27.0	35.8	40.5	37.4
Employment Share	1983	8.1	34.7	3.6	22.9	30.7	100.0
	2001	13.6	35.9	2.9	20.5	27.1	100.0
Employment Growth, 1983-2001		208.0	127.9	99.4	110.4	108.9	123.5
			Panel B: Private Sector				
Union Density	1983	4.2	7.1	11.5	9.7	25.6	16.5
	2001	2.6	4.9	8.7	5.8	14.7	9.0
Employment Share	1983	9.4	21.3	3.4	16.8	49.3	100.0
	2001	14.1	25.7	3.8	13.8	42.7	100.0
Employment Growth, 1983-2001		210.3	168.7	157.0	114.2	121.0	139.5

Source: U.S. Department of Labor (1983 and 2001).

Geographic Location. Another structural-change argument is that private sector employment has moved from highly organized northeastern and midwestern states to less labor friendly southern and western states. The data in Table 7 show that, in fact, there is a rough correlation between union density and employment growth by region in the private sector. For example, the highest union penetration rates in 1983 were found in the Middle Atlantic and Great Lakes states, which had the second- and third-lowest rates of employment growth over the period, while the second-to-lowest unionization rate and second-fastest employment growth occurred in the South Atlantic states. There are obvious exceptions in the private sector, however, to the inverse relationship between union density in 1983 and subsequent employment growth: the Pacific states had both high density and high growth, while the Southwest states had low density and employment growth below the national average.

The same union density and employment patterns found in the private sector exist in the public sector. Three of the four regions with the highest union density (New England, Middle Atlantic, and Great Lakes) had the lowest growth rates; the Pacific states were once again the major anomaly. This pattern suggests that structural change has some relevance for the public sector. Nonetheless, the overall rate of public sector organization did not change significantly over the 20 years because the lower employment growth in high-density states was offset by increasing density within four regions, including the Pacific states. Overall, the structural hypothesis as applied to geographical shifts in employment provides only a very limited part of the explanation for developments in union density in the private and public sectors since 1983.

Race and Gender. One of the most striking changes in employment composition in the post–World War II era has been the dramatic increase in female labor-force participation rates. Because women have historically been less likely to organize than men, some argue that this demographic change is partially responsible for the erosion of union density. Racial composition of employment has also changed in recent years—as nonwhites make up an increasingly larger segment of the workforce. Furthermore, African Americans, who until recently made up the largest segment of the nonwhite population, have had higher rates of union density than whites, at least in the post–World War II period. Presumably this means that changes in racial composition should have increased the union density rate.

TABLE 7
Union Density and Employment, by Census Region and Sector
(All figures in percentages)

Variable	Year	New England	Middle Atlantic	Great Lakes	Mid-west	South Atlantic	South Central	South-west	Moun-tain	Pacific	All areas
				Panel A: Public Sector							
Union Density	1983	58.0	61.7	41.5	29.2	21.7	21.4	19.6	25.2	44.8	36.7
	2001	51.5	65.5	48.4	30.5	20.8	18.4	17.3	22.6	50.7	37.4
Employment Share	1983	5.0	15.4	15.8	8.1	19.1	6.1	10.3	5.8	14.4	100.0
	2001	4.6	13.5	14.4	7.3	19.3	6.0	11.6	7.1	16.4	100.0
Employment Growth, 1983-2001		113.2	108.4	112.3	110.7	124.9	121.1	138.4	150.7	140.2	123.5
				Panel B: Private Sector							
Union Density	1983	15.6	23.2	22.9	16.1	9.5	14.1	8.8	11.4	18.2	16.5
	2001	8.1	14.0	13.4	9.8	4.5	7.0	4.0	5.9	10.3	9.0
Employment Share	1983	6.3	16.0	18.2	7.2	16.3	5.7	10.7	5.1	14.5	100.0
	2001	5.2	13.7	17.2	7.3	18.2	5.8	10.6	6.2	15.9	100.0
Employment Growth, 1983-2001		115.8	119.0	131.7	140.5	155.1	141.9	138.7	171.0	153.0	139.5

Source: U.S. Department of Labor (1983 and 2001).

Data on union density and employment by race and gender during the study period are exhibited in Table 8. The data confirm that in the private sector, women were less likely to be organized than men, and nonwhites had higher unionization rates than whites, particularly at the beginning of the period. In addition, employment growth in the private sector was greater for nonwhites than for whites, and for females than for males. However, the union density rate in that sector declined substantially for all the race and gender categories shown, more than offsetting the few favorable shifts in employment (such as the relatively greater growth of nonwhite employment). Therefore, the structural-change hypothesis is only weakly supported.

There were some particularly interesting differences between the public and private sectors. In general, there were smaller variations among the different demographic groups in the public than in the private sector. For example, the level of unionization among women was much more similar to the level for men in the public than the private sector. Moreover, differences in union density by race were smaller in the public sector; in fact, in 2001 white public sector employees were as likely to be organized as nonwhites. Significantly, women and nonwhites represented a larger proportion of the public sector workforce than of the private sector workforce. In the public sector, the union density rates among the gender and racial categories were relatively stable from 1983 to 2001, helping to explain the overall stability in public sector unionization over the period. Again, the structural-change hypothesis as applied to racial and gender categories of the workforce provides some assistance in understanding developments in private sector union density since 1983 but is of little value for the public sector.

Conclusions on Structural Change

The structural-change hypothesis provides some limited help in explaining the continuing decline in union density in the private sector, because many of the segments of the workforce that have traditionally been relatively unorganized, such as white-collar workers and workers in the sun belt, have grown relatively rapidly. The major limitation of the structural-change hypothesis for the private sector is that union density declined significantly within every category of the workforce shown in Tables 6 to 8. In essence, the union density rate for the entire private sector would have declined between 1983 and 2001 even if there had been absolutely no change in the structure of employment over those 20 years.

TABLE 8

Union Density and Employment, by Race, Gender, and Sector
(All figures in percentages)

Variable	Year	Race		Gender		Nonwhite		White		Total
		Nonwhite	White	Male	Female	Male	Female	Male	Female	
				Panel A: Public Sector						
Union Density	1983	37.3	36.6	39.8	33.7	40.5	34.7	39.6	33.5	36.7
	2001	37.3	37.4	38.9	36.2	41.1	34.6	38.3	36.7	37.4
Employment Share	1983	17.1	82.9	49.1	50.9	7.7	9.4	41.4	41.5	100.0
	2001	19.9	80.1	43.2	56.8	8.1	11.8	35.1	45.1	100.0
Employment Growth, 1983–2001		143.4	119.4	108.7	137.7	129.9	154.5	104.7	133.9	123.5
				Panel B: Private Sector						
Union Density	1983	21.9	15.8	21.8	10.0	26.5	16.9	21.2	9.0	16.5
	2001	10.5	8.7	11.6	6.0	12.6	8.5	11.5	5.4	9.0
Employment Share	1983	11.8	88.2	55.3	44.7	6.2	5.6	49.1	39.1	100.0
	2001	16.3	83.7	53.6	46.4	8.1	8.2	45.5	38.2	100.0
Employment Growth, 1983–2001		192.8	132.4	135.2	144.9	182.3	204.2	129.3	136.4	139.5

Source: U.S. Department of Labor (1983 and 2001).

The structural-change hypothesis is also of very limited assistance in understanding union density developments in the public sector. Only a few components of the public sector workforce that have traditionally been relatively unorganized—such as managers—have grown faster than the overall public sector workforce. Of more significance, union density has increased among most of the components of the public sector workforce shown in Tables 6 to 8. In essence, the union density rate for the entire public sector would have increased between 1983 and 2001 even if there had been absolutely no change in the structure of employment over those years.

The explanations for the declining density in the private sector in recent decades must lie with factors other than changes in the structure of the workforce, such as increasing employer resistance to unions or a legal environment that provides less protection to workers seeking to organize. For the public sector, the limited contribution of the structural-change hypothesis to understanding developments in union density in recent decades suggests that for the near-term future, changes among the components of the workforce are unlikely to have a major impact on overall public sector density.

Union Employment Effects

The likelihood that union density will remain high in the public sector means that efforts to improve the effectiveness and efficiency of government functions will often require union-management cooperation. We examine two factors that provide a context for efforts to achieve such cooperation: the tendency of public sector unions to increase employment and the tendency for governments to privatize the provision of certain services.

Studies of the wage elasticity of labor demand in the public sector have generally found that the labor demand curve is relatively inelastic: elasticity estimates typically are significantly much less than one (Ehrenberg and Schwarz 1986).[9] These results suggest that government employees may be able to take advantage of the fact that their employers have few direct competitors for their services. However, any conclusions drawn from these public sector labor demand studies must be tempered by the knowledge that these estimates do not appear to be substantially different from those found for private sector firms.

More to the point, however, are a number of other studies from the first few decades of significant unionization in the public sector indicating that unions were able to shift the labor demand curve to the right, increasing both employment and wages. Zax and Ichniowski (1988), using data from the Survey of Governments for the years 1977–80 and 1982, estimated a recursive system of equations predicting wage, employment, and expenditures for four municipal functions: highway and street maintenance, police, fire, and sanitation.[10] They found that employment in a function was positively related to union representation in that function and negatively related to union representation in other functions. Their findings suggest, for example, that police employment will be higher when the police department is organized, but lower to the extent that other departments (i.e., fire, maintenance, and sanitation) are organized. They also found that both own-function and other-function union representation was positively associated with higher wages. That is, union representation by police was associated with higher wages for both police and firefighters.

Other studies have also found a positive relationship between the number of employees and union organization. Zax (1989) examined data from the 1977 and 1982 Census of Governments and found that union representation increased per capita employment in 1982, after they had controlled for 1977 per capita employment levels and a number of other labor market, public service demand, and legal environment variables.[11] Similarly, Mehay and Gonzalez (1994) estimated the impact of unions and the electoral system in cities with populations greater than 25,000. They hypothesized that public sector unions would have more influence over employment levels in cities where council members are elected by district elections than on an at-large basis, since the cost of influence is lower. They found that a union dummy was positively related to employment and statistically significant and, consistent with their hypothesis, a dummy indicating that the city had an at-large electoral system was significantly and negatively related to city employment.

Freeman and Valletta (1988) estimated the joint effects of collective bargaining coverage and the state's legal environment for collective bargaining on both wages and employment using data on cities from the Survey of Governments. Consistent with Zax and Ichniowski, they found that union representation increased both wages and employment. They also found that a legal environment favorable to collective bargaining was associated with higher wages. However, the relationship with the legal environment was complex: unexpectedly, a favorable legal environment was negatively related to employment, although employment was positively related to the interaction between collective bargaining coverage and the legal environment. While they indicate that their results are complex and subject to other interpretations, Freeman and Valletta offer two possible explanations for them. Either a favorable legal environment induces municipalities to increase wages in order to avoid unionization or a favorable environment increases union power more at the bargaining table than in the political arena, so that wages increase at the expense of employment.

Using teacher collective bargaining data from New York for the years 1972–73 and 1976–77, Eberts and Stone (1986) estimated wage equations. Dummy variables representing various contract provisions affecting employment (specifically, provisions for teacher tenure, limitations on reductions in force, and class size) and other measures of contractually provided nonwage outcomes (i.e., paid leave, health benefits, and other pecuniary benefits) were used as regressors. Eberts and Stone found a positive relationship between these employment security dummies and teacher wages, indicating that unions bargain wages and employment simultaneously.[12]

A more direct test of the impact of union political lobbying on wage and employment outcomes was provided by O'Brien (1994), who used data collected by the International City Management Association (ICMA) to estimate the effects of police and fire union political activity on a number of municipal outcomes. The ICMA survey collected data on seven political activities pursued by municipal police and fire unions: candidate endorsement, candidate financial contributions, manpower or in-kind campaign contributions, threats to disclose mismanagement, publicity campaigns, state-level lobbying, and initiatives to take issues to referendum. O'Brien found that higher levels of these political activities increased the level of a city's police and fire expenditures and departmental employment, but they had little or no effect on wage levels. Collective bargaining, as indicated by the presence of a collective bargaining agreement, appeared to have no effect on department spending but was positively associated with wage levels and negatively associated with employment.

These studies suggest that public sector unions employ a mix of collective bargaining and political-lobbying strategies. Through lobbying, unions are able to increase the budgetary allocation flowing to their departments and thus increase employment.[13] Once the level of public expenditures has been determined, unions are able to increase wage levels for their members at the bargaining table. While this necessarily comes at the expense of employment for a given labor demand curve, the employment reduction resulting from the wage increase does not,

on average, offset the higher levels of employment obtained through
political activity that shifts out the labor demand curve.

These results from the initial decades of extensive unionization of
the public sector indicate that a normal goal of public sector unions is to
increase employment. This suggests a dilemma—efforts to improve the
effectiveness and efficiency of public sector functions through labor-
management cooperation plans that seek to maintain or perhaps even
reduce employment must contend with the tendency of public sector
unions to increase employment.

Privatization

Efforts to Privatize

A hallmark of the conservative agenda inaugurated by Ronald Reagan at the dawn of the 1980s was the initiative to reduce the size and
scope of government. In part this initiative manifested itself as a call for
the privatization of services formerly offered exclusively by government
agencies. In many cases, these efforts were tinged with an anti-union
animus, perhaps in part as a response to the tendency of public sector
unions to increase both wages and employment through their bargaining and political activities.

Proposals for privatization were advanced at all levels of government
and involved nearly all government functions. Privatization comes in many
forms, including the contracting out or outsourcing of support services,
such as janitorial or maintenance services; vouchers, whereby government pays for the service but voucher recipients are allowed to purchase
from private sector providers; management contracts, under which the
operation of an agency or facility, such as an airport, is contracted out to
a private company; managed competition, in which the right to provide
public services is auctioned to private sector and public organization
bidders alike; the reorganization of a government entity as a for-profit
business; and the wholesale divestiture of assets to an existing private
sector firm.

As can be expected, government unions strongly opposed privatization. The president and secretary-treasurer of the American Federation
of State, County, and Municipal Employees (AFSCME) (McEntee and
Lucy 2003) stated:

> For public employees and the people we serve, the price of pri-
> vatization is high—and getting higher. For workers, privatiza-
> tion threatens job security, pay and benefits, working conditions

and career opportunities. For the public, it means less quality, less access and less accountability. For local economies, because the privatizers are often non-union, it means fewer good jobs and a reduced tax base. That is why we all must fight privatization—before the first warning sign and with every resource.

At the federal government level, the president of the American Federation of Government Employees expressed a similar concern about privatization (Harnage 2003):

> At the rate things are going, federal workers serving in the armed forces reserves in Iraq may come home to find their jobs eliminated—sold off to private contractors. . . . Meanwhile, the administration's privatization plans could turn the federal workplace into a gargantuan spoils system for campaign contributors and others who have ingratiated themselves with the party in power.

These passages reveal that job loss (and consequently the loss of union members) is one of the principal concerns of public sector unions with respect to privatization, but we have been able to discover only one statistical study directly examining the impact of unions on decisions to privatize. Chandler and Feuille (1994) combined data from public sources with data on the provision and production of sanitation services by municipalities with a population of 10,000 or more that they collected.[14] They found that the effect of union organization or the existence of a collective bargaining agreement was mediated by the quality of labor-management relations. In those municipalities where cooperative relations existed between the city and the sanitation union, union organization or the existence of a collective bargaining agreement was associated with a lower probability that the city would consider or adopt contracting out. Where the relationship was adversarial, union organization or the existence of an agreement was positively related to the probability that the city would consider or adopt contracting out.

This statistical study is consistent with case studies indicating that the reactions of unions to the possibility of privatization and the ability to achieve improvements in the effectiveness of government services without privatization are closely tied to the nature of the relationship between unions and management. The U.S. Secretary of Labor's Task Force on Excellence in State and Local Government Through Labor-Management Cooperation (1996) and Sclar (2000) provide examples of labor-management cooperation that resulted in improved service quality and better efficiencies, often coupled with no-layoff clauses that protected current workers.

Trends in Privatization

We now examine the relationship between union density and the mix of public and private sector employment in four industries: hospitals, bus and urban transit, sanitary services, and elementary and secondary education. We have chosen these industries because each has a substantial proportion of employment in both sectors and each has experienced an increasing share of employment in the private sector over the last 20 years, which we attribute largely to privatization.[15]

Privatization does not necessarily lead to a decline in union density for the total industry. If, for example, a hospital that moved from the public sector to the private sector was unorganized both before and after privatization, the shift will result in a higher unionization rate in the public sector, a lower rate in the private sector, and no change in the rate for the entire industry. In contrast, if a unionized hospital in the public sector is converted into a nonunionized private sector hospital, union density will decline in the public sector, the private sector, and in the entire industry. The data will help clarify what has happened as the private sector share of employment has grown.

Hospitals. Figure 4 and Table 9 (Panel A) display data on union densities in the public, private, and total hospital industry, as well as the public sector share of employment for hospitals (SIC 831) for the period 1983 to 2002. These data show slight but steady declines in union density among both public sector and private sector hospital workers during this period. There was also a more pronounced decrease in the public sector share of employment over the 20 years, from about 25 percent of total employment in the early years to about 13 percent in more recent years. As a result of these trends, the union density for the entire hospital industry declined from about 17 percent in 1983–84 to about 14 percent in 2001–02.

Bus and Urban Transit. Table 9, Panel A, also shows the level of union organization in both the private and public sectors of the bus and urban mass transit industry (SIC 401), as well as the proportion of the industry workforce engaged in public sector employment. Over the entire period, union density in the public sector fluctuated markedly, generally declining from about 69 percent in 1983–84 to about 65 percent in 2001–02. Union density in the private sector also declined, from around 36 percent during the first two years to about 25 percent during the last two. The proportion of public sector employment decreased, although unevenly, from about 36 percent of total employment in

FIGURE 4

Union Density and Employment, Hospitals, 1983–2002

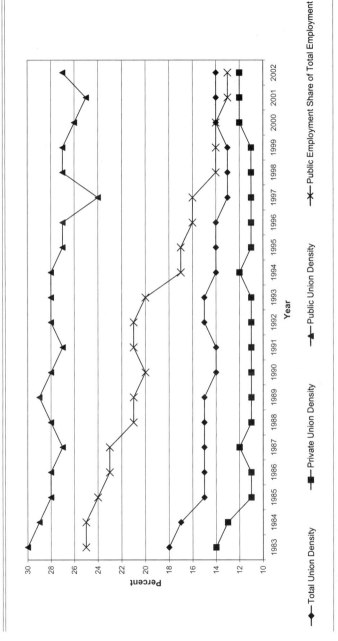

Source: Table 9, Panel A.

TABLE 9

Union Density and Privatization, Selected Industries, 1983–2002

Year	Public sector employment as percent of total employment	Union density (percent) Private	Public	Total	Public sector employment as percent of total employment	Union density (percent) Private	Public	Total
			Panel A					
		Hospitals				Bus and urban transit		
1983	24.6	13.7	29.5	17.6	38.4	37.6	70.4	50.2
1984	24.8	13.0	29.2	17.0	34.2	35.7	68.2	46.8
1985	23.9	10.6	28.0	14.7	34.5	39.9	69.1	50.0
1986	22.7	10.8	28.1	14.7	34.9	32.6	68.8	45.3
1987	23.1	11.6	26.8	15.1	37.7	31.1	63.5	43.3
1988	20.8	11.2	28.4	14.7	32.7	30.6	64.9	41.8
1989	21.2	11.2	28.9	14.9	33.3	26.8	62.6	38.7
1990	20.1	11.1	27.6	14.4	33.7	28.7	58.6	38.7
1991	20.8	10.8	27.2	14.2	37.8	25.4	72.6	43.2
1992	20.8	10.9	28.4	14.5	35.5	27.2	70.4	42.6
1993	20.5	11.3	27.7	14.7	38.0	23.5	63.7	38.8
1994	17.5	11.6	28.0	14.5	33.0	27.6	62.9	39.3
1995	16.6	11.4	26.9	14.0	29.0	27.2	68.2	39.1
1996	16.1	11.3	27.2	13.8	31.2	24.2	63.4	36.4
1997	15.7	11.0	24.4	13.1	24.9	27.6	64.5	36.8
1998	14.4	10.6	26.6	12.9	28.8	21.9	60.0	32.8
1999	14.3	10.8	26.7	13.0	30.4	23.3	55.7	33.2
2000	13.5	11.8	26.5	13.8	31.1	24.4	62.5	36.3
2001	12.9	11.9	25.3	13.6	31.1	23.5	63.2	35.8
2002P	13.0	12.2	27.3	14.2	27.0	27.3	66.2	37.8
			Panel B					
		Sanitary services				Elementary and secondary education		
1983	78.0	19.4	40.6	36.0	86.4	12.3	49.2	44.2
1984	74.4	29.0	37.1	35.0	87.1	12.5	48.8	44.1
1985	75.0	19.0	41.6	35.9	87.1	13.7	49.0	44.5
1986	73.4	9.4	37.0	29.7	86.9	13.2	48.0	43.4
1987	69.3	12.5	36.4	29.0	87.4	13.9	48.1	43.8
1988	62.6	16.5	38.1	30.0	88.1	12.2	49.4	45.0
1989	61.6	11.5	42.1	30.3	87.5	12.8	49.7	45.1
1990	57.3	18.5	44.4	33.3	87.4	12.4	49.6	44.9
1991	57.7	18.4	38.2	29.8	87.5	12.1	49.5	44.8
1992	54.9	12.3	45.5	30.5	87.6	13.1	49.1	44.6
1993	58.5	11.4	35.8	25.7	88.2	13.5	51.0	46.5
1994	56.4	8.8	40.1	26.5	85.6	18.9	51.0	46.3
1995	50.0	10.6	41.6	26.1	85.0	18.3	50.1	45.3
1996	49.3	15.6	39.8	27.5	84.8	19.6	49.8	45.2
1997	52.7	14.9	35.7	25.9	84.3	20.0	49.3	44.7
1998	57.4	13.0	38.6	27.7	83.1	19.4	49.2	44.1
1999	52.0	13.5	39.2	26.8	83.0	18.7	49.9	44.6
2000	48.9	14.7	45.5	29.8	83.3	19.0	48.9	43.9
2001	45.9	16.3	40.9	27.6	81.5	20.8	48.7	43.5
2002P	44.3	15.7	40.6	26.7	81.6	22.0	49.0	44.0

Source: U.S. Department of Labor (1983–2002). *Note:* 2002P are preliminary data for 11 months.

1983–84 to a little under 30 percent in 2001–02. The data for this industry indicate that privatization had only a limited effect on the level of union density in the public sector. However, because unionized public sector jobs were converted to nonunion private sector jobs throughout the period, the overall density declined significantly, from about 49 percent in the first two years to about 37 percent in the last two.

Sanitary Services. Union density and employment data for sanitary services (SIC 470) are presented in Panel B of Table 9. The data indicate that public sector employment decreased from about 76 percent of total employment in 1983–84 to about 45 percent by 2001–02. Over the same period, private sector unionization sporadically declined from around 20 percent to about 16 percent. Public sector density was apparently unaffected by the shift of jobs to the private sector, since union density in the public sector fluctuated around 40 percent throughout the period. As a result of the increasing importance of the private sector and the declining union density in that sector, however, the total union density for sanitary services declined from about 36 percent in 1983–84 to about 27 percent in 2001–02.

Education. Data on union density and the public sector share of employment for elementary and secondary education (SIC 842), presented in Table 9, Panel B, show that the public sector share of employment fluctuated in a narrow range of 86 to 88 percent from 1983 to 1993, before a decline began that reduced it to about 82 percent in 2001–02. However, unlike the other industries discussed in this section, private sector union density for this group actually grew over the 20 years, from about 12 percent to about 21 percent in the two most recent years. Moreover, the extent of public sector unionization essentially remained unchanged throughout the period, hovering in a narrow band around 49 percent. As a result, union density for elementary and secondary education started and ended the 20-year period at about 44 percent.

The Four Industries. Taken together, the data in Table 9 indicate that each of these industries became increasingly privatized during the past 20 years. The effects of this privatization on public sector density, however, were mixed. For hospitals and mass transit, the increasing privatization was associated with declines in union density in both the public and private sectors, as well as a decline in unionization for the entire industry. These results suggest that privatization was associated with loss of union protection for the affected workers. For sanitary services, the increasing privatization did not reduce union density in the public sector, but the declining unionization in the private sector and the shift of jobs to that sector led to a decline in union density for the entire industry. One possible explanation of these results is that both unionized and nonunionized sanitary units in the public sector were privatized, and at least some of the privatization was associated with the shedding of unions.

Education was the most distinctive sector: the increasing share of jobs in the private sector after 1993 was associated with increased union density in the private sector and stable union densities in the public sector and the entire industry. The increasing share of the generally less-organized education private sector was balanced by the increasing proportion of private sector teachers who were organized.

These four industries differ considerably in size, with employment in 2001 ranging from 7.7 million in elementary and secondary education to 5.1 million in hospitals to 0.6 million in urban transit to 0.3 million in sanitary services. In essence, the increasing privatization of education did not contribute to the total workforce decline in union density after 1983 that is shown in Figure 2, while the privatization in the other three industries that resulted in a declining share of their unionized employment was a factor in the total workforce decline in union density. The greatest significance of these results is that they make clear that privatization has been, and is likely to remain, a threat to public sector unions.

Conclusions and Prognostications

Union density developments since the early 1980s have occurred in two different worlds. The private sector has experienced a sharp overall decline in union strength, as well as losses among almost all categories of the workforce. The public sector has experienced almost no change in union density overall, or at the federal, state, and local government levels. Moreover, while some categories of the public sector workforce have lost union density, other categories have seen an increasing proportion of workers organized. These divergent developments suggest that unions will retain a significant presence in the public sector regardless of the waning fortunes of private sector unions and regardless of shifts in the occupational and personal characteristics of public sector workers.

The continuing importance of public sector unions indicates that improvements in the effectiveness and efficiency of the delivery of government services will require the involvement of unions and the development of constructive labor-management relations. While there have been notable examples of such cooperation between unions and management in the public sector, there are two factors that complicate such gains. First, most studies of the first few decades of extensive unionization in the public sector indicate that unions used their economic and political influence to increase employment, not just to enhance wages for current membership. There is an obvious tension between efforts to improve efficiency through labor-management cooperation and union bargaining strategies designed to increase employment. The second factor inhibiting cooperative labor-management relations is the continuing loss of jobs in the public sector as a result of privatization. We have shown that significant inroads into public sector employment have occurred since the 1980s in several important functions. The threat of privatization often results in bitter confrontations between unions and management that can undermine efforts to achieve cooperation.

There are, to be sure, three choices for a government considering privatization, as discussed by Sclar (2000:162): stay with the current method of providing the service, contract with a private firm, or retain the service in the government but improve its delivery through the adoption of best practices, preferably (from the unions' standpoint) with guarantees that jobs will be preserved. Ideally, all three options will be considered in a constructive manner by management and unions when privatization is considered. In practice, some governments use the threat of privatization as a weapon to wring concessions from unions, which not surprisingly provokes the types of hostile reactions shown in the AFSCME and AFGE statements, making the chances for cooperation slim.

While union density for state and local governments is apt to remain at current levels in the next decade, privatization is likely to remain a contentious issue, particularly because of the charter school movement in elementary and secondary education. However, the greatest threat to the continued stability of union density and to constructive labor-management relations involves federal unions, which are experiencing a two-front assault from the Bush administration. One attack involves privatization: the administration has announced that it will place as many as 850,000 jobs—almost half of the federal civilian workforce—up for bids from private contractors (Stevenson 2002). The policy, which does not require congressional approval and therefore will be harder to resist, will focus on jobs that are not "inherently governmental," such as trash collection and printing. Whether the wholesale privatization of federal jobs actually occurs remains to be seen, but unions representing federal employees are understandably agitated. The other attack involves the limitations on collective bargaining rights for employees of the Department of Homeland Security. The administration has blocked efforts to unionize the 56,000 federal screeners at airports because of the assertion that collective bargaining for these workers is "not compatible" with the fight against terrorism (Marquis 2003). A policy of saving democracy by limiting workers' rights does not portend well for the organizing efforts of federal sector unions.

Acknowledgements

Terry Thomason was the primary author of the initial drafts of this chapter and prepared preliminary versions of the tables and figures using CPS data from 1983 to 1999 prior to his death in April 2002. Douglas Kruse of the School of Management and Labor Relations (SMLR) at Rutgers University provided valuable assistance in updating the tables and figures used in the current version of the chapter. I also appreciate the assistance of Eugene McElroy in the SMLR library in obtaining research material and Florence Blum in preparing the tables and figures. I accept responsibility for any errors of fact or analysis.   John F. Burton, Jr.

Notes

[1] The relationship between the extent of unionization and the level of employee benefits paid for by employers during the 20th century is one of the issues examined by Burton and Mitchell (2003).

[2] Burton and Thomason (1988:45) expressed even more skepticism about the role of public policy in explaining developments in public sector unionism than had Burton (1979) in his earlier study.

[3] We note, with sorrow, that the phenomenon of "disappearing data" has continued unabated since we decried it in 1988. At that time, we reported aggregate national union density statistics using three data sources, albeit one of which had already been discontinued. In addition, we were able to report state and local unionization rates disaggregated by function, using data from the Census of Governments. The union membership portion of this data set has likewise been discontinued. Consequently, we rely solely on data from the Current Population Survey (CPS) for the national and disaggregated data for 1983 to 2002 presented in this chapter.

[4] Tables 3 to 8, which contain only one or two years of data, end with 2001 since that is the last year with complete CPS data. Preliminary 2002 data are shown in Tables 1, 2, and 9 because those tables include data for all years from 1983 to 2002 and so any anomalies in the 2002 data can be readily identified.

[5] Functions were chosen if there were at least 100 respondents in the national sample who worked in that classification.

[6] Several functions with fewer than 2,500 workers and no union members are also shown in Table 5.

[7] As previously mentioned, Burton (1979) and Burton and Thomason (1988) examined the determinants of public sector union density from the 1950s to the 1980s, including (1) changes in the structure of employment, (2) the demand for union services among workers, (3) employer resistance to unionization, and (4) public policy.

[8] Farber (1985) and Dickens and Leonard (1985) estimated that structural change was potentially responsible for between 35 and 40 percent of the decline in union density in the late 1970s and early 1980s.

[9] An elasticity of less than one means that a 10 percent increase in wages is associated with less than a 10 percent decline in employment.

[10] This recursive system assumes a three-stage decision-making process. Public sector managers first determine the overall budget for the municipality. They then determine expenditure levels for each function within the municipality. Zax and Ichniowski (1988) hypothesize that during this second stage, unions that represent employees in a particular function lobby politicians to influence expenditure levels for their function. Finally, in the third stage, managers and unions negotiate wages and determine employment levels.

[11] Zax and Ichniowski (1988) also found that a nonbargaining public employee association representing employees did not have a statistically significant impact on employment.

[12] Eberts and Stone (1986) found negative relationships between wages and paid leave, health benefits, and other benefits, indicating that the relationship between wages and employment security was not a spurious result of greater union bargaining power. In addition, the use of first-difference equations controlled for time-invariant variation in union bargaining power across contracts.

[13] Trejo (1991) argued for an alternative explanation for the positive relationship between employment and unionization—namely, that due to scale economies in the organizing process, larger cities are more likely to be attractive targets for unionization than smaller cities. To test this hypothesis, Trejo estimated structural equations where unionization and employment were jointly determined using data from the 1980 annual Survey of Governments. He found that while employment had a statistically significant, positive impact on the probability of unionization, the impact of unionization on employment, while positive, was not statistically significant.

[14] Chandler and Feuille (1994) estimated two sets of equations related to the contracting out of sanitation services: those predicting the placement of contracting out on the government's decision agenda (indicating that the government was seriously considering sanitation contracting) and those predicting the adoption of contracting out. They estimated two different specifications: one designed to measure the effect of union organization of the service and the other designed to measure the effect of an existing collective bargaining agreement.

[15] The increasing share of private sector employment in each of these industries does not necessarily represent privatization in the sense of a function being moved from the public sector to the private sector. The decreasing share of employment in the public sector may be due to slower growth of government units compared to the faster

growth of private sector firms without, for example, converting a hospital from public to private ownership. The CPS data do not allow us to separate these scenarios. In order to simplify the exposition, we treat both types of developments as privatization.

References

Burton, John F., Jr. 1979. "The Extent of Collective Bargaining in the Public Sector." In Benjamin Aaron, Joseph R. Grodin, and James L. Stern, eds., *Public-Sector Bargaining.* Madison, WI: Industrial Relations Research Association, pp. 1–43.
Burton, John F., Jr., and Daniel J. B. Mitchell. 2003. "Employee Benefits and Social Insurance: The Welfare Side of Employee Relations." In Bruce E. Kaufman, Richard A. Beaumont, and Roy B. Helfgott, eds., *From Industrial Relations to Human Resources and Beyond: The Evolving Management of Employee Relations.* Armonk, NY: M. E. Sharpe.
Burton, John F., Jr., and Terry Thomason. 1988. "The Extent of Collective Bargaining in the Public Sector." In Benjamin Aaron, Joyce M. Najita, and James L. Stern, eds., *Public-Sector Bargaining*, 2d ed. Madison, WI: Industrial Relations Research Association, pp. 1–51.
Chandler, Timothy D., and Peter Feuille. 1994. "Cities, Unions, and the Privatization of Sanitation Services." *Journal of Labor Research*, Vol. 15, no. 1 (Winter), pp. 53–71.
Dickens, William T., and Jonathan S. Leonard. 1985. "Accounting for the Decline in Union Membership, 1950–1980." *Industrial and Labor Relations Review*, Vol. 38, no. 3 (April), pp. 323–442.
Eberts, Randall, and Joe Stone. 1986. "On the Contract Curve: A Test of Alternative Models of Collective Bargaining." *Journal of Labor Economics*, Vol. 4, no. 1 (January), pp. 66–81.
Ehrenberg, Ronald G., and Joshua L. Schwarz. 1986. "Public Sector Labor Markets." In Orley C. Ashenfelter and Richard Layard, eds., *Handbook of Labor Economics*, Volume II. Amsterdam: North-Holland Press, pp. 1219–68.
Farber, Henry S. 1985. "The Extent of Unionization in the United States." In Thomas Kochan, ed., *Challenges and Choices Facing American Labor.* Cambridge, MA.: MIT Press, pp. 15–43.
Freeman, Richard B., and Robert G. Valletta. 1988. "The Effects of Public Sector Labor Laws on Labor Market Institutions and Outcomes." In Richard B. Freeman and Casey Ichniowski, eds., *When Public Sector Workers Unionize.* Chicago: University of Chicago Press, pp. 81–103.
Harnage, Bobby L. 2003. "Rally to Stop the Privatization of Public Sector Jobs." American Federation of Government Employees (AFGE) News Release, March 28, 2003. URL http://www.afge.org/Index.cfm?Page=PressReleases$PressReleaseID=218 [April 19, 2003].
Marquis, Christopher. 2003. "Threats and Responses: Airline Security; U.S. Transportation Leader Acts to Stop Screeners' Union Effort." *New York Times,* January 10, p. A12.
McEntee, Gerald W., and William Lucy. 2003. "Privatization: The Public Pays." American Federation of State, County, and Municipal Employees (AFSCME). URL http://www.afscme.org/private/index.html [April 19, 2003].

Mehay, Stephen L., and Rodolfo Gonzalez. 1994. "District Elections and the Power of Municipal Employee Unions." *Journal of Labor Research,* Vol. 15, no. 4 (Fall), pp. 387–402.

O'Brien, Kevin M. 1994. "The Impact of Union Political Activities on Public-Sector Pay, Employment, and Budgets." *Industrial Relations,* Vol. 33, no. 3 (July), pp. 322–45.

Sclar, Elliott D. 2000. *You Don't Always Get What You Pay For: The Economics of Privatization.* Ithaca, NY: Cornell University Press.

Stevenson, Richard W. 2002. "Government May Make Private Nearly Half of Its Civilian Jobs." *New York Times,* November 15, p. A1.

Trejo, Stephen. 1991. "Public Sector Unions and Municipal Employment." *Industrial and Labor Relations Review,* Vol. 45, no. 1 (October), pp. 166–80.

U.S. Department of Labor. Bureau of Labor Statistics. 1983–2002. *Current Population Survey* (CPS). The CPS data used in this chapter were downloaded from the National Bureau of Economic Research, for which the URL is http://www.nber.org/cps/.

U.S. Secretary of Labor's Task Force on Excellence in State and Local Government Through Labor-Management Cooperation. 1996. *Working Together for Public Service.* Washington, DC: GPO.

Zax, Jeffrey. 1989. "Employment and Local Public Sector Unions." *Industrial Relations,* Vol. 28, no. 1 (Winter), pp. 21–31.

Zax, Jeffrey, and Casey Ichniowski. 1988. "The Effects of Public Sector Unionism on Pay, Employment, Department Budgets, and Municipal Expenditures." In Richard B. Freeman and Casey Ichniowski, eds., *When Public Sector Workers Unionize.* Chicago: University of Chicago Press, pp. 323–64.

CHAPTER 3

Restructuring Labor-Management Relations to Improve Government Services

STEPHEN GOLDSMITH

Harvard University and Former Mayor, City of Indianapolis

In 1994 the city of Indianapolis faced a problem mayors dread: tax revenues available for the fire department had reached the maximum allowed by law, significant needs remained, and allowing the natural growth of salaries and pensions would have burst the statutory cap. Only closing firehouses in areas with substantial population decline would have resolved the matter, but station closings traditionally had led to enormous community, firefighter, and city hall arguments. In a remarkable meeting the International Association of Firefighters Association (IAFF) local leadership, and the fire chief and public safety director, jointly presented to me an enormously creative proposal that would enhance safety, reduce costs including some closings, and reward hardworking firefighters.

At about the same time the fire chief and union president were presenting this proposed solution, Indianapolis officials were on the stage with another no-nonsense local union president, Steven Quick, jointly accepting an award from Harvard's Innovation in American Government Program for creative partnering. Quick headed the same union whose members had picketed and hand-billed against me, lobbied the city council, and engaged in isolated instances of sabotage during my first year in office—the American Federation of State, County, and Municipal Employees (AFSCME). How we got to these unusual points provides an interesting illustration of cooperative principles.

My two campaigns for mayor highlight this transition. As in many big city elections labor issues played a prominent part in the 1991 Indianapolis mayoral election campaign. After hearing my campaign pledge to privatize some services and shrink government, AFSCME, the union most directly affected, vehemently opposed my election.

During periods of budget difficulty, campaigns tend to generate zero-sum politics of labor-management relations. AFSCME, fearing the loss of jobs, spent money, organized volunteers, and did everything legally possible to defeat me. The IAFF, on the other hand—the other major player in this story—displeased with existing working conditions but somewhat more hopeful about me, infused my campaign with off-duty, articulate firefighters, who—while volunteering—made sure that I saw the world through their eyes.

A great deal occurred over the next four years and, when the following election came around, the enthusiastic support of both these unions for my reelection was a point of pride for me, and perhaps even for them. Their unqualified support was not based on a series of specific promises for future action, but rather was an endorsement of a relationship about which they had confidence.

I certainly never would have predicted this happy outcome when on my first day in office I visited AFSCME solid waste department workers before they left to pick up the city's trash. We met in a small area near their time clock and, despite my overtures about working together, the anger and tension were palpable. The city would not balance its budget on their backs and my approach demeaned them and their work, they contended. Mindful of other well-intentioned mayors, like John Lindsay, who had started their terms with labor strife, I wanted to avert a strike or slowdown, but without undermining my campaign pledge to increase the productivity and quality of the city workforce. In circumstances like these I knew it was easy to get sidetracked arguing about who is right, or wrong, or winning on process points. I needed to keep reminding myself that the issue was not about who appeared to win or back down, but rather about fulfilling citizens' demands that required increased productivity. So I promised literally to work alongside them, picking up trash, cleaning areas in public housing, cutting grass in parks, and listening to their unfiltered comments.

The evolution of my relationship with the fire department started differently but ended with a similarly deep partnership. Firefighters always present challenges to mayors. They are local, and now national, heroes. They provide a service that all citizens believe is vital, and voters insist that in case of both fire and emergency medical services, the more proximate the firehouse the better. Firefighters are a very tight family, passing problems, issues, and even rumors at the speed of sound. Fire unions tend to be well organized and often very demanding. Yet the services firefighters perform are quite expensive, and cities with a declining tax base face considerable challenges in financing a rational but well-equipped response.

In the several years preceding 1992, when I first took office, the relationship between the IAFF and the city leaders had been poor. The firefighters and their union leaders did not believe the city, or even their own upper management, appreciated their efforts or made good decisions. The city's main fire goal had been simply to limit expense, without sufficient regard for worker safety or the expertise firefighters could bring to these complicated issues. During my first campaign I remember visiting even new firehouses where the firefighters who supposedly benefited from their new facilities more often complained that avoidable design defects occurred because they had not been consulted. Because city officials had viewed fire union officials as disruptive and overly demanding, the then–fire chief avoided consulting with them. The result (as firefighters later described to me) was a strong sense among them that the city simply did not respect them for their expertise or commitment to mission.

In early February 1992 a high-rise fire at the Indianapolis Athletic Club claimed the lives of two firefighters, a highly unusual event for the city. This experience exposed a number of management and equipment problems, and the resulting recriminations provided a seminal event in labor-management relations. The change in administration and the tragedy led me to appoint a new fire chief—who had risen through the ranks as "one of us." The changes over the next several years eventually brought about the bold 1994 fire station solution, illustrating the best of labor-management collaboration.

So when faced with a crisis requiring station closings in 1994, and based on a solid foundation of trust, firefighters' union officials Tom Hanify and Tom Miller approached the city administration with a startling request: they proposed to help solve the problem, identify where closures would not harm safety, and communicate to the neighbors with us *if* they could share in the benefits.

Over the ensuing months these labor-management teams identified areas with population losses and studied run reports and digital maps to determine where stations could be consolidated or enhanced. They provided suggestions on emergency medical service (EMS) responses and, after negotiations, helped the city "sell" the closings. Of course union officials could not advocate laying off their members and this created tension in all union dealings. The city's previous approach to manpower had involved authorizing a relatively high number of firefighters but then not filling all the jobs. This time, though, the city and union faced actual jobs that exceeded available revenues. Thus, the parties worked to arrive at a manpower number everyone could support, an agreement that no one would be laid off, and a decision that once attrition dropped below the agreed-on number, hiring would commence again. The clarity of the plan helped, as did the commitment by the city to apply some of the savings to safety equipment, enhanced training, and a very important schedule change that reduced the hours in a year slightly but also helped scheduling personal and family time. In the end, the community continued to receive a high-quality response, and from a public-spirited, high-morale group.

Large Purposes, Small Steps

The platform for partnership needed a clearly articulated, shared vision that would cause both sides to understand that cooperating would be advantageous if the points of cooperation exceeded the areas of friction. The overall purpose for changing labor relations practices was a new vision for the city: that Indianapolis be a competitive city with safe streets, strong neighborhoods, and a thriving economy.

Increasing tax rates, deteriorating city services, and comparatively poor education and crime control were pushing people and their capital to the suburbs. We needed to freeze or reduce taxes in order to close the gap with the suburbs; yet the business community urgently requested a one-billion-dollar program to repair the city's infrastructure. These demands and important neighborhood revitalization could not be accomplished without major changes in how the city conducted its business. We could not save enough money simply by doing existing chores somewhat better. The city's early implementations of total-quality management had led to only marginal improvements. To interrupt the status quo, labor and management needed an incentive to change under which the benefits would exceed the risks. Developing this incentive, we hoped, would depend on the unions' understanding both the "macro" of the region's economics and the "micro" of how changes would affect their members.

In the early months of my term, long-standing Republican middle managers assumed that change meant eliminating large numbers of union jobs through privatization and leaving most of the managers in place as contract monitors. When I saw the value the laborers and their ideas could contribute, however, my commitment to conduct the process in a way that treated everyone fairly became stronger. As we did that, management was actually put at risk more than labor.

Early efforts demonstrated that we had many good people trapped in bad systems, and that the only way to produce higher-quality services within appropriate budgets would be to convert the workers' frustration with management into a new responsiveness that sent the correct signals and, in turn, increased productivity. In those cases where I was fortunate enough to have thoughtful union leaders like Steve Fantauzzo and Steve Quick from AFSCME and Tom Miller and Tom Hanify from IAFF, the unions quickly moved from the problem side of the ledger to the asset side: they were not a problem to be managed but a partner with many of the same goals.

The Overtures

We needed a coherent, well-understood process to produce the necessary change. We presented two very different proposals to the two major union players, AFSCME and IAFF, because our relationship with one had been adversarial and our relationship with the other more open.

AFSCME had been lobbying vigorously against privatization reforms by picketing, contacting legislators, and holding public events. We already had the support necessary to proceed, but the process was slow and the human cost in anxiety and morale was high. My supporters, who were in large part Republicans, could see the vigor of the organized-union efforts to defeat us at almost every election, including mine. They saw privatization as a sure way to improve efficiency at the expense of an already very unfriendly political group. The nonunionized city managers, many good people appointed under the patronage process, would be supportive of any system under which they retained their influence. They expected to see outsourcing with them as contract managers.

These thoughts plus many small unpleasant events with each side led us to conclude that if we could drive dramatic improvements in efficiency and reduce costs at the same time, public support would be wide and strong enough for the city council to back us over entrenched interests. We presented a plan to the unions that, at the time, felt like a concession in terms of methodology but not principle: the city would allow its workers a window to bid on any work before outsourcing and provide them access to all information and financials, full authority to propose changes in how they did their work, and a city-funded independent consultant to assist them.

Since AFSCME had so vigorously claimed their superiority over the private sector, they were somewhat hard-pressed to reject the concept.

The long-standing mistrust among the parties precluded an immediate acceptance of the offer, however. Winning trust and convincing union members that the status quo was truly unacceptable became the critical prerequisites of change.

The firefighters were also distrustful, but for them the recent tragedy demanded changes in the status quo. The fire chief commissioned a major outside evaluation, placed IAFF leaders on the oversight committee for the study, and reached out to these leaders on all questions dealing with implementation. Over the next two years the firefighters with their union leadership became full partners with management. Neither side co-opted the other. The defining issue that brought the parties together was a shared concern: safety. The city administration invested substantially in purchasing safety equipment recommended by the joint union-management team. The men and women of the department eventually concluded that city officials did, in fact, care about them.

Respect and Trust

Indianapolis government in the 1970s and '80s had been a relatively well run, professional implementation of traditional public administration: lots of hierarchical systems, detailed input, and management, institutional, and personal distrust of discretion. These older processes, layered with collective bargaining and legal protections, created a relationship that guaranteed friction: most of the effort reinforced the belief that but for management supervision, detailed audits, and input measures, the laborers would malinger, or worse.

Earning the trust necessary to move forward on large, sometimes painful, issues required management's demonstrable progress on smaller issues. Working with labor crews provided me direct access to their ideas and attitudes, unfiltered by layers of management. The consistently good ideas they raised changed my stereotyped opinion of labor but reinforced my suspicion that many layers of management unnecessarily added costs and little value. The public housing union president one day helped me understand both the distrust and the waste. He claimed that public housing managers who supervised craft laborers, such as plumbers and electricians, had not done the actual jobs either ever, or in years. He reasonably claimed that those managers standing over the workers and instructing them served no constructive purpose and that, in fact, the orders they gave were often counterproductive. The hierarchical system told the workers the city did not trust them with more discretion and thus harmed motivation and reduced productivity.

Similarly instructive was an event after a large snowfall that had hundreds of residents complaining. I went to the headquarters of the snow removal effort, visiting with managers in one room and the men and women who drove the snowplows in another. The first group had many reasonable explanations for the effort's poor performance, ranging from equipment breakdowns to the temperature and time of day the snow fell. The drivers, however, had a dozen specific ways to improve the results, including changes in the route maps, the type of salt purchased, the way mechanics were deployed, and so forth. Translating the drivers' ideas into better productivity and worker satisfaction became a high priority for me.

After the election the unions had no expectation other than of a four-year fight. They had strongly opposed me, whereas the upper and middle managers, mostly of my political party, had supported me. Thus, any suggestion I made about competition was interpreted as a cleverly disguised act of war. In an early managed competition to decide whether to outsource the central garage, union leader Steve Fantauzzo demanded that we "get these guys off our backs. We are not going to lose bids because you are making us carry managers we don't need." He was advocating that I remove most of the managers who supported me, of course, in order to help those union members who opposed me with competitive bids. For the managed competition model to be accepted by the unions I had to respond by offering to transfer, retire, or lay off the unnecessary managers. I did so, and the remaining managers became more like partners, helping to find ways to increase performance and drive costs down in their work activities.

Translating this vision throughout the departments in a way that engaged labor with management on its importance was critical. Tom Hanify started out as a firebrand union leader, finding no issue too small for a fight. His comments concerning the mission statement that followed the vision illustrate the change:

> One of the first things the public safety director (Mike Beaver) did was that he brought a wide range of people in to produce a strategic plan. The union played a significant role in creating the mission statement and the strategic plan. The strategic planning process was foreign to me, but what was really foreign to me was that the union was included. When the mission statement and strategic plan came out, you had nearly 10 percent of the department already involved and selling it. We had people intimately involved with it who went back to their fire stations and would talk about it.

Chief Smith's view was similar: "Those 60 people became stakeholders. They had ownership in what we were trying to accomplish. These people really liked being involved in that, and they took ownership of the mission statement. I thought, 'If this works for producing a mission statement, it will work for other things'."

Common Ground. Before these efforts, labor and management leaders in Indianapolis engaged each other only around complaints or contract negotiations. Developing trust required that the sides interact before problems reached the grievance stage. Over time AFSCME local presidents became quite adept at looking for solutions when issues first arose and engaging management constructively. And management got much better at responding quickly and effectively. Joint labor-management teams participated in all aspects of work-related decisions. For example, after years of labor's complaining that city procurement officials purchased equipment that was not optimally designed for use, labor started assisting in developing specifications.

Solving small problems helped create trust. If workers needed better safety gloves, or more water breaks in hot weather, or different schedules, those things were solved quickly and jointly. Firefighters had far-ranging issues because they live at work, often not in very good situations. Thus, repairing kitchens and windows that leaked in their stations, and apparatus that was apt to break down, quickly and cooperatively was important. Firefighters were included in oversight committees advising on the design of their firehouses and the choice of equipment. They found that when they complained, something actually happened. Eventually, enough progress occurred that it pressured a change in the collective bargaining process. After the start of negotiations in 1994, firefighters' officials Tom Hanify and Tom Miller arrived in my office with an ultimatum: either replace or reeducate the negotiator or they would return to the old style of confrontation. The city's very good outside labor lawyer had begun the first session with a typical hard-edged style and a list of demands, but the union had expected the city to negotiate as a partner working through issues cooperatively. The city team immediately changed its approach, allowing for a successful, albeit long and sometimes unpleasant, negotiation.

Investing in Training and Equipment. Even if the long-term goal is to do more with less, building a sustained partnership requires early expenditures, some simply to show good faith, even before there is an agreement on the specifics of the partnership. When management reduces its investment in training and equipment, it further demeans the workers and erodes their confidence that there is a team dedicated to the common good. If in fact bad equipment costs time and productivity, then pushing the unions to do more with less with this equipment will not be well received. Since we believed a well-trained, empowered workforce was the source of many ideas, even as we attempted to reduce expenditures we increased training in a range of skills, from costing to how to avoid accidents or use equipment better. Intensive training not only on safety but also on business principles, like activity-based costing, helped put the unions in a better place to participate.

A good partnership does not rest on bad information. Neither unions nor management originally had true costing information. They did not know how much it cost to fill a pothole, how to calculate overhead, or what the cost of using one type of machinery versus another was. Reforming city financial systems to support productivity, providing access to all such information, and training union and management leaders on how to use the information became critical, especially as competitive outsourcing became more frequent. The city brought in outside consultants, KPMG (not the organization doing the city's standard annual audit), to construct an activity-based costing approach and to train city department CFOs in its application. Training was also provided to union leaders.

Eventually Indianapolis officials listened carefully to worker suggestions about equipment, looking at the cost of capital and its effect on production, and invested more frequently than had previously been the case. Both unions became expert on understanding how the large equipment purchases could, if designed correctly, increase productivity. AFSCME found ways to run road repair crews with fewer people and better equipment, calculating how it brought down their unit costs. The labor-management game had changed. Even on the small matters, I recollect visiting fire stations where those stationed there would tell me how much it cost to repair the roof or cut the grass and explain how we could save money.

These changes allowed the parties to measure progress on accepted metrics. For example, solid waste workers noted that since the system began in 1994, the cost per household for trash pick-up dropped from $85 to $72, the amount of refuse collected daily per worker increased from 14 tons to more than 24, and complaints dropped by two thirds.

Two-Way Street. In this chapter I look at what management might do to create a productive partnership with labor. Of course, if labor leaders do not want such a partnership, the effort cannot succeed. The cases studied here concerning AFSCME and IAFF involved union leaders with vision. The state president of AFSCME was a tough advocate who often took positions I found quite unreasonable, but he had been with a local in another state that represented workers who lost their jobs when de-institutionalization closed many state hospitals. He thus understood the need to help reposition the city, for an eroding tax base could never support the numbers of union workers, nor the pay levels, he demanded. In contrast, I was not able to convince the teachers' union that a similar approach based on employee empowerment and direct management-employee communication was worth the risk to the union.

Safety and Symbolism. With many public employees and particularly firefighters, safety is the most important issue. It also is a symbolic issue, however. Perceived indifference to the chance of accident or death contaminates discussion of other issues. For us, the constant attention to safety, addressed visibly and jointly, enhanced safety and became symbolic of a new partnership with the firefighters.

Symbolism contributes to the reservoir of good will even when smaller, less-expensive matters are involved. A small act proposed by the fire chief helped enhance our partnership's value:

> The issue of the emblem on the side of the fire truck had more impact than I would have thought. The union suggested and I agreed that the new emblems on the sides of the fire trucks say "Partners in progress for a safer city." It consisted of the union emblem, the fire department emblem, and a picture of Monument Circle. We had more positive comments over that issue, and the firefighters took more pride in that emblem to the point it became part of our reputation nationally.

City officials needed constantly to work on sending the right signals because issues inevitably could take on quite counterproductive lives. The discipline of a popular co-worker or an exaggerated story about a proposed cut, for example, could undermine good will quickly. Therefore I personally delivered the bonus checks to work groups and attended events the workers viewed as important. Equally important, whenever we "managed by walking around," any reasonable suggestion was given a response within two weeks. People needed to see their ideas taken seriously.

Moreover, the union-management cooperation encouraged by the competition fundamentally changed the quality of work life. For example, in the fleet management local, the number of days lost to worker's compensation injuries dropped from over 500 in 1992 to just 4 in 1998 and grievances plummeted 80 percent.

Communication and Partnership. Better communication is a common refrain, but Indianapolis and many other government employers do not accomplish it in a pervasive and effective manner. Government is filled with gatekeepers and none work with more vigilance than those who hold the keys to information. So shopping ideas inside a government is rough going. Good ideas require an open market where workers can compare notes, talk to others with different assets, and finally try their ideas out on someone other than their immediate boss. Chief Smith recognized this when he noted:

> I'm a little different model of a fire chief because I had five years as the assistant chief. The adversarial relationship was obviously not working. The previous chief said, "I don't want to talk to them (the union), because all they do is embarrass me or surprise me. As the assistant chief, your role is to talk to the union." The union would say to me, "Here's what we're trying to accomplish. Why does he disagree with us?"

Tom Hanify described the relationship he had with the new chief in this manner:

> He listened to people. He engaged people. It took time, but good management takes time, and bad management is easy. He sat there and he would engage people and make people feel that he cared about their concerns. That is extremely important for anyone who manages a huge workforce. He did recognize that he had multiple customers. His job was to facilitate, but the product he was delivering was, "How do I get the rank and file to serve the people and keep them safe?" He recognized the mission and he identified the tools to get there.

Mid-management, often acting as the preservers of the status quo, often take the side of labor in their common complaint about some superior level of government or management. They blame higher-ups for circumstances rather than take the more-difficult steps to solve a particular issue. Therefore, small problems that could be corrected are not, and the failure to respond is taken as indifference to the quality of the workplace and the product. Some union and management leaders prefer that information pass through them and then to members. Both groups often believe that control of information is one way to control others.

Real communication is real work; it takes time and multiple channels. More importantly, communication is not merely management dissemination. Listening is not enough. There needs to be an agreement on specific forums for, and energy devoted to, sustained action and problem solving. As Mike Beaver explained: "You walk away from every meeting with action steps that you will accomplish before meeting next. You don't just meet." Each small problem resolved built up the reservoir of trust that would be necessary. We tried many channels for this communication, some of which worked, like those described in the next subsections, and some of which did not, like a bonus for hot ideas. Who listens and how became critical.

Meetings and Mayor's Office Attention. None of these changes occurs easily or naturally. Bureaucracies, whether union or management, fight off these reforms as if they were infections. We established a small group in the mayor's office to power the changes, oversee the analytical work, and interact directly with labor. In addition, we imposed a chief operating officer who had direct access to the mayor's office over the civilian blue-collar workers. This official had specific instructions to solve every reasonable labor complaint quickly and in a way that proved to union members that their leaders' participation in our cooperative partnerships would translate into much faster and better resolution of issues than the previous grievance and lawsuit procedure.

Each month for our regular meeting, an AFSCME local president, along with his or her officers, would arrive in the mayor's office with an agenda of suggestions and complaints. The mayor's staff, but no other managers, attended these meetings. The items discussed provided insights into how middle management operated. We pledged a solution or a thorough answer of why not, by the next meeting. The fact that these meetings occurred regularly had a therapeutic effect on middle management, who knew that access to the top existed.

The meetings helped focus sustained attention by the city's staff on the importance of labor issues. Absent meetings at this level, the natural tendency is to push issues farther down in the organization, a tactic that may seem best but results in constant backsliding. Some managers began to understand that the program had changed, but many remained convinced of their superiority over labor. In fact, that was how they defined their worth. Without high-level attention they could not be convinced to change.

Deputy Mayor Skip Stitt was in charge of the city's managed competition. He had access to all performance metrics and cost records and could see whether management was truly interested in change. He could evaluate a union suggestion for cost effectiveness quickly. Even so, many managers could or would not change their autocratic behavior. That made us create a new senior administrative position so we could add a person with operations experience, giving him authority over blue-collar lines of business. Specifically, he was charged with quickly solving even small workplace problems that had previously eroded trust and prevented a partnership from flourishing.

Web Boundary Busting. Empowering workers required that we find as many ways as possible to provide them with access to information and upper management. During one interesting collective bargaining session, AFSCME solid waste workers asked for access to e-mail next to their time clocks in the morning. They wanted both to see on-line the customer complaints and to send reform ideas directly to the mayor's office. If they were to be held accountable for results, they wanted to make sure senior management saw their ideas and understood their frustrations. Digital file sharing and e-mail caused rigid boundaries to become permeable and eroded the gatekeeper's control. Similarly, intra- and Internet expansion allowed us to move to decentralized electronic systems without loss of accountability. Older command and control procurement systems, tightly managed from the top in a way that reduced worker discretion, for example, were replaced with purchasing systems that allowed many more individuals, at all levels, to procure through web tools. At the same time, those electronic systems enhanced auditing trails.

Transparency. The city financial office used to protect financial information closely on the belief it helped them manage union leaders more completely. This game-like atmosphere produced and reinforced predictable distrust. We tried the opposite: maximum and timely disclosure of financial information, performance data, and everything else that would aid the unions in better production. No longer was the goal to reduce the chances that labor would earn more, but rather to increase the likelihood that productivity would increase by more than labor costs. Armed with costing data and sharing in the benefits, union members offered suggestions concerning waste in materials, equipment, route structures, management, and more.

Moving from a System Designed Not to Work

These early dysfunctional relationships did not simply result from short-sighted approaches; rather, they were baked into the government.

The relationship structures reinforced hierarchical and program-matic boundaries, reduced discretion, micromanaged inputs, and cen-tralized decisions.

Rigid pay systems did not allow bonuses, but the pay systems could not be changed until the city created better approaches to measuring performance. Worker empowerment meant that purchasing needed to be devolved to the lowest practical level, which in turn necessitated changes to internal audit practices and major changes to procurement software. Personalities and attitudes aggravated these structures: many employees found it difficult to move from a command-and-control atmosphere to a coaching atmosphere. Racial biases, and the view by many bureaucrats that power is positional and that if you are superior in rank you need to act that way, erode good will. The fire chief was clearly aware of this as his comments about his appointed deputy chiefs reveals:

> I also wanted them to think like me. I wanted them to have common sense, but not be Mr. Muscle either. Any sign of arro-gance, and they were out. I told each one of them, "I'm going to give you the tools and resources. The first thing you've gotta do is be nice, and you've gotta work with the union."

A labor-management agenda based on empowerment cannot suc-ceed without major internal governance changes. The outdated bureau-cratic mold needs to be replaced by a much more flexible, networked, decentralized, and performance-driven system. Here are some of the structural changes we undertook.

Close to the Customer (or Customer's Data)

We knew that our vision for the city would not motivate employees unless they viewed it as important to them. Although most public em-ployees I had met over the last 20 years work for government in order to contribute to the public good, most of the municipal workforce at the time performed in hierarchical systems, in narrow jobs, with inadequate training, and disconnected from solving tangible public problems.

Celebrating this public service role, we thought, would motivate em-ployees to do better and cause them to engage in changes that would im-prove results. It became important to increase both employee discretion and their connection with citizens. Workers needed to be reorganized around problems and neighborhoods; they needed to fight their way out of prescriptive motions and measured activities. We thought the way the union workers thought of themselves, and us, could change dramatically from the reinforced pride that went with making their city a better place.

So city officials needed to cultivate this sense of public service and shared goal of making the city competitive. Employees needed more opportunity to have firsthand citizen feedback. A series of reforms allowed this to occur. Broadbanding replaced narrow job descriptions, allowing workers much more discretion. In addition, city employees from different specialties were assigned to projects involving a specific neighborhood and its leadership. These employees moved from situations that were functionally specific but geographically general to work that was more the opposite, allowing them to see and feel the results of their efforts.

Citizens have always complained to city hall, but traditionally that information was neither integrated with broader performance data nor adequately decentralized. We started by centralizing the call centers and securing software that allowed the call taker easily to answer and route complaints. But at first the front office was disconnected from the back office, and officials could not determine when, or even whether, a complaint was resolved. Eventually enhancements allowed the information to be compiled and distributed to the work groups.

A continuing and difficult effort to establish performance measures included attempts to gather information on customer satisfaction, for example, how many homes were missed by trash collectors or how long it took to tow an abandoned car. Electronic tools allowed all of these data to be disaggregated easily and distributed in a way that enabled each work team to see the results of its efforts. Internal customer satisfaction mattered as well. The fleet services group, for example, proudly claimed that even with *fewer* workers than there were before the competition the number of vehicles serviced within eight hours had jumped from 70 percent to over 80 percent. The complaints thus evolved to a more-integrated citizen satisfaction measurement, which showed dramatic improvement in how the public viewed most of its services and infused workers with pride, reinforcing the collaborative commitment to the city's vision.

Pay and Progress

Weaving these numerous changes together produced tangible results that further encouraged labor and management to operate as a team. Increased productivity exceeded attrition by enough that we could offer performance pay resulting from gain sharing. In 1995 and 1996, for example, the Department of Public Works' employees fulfilled their contractual obligations for even less money than they bid and therefore received year-end bonuses negotiated under the gain-sharing formula. As one union leader explained, "We corrected problems and found ways to save money that we hadn't thought of before. Employees started turning out lights when they weren't in the rooms to save on electricity; it's amazing how much money you can save through little things."

Another city union worker added:

> We didn't do preventive stuff in the past. We let things run, and then fix them when they broke. We realized if we do preventive maintenance, that makes costs cheaper. In the past, nobody cared if the nut on that machine was loose—you worried about it when the machine broke. Now, a guy tightens it as soon as he notices it because that saves money.

The structural change in the pay system, coupled with the empowerment to affect how work was done, produced a dynamic that encouraged both sides to solve problems quickly. The president of the largest local, Steve Quick, explained how his local went from 300 grievances a year to none:

> Grievances vanished overnight, because now the union managed itself. Attitudes changed dramatically, because again, people had ownership of their jobs. They made the decisions, they did the work, and they suffered the consequences when they did something wrong. But people took a lot more pride in what they did.

When procurement, classification, and supervision reduce work to carefully controlled tasks, and pay is disassociated from performance, individuals with little discretion have equally little job satisfaction. Conversely, when these reforms converge, as they did in one of the first years after competition, the employees can receive bonuses—like the mechanics' $1,900 each—which motivate even greater commitment the next year.

Conclusion

I campaigned committed to providing higher-quality services, especially to those in the most neglected areas, and to increasing the economic base of the city. Yet competition from our own suburbs limited our resources. Privatization as the first solution conceived quickly gave way to competition when the workers recognized that most city services could continue to be provided by city employees. Surprisingly, it became apparent that most of the city's unions, if engaged correctly, would help provide the necessary service levels. The ever-present risk of outsourcing provided motivation, of course, but conversion to a managed-competition model brought out the best in union initiative and forced the managers to pay attention. Working together in managed competition under new empowering internal rules led to service-oriented partnerships.

The results of this partnership were impressive:

- From 1992 to 1998 the city went from a deficit to a 102-million-dollar surplus in its half-billion-dollar base budget.
- Property tax rates were reduced four times.
- No union employee was laid off.
- Over 90 percent reduction in labor grievances.
- Over 80 percent reduction in accident rates and lost days from injuries in areas of competition.
- Pay and benefits increased in every case.
- Customer satisfaction increased.
- The unions won two thirds of the work they chose to bid on.

The transformation was neither easy nor quick. It took over two years of demonstrable and reciprocal good faith and then sustained follow-up to maintain trust and get results. En route strong union leadership facing management with a failing status quo engaged around a new vision. We were able to improve services to the citizens and working conditions for labor because of increased productivity. The productivity increases made it possible to continue to fund performance pay and training. Eroding boundaries played a key role, both vertically as workers could speak with the mayor or other policy makers and horizontally as teams came together to furnish cross-department services to citizens of a specific area.

One day while working alongside a transportation worker sealing cracks, I asked him what he thought about all these changes and the pressures of competition. His response spoke volumes: "Mayor, you can bid this all you want, but we are the very best at this work in the entire state, we are making you proud, and we will win every time you bid something out." This terrific response explained how almost everyone managed to win: better services for less money combined with more-satisfying and better-paying work.

CHAPTER 4

The Role and Responsibility of Union Leaders for Effective Service Delivery

ROBERT M. TOBIAS
American University

The role of a union leader is to organize employees to act collectively, and the responsibility of a union leader is to leverage the collective voice to ensure individual member satisfaction in the workplace. Employee satisfaction has been shown to correlate directly with improved productivity. Therefore, meeting member needs can coincide with management's responsibility to provide more effective, efficient service in the public sector.

What constitutes employee satisfaction has changed dramatically over time with the change in workforce composition. The federal sector workplace in 1950, for example, was 70 percent clerical, while today it is 70 percent knowledge workers (James 2002a:5). Knowledge workers want more than the reactive voice promised by unions and the security promised by public employers.

Unions have traditionally used the collective employee voice to provide aggressive use of the grievance procedure and collectively bargained protections from harm. Knowledge workers believe they will never need a grievance procedure, however. They want interesting, challenging work that includes planning, designing, and implementing more effective work processes, together with the opportunity to participate in day-to-day decision making concerning how best to accomplish organizational goals. For unions to remain relevant to the new workforce, they must use the collective employee voice to satisfy knowledge-worker needs.

The traditional public manager mantra of promising security while recruiting employees is no longer viable, at least not for knowledge workers. They do not necessarily see public service as a career. They are looking for challenging work, whether it be in the public service, nonprofit organizations, consulting, or the many other opportunities available to them (Chetkovich 2001; Britt 2003). In addition, in light of the pressure to outsource and to reduce the number of public employees, a promise of security is hollow.

The federal government needs knowledge workers, however. As the problems government addresses become more difficult and the complexity of the methods used to address them increases, the government must attract and hire more people with college and advanced degrees. The simple government solution of the past—create a program—has been replaced by an array of methods and tools (e.g., federal-state-local partnerships, grants, loans, vouchers, and contracting) that require sophisticated management, evaluative, and implementation skills (Salamon 2002). Federal managers must tap the expertise of the knowledge workers in order to fulfill legislative promises and taxpayer expectations. In addition, with 50 percent of the federal workforce eligible to retire in the next five years, managers must make attracting, creating, and retaining a productive knowledge workforce a very high priority.

Public sector managers and union leaders are also faced with growing pressure exerted by the executive and legislative branches and the public to do more with less and to outsource work currently performed by government employees to the private sector. There is a growing recognition by union leaders that they can no longer address the threat of job loss and member satisfaction solely through the creation and enforcement of rights. Many of them recognize the need to create a new, more-collaborative relationship.

The theory behind this new understanding is as follows: if unions can enhance knowledge-worker satisfaction by creating opportunities for meaningful participation, worker productivity will be enhanced, thereby satisfying management needs. There is no question that public sector knowledge workers have information and ideas on how to address the intractable problems of public policy implementation. And there is no question that increasing employee satisfaction improves employee and agency productivity.

The intuitive link one might make between employee satisfaction and productivity and customer satisfaction has now been replaced with hard data. In *First Break All the Rules,* Marcus Buckingham and Curt Coffman of the Gallup organization proved a relationship between employee satisfaction and employee productivity (Buckingham and Coffman 1999). They found they could predict the level of increased productivity and customer satisfaction from an increase in employee satisfaction (Tobias 2000; Ricci, Kirn, and Quinn 1998; Kahn and Smith 1992).

In order for unions to fulfill their responsibility to the knowledge workers while remaining relevant to the needs of all those they represent, and for managers to attract and maximize what knowledge workers have to give, however, significant barriers must be addressed successfully.

Initial Organizing Campaigns

A competitive and adversarial labor-management relationship most often begins in the context of the initial union-organizing campaign and rarely changes. In every organizing campaign, employee discontent and management mistakes are highlighted. The union promises a better future in a negotiated collective bargaining agreement that will substitute rules that are clear and enforceable through a grievance procedure for arbitrary, subjective management decision making. The union pattern is to define member needs in response to management actions. The focus is on fixing the past by creating rights enforceable in the future.

Management typically sees the union as an interloper to be defeated for a number of reasons. First, management's ability to make unilateral decisions concerning conditions of employment will be eliminated. Second, decision making may be delayed because of the need to inform and negotiate substantive decisions with non-employee union organizers who may know little about agency business. Third, costs may be increased because of the time involved in negotiating and administering a collective bargaining agreement. As a result, the management focus is on minimizing the role and impact of the union on management decision making.

At this point in a relationship, neither party sees how it can advance its interests in collaboration with the other. Each party sees only how it can win if the other loses. Therefore, when a union wins an organizing campaign, management sees it as a loss. The win-lose relationship is established. The respective roles are set, constituent expectations are established, and the hostile dance of an adversarial labor-management relationship begins.

This is certainly true in the federal sector. Almost 30 years of the possibility of public sector organizing has yielded a workforce in which 80 percent of those eligible to join unions have elected union representation (National Performance Review 1993:83). The General Accounting Office concluded in 1991 that the federal labor-management relations program "suffers from excessive litigation and adversarial proceedings" (U.S. General Accounting Office 1991:76). Parties at war cannot fulfill the needs of knowledge workers.

Organizational Structure

Both managers and unions need changed organizational structures to meet the needs of knowledge workers. Federal sector political appointees have often called for increased employee satisfaction and productivity, yet they refuse to alter or flatten the traditional hierarchical structures in their organizations that are inconsistent with creating the discretion needed to maximize knowledge workers' productivity.

As Peter Drucker recently commented, "In a traditional workforce, the worker serves the system; in a knowledge workforce, the system must serve the worker" (Drucker 2002:76). In the federal workforce, however, many knowledge workers still serve the system.

Union organizational structures have also traditionally been hierarchical, service-based organizations. A few elected officers, stewards, and union staff represent member interests to management: they negotiate the collective bargaining agreements, process the grievances, and provide protection from arbitrary management actions. In exchange, employees are asked to join the union and pay dues. Members are rarely called upon to be involved in day-to-day union activities or in workplace change efforts. Perhaps 5 percent of the workforce may file a grievance, but 95 percent never call upon that union "insurance policy."

To identify and meet knowledge-worker needs, union leaders must shift from a hierarchical, service-based organizational structure where the few decide for the many, to a flatter model where the many participate, decide, and implement agreed-upon changes together. This means that union leaders must proactively identify the interests of the 95 percent and provide them with opportunities to be involved in addressing those interests.

Union leaders must also create and manage more opportunities for members to participate in internal union affairs (e.g., creating budgets, planning social events, and crafting internal and external communication programs). In an organizing model, union leaders know and act in conjunction with union members to realize member dreams while still creating and protecting member rights.

Scope of Bargaining

The scope of bargaining in the federal sector is narrow (Labor Management and Employee Relations Act, U.S. Code 1978, vol. 5, sec. 7106(a)), and federal managers have traditionally guarded the exercise of protected management rights, particularly decisions to determine what work will be contracted out and how existing work may be reorganized to increase efficiency. This approach is consistent with a hierarchically controlled work environment where management creates a work system and fungible employees do the work. But this narrow scope is ineffective in a workplace that relies on knowledge workers. There, it is the knowledge of the workers, not the management-created system, that maximizes employee productivity.

Union leaders cannot wait for a change in the statute to guarantee an expanded scope of bargaining. They must create the opportunity for knowledge-worker involvement as an adjunct to the statutory collective bargaining rights.

Fear of Failure

Many union leaders construct reelection campaigns based on what has been successful in the past: tough bargaining, aggressive grievance processing, and never being found guilty of trusting a manager. Changing a successful reelection formula for any politician is very risky.

It is so easy and safe for a union leader to wait for management mistakes because they always happen. It requires the leader to make a significant change—to think and act proactively and strategically. It takes time, energy, and patience to include and involve union members in shaping a vision for the future. Rather than reacting to management, a union leader seeking to change a labor-management relationship must spend time creating and maintaining a consensus for action, often among employees with different goals and objectives. A union leader must see that the value of acting rather than reacting is greater than the comfortable, predictable status quo.

It is also easy and safe for managers to maintain the status quo. Managers in the public sector are wisely risk averse—success is so expected it is unacknowledged—but a mistake is punished severely, often with public humiliation by Congress and the press. Therefore, it is understandable for managers to create work processes with high control and low employee discretion. But maximizing knowledge-worker productivity is inconsistent with a highly controlled workplace.

Either a manager or a union leader may be first to recognize that his or her individual interests cannot be achieved without the collaboration of the other party. But both parties must see the value of changing. A unilateral change by a union leader from a competitive and adversarial posture to a collaborative one will not create a collaborative relationship. Nor will a management leader's suddenly becoming more inclusive. Each must change in relation to a change by the other.

It is commonly believed that it is impossible to align a union's responsibility to serve its members with the government's responsibility to provide effective public service to the community. There is ample evidence to support this belief. There is also evidence, however, that a labor-management relationship can evolve from its competitive and adversarial roots with a focus on the past to a relationship between union and agency that is capable of creating a vision for the future. Such a vision can meet both union-member needs and management responsibility to provide more effective, efficient public service. The key is for both union and management to understand that they have a mutual interest to work jointly to improve employee satisfaction.

President William J. Clinton recognized the difficulty of changing labor-management relationships and the link of collaborative labor-management relationships to successful organizational change when he issued Executive Order 12871 mandating the creation of labor-management partnerships:

> Only by changing the nature of Federal labor management relations so that managers, employees, and employees' elected union representatives serve as partners will it be possible to design and implement comprehensive changes necessary to reform Government. (Clinton 1993)

The president also made clear that the partnerships must "involve employees and their union representatives as full partners with management representatives to identify problems and craft solutions to better serve the agency's customers and mission" (Clinton 1993: Section (4)(b)). The National Partnership Council, created by Executive Order 12871, issued annual reports that contained examples of agencies and unions creating successful partnership efforts that improved agency productivity (National Partnership Council 1995, 1996, 1997).

The history of the National Treasury Employees Union (NTEU) and U.S. Customs Department's labor-management relationship fits the federal sector pattern of change from an adversarial to a collaborative relationship as a result of Executive Order 12871. It also shows the difficulty and fragility of change efforts.

NTEU won elections against incumbent, often passive, rival unions during the 1970s. The organizing campaigns were long and bitter, with the Customs management explicitly supporting the incumbents. The resulting labor-management relationships were extremely adversarial. The NTEU-Customs adversarial relationship began to change in 1993.

On June 3, 1994, in response to President Clinton's executive order and the need for the U.S. Customs Service to initiate extensive restructuring and organizational change in order to increase its productivity, NTEU and George Weise, the newly appointed Customs Commissioner, created a labor-management partnership agreement. The partnership agreement covered all bargaining-unit employees.

NTEU was given a role in designing the new Customs organization, creating new business processes, and implementing the changes. Although most of the decisions were outside the scope of bargaining, the agreement provided for a "strive for consensus" decision-making model with union participation. Few decisions were not reached by consensus.

Although local union leaders expressed an intellectual understanding and acceptance of the opportunity to be involved and to involve their members, many were reluctant to discuss the future until all past wrongs were righted. NTEU devoted thousands of hours of union resources conducting union leader–training sessions, talking individually to union leaders, facilitating meetings between union leaders and managers, and supporting relationships that looked forward as well as back. In addition, the Customs Service and NTEU trained a cadre of facilitators and made them available to local union leaders and managers. All these efforts were necessary to begin solving the problems of the past, creating experiences that showed that problems could be solved outside the traditional collective bargaining arena, and breeding trust that significant change efforts could be managed together.

As the union became increasingly involved with change efforts, the labor-management relationship began to shift from union leaders and labor-management relations specialists to union leaders and operations managers. In an adversarial relationship, operations managers delegate contact with union leaders to lawyers or labor-management relations professionals. Under that scenario the labor-management relationship becomes separate from agency operations managers, and union leaders have no impact on agency operations.

As Customs operations managers began to develop processes to improve employee productivity, they were working with employees through the NTEU. The union was viewed as an extension of the employees, rather than an institution separate from them. Agency operations managers, heretofore protective of "management rights" and unilateral decision making, included union leaders and employees appointed by their union as part of the operations decision-making process. Union leaders had a significant and meaningful opportunity to influence decision makers on all operational matters before final decisions were made. Operations managers, and employees through their union, were aligned to increase individual and agency productivity and employee satisfaction.

A specific example of the results of this effort was apparent when drug interdiction efforts fell dramatically and Customs operations managers asked NTEU and Customs employees to address the problem. Customs management and NTEU agreed at the national level to delegate authority to local union leaders and local managers to develop plans to improve drug interdiction in their locale.

Local union leaders were extremely pleased to be asked to participate for the first time in creating a significant agency operation plan. But they were confronted with the need to recruit, train, and select a large cadre of members who were willing to serve on the union-management teams created in the collaborative relationship. They were challenged to establish an elaborate two-way communication system that would allow members to participate in the expanded decision-making opportunities as they were occurring.

The local union leaders were required to manage participation, consensus building, vision creation, and results while maintaining their adversarial skills, just in case they should be needed. They ran the risk that the newly involved members, who had little history with the union, would want to change its leadership. Changing an organizational structure and continuing in office require skills many union leaders do not possess.

The vast majority of local union leaders recognized the need to change and did change. Old, inactive members volunteered for labor-management teams. Nonmembers became union members so they could participate in the union-management teams. The national and local unions publicized their role in creating the opportunity for participation. Customs service knowledge workers were maximizing the use of their expertise, and they were giving NTEU credit for the opportunity to participate.

There were some union leaders who resisted creating a new union organizational structure, however. Some were persuaded to change in conjunction with union staff support, some gave only grudging acceptance, and some never changed. Some of those in the never-change category were defeated in local elections by members who wanted to work as the knowledge workers they envisioned themselves to be and had experienced in other locations. Those who supported the effort received credit for the change and were reelected. And NTEU increased its percentage of membership in the bargaining unit by 7 percent.

Managers were also challenged in using the newly delegated discretion. Those who had made a career of testing the wind before doing anything were now responsible for creating a complex operations plan. For the work system, once established, to serve the knowledge worker—as Peter Drucker suggested it must—the knowledge worker and the manager must be able to exercise discretion. Both union leaders and managers had used discretion in creating it.

Granting local managers and union leaders discretion, however, was like bringing water to a desert. When Customs and NTEU headquarters offices gave local managers and union leaders the discretion to devise and implement efforts to improve drug-interdiction efforts, many flowers sprung up all around. Discretion is the substance that feeds successful collaborative efforts.

Once the system was activated, both Customs management and NTEU believed the new relationship had achieved significant cost benefits for the Customs Service. To verify the anecdotal evidence, they engaged the consulting firm of Booz-Allen and Hamilton (BAH) to conduct a cost-benefit analysis of the labor-management partnership for the fiscal years 1994 through 1998. The identified costs included training, partnership-development activities, and interventions to facilitate problem solving. The benefits included cost avoidance—reductions in the number of grievances and unfair labor practices filed and the number of days spent bargaining collectively—together with the measured results from process improvement teams, strategic problem-solving teams, and work groups that identified operational improvement activities. The BAH report concluded that "for each $1.00 Customs invests in these activities, it receives approximately $1.25 in benefits" (Booz-Allen and Hamilton 1998:10). The alignment of Customs management and NTEU, as hoped, did significantly increase the productivity of the U.S. Customs Service.

Notwithstanding the measurable return on investment to the Customs Service, the end result of the Customs experience is an example of how difficult it is for labor and management leaders to create and maintain alignment and how easy it is to destroy what is created. A new Customs commissioner, who had a philosophical aversion to delegation, took over in 1998 and immediately eliminated the discretion and reinstated the preexisting hierarchical management structure. Without a focus on increasing agency productivity and employee satisfaction, there was no longer an alignment between managers and union leaders.

As a result, the parties began a slow but inevitable slide back to the adversarial relationship they are stewing in today. With no discretion, the local Customs managers have no way to involve the local union and employees. They are stuck with implementing whatever policy is adopted in Customs headquarters, and employees are stuck with resisting. The number of grievances filed and time spent in bargaining have once again increased. In addition, the time to implement changes has increased.

In contrast, the Internal Revenue Service (IRS) and NTEU began to transform their adversarial labor-management relationship in 1987, in response to the 1986 filing-season fiasco of bad publicity associated with destroyed returns and overworked employees who were responding to management pressure for more production while ignoring the quality of the work (Tobias 1995). The parties have continued, in fits and starts, to expand the role and responsibility of the NTEU. The difference between the Customs and IRS experience is that Congress, the three presidents since 1987, and the press have constantly focused on the need for the IRS to improve its productivity and customer satisfaction. While the Customs service had the option to ignore its productivity obligation and the satisfaction of its employees, the IRS did not. An agency seriously seeking to maximize the productivity of its knowledge workers in an organized workplace must create a more collaborative labor-management relationship in order to be successful.

In 2001, shortly after President George W. Bush was inaugurated, he revoked Executive Order 12871 (Bush 2001). Agencies were no longer required to create labor-management partnerships. Office of Personnel Management Director Kay Coles James (2002b) issued a memorandum to all heads of departments and agencies on June 21, 2002, clarifying the revocation:

> The President was motivated by his conviction that partnership is not something that should be mandated for every agency in every situation. But while agencies are no longer *required* [emphasis in original] to form partnerships with their unions, they are strongly encouraged to establish cooperative labor-management relations.

Without strong support from the chief executive officer of the executive branch, there are very few new labor-management partnerships being created, and those without a strong performance focus are dying. President Bush risks a return to the adversarial labor-management relationships of the past, in spite of his highly publicized management agenda (Executive Office of the President 2001).

Conclusion

Adversarial, unproductive labor-management relationships can change when managers and union leaders recognize that employee satisfaction can generate increased productivity and active, involved, committed union members. To accomplish this in the federal sector, the parties need the support of a president who encourages them to take the risks necessary for success. The changes for both sides are difficult but critical to an effective, relevant public sector labor movement and a viable public sector able to implement the promises made by the president and Congress to the public.

References

Booz-Allen and Hamilton. 1998. "Cost Benefit Analysis of the Labor-Management Partnership." Washington, DC: Booz-Allen and Hamilton (October).

Britt, Thomas W. 2003. "Black Hawk Down at Work: When Your Most Motivated Employees Can't Do Their Jobs, Get Ready for an Exodus." *Harvard Business Review,* Vol. 81, no. 1 (January), pp. 16–17.

Buckingham, Marcus, and Curt Coffman. 1999. *First Break All the Rules.* New York: Simon and Schuster.

Bush, George W. 2001. "Revocation of Executive Order and Presidential Memorandum Concerning Labor-Management Partnerships." Executive Order 13203. *Federal Register,* no. 37 (February 26), p. 311. <www.whitehouse.gov/news/releases/2001/02/20010221-1.html> [February 17, 2001].

Chetkovich, Carol. 2001. *Winning the Best and Brightest: Increasing the Attraction of Public Service.* Washington, DC: PricewaterhouseCoopers Endowment for the Business of Government (July).

Clinton, William J. 1993. "Labor-Management Partnerships." Executive Order 12871. *Federal Register,* Vol. 58, no. 192 (October 6).

Drucker, Peter. 2002. "They're Not Employees, They're People." *Harvard Business Review,* Vol. 80, no. 2 (February), pp. 70–77.

Executive Office of the President. Office of Management and Budget. 2001. *President's Management Agenda.* Washington, DC: GPO (July). <www.whitehouse.gov/omb/budget/fy2002/pmo-index.html> [April 22, 2003].

James, Kay Coles. 2002a. *A Fresh Start for Federal Pay: The Case for Modernization.* Washington, DC: GPO (April).

———. 2002b. "Labor Management Relations." Memorandum for Heads of Agencies. Office of Personnel Management. <http://opm.gov/lmr/LMR_memo.asp> [June 21, 2002].

Kahn, Lynn Sandra, and Ron H. Smith. 1992. "Recruitment, Attrition and Retention at the IRS: Coming, Going and Staying in Collection." *IRS Research Bulletin.* Publication 1500, Assistant Commissioner Collection. Washington, DC: IRS.

Labor Management and Employee Relations Act. 1978. U.S. Code, Vol. 5, sec. 7101 *et seq.*

National Partnership Council. 1995. *A Report to the President on Progress in Labor-Management Partnerships.* Washington, DC: GPO (September).

————. 1996. *A Report to the President on Progress in Labor-Management Partnerships*. Washington, DC: GPO (October).

————. 1997. *A Report to the President on Progress in Labor-Management Partnerships*. Washington, DC: GPO (December).

National Performance Review. 1993. *From Red Tape to Results: Creating a Government that Works Better and Costs Less*. Washington, DC: GPO.

Ricci, Anthony J., Steven P. Kirn, and Richard T. Quinn. 1998. "The Employee-Customer- Profit Chain at Sears." *Harvard Business Review*, Vol. 76, no. 1 (January-February), pp. 82–99.

Salamon, Lester M. 2002. *The Tools of Government*. Oxford: Oxford University Press.

Tobias, Robert M. 1995. "National Treasury Employees Union and the Internal Revenue Service: Creating a Total Quality Organization." In Edward Cohen-Rosenthal, ed., *Unions, Management, and Quality*. Chicago: Irwin.

————. 2000. "Survey Provides Map to Better Service." *Government Executive* (February), pp. 78–79.

U.S. General Accounting Office. 1991. *Federal Labor Relations: A Program in Need of Reform*. Report no. 660-91-101. Washington, DC: GAO (July).

Chapter 5

Enacting Labor-Management Cooperation: New Competencies for New Times

Sonia Ospina and Allon Yaroni
New York University

The management literature suggests that a participatory, collaborative, service-oriented approach to labor relations may produce tangible positive results, such as better service, more cost effectiveness, better quality of work life, and improved labor-management relations (U.S. Department of Labor 1996; Delaney 1996; Cooke 1994). According to the participative decision-making literature these outcomes are a result of a synergy among the positive societal, organizational, and personal benefits of workplace participation (Kearney 1996).

From this perspective, labor-management cooperation (LMC) is preferred to the traditional adversarial labor relations, especially when it adds value to constrained organizational resources. The challenge therefore is to make this approach the norm rather than the exception in government (U.S. DOL 1996; Kearney 1996). Some argue, and we agree, that LMC may not be a permanent state. However, developing a strategy to increase the occurrence of instances of cooperation and sustaining those that exist are important and desirable public policy and public management goals. A better understanding of the behavioral dimension of cooperation can help fulfill these goals.

This chapter reports on an exploratory study of the roles and competencies associated with LMC efforts. The goal was to identify behavioral changes associated with a shift in labor relations from traditional adversarial toward more-cooperative relations. In particular, we explored changes in interactions, work roles, attitudes, knowledge, and skills associated with the implementation of three successful LMC initiatives. To do this we captured the experience of pairs of participants in these successful efforts, three managers and three labor representatives. The core question underlying the study was: What cognitive and behavioral competencies allowed managers and employees to interact differently, thus achieving success in their efforts to pursue collaborative projects over time?

Most of the studies of LMC focus either on the conditions under which cooperation is more likely to occur or on the outcomes of cooperation (Larson 1989; Rubin, Rubin, and Rolle 1999; Rubin and Rubin 2001). This focus is important but incomplete, because it undermines the relevance of interactions and behaviors that help us understand LMC. The behavioral dimensions of cooperation must be further developed and explored in the literature of LMC. Our work tries to address this gap by exploring the nature of the competencies associated with effective behavior in the context of successful efforts. Specifically, in this chapter we approach two empirical questions: What is the nature of the changes in the work roles of labor and management in the context of cooperation? and, Given the nature of these changes, what competencies are required for successful LMC to be sustained over time?

We tried to answer these questions using the experience reported by participants in LMC. In doing so, we learned that when cooperation happens at its best, a blurring of the traditional lines between the tasks performed by labor[1] and management occurs. This eventually produces a shift in the traditional work roles of the employee, labor leader, and manager. The core of this transformation is a redistribution of symbolic resources—such as responsibilities and information—that, before, were traditionally monopolized by managers.

The accounts of participants in the initiatives studied suggest that stakeholders must, accordingly, adjust the attitudes, knowledge, and skills required to do the job well in the new context of LMC. When we explored the competency characteristics associated with the shift in roles, employees and labor representatives reported a need to develop additional knowledge competencies that were not dominant in their traditional role, in order to engage in the collaboration. In contrast, managers seemed to require the development of additional skill competencies. More specifically, in this new environment labor had to learn new technical knowledge, while managers had to learn new "soft," people-oriented skills that were not as central in their traditional role. These competencies represent the mirror image of what is normally emphasized for the worker and managerial roles, respectively, in more traditional environments.

From these observations we conclude tentatively—given the exploratory nature of our research—that with the shift in the nature of the roles, there is also a shift in the nature of the competency requirements for both labor and managers. The shift is from technical knowledge to people skills in the case of management and from people skills to technical knowledge in the case of labor.[2] We argue that the nature of this shift has important implications for training and development aimed at supporting LMC.

The chapter is structured as follows. We start by making a case for the need to explore the behavioral dimensions of cooperation in the LMC literature. After describing how we went about doing so empirically, we present the findings of our study. We first analyze the changes in interactions and communication patterns that occurred during LMC and describe the consequent shift in work roles that we identified. We then explore the competencies required for cooperation, discussing the types of skill and knowledge requirements demanded by the new environment. We complement the analysis with a brief discussion of the temporary nature of cooperation and the implications for training and development.

Opening the Black Box: The Behavioral Dimension of LMC

LMC has a wide range of definitions: from a philosophy or an attitude regarding labor relations to a process involving efforts or activities with measurable results. At its best, cooperation between labor and management is a "process that provides a vehicle for participation in problem-solving and decision-making to improve the effectiveness of an organization and to enhance the quality of work life" (State and Local Government Labor-Management Committee, no date). It provides "organizational structures or mechanisms that give employees a voice in workplace decisions" (Delaney 1996:45).

Even though a great deal has been written about LMC, the behavioral dimension of this phenomenon has been underexplored. The practice-oriented LMC literature provides advice to managers and labor leaders about how to foster cooperation and train stakeholders in developing successful partnerships (Dinnocenzo 1989). This literature consists mostly of government and union reports. It is based on anecdotal evidence and selected stories of success, rather than on systematic research (Cooke 1990; Dunlop 1993). Academic research emphasizes the advantages of participatory decision making and cooperative approaches. Building on the long scholarly tradition of workplace democracy, this literature has focused mostly on the context and impact of cooperation and participation, rather than on the specific dynamics of cooperation (Kearney and Hays 1994).

Moreover, the practice-oriented literature mentions in passing the most obvious types of organizational conditions and the skills needed for improving cooperation. These include strong organizational leadership, definition of mutual goals and team building, openness, effective communication skills, and, above all, trust (Dinnocenzo 1989; Cavanagh et al. 1999; U.S. DOL 1996). Successful collaborative labor relations require that both management and labor be competent and trained (State and Local Government Labor-Management Committee, no date; U.S. DOL 1996). These general statements are normative rather than positively derived, however, and the specific meaning they have for the actors involved is not explored. The absence of information about the behavioral dimensions of LMC suggests that this represents a "black box" in our understanding of the way the shift from adversarial to cooperative relations takes place.

Entering the Black Box: Exploring the Competency Requirements of Cooperation

Insights from the competency movement in the industrial-organizational psychology literature provide a heuristic device to explore the behavioral dimensions of cooperation. This literature suggests that superior performance in a job or a situation can be explained by identifying a set of underlying characteristics of the individual involved, that is, the competencies needed to perform (Spencer, McClelland, and Spencer 1994). These competencies indicate enduring "ways of behaving or thinking" that individuals generalize across situations (Spencer and Spencer 1993:9). These authors identify five types of competency characteristics: motives, traits, self-concepts (or attitudes), knowledge, and skills. According to their causal model, motives, traits, self-concept, and knowledge competencies predict skill behavior actions, which in turn predict job or task performance outcomes.

If we think of cooperation as a desirable performance outcome, there is a value in identifying the underlying characteristics that can help make it happen. In this study we use the descriptions of individuals' experience during participation in successful efforts, compared to their account of the experience in traditional roles, to extrapolate the competencies—attitudes, knowledge, and skills—required to maximize the likelihood of successful cooperation.[3] We frame this analysis with an account of the ways in which interactions and roles changed as the context shifted from adversarial to cooperative relations. With changes in responsibilities and roles, one would expect to see changes in attitudes and behaviors required to interact effectively in this different context. Exploring what the required competencies for successful LMC are, given the nature of the new roles, thus represents an important contribution to the literature.

An Empirical Exploration: Three Successful Efforts of LMC. Our analysis is based on lengthy transcriptions of more than nine hours of interviews with participants of three successful efforts of LMC. In this chapter we identify the efforts according to their geographical location: Indianapolis, Charlotte, and Bridgeport. The scope of this chapter is limited to local government labor-management cooperation. Thus, it complements the report of the U.S. Secretary of Labor's Task Force on Excellence in State and Local Government through LMC (U.S. DOL 1996). LMC efforts are also found in the private sector and in the federal government (Perline 1999). Although indirectly influenced by these arenas, LMC in state and local government has emerged within a different policy context characterized by devolution, privatization, and managerialism (total quality management [TQM] and the new public management applications). It is within this context that change from adversarial to cooperative relations in the cases studied must be understood.

In Indianapolis we interviewed an executive-level representative from the mayor's office to capture the managerial experience and a high-level representative of the local union (AFSCME) to capture the labor experience. The goals of the LMC in this effort were to improve the quality of service delivery and to reduce costs. The new mayor, Stephen Goldsmith, launched a comprehensive LMC initiative, along with promoting competition between public agencies and private contractors. The city workers bid for new work and for jobs previously contracted out, the new goal being to "provide the best cost services regardless of the source" (U.S. DOL 1996:158). Since 1992 the city's operating budget has been reduced by $26 million, without any rank-and-file workers losing their jobs. A gains-sharing program was a major component of the LMC effort.

In Charlotte, North Carolina, we interviewed a manager from the city's human resource (HR) department and a representative from the Charlotte Police Department's employee association. In this city, LMC efforts were initiated to solve the city's problem with the collapsing pay system of the police and fire departments. The LMC was focused on human resources' giving the employees a voice in determining their performance-pay system and using the process to introduce better customer orientation and a problem-solving approach to service delivery and workplace issues. The interviews focused on the police department initiative.

In Bridgeport, Connecticut, we interviewed a representative of the
mayor's office and a high-level representative of the fire department's
local union. The city of Bridgeport filed for bankruptcy in 1992. Most of
the city's employees (about 4,000) belonged to one of 15 local unions.
When the city health care plan was canceled, cooperation efforts
brought management and union members together. The effort produced a single-provider plan, equal benefits to all union members, and
savings of over $8 million annually. Our interviews focused on the fire
department's experience.[4]

We asked the respondents to describe the events that led to the
development of successful collaboration and to tell stories describing
the nature of the labor relations before and during the time the LMC
initiative was implemented in their city. From these accounts emerged
patterns that point to a critical transformation of the interactions among
the various stakeholders and their work-related roles. Before describing
the particular changes, we offer an overview of the broad findings,
which we report more fully in another publication (Ospina and Yaroni,
forthcoming). This overview will be helpful to frame the detailed
descriptions of the shifts in roles and competencies that are the primary
subject of this chapter.

The Great Transformation: From Mandated to Genuine Cooperation

In all three efforts, LMC started with an organizational crisis imposed
by an external threat. The nature of this crisis and the consequent need
for survival led managers to believe that solutions required employees'
cooperation, more specifically their involvement in the decision-making
process. Organizational survival also motivated union representatives and
employees to cooperate with managers. In Indianapolis the problem was
related to the high costs of service and the political intention to contract
out the delivery of services. In Charlotte the problem was related to the
collapsing pay system in the police and fire departments. In Bridgeport
the city filed for bankruptcy and the employees' health care plan was
canceled.

At first, cooperation was "imposed" within the context of the need
for organizational survival. Both managers and labor realized that there
was a need to seek solutions "outside the box," solutions that would
require opening up the boundaries of the traditional work arrangements
within which labor and management interacted under normal circumstances. This "mandated" collaborative behavior and the development of

new expectations around the traditional division of labor blurred the boundaries of the existing work roles and, in turn, reshaped them over time. The shift occurred progressively, following a cyclical process—as the interactions that developed from the new behavior produced positive outcomes, the new work roles were tested and reshaped and trust developed gradually. Over time, cooperation became more natural and was reinforced.[5] In the next sections we describe the new interactions and the new roles that emerged in the context of successful LMC and that were at the base of the transformation from mandated to genuine cooperation.

Constructing the Cooperative Relationship: From New Interactions to Shifting Roles

> *Before, it was professional and courteous but distant, untrustworthy, occasionally antagonistic and not particularly warm. Afterwards, it was a very close relationship, daily contacting, communication, complete trust; we did everything on a handshake, forgave each other's mistakes along the way and were focused on a set of goals that were congruent. So, I don't want to be too dramatic here, but it was a night and day change.* (M:11–12)[6]

This quote from a manager illustrates vividly the extent of the transformation that took place as the LMC efforts developed. The nature of the interactions between individuals enacting managerial and worker roles; the frequency, scope, and nature of the communication among them; and the tasks and functions they performed changed dramatically as the LMC effort developed. The changes were so dramatic that the contrast of the interactions, before and after, was like the difference between night and day.

New Interactions and Communication Patterns

The external threat that brought labor and management to change their traditional behavior and to seek solutions to the crisis produced striking differences in the nature, scope, and frequency of their interactions. One manager described the interaction between labor and management before cooperation as hostile regardless of the issue at hand. He argued that any attempt *"to do something innovative, and irrespective of its merits, labor would diligently work to block that effort"* (M1:5). After engaging in cooperative efforts, interactions became much more positive. Even when the relations were not hostile in the first place, as one of the managers explained, the relationship shifted *"from being civil…to friendly"* (M2:17).

In Bridgeport, cooperation affected not only the relationship between labor and management, but also the relationship among different unions. The manager in this case recounted how at the early stages of the process one of the unions refused to sit in the same room with other union representatives. The unions were very competitive over the deals they could negotiate. Over time, "*They all came to the table and said, OK, let's carve out those issues that we can all agree upon as...having...deep commonality across the board of all bargaining units...and put that kind of competition aside*" (M3:29).

Respondents reported that even the quality of personal interactions changed. Personal relationships developed as the individuals participating in the cooperative process got to see each other in a different light. The manager in Indianapolis described this as follows: "*This may sound a little hokey, but we got to know each other outside of work....I began going to ball games with these guys and I began to go to their AFSCME picnics and they began coming to basketball games with me and my girlfriend*" (M1:14). The labor representative in Bridgeport affirmed that he still keeps in touch at a social level with some of the managers he befriended during the cooperation efforts. He attributed this to honesty: "*If you are honest with each other, personal friendships like I've developed will blossom*" (L2:28).

In Charlotte, the HR manager rode patrol cars with police officers to get a sense of their work firsthand. She described how the nature of communication changed once she "broke the ice": "*Once I made the effort to get to know them, it was pretty instantaneous*" (M2:17). She argued that once she started to interact with them while they were on duty, they started disclosing candid opinions and discussing issues that evidenced a new openness. Alluding to a conversation during which employees disclosed their negative opinion of some critical actors, the manager concluded: "*As we worked together...they would start telling me things like that*" (M2:18). Indeed, this type of disclosure suggests a degree of openness in communication that is not common among managers and employees involved in a more traditional relationship. Similarly, several respondents talked about how, once the interactions changed, work became much more enjoyable and even fun.

Changes in the Patterns of Communication. The new interactions were evident in the nature of communication. The new communication patterns were not only friendlier but also significantly different in frequency, nature, and scope. One of the managers described the type of communication before and after engaging in cooperative efforts as follows: before, *"they said something mean about me in the morning paper and I said something mean about them in the afternoon paper. Employees had zero access to me....We knew each others' names...all communication beyond that was certified mail"* (M1:12). After LMC was in place, employees and union representatives had *"24 hour a day access on my pager and cell phone, [and] an open door policy in the mayor's office"* (M1:13). The labor representative described how communication went *"from a relationship where my contact with the mayor's office was probably once, two, maybe three times a year, to the point where our contact was regular, at least weekly, at that point, more often, daily, quite frankly"* (L1:19), explaining later that *"there was a whole different system of communication"* (L1:26).

This labor representative described the change in the frequency of communication in ways that highlight the change of managerial responsiveness. Before, he would call a manager and *"it would be a couple of days before I might get a return phone call."* After, he could not think of any time when he didn't get *"a phone call returned within two or three hours."* Similar changes were also reported in the nonunionized context of Charlotte, and in reverse direction where the manager tried calling an employee representative. Before, *"it used to be impossible to get somebody on the phone....They would just kind of do their own thing,"* while later, people were more involved and responsive (M2:32).

The issues discussed also changed considerably. According to a manager, *"Before,...it was exclusively procedural and legal in its nature. And everybody always carried a copy of the contract in their pocket and we would argue about Article 5, Section 3, Clause 32, Subpart J"* (M1:16). In contrast, the types of issues discussed afterward were not only different in nature, but also broader in scope: *"We talked about operational issues, we talked about strategic issues, we talked about financial issues, we talked about solving operating problems as opposed to bickering over grievances"* (M1:17).

These changes had to do with the new meaning of work and the impact this had on the quality of the interaction: *"Before, we talked about what the contract said....After...we talked very little about process. We established some baseline rules of engagement. Once that foundation was built, the interaction was very different. Rather than procedural arguments and nuances, we talked about how to deliver services more cost effectively"* (M1:16–17). Indeed, his labor counterpart described how in the early part of the cooperative relationship *"much of the issues dealt with...either bureaucratic barriers—purchasing...personnel—or person-alities.*" Later this changed, moving from "*defensive issues to offensive issues,*" issues that allowed them to think about "*How can we create a system where we not only survive, but we can actually thrive*" (L1:21). In this context, issues like gain sharing appeared in the conversations, which became more about "*how we could find more win-win situations, as opposed to how we could simply stem the threat*" (L1:22). Another labor representative qualified the discussion on "issues" by saying: "*I'm not sure there was a change in the nature of the issues, but there was certainly a change in the understanding of the issues*" (L2:15).

Because the emphasis now was on organizational problem solving and service improvements, changes in communication also occurred within and among the unions, mirroring the changes in relationships described above. One of the labor representatives described how "*All of a sudden the local president in Fleet Services was talking to the local president in Public Works, figuring out how to get the trucks back on the road*" (L1:35). He also described how in the new context, the local president would go "*from work site to work site*" meeting "*on a monthly basis with small groups of workers*" (L1:50) to discuss issues, ideas, and concerns. These meetings were quite different from the monthly local union meetings and they had become "*the conduit of information from the rank and files up through the system*" (L1:60). In a different city, the manager interviewed saw the same shift: "*They had to perhaps communicate more often through this period because there was a lot going on and because they needed to assure the constituency that the changes going through were in their best interest*" (M3:26).

An Increase in the Flow and Sharing of Information. At the heart of the new communication patterns was a significant increase in information sharing. Describing this change, one of the union leaders explained: "*Union members were in a position where we were dealing with all of the information that the City had at its disposal, not just the information that the City chose to bring to the table with them*" (L2:9). This "*freer sharing of information*" (L1:56) was also different in the manner the information could be accessed in the new environment. In one of the cases management gave the union direct access from the local union office to the city financial database, so they "*no longer even have to ask for permission*" (L1:56).

The changes in information flow were not merely technical but also linked to an increase in trust between the two sides. Managers were willing to share information that traditionally would have been withheld. Similarly, labor understood that access to information represented a critical tool for problem solving. Related to these changes is a sense that both managers and employees became more responsive, more willing to support one another, and more open to give one another the benefit of the doubt when needed. One labor representative said: "*When I was able to sit down with them and actually see the paperwork that they were working with, and basing their opinions on, and facts, I realized that these people weren't trying to mislead me. And I look for those things in people today, rather than just assuming that someone is not telling me the truth*" (L2:24).

The new cooperative interactions between labor and management were possible because both sides suspended the expectations they had about the work each had to do and how they would go about accomplishing it. This represents a shift in the work roles of managers, employees, and their union representatives. Exploring this shift is the subject of the next section.

A Change in Mental Models and a Shift in Work Roles

A role is a cohesive group of values and attitudes that provides individuals with a stable set of expectations about the responsibilities and rights inherent in a given social position (Selden, Brewer, and Brudney 1999; Merton 1968). Roles can also be understood as the ways in which these sets of expectations are put into practice. Since a role depends on the translation of these expectations and value sets into practice, a role *change* depends on the transformation of the value sets that supported its original nature. Senge (1990) argues that organizational learning, and thus a willingness to participate in change, requires individuals to question their "mental models," that is, the basic assumptions and expectations people carry around with them as they interact in the world.

In all three instances of LMC studied, participants described a strong and noticeable shift in the mental models of the participating individuals. This transformation seemed to allow for new attitudes and behaviors to emerge and be sustained over time. We identified three interconnected shifts in the mind-sets of participants, which colored differently their approach to work: a new way of thinking about the purpose of work, an improved ability to view the world from the other's perspective, and a new understanding of the labor relationship as a partnership.

Consistent with accounts in the task force report (U.S. DOL 1996), our respondents said that over time managers and labor started to share the sense that the value of their work depended on its contribution to the quality of services the taxpayers deserved. As one manager suggested, they agreed that work should be *"outcome-related, problem-based"* (L1:50). This meant redefining the meaning of work to give priority to shared organizational goals concerning service delivery.

The redefinition of the meaning of work was also related to the stakeholders' ability to view and appreciate the world from the perspective of the other side. For the managers this meant a higher sense of trust in the motives and competencies of public employees, a sharp contrast with the traditional view of public employees as incompetent and uncaring. For the union representatives and employees the new assumptions about "the other" were expressed as a "revolutionary" understanding of the constraints managers faced in trying to do their jobs.

The redefinition of the meaning of work and the new understanding of the others' perspective helped transform the mental image of the labor-management relationship from a contractual relationship into a partnership. There was a realization that the old assumptions characterizing labor relations as confrontational and based on a zero-sum game could be replaced with a new collaborative win-win approach based on *"overlapping circles of opportunity"* (M1:29b). For the managers this meant that *"if our goal is to serve citizens then we need to be on the same side...."* (M1:34–35). For the union leaders this meant trying to reach the same goal they had before but now *"addressing the cost associated with these demands"* (L2:44)—a factor previously considered solely a managerial concern. This was a temporary shift, of course, that was applied to the LMC effort. Both managers and labor understood that parallel to this partnership, the more traditional relationship to be used in renegotiating the contracts when the time came lay dormant, but alive. We will come back to this contradiction toward the end of the chapter.

These shifts in mental models contributed to a change in the work roles of managers, employees, and union representatives. The redefinition of the meaning of work (the results orientation) contributed to the adjustments of job-related expectations. The ability to view the world from the others' perspective allowed managers to *"turn [employees] loose"* (M2:23) and give them more autonomy and responsibility to do their jobs. It also allowed labor representatives to suspend assumptions about the motives of managers more easily. The overall new win-win mentality resulted in more flexibility. For example, labor stopped behaving as if they just had to win every fight and began questioning the idea that *"every fight stands on its own"* (L1:70). They started adopting a long-term vision and a wider perspective of the relationship as a partnership. These changes in mental models facilitated and supported a dramatic shift in the work roles the main stakeholders played.

The change in the managerial role was from a more directive and authoritarian figure toward becoming *"a coach and a team member"* (M1:38). For example, one manager described how he started challenging the assumption that *"if you don't stand over these guys and yell at them all day long, they won't do the work."* He replaced this belief with the notion that *"you are on their team"* (M1:36) and you must *"turn your work chart upside down and say, my job as a manager is to work for my employee team"* (M1:19).

The role of union representatives also changed because leadership over organizational problems was now shared with them. *"The union became an equal partner in moving change within the bureaucracy of city government....if there was a problem, we were now part of the problem, because we had up-front input into all of the changes"* (L1:15). Their role became more proactive rather than reactive, and they acquired a wider perspective in contrast to the detailed orientation they used before. As one of the union representatives explained, *"When you have to lead...it requires a much broader view of the potential problems"* (L1:25). Union representatives assumed responsibilities that until then were exclusively managerial. The same representative reported that *"the Local...now assumes responsibility for calling out the workforce when there is a snow emergency....That's a responsibility that's considered a managerial one"* (L1:49).

Interestingly, the role of labor leaders changed not only vis-à-vis management, but also in reference to the union members. These leaders understood that from the perspective of the rank-and-file membership, the new proposals would sound managerial in tone. Hence, the union leaders had to work harder to mobilize their membership. One labor leader commented that *"it became more difficult....[Before] it was easy to agitate and lead a single focused agenda, because you could identify the enemy. [Now you need to] convince your membership that creating a new program, and...cooperating with [the enemy] was ultimately going to be the best course of action, in terms of their own self-interest"* (L1:29). In these efforts union representatives had to lead their constituencies through uncertain organizational changes rather than organize them to block managerial initiatives.

Finally, a dramatic change in the workers' role also took place, because decision making and accountability were now shared among managers and employees. One of the managers describing the process explained that *"that kind of a shared decision making was a fundamentally different thing; it was a profound departure from what they had previously...where management was just telling them what they were going to do"* (M3:18). Another manager described the new mode of operation in terms of *"distributed leadership"* where *"employees...are being given a lot more autonomy to make decisions in the field: they are being given more autonomy to make suggestions about how things might be done differently"* (M1:8b). Mirroring the changes in managerial roles, employees in this new context were expected to come up with the ideas, while *"the manager's job is then to go facilitate those changes"* (M1:42b). Employees were asked to move away *"from rigid, bureaucratic rule-driven behaviors"* (M1:37b). As was the case with managers, the role of the employees became more fluid and less fixed, more open-ended, more adaptive to the requirements of the problem-solving tasks at hand. Overall, work during successful LMC seemed to be more enjoyable and satisfying than it was within the traditional framework, according the respondents' accounts.

In sum, we found that in all three cases the shift from a traditional to a more cooperative labor relationship was associated with a change in the mental models of the main stakeholders involved and adjustments in their work-related expectations. These changes seemed to go hand in hand with a shift in mental models about service delivery and about the approach toward one another. They also paralleled a dramatic shift in the roles of managers, union representatives, and employees. In the next section we address the underlying competencies for managers and labor required to respond successfully to the demands of the changed task environment.

New Competencies at Work: Attitudes, Knowledge, and Skills for Cooperation

As noted earlier, Spencer and Spencer (1993) identified five types of competency characteristics associated with high performance: motives, traits, self-concepts, knowledge, and skills. Motives are "wants" or "drives" that cause action, and traits are physical or psychological characteristics that help individuals respond to situations. Although motives and traits affect behavior, they are hidden "deeper" and more central to personality and thus are more difficult to assess and develop. In contrast, knowledge and skill competencies are easier to observe and to develop. Knowledge refers to information a person has about a specific content area, and skills are the cognitive and behavioral abilities to perform a given task.

Self-concept competencies, that is, a person's attitudes and values, his or her self-image, lie somewhere in the middle of these two sets of characteristics. They can be influenced, but with more time and difficulty. For the purpose of this chapter, we will loosely apply insights only about self-concept (attitudes), skills, and knowledge competencies to answer the questions proposed, as motives and traits are harder to observe, measure, and manipulate. We will also briefly address the motivational context of LMC by reviewing the triggers to cooperation because these are relevant to understanding the competency needs.

In this section we identify bundles of attitudes, knowledge, and skills specifically associated with the respondents' experience in the cooperative effort or with one of the processes derived from it, such as joint decision-making or gain-sharing programs. The competencies we identify and describe were drawn from direct suggestions of our respondents and from our inferences based on the broader stories they told us.[7]

Our discussion of the changes in interactions and roles has already illustrated some of the new types of competencies required for successful LMC. Here we name them and document an important finding. For our respondents, employee needs seemed to be more associated with knowledge competencies, while managerial needs were associated with skill competencies. Moreover, the knowledge our respondents believed labor required in the new environment was of a technical (formal) nature, while the skills managers required were people-oriented.

New Attitudes for Cooperation: Openness, Reciprocity, and Respect

In the competency-model literature, attitudes and values are treated under the broader category of self-concept. This idea refers to the underlying assumptions and beliefs that drive a person to act in the short run and under situations where others are in charge. They are different from motives and drives that operate in the longer run and under situations without close supervision. They also differ from mental models in that the latter are broader in scope and most likely encompass both motives and self-concepts.

Given the exploratory nature of this work and our choice of methods, we have limited the scope of our analysis of this type of competency characteristic considerably.[8] Instead we concentrate on attitudes.[9] The concepts discussed below may be viewed, loosely, as a set of attitudes through which respondents captured the broader values of trust and cooperation as they described their experiences.

The dominant attitude was the willingness to be open throughout the process, as the collaboration developed. Two other attitudes, reciprocity and respect, were also mentioned consistently. The values of openness and reciprocity were present in the accounts of managers and labor. Respect toward employees and their unions was a value specifically mentioned by managers. Openness manifested itself with three different, but related, connotations: as the willingness to share information, to be more flexible, and to be more tolerant.

- *Openness as the willingness to share information:* Managers talked about the need to provide labor representatives and employees *"much greater access to gathered information"* (M1:31b). Union representatives saw sharing information as a critical condition for long-term cooperation: *"If they [managers] hide bad news, they will never be able to successfully go to unions and try to get cooperation to solve problems...."* (L3:16).

- *Openness as the willingness to be more flexible:* Line and HR managers emphasized the need for *"great[er] flexibility"*—the willingness to throw away the old rules (M1:39) and the need to develop the *"ability to change your position, to not take [fixed] positions"* (M3:25). Union representatives linked the need for flexibility with the need to search for *"solutions outside of [the] typical box"* (L1:65). For both labor and management this meant being able *"to say you are wrong if you are wrong, and to act it, [to]... change direction or whatever"* (M3:26). But greater flexibility was now required not just from program managers. The attitudes of HR managers had to change too in the context of LMC. For example, a manager told a story about how he approved management development training for union leaders and the HR department denied it because they said *"that's for managers"* (M1:44).

- *Openness as the willingness to be more tolerant:* For managers it meant giving employees the benefit of the doubt. A manager talked about keeping *"a very open mind and not [getting] threatened by whatever [the employees] are doing"* (M2:24). Talking about the union's traditional role, a manager commented: *"I fully respect the fact that...they had to take a position...to fight certain things. And that's fine, that's their role,...that's what unions are there for, to take those positions that are driven by the membership demands"* (M3:22). But tolerance was even more recognized as a change in the labor side. For union representatives it meant giving managers the benefit of the doubt: *"So I've become a little bit slower, I guess, at pointing my fingers at somebody"* (L2:19). For both employees and their representatives it also meant being *"receptive"* to ideas and to change (M2:31) even when they come from management. The willingness to be more tolerant also resulted in the willingness to accept each other's mistakes and not to hold them against each other (M1:15).

Reciprocity, an attitude of mutuality, meant for both managers and labor the willingness to put themselves in the others' role (M2:45–46). As they were able to transcend their own interests, they could *"take an organizational perspective as opposed to a personal perspective"* (M2:45). This made it more possible to believe that acceptable compromise solutions could be found (L1:77). One manager said: *"There were times when, you know, we would hit a road block and I would call the union and say, you guys got to give me this one....They would say OK but 'next close' one, we get"* (M1:49b). Finally, reciprocity helped increase tolerance, as people would not hold mistakes against one another (M1:15).

The third identified value was respect. This attitude appeared as a new managerial disposition toward employees and unions. Managers talked about the need to *"turn line employees loose, to do their job"* (M1:35; M2:21) and *"trust [employees'] suggestions"* (M3:45). Managers recognized the importance of spending more time in the field with employees *"not as a follow-up but as a way to gather ideas"* (M1:50).

In sum, managers and labor identified openness and reciprocity as critical attitudes needed for both roles to engage in successful LMC. Respect for employees and their unions was a third critical attitude for managers engaging in LMC. We do not know whether these attitudes were predispositions already present in our respondents' psyche, or whether they developed within the new environment. Nevertheless, it is clear that these attitudes were relevant for LMC and that they became reinforced in the transformative cycle described earlier. At least for this group of players, openness, reciprocity, and respect (and probably other attitudes we did not identify) provided the grounding for the knowledge and skills our participants reported as critical for effective cooperation.

Knowledge Requirements for Cooperation: The Need for Employee Technical Expertise

In the competency literature, knowledge refers to learned facts, procedures, or technical information in specific content areas. Studies suggest that content knowledge by itself rarely distinguishes superior from average performers, because it predicts what someone can do rather than what they will do (Spencer and Spencer 1993). Nevertheless, content knowledge is critical to performing specific work-related tasks, and, therefore, it is important to identify critical contents needed for effective LMC. This is particularly true because with the shift in the roles documented earlier, knowledge associated with traditional tasks may no longer be sufficient to perform effectively.

Indeed, the amount of information management shared with labor under a LMC effort created a new knowledge demand for employees. Our participants' accounts suggest that successful performance in a cooperative context placed a direct demand on labor representatives and employees to learn how to find and process information relevant to the problems at hand. Most of the direct suggestions offered by respondents about what they would want to see taught in a training program for LMC focused on new knowledge for employees rather than for managers. We drew a similar conclusion from the respondents' general descriptions of their experiences.

The interviews suggested that the specific content knowledge required for success in LMC varied with the particular issue addressed under a cooperative strategy. Although both parties would have to learn this knowledge as the cooperative effort unfolded, it was more likely that managers already had this knowledge, while labor experienced a stronger knowledge need. For example, in the case of Charlotte's new performance appraisal system, workers "got kind of a mini-HR education during the development phase" (M2:27). Indeed, they needed to understand "the theories behind the things that HR people are doing" (L3:48). In Bridgeport's effort to develop an insurance scheme for city employees, they had to learn the "actual insurance business...and the ways the insurance industry is run" (L2:30). Finally, for Indianapolis's effort to introduce competition, union leaders had to learn how to "sell" city services to other government units and employees had to learn how to "cost" their operations (L1:41–42).

In addition to specific knowledge related to the core problem that motivated the collaborative efforts, we identified critical knowledge needs in three broad areas: basic knowledge, managerial and technical knowledge, and local government administration knowledge. These sets of knowledge needs are by no means complete. Nevertheless, they represent a springboard for creating a more complete inventory as new studies are developed in the future.

- *Basic knowledge* includes generic knowledge that is required as the foundation to acquire or process more complex information. The areas mentioned in this category are improved math skills needed for public budgeting and municipal financial management (L1:30), computer literacy (L1:57), and understanding organizational dynamics (M1:20b).

- *Managerial-technical knowledge* includes content associated with knowledge traditionally required for managerial jobs but now also needed for labor. The participants mentioned the need for union leaders *"to understand up front how a budget is created, how taxes are collected, how our budgets are built"* (M3:47; L3:46); details about municipal finances (L2:26); and an understanding of information systems for the use of the city financial database (L1:56–57).

- *Local government administration knowledge* refers to information about the administration of the jurisdiction where the effort is taking place (in our cases, city government). Participants felt employees and union leaders needed knowledge about topics required in a broader context for the operation of the city or the jurisdiction where they worked, such as *"finance, health care, accounting issues, budget creation issues, the economy, the industries of the town, the utility billings, all those things"* (M3:46).

Our study suggests that employees must acquire a considerable amount of new technical knowledge, in addition to new skills and attitudes, to get involved successfully in cooperative efforts. In contrast, participants did not identify many new content areas as knowledge needs for managers. As one of respondents explained: *"A manager still needs to understand how to handle human resources, legal, finance and procurement. But it is going to become less significant than the people side of the equation"* (M1:36b). One could speculate, and propose for future research, that in the new context of cooperation, labor, more than management, will need new specialized knowledge. In contrast, given their experience, managers may already have most of the technical knowledge required to participate in problem solving and decision making by virtue of their structural position in the traditional system. In fact, many managers traditionally come from technical backgrounds. They now are faced with the novel demand of acquiring people skills to interact successfully with labor in this new, and more-equalized, environment.

A New Skill Set for Cooperation: From Problem Solving to Persuasion

In the competency literature, skills are the abilities required to perform a physical or mental task. There are cognitive and behavioral skills, and there are covert and observable skills. They differ from knowledge in that they are directly associated with action rather than intent. They are the competency characteristics that are most easily changeable and they are the ones that most directly predict successful performance. The practice-oriented literature on LMC has tended to identify several skill sets that are critical for successful LMC. However, in most cases, the skills are mentioned in generic terms. In particular, negotiation skills, conflict-resolution skills, and communications skills appear often in the literature. The contribution of this chapter lies in starting to fill in the blanks by providing speific examples and abilities that can be associated with each generic concept. Even though more research is required to refine them, we illustrate the type of abilities managers and employees need for successful LMC.

In general, the skill needs our respondents identified for successfully engaging in LMC are all related to the problem-solving ability of the team associated with the new partnership. Specifically, the skills are related to the ability to define the organizational problem and search for valid solutions (needed for labor), persuasion skills for promoting the solutions found (needed mostly for labor), and negotiation and conflict-resolution skills for implementing the organizational solution (needed for labor and management). With respect to persuasion and negotiation skills, participants also identified formal and informal communication-skill needs. In the new collaborative context, labor needed more formal communication skills while managers needed more informal and team-related skills.

Problem-solving skills, *"the kind of problem solving...that management has been exposed to"* (L3:45), were the most frequently mentioned skill requirements for both managers and labor. This specifically meant *"the ability to take an issue and develop solutions or options"* (M2:38–39). Respondents emphasized not only the importance of critical thinking for problem solving—*"how to get to the root cause of problems through a very structured investigation"* (M3:41)—but also the importance of developing a wider managerial-like perspective that is focused on *"systemic solutions rather than individual solutions"* (L1:65). This respondent later explained the difference: *"rather than just looking to solve a problem...[looking at] how to change a system to solve its own problems, or continue to solve problems"* (L1:24). The HR manager also explained this as the ability to *"switch back and forth from the big picture to the details"* (M2:50) while keeping *"your eyes to the horizon [and] focus on the long-term vision of where you want to be"* (M3:32). Although improved problem-solving ability is clearly relevant to managerial jobs, it is more likely that managers already have this skill and, thus, the managers we interviewed mentioned this as something labor needed to acquire.

The problem-solving skills employees needed in the partnership context specifically included the ability to define organizational problems, the *"ability to see the big picture, work on reaching an agreement on it, and then working on the details"* (M2:50) and the ability to search for solutions, that is, the ability *"to present options that are viable"* (L3:23). For labor this also meant the ability to *"draw out...information from management"* and to know what type of information to look for and what types of questions to ask (L2:19).

In the new partnership context, the ability to define an organizational problem and propose solutions also required stronger and more-convincing persuasion skills. Union leaders bringing managerially toned proposals needed persuasion skills to *"relay that information to [their] membership"* (L2:16) and mobilize them. For managers these skills were required to *"bring people along collaboratively and direct them without it being dictatorial"* (M1:57) and *"constantly trying to sell...the idea of collaboration, not confrontation"* (M3:32).

Furthermore, in the new collaborative environment the implementation of novel ideas as solutions placed a premium on developing negotiation and conflict-resolution skills. These were again major skill needs respondents assigned to both managers and labor. One of the managers explained that negotiation and conflict-resolution skills were *"skills that I use on a daily basis"* in the new partnership (L3:24). These skills were now needed beyond the traditional contract negotiations. As the manager in Charlotte argued, *"Even in [this] right-to-work state, management needs to be more skilled at negotiation"* (L3:28).

Better persuasion and negotiation skills were linked to the need to improve both formal and informal communication. These skills would allow the players in their new roles to frame, package, and sell their ideas more effectively while *"work[ing] toward consensus and compromise"* (L3:44) Improvement of formal communication skills seemed to be more critical for labor. It included *"public speaking skills and presentation skills"* (M3:40) to better sell an idea (M2:26, 49). A labor representative commented that LMC required from him *"a lot more writing than I thought I would have to [do]"* (L3:23).

Informal communication and interpersonal skills were also more important in the new environment for getting *"below the surface as to why somebody seemed to be unhappy with the discussion, or not like an idea, or seemed to be resistant to something"* (M2:48) and for understanding *"why they communicate the way they do...."* (L3:43). For both management and labor this meant the ability to listen to the other side and specifically focus on the arguments to understand the *"reasons why someone might tell me what we are asking for is not possible"* (L2:54). The informal and interpersonal communication skills for managers included the *"the ability to speak [the employees'] language...to understand what they were doing and what their work was like"* (M2:17) and *"read their body language and understand how they were reacting to what [managers] were saying"* (L3:26). For labor, informal communication skills were related to *"becoming...savvy about the importance of networking and social interactions to do things [and] have things done"* (L2:29).

For managers, in their new role as coaches and team players, there was a specific need to learn team-related skills. In one respondent's words, managers needed strong *"leadership skills."* As he argued, *"Coaching skills are essential...interpersonal skills, the type of skills that football coaches and officers in the Marine Corps have"* (M1:57). For this respondent this meant knowing *"how to make the people in your team stars...how to get them paid more, how to get them better training and how to expand their role"* (M1:18b). For another it also meant the ability to *"elicit cooperation from people...[and] draw on everybody's strong points"* (L2:62). One of our respondents argued that *"managers' understanding how to run Lexus spreadsheet on your finances is important, but understanding how to motivate and encourage people is far more important than that"* (M1:57). This once again points to the importance of the stronger people skills managers needed in the new cooperative environment. As team players, managers had to learn how to work with their employees as a team and how to make team decisions. This specifically required *"to learn when to pull back, just be a member of the team and not trash an idea"* (M2:24) and to allow the responsibility to move around the team (M2:47).

Respondents also identified similar team-related skills for HR managers but with a stronger emphasis on facilitation skills, that is, *"getting the group talking and then gleaning from the discussion what were the key points and feeding them back to the group to get confirmation"* (M2:23). In particular, facilitation required the ability to provide information, translate ideas from knowledge base to clients and from clients to others, and package ideas for discussion (M2:5, 20–21) and a general *"responsibility for keeping a process moving"* (M2:47).

Wheelan (1999) argued that the demand for work teams increases with the complexity of organizational problems. This was also the case in the efforts we studied. The managerial need to *"focus on teams,"* as one of our respondents phrased it, was associated with the crisis that triggered cooperation in the first place. The need for teamwork stemmed from the circumstances that brought managers to search for solutions outside the traditional box and to cooperate with their employees.

A New Profile Emerges

From the analysis of the changes in interactions and roles we described earlier, and from the bundles of competency characteristics identified in this section, we can infer the profile of the new type of actor who would thrive in a cooperative environment. The attributes associated with this profile help us answer the original question posed about the cognitive and behavioral competencies that allowed management and labor to interact differently and thus achieve success in their efforts to pursue collaborative projects over time. Table 1 summarizes the main additional competencies labor and managers engaging in successful LMC need to reinforce if they want to perform well in the new environment. Of course both labor and management would need all the competencies listed: the table notes only the gaps found for each actor between the competencies associated with the traditional roles and those needed in the new roles for cooperation.

TABLE 1

Required Additional or Enhanced Competencies for Successful LMC

Competencies	Labor	Management
Attitudes:		
Openness	+	+
Reciprocity	+	+
Respect		+
Knowledge:		
Knowledge regarding core problem	+	
Basic knowledge	+	
Managerial-technical knowledge	+	
Local govt. administration knowledge	+	
Skills:		
Problem-solving skills	+	
Formal persuasion and negotiations skills	+	
Informal communication, interpersonal skills		+
Team-related skills		+

The ideal new manager and new employee (as the new labor leader) share values and attitudes that place a premium on a public service that is problem solving, value adding, and results oriented. Both sets of actors would be more open, flexible, and willing to engage in reciprocal cooperative behaviors and to place themselves in the shoes of the other. The new managers would be more people-oriented than their traditional counterparts, and they would need more soft skill competencies associated with coaching and team building. HR managers in this new context would be more service oriented and more flexible and would use a new client-base approach to developing their work in partnership with management and labor. In contrast, employees and labor representatives would become more technical in their orientation, compared to their traditional counterparts, requiring new knowledge competencies and formal skills traditionally associated with management.

An important question for further consideration is the extent to which the attitudes, knowledge, and skills identified in these profiles are a function of the specific types of activities and strategies developed in the three cases studied. Are entrepreneurial skills important in all instances of LMC or only in cases when introducing competition is an important strategy? Are some of the competencies identified generic to LMC or are they more typical of cases of innovation where employees belong to a uniform force like police and fire departments (as is the case in two of the efforts studied)? Moreover, what are the implications of the fact that the three managers in our study have specific attributes, such as having recently arrived to their positions when LMC took place?

Two new stages in a future research agenda are thus foreseeable to refine these profiles. In a first stage, we would propose adding more cases and continuing to do qualitative work, to refine the lists and to try to look for more generalizable patterns, while still exploring these patterns in depth. With enough additional material to generate testable hypotheses, we would then propose using the existing competency assessment methodologies to develop a framework of competencies for LMC. For example, we could compare LMC-based competencies with some of the other managerial and occupational profiles of the generic competency dictionary assembled by Spencer and Spencer (1993). We could also explore the implications of the findings with the work of other scholars in the competency movement, such as the recently developed emotional intelligence framework (Goleman, Boyatzis, and McKee 2002), which also emphasized the relational dimensions of effective performance.

For now these profiles are ideal types based on a composite of characteristics from the various stories in our sample.[10] The successful cases upon which they are based do provide partial portraits of real individuals who, with great effort, have in fact enacted many aspects of these profiles. Yet a final issue must still be addressed before we can discuss the implications of these findings for training and development. It has to do with the sustainability of the cooperative behavior these competencies help support. We turn to this next.

The Cyclical Nature of Cooperation: Developing Competencies to Sustain It

As the literature suggests, the changes associated with LMC do not happen overnight. Two respondents in our study described LMC as a hard, joint *"evolutionary, not revolutionary, process"* (L1:15; M1:19). Another manager commented: *"I learned it is not an easy process. It can be very grueling and you need to demonstrate patience, perseverance and maintain a sustained course of action for it to work....It takes quite a number of years for it to evolve into a productive relationship"* (M3:48). A critical question, with important behavioral implications, is the extent to which this process is irreversible and the impact that potential reversibility has for the maintenance of cooperative behavior at an individual level.

Some definitions of LMC conceptualize it as a new stage in labor relations, a definite shift from an adversarial to a cooperative mode of interaction between labor and management. Some talk about a shift in paradigm—a revolutionary transformation in the way labor and management relate to each other (Loney 1996). As experts in labor-management relations well know, and as a few studies suggest, there is no reason to believe that the transformation can be self-sustained over time (Delaney 1996; Cooke 1990; Rubin and Rubin 2001). For example, Cooke (1990) argues that cooperation is a fluid state, reversible rather than permanent. In his view, only when both parties derive greater benefit from joint efforts will there be a continued incentive for cooperation. When these benefits are exhausted, Cooke predicts, the relations will tend to shift back toward a traditional approach.

Our interviews support Cooke's (1990) insights that LMC is a fluid and transitory process rather than a permanent state. They also suggest that adversarial relations might be more stable and easier to maintain than cooperative ones. As stated by one of the labor representatives, *"Change is never forever"* (L3:39). Those involved in LMC efforts may expect to find cyclical effects, as described by one of the managers: "*I think things went in cycles. I think that it had a real positive effect for two to three years and then there was backsliding into more traditional roles....I think you have to keep doing it over and over again but you also need to have a good reason to do it over and over again*" (M2:53). Furthermore, the cyclical effect might also be associated with the nature of the issues addressed by LMC: "*Paying for performance is an issue that comes and goes*" (L3:21), said one of the respondents.

The cyclical nature of LMC implies that cooperative behavior is something that must be maintained (L3:41) in order to be kept alive. One of the managers compared LMC to a friendship: "*Like a relationship or a friendship, it can be challenged and it can be broken. And I think it does need to be nurtured*" (M3:51). Such "*nurturing*" requires "*a constant refreshment of vitality, of honesty, of movement*" (M3:49). One of the union representatives saw it as a joint responsibility: "*Both sides have to work on it, constantly maintaining [the relationship]*" (L3:41).

At the end of the day, successful LMC cannot be viewed as a point of no return. One respondent said: "*I do not think it is something like a smallpox vaccination that stays forever. I think you have to keep doing it over and over*" (M2:55). Another said, "*It is like a friendship or any relationship that needs to be maintained or else they grow stale*" (M3:49). This statement is even more dramatic when one considers that today LMC efforts are still based on a structural arrangement that maintains intact the traditional structure for collective bargaining. The question is, then, the extent to which cooperative behaviors can be sustained in that context. We would argue that enacting collaborative behavior after the formal LMC ends requires deliberate will and the solidification of the competencies associated with it.

In other words, LMC requires a cultural shift (Wasilisin 1994). Sustaining the collaborative behaviors afterward also requires an environment that fosters and rewards competencies that allow the new values to continue to be expressed. Gaining and reinforcing the right competencies are critical for the benefits of LMC to persist in the more-traditional environment. The findings in our study suggest there is room for some optimism. Our respondents suggested that in the process of participating in the LMC effort they had become new individuals. They developed new relationships that nourished them in the workplace and that were often maintained outside of work. Furthermore, they reported gaining new competencies that enabled them to approach their job (independent of what it was) at a higher level of performance. Finally, they reported that they would never see themselves or their counterparts in the same light as they had before LMC. In other words, even if the structural conditions changed, the value added by the effort and the learning gained would stay with them at a personal level. The experience would inform the way they would approach others and their work from there on.

Indeed, in addition to the direct perceived benefits (and costs) of LMC, cooperative behavior had a spillover effect outside the scope of the effort, because the gained competencies were transferable. Some examples of this type of learning from our interviews include employees' new ability to develop solutions around issues not originally connected to the LMC effort, enhanced communication with other employees and other departments, and a sense of belonging that improved employees' self-esteem in the organization (M2:38; M3:42). The learning process associated with LMC produced better-rounded individuals, both in the managerial and labor roles.

Implications for Training and Development

The fine line between adversarial and cooperative behavior represents a critical factor in the environment within which motives, attitudes, and behaviors emerge. In fact, the impact of the fluidity of cooperation on the competencies required to make it successful represents an important agenda for future empirical research. But we can say for sure at this point that this fluid nature highlights the necessity of paying deliberate attention to the developmental needs of the individual actors involved in the initiative, as it is unfolding. This is a critical point to keep in mind when designing and implementing training and development initiatives to support successful labor-management cooperation.

What are then the specific implications of our work for training and development? Formal training about the identified competencies can be helpful for any individual involved in a public sector job. However, we believe that the synergy that converts these competencies into genuine cooperative behavior comes from a more-complex scenario that is context specific. During the LMC initiative, middle managers, line employees, and labor representatives shared the problem at hand, the information required to solve it, and the decision-making authority. They also shared leadership capacity and accountability for the consequences of the choices made. This blurring of the traditional lines between labor and management becomes fertile ground for learning and using competencies unfamiliar to them. Managers and labor seized the opportunity to learn and practice the demanded competencies over time and continued to use them even when the structures reversed back to the relationships associated with traditional collective bargaining. It was the recurrent process by which individuals engaged in team problem solving that helped build new relationships, higher levels of trust and reciprocity, and, in the long run, higher levels of performance.

This suggests that the competencies required for cooperative behavior (for both labor and management) may be more effectively developed within the context of a LMC initiative than in formal training. It is in the unfolding of the relationship that both managers and labor become motivated to learn the new knowledge and skills required to respond to the new expectations and demands of their work. In this relational context they are able to rehearse and practice the new knowledge and skills over and over, to internalize them and produce genuine learning.

Winterton and Winterton (1999) argue that management development is more likely to be successful than formal training. They further argue that effective development involves action–learning—that is, when competency development is related to the experience in which the individual feels committed and motivated and experiences ownership over the organizational process. Action–learning also implies that the target of the development efforts should be the team or the organization rather than the individual manager (Winterton and Winterton 1999). Action–learning may also represent the best tool to develop competencies for successful LMC. In our context, this argument extends to the developmental needs of labor, as employees and union leaders step away from their traditional role toward the managerial domain. From an HR training perspective, it may mean targeting the LMC effort, rather than the individuals, as the locus of learning.

Once labor and managers learn in this context, it is more likely that learning will become irreversible, even when the formal relationships go back to a traditional style. The best schooling for collaboration, we argue here, is an environment that demands sustained interactions from individuals in different structural roles toward finding common-ground solutions to address service-delivery problems. In this environment, demands for new competencies, and the opportunities to gain access to them, will help produce a different human resource profile for the public sector. If this is the case, targeted opportunities for training and development in LMC competency must be embedded in the process itself, rather than independent of it. This suggests that leaders of a LMC initiative should devote energy and resources to building a developmental strategy to support employees involved in the process. This strategy would consider formal training as one of several possible mechanisms to support if, for example, employees need to learn technical knowledge. But it would also incorporate other action–learning tools that would strengthen the relationship between the stakeholders involved, such as cooperative inquiry, peer-review audits, and peer support groups (Heron 2000).

Summary and Conclusions

Collaboration is often proposed as a strategy for dealing with new and complex environments. This is the case at the societal level in the new environment facing businesses, nonprofits, and government (Cavanagh et al. 1999), as well as at the organizational level in the new environment facing organizational actors (U.S. DOL 1996; Wheelan 1999; Kettl 2000). At both levels the decision to cooperate produces changes in the way stakeholders relate to one another and communicate. We know very little about this dimension of LMC, or about the new competencies demanded for successful engagement in this new environment. Our study has tried to address this gap.

We studied three municipal instances of successful cooperative labor relations. In the three cases, managers proposed collaboration as a strategy to deal with an external threat facing the organization. In all instances, labor engaged wholeheartedly. Exploring the experience of our respondents—before, during, and after participation in successful LMC efforts—provided insights about the types of roles and competencies associated with cooperation.

We found that in the new environment of cooperation, labor and management both developed similar collaborative mind-sets. They shared an understanding of the nature of public service as problem solving, value adding, and results oriented. But the new line manager became more people oriented than the traditional one, and coaching and teamwork became the predominant functions in this new role. In contrast, labor leaders became more technical in their expertise, thus gaining new competencies that used to be associated mostly with the managerial role. The new rank-and-file employee, in turn, also held more technical knowledge, was more autonomous, and felt empowered and accountable.

Based on these changes, we identified bundles of attitudes, knowledge, and skill competencies critical for success in LMC, at least according to the respondents in our study. In terms of attitudes, openness, reciprocity, and respect stood out. In terms of knowledge, four content areas emerged: knowledge about the core problem that motivated cooperation, basic knowledge related to the ability to acquire and process complex information, managerial-technical knowledge, and knowledge about local government administration. Finally, the skill competencies we identified related to team problem solving. These included cognitive skills to frame and define the organizational problem, persuasion and negotiations skills, communications, and team-related skills.

Consistent with the findings that LMC produced changes in roles, we conclude that it also produced a shift in developmental needs, based on the competency requirements. It created demands for managers to pay attention to people skills and demands for employees and union representatives to shift toward more formal and technical knowledge and skill competencies. The new required competencies represented areas where the actors would need additional reinforcement, because these were competencies traditionally associated with the role of the other side. In the context of cooperation at its best, new competency profiles emerged for the new manager and the new employee.

Overall, the new environment of cooperation is one where the competencies traditionally associated with managerial effectiveness are now shared by labor and management. This is consistent with the definition of LMC as a joint process in which both employees and their employers share managerial decision making (Rubin, Rubin, and Rolle 1999; Perline 1999). But since the shift toward more cooperative behavior is not permanent, there is a need to ensure that the competencies gained during this unfolding be sufficiently internalized to become transferable. We argue that isolated formal training is less effective than offering developmental interventions within the LMC initiative itself. We suggest using action–learning techniques as a means of creating a developmental strategy to strengthen and solidify the competencies learned during the cooperation effort.

The bundles of competencies proposed, as well as the ideal profiles derived from them, represent only the very early draft of a possible competency-based framework to be developed in future research. However, given the predominance of a managerial focus for all actors in LMC, it is reassuring to see that the competencies we identified are consistent with the findings of other studies that explored requirements for managerial effectiveness (Quinn, Faerman, Thompson, and McGrath 2002; Whetten and Cameron 2002; Winterton and Winterton 1999). These studies stressed the seemingly conflicting demands the modern manager faces and the need to use what may appear to be conflicting competencies in a balanced manner. The image in this literature is one of a well-rounded individual who must master both hard and soft competencies. The exploratory nature of our work requires taking these conclusions with caution. The findings cannot be generalized to a broader public sector population because they are based on only three initiatives. At the same time, we believe that the value of our study is precisely having only a few cases for an in-depth exploration of each of the individual experiences. This helps us deepen our understanding of the details associated with the behavioral dimension of cooperation, an aspect of LMC that has been left unexplored until now. We hope to have contributed to generating insights and ideas that can be tested in future studies aimed at developing a framework of competencies for LMC.

In sum, our findings suggest that LMC initiatives represent excellent developmental laboratories to help all stakeholders involved learn the appropriate combination of attitudes, knowledge, and skills for effective individual and organizational performance. They also help observers study the change in roles necessary for effective service and quality-of-work-life outcomes. Our study suggests that successful initiatives of LMC produce a work environment in which symbolic resources traditionally associated with the managerial role become redistributed in a more equitable way. In addition, the new roles for labor and management have in common a focus on better human understanding and interaction. This, in turn, seems to produce a more-democratic and effective workplace altogether. As the global revolution of public management continues to unfold (Kettl 2000), we wonder whether the competencies associated with cooperative behavior represent the competencies required for these new times.

Appendix:
Methodological Considerations

This chapter draws from an in-depth study of the experience of six individuals who took part in three successful efforts of LMC. We chose the three out of a pool of previously identified "successful" cases of LMC by the Department of Labor Task Force (U.S. DOL 1996). Each instance has unique characteristics that provide variation in the context of cooperation. Two of the cooperation efforts occurred within a paramilitary context (police and fire departments) and one in a civilian context (office of the mayor); two of the efforts took place in unionized settings and one was developed in a nonunionized state. This case represents an effort of cooperation between the human resources department of a city and nonunionized employees in one of its agencies. The other two represent broader efforts of cooperation between city managers and unions. In one case the context was the introduction of competition within public service operations; in the other case the context was the choice of a new insurance scheme for the city workforce. The three cases have in common the fact that all represent the municipal level of government. They provide enough variation in context, however, to be used as the base to search for patterns associated with what is common to all: LMC.

We conducted six in-depth telephone interviews with three pairs of labor and management representatives who were key actors involved in the same LMC effort in their agency. We asked all individuals to compare their own and their counterparts' attitudes and behaviors before and after the cooperative efforts had started. We also asked them to provide specific suggestions about the types of attitudes, knowledge, and skills they would want to see managers, labor representatives, and employees gain in training programs designed to help them become more proficient in LMC.

The three pairs of interviewees were a convenience sample based on a list of suggestions from an expert source.[11] The goal was to use their accounts to characterize the nature of LMC and capture changes in the mental models, roles, interactions, and competencies associated with the shift from traditional to cooperative labor relations. We identified similar and contrasting characteristics across labor and management representatives and within each group. We also compared these using accounts from before and after the occurrence of LMC efforts. We assumed that all three cases were successful instances of LMC and thus focused on the changes at the individual level. We did not measure the level of cooperation or the organizational outcomes of such efforts.

Notes

[1] Throughout the paper, we use the generic term "labor" to refer to both employees and labor representatives.

[2] The argument we make refers to the need for new or enhanced competencies for new role demands, not to the need for improving "less-competent" individuals or groups. Arguing that labor and managers require new skill and knowledge competencies for a new role does not preclude the possibility that some individual employees, labor leaders, or managers in those roles may have already possessed the new competencies. The point is that they did not need to use them before in their traditional role.

[3] For a brief description of the methods used and the study's limitations, see the appendix.

[4] The case description is based on the U.S. Department of Labor Task Force Report (1996).

[5] For a detailed account of this process, see Ospina and Yaroni (forthcoming).

[6] Citations in *italics* are direct quotes from the interviews. The information in parentheses after each quote refers to the respondent (labor representatives: L1, L2, L3; and managers: M1, M2, M3) and the page number(s) in the transcript from which the quote was extracted.

[7] In order to capture as many potentially useful ideas as possible, while looking for patterns, we also included items that were mentioned by single individuals if they were interesting or relevant.

[8] In competency studies, self-concept is normally measured with respondent tests, such as occupational preference or psychological inventories.

[9] For obvious reasons we avoided focusing attention on such words as "trust" and "cooperation," even though they represent values that were mentioned many times during the interviews and thus may "inform" many other attitudes. Instead, we searched for patterns to infer about attitudes underlying trust and cooperation.

[10] For a discussion of limitations, see the methodological appendix.

[11] Jonathan Brock, Executive Director of the Department of Labor Task Force, The Cascade Center for Public Service, Daniel J. Evans School of Public Affairs, University of Washington.

References

Cavanagh, Richard E., Dorothy S. Ridings, Sarah E. Melendez, Scott R. Fosler, Robert T. Jones, and Raymond Sheppach. 1999. *Changing Roles, Changing Relationships: The New Challenge for Business, Nonprofit Organizations, and Government.* A Three Sector Collaborative Project <http://www.independentsector.org/programs/leadership/changeroles.pdf> [April 18, 2003].

Cooke, William N. 1990. *Labor Management Cooperation: New Partnership or Going in Circles?* Kalamazoo, MI: Upjohn Institute for Employment Research.

———. 1994. "Employee Participation Programs, Group-Based Incentives and Company Performance: A Union-Nonunion Comparison." *International Labor Relations Review,* Vol. 47, no. 4 (July), pp. 594–609.

Delaney, John T. 1996. "Workplace Cooperation: Current Problems, New Approaches." *Journal of Labor Research,* Vol. 17, no. 1 (Winter), pp. 45–61.

Dinnocenzo, Debra A. 1989. "Labor Management Cooperation." *Training and Development Journal,* Vol. 43, no. 5, pp. 34–40.

Dunlop, John T. 1993. "The Future of Labor-Management Relations." In James A. Auerbach and Jerome T. Barrett, eds., *The Future of Labor Management Innovation in the United States.* Washington, DC: National Planning Association, pp. 82–92.

Goleman, Daniel, Richard Boyatzis, and Annie McKee. 2002. *Primal Leadership— Realizing the Power of Emotional Intelligence.* Boston, MA: Harvard Business School Press.

Heron, John. 2000. *The Complete Facilitators' Handbook.* London: Kogan Page.

Kearney, Richard C. 1996. "Managing Relations with Organized Employees." In James L. Perry, ed., *Handbook of Public Administration.* San Francisco: Jossey-Bass, pp. 460–74.

Kearney, Richard C., and Steven W. Hays. 1994. "Labor Management Relations and Participative Decision-Making: Towards a New Paradigm." *Public Administration Review,* Vol. 54, no. 1 (January/February), pp. 44–51.

Kettl, Donald F. 2000. *The Global Public Management Revolution: A Report on the Transformation of Governance.* Washington, DC: Brookings Institution Press.

Larson, James S. 1989. "Employee Participation in Federal Management." *Public Personnel Management,* Vol. 18, no. 4 (Winter), pp. 404–14.

Loney, Timothy J. 1996. "TQM and Labor Management Cooperation: A Noble Experiment for the Public Sector." *International Journal of Public Administration,* Vol. 19, no. 10 (October), pp. 1845–63.

Merton, Robert K. 1968. *Social Theory and Social Structure*. New York: Free Press.

Ospina, Sonia, and Allon Yaroni. Forthcoming. "Understanding Cooperative Behavior in Labor Management Cooperation: A Theory Building Excercise." *Public Administration Review*.

Perline, Martin M. 1999. "Union Views of Managerial Prerogatives Revisited: The Prospects for Labor Management Cooperation." *Journal of Labor Research*, Vol. 20, no. 1 (Winter), pp. 147–54.

Quinn, Robert E., Sue R. Faerman, Michael P. Thompson, and Michael McGrath. 2002. *Becoming a Master Manager: A Competency Framework*. New York: John Wiley & Sons.

Rubin, Barry M., and Richard S. Rubin, 2001. "Labor-Management Partnerships: A New Approach to Collaborative Management." *The PricewaterhouseCoopers Endowment for the Business of Government—Grant Report*. Arlington, VA: PricewaterhouseCoopers, 1616 North Fort Myer Dr., 22209.

Rubin, Barry M., Richard S. Rubin, and Anthony R. Rolle. 1999. "Successful Collaborative Management and Collective Bargaining in the Public Sector: An Empirical Analysis." *Public Productivity & Management Review*, Vol. 22, no. 4 (June), pp. 517–35.

Selden, Sally C., Gene A. Brewer, and Jeffrey L. Brudney. 1999. "Reconciling Competing Values in Public Administration: Understanding the Administrative Role Concept." *Administration & Society*, Vol. 31, no. 2 (May), pp. 171–204.

Senge, Peter M. 1990. *The Fifth Discipline: The Art and Practice of the Learning Organization*. New York: Doubleday.

Spencer, Lyle M., David C. McClelland, and Signe M. Spencer. 1994. *Competency Assessment Methods: History and State of the Art*. Boston: Hay/McBer Research Press.

Spencer, Lyle M., and Signe M. Spencer. 1993. *Competence at Work: Models for Superior Performance*. New York: John Wiley & Sons.

State and Local Government Labor-Management Committee. No date, circa 1993. *Working Together—An Instructor Guide*. Washington, DC.

U.S. Department of Labor. Secretary of Labor. Task Force on Excellence in State and Local Government Through Labor-Management Cooperation. 1996. *Working Together for Public Service*. Washington, DC: GPO.

Wasilisin, Andrew M. 1994. "Go Forward and Partner!" Introduction to the Mini-Forum. *Public Manager*, Vol. 23, no. 2 (Summer), pp. 17–21.

Wheelan, Susan A. 1999. *Creating Effective Teams—A Guide for Members and Leaders*. Thousand Oaks, CA: Sage Publications.

Whetten, David A., and Kim S. Cameron. 2002. *Developing Management Skills*. Upper Saddle River, NJ: Prentice Hall.

Winterton, Jonathan, and Ruth Winterton. 1999. *Developing Managerial Competence*. New York: Routledge.

Chapter 6

Federal Labor-Management Partnerships: Perspectives, Performance, and Possibilities

Marick F. Masters
University of Pittsburgh

Robert R. Albright
Rensselaer Polytechnic Institute

Federal sector labor-management relations stood at the center of the recent debate to create a federal Department of Homeland Security (DHS; see Harnage 2002; Ballard 2001; Cummings and Tejada 2002). Rarely does federal labor relations receive so much attention except when something goes seriously wrong, as was the case in the 1981 strike by the former Professional Air Traffic Controllers Organization (PATCO; see Northrup and Thornton 1988; Hurd and Kriesky 1986). The DHS debate revolved around whether or not employees of the proposed department should have the right to join unions and bargain collectively; President Bush and Congress were at loggerheads, stalling the DHS proposal until after the November 2002 elections. While the media attention given to federal labor relations is unusual, the controversy about the power to grant federal-employee unions is long-standing (Hart 1961; Nesbitt 1976). One perspective, embraced by the Bush administration, is that management needs maximum flexibility, particularly in areas involving national security, a uniquely federal role. Another, which most Democrats hold, is that the empowerment of employees through unions is essential to realizing their full potential (Goldberg 1961; Tobias 2002). At a minimum, except under special circumstances, federal employees should be given the basic rights to unionize and bargain collectively, as provided in current law. While the former view prevailed in the eventual outcome creating the DHS, the debate itself reflected a deeper philosophical conflict about how federal labor-management relations should be conducted in the future on a governmentwide scale (Nesterczuk, Devine, and Moffit 2001).

In the 1990s, under a Democratic administration, the federal government adopted a policy that promoted the empowerment of federal-employee unions in co-equal partnership with management (National Performance Review 1993). On October 1, 1993, then-President Clinton issued Executive Order 12871, establishing the National Partnership Council (NPC) and mandating that federal agency and department heads partner with their unions to improve government service and performance. The order reflected an underlying labor relations policy that departed dramatically from the state of adversarialism that beset much of the federal service, to the detriment of labor, management, and the public.

For over seven years, the federal government operated under this presidential mandate. Despite the policy's unique nature and scope, however, little research investigated federal labor-management partnerships (see Doeringer, Kaboolian, Watkins, and Watson 1996; Verma and Cutcher-Gershenfeld 1996; Suntrup and Barnum 1997). We address this void. Specifically, we examine the origin, nature, and performance of labor-management partnerships, including evidence about their perceived impact on the labor-management climate, indicators of labor-management conflict, and the institutional strength of federal-employee unions. In the process, we explore the barriers to realizing the full potential of partnership, show how it represented a distinctive political compromise between somewhat competing perspectives about both management and public administration, and speculate about the future direction of federal sector labor-management relations, particularly in light of President Bush's rescission of the 1993 Clinton mandate and the recent debate over the DHS.

We rely on several sources of data for this assessment. In addition to having reviewed the relevant literature in industrial relations and related fields and appropriate government reports (e.g., Cooke 1989, 1994; U.S. General Accounting Office 1991), we use the results of a comprehensive study on labor-management partnerships conducted in the 1999–2000 period for the National Partnership Council under the auspices of the U.S. Office of Personnel Management (OPM). In that study we examined 60 labor-management partnerships across eight federal agencies that differed widely in mission and composition, as well as size, although each is well recognized.[1] The study involved almost 300 interviews of union and management participants on partnership councils; surveys of labor-management partnership council members, employees covered by councils, and local and national leaders of the three major unions representing federal workers; a review of council and agency records; and about 20 targeted interviews with union, management, and government representatives involved in the development and implementation of partnership policy and practice. We organize this chapter in several parts. In the first part we provide relevant background information about federal sector labor relations and union representation. In the second, we examine the basic conceptual foundations of the initiative to reinvent government. Part three addresses how partnership fits into reinvention. In part four, we examine the apparent effects of partnership on labor-management relations and union strength in the federal government. Part five explores barriers to achieving the potential of partnership. In the sixth, we speculate about the future of labor-management relations in light of recent policy developments and the enactment of DHS in November 2002. We end the chapter with a discussion section.

Background

Federal sector labor-management relations have reflected a continuing contest of ideas about management, public administration, and unions (Kearney and Hays 1994; deLeon and Denhardt 2000). Generally speaking, the debate has occurred along a conservative-to-liberal ideological spectrum (Nesterczuk, Devine, and Moffit 2001). Conservatives have favored a managerially oriented, politically responsive civil service, while liberals have found employee empowerment, through unions, more desirable. These views have often competed in a broader discussion about reforming government to make it more effective and efficient. In the early 1990s, the forces of reform joined hands with proponents of employee empowerment to change the prevailing federal labor relations paradigm (National Performance Review 1993). The emergence of a partnership initiative occurred, however, in a political context in which strongly differing views about the appropriate role of federal-employee unions made it impractical to change the paradigm legislatively, even when Democrats controlled Congress and the White House (Ban 1995).

Several major developments have shaped federal sector labor relations over the past 40 years (see Figure 1). Various policies, emanating in the form either of legislation or presidential order, have defined the rights and powers of federal employees and their union representatives. In the main, they have had governmentwide applicability, but two policies have partitioned the federal sector and conferred expanded bargaining rights on certain unions that have emerged as politically influential and

organizationally strategic. While much has arguably changed over the past
four decades, a lot has remained more or less the same for extended periods of time. For example, for the past 25 years or so, the level of aggregate union representation in the nonpostal federal service has held steady
at 60 percent. (Within this overall picture, however, there has been a
great deal of movement among and between the unions.) In addition, no
governmentwide statute involving labor-management relations has been
enacted in almost a quarter of a century.

FIGURE 1

Federal Sector Labor-Management Relations Timeline

November 1961	—	Goldberg Task Force Report
January 1962	—	E.O. 10988
1966	—	Union Recognition Passes 20 Percent
October 1969	—	E.O. 11491
August 1970	—	Postal Workers Strike
August 1970	—	Postal Reorganization Act
1978	—	Union Recognition Reaches 60 Percent
October 1978	—	Civil Service Reform Act (FSLMRS)
August 1981	—	PATCO Strike
October 1993	—	E.O. 12871
October 1996	—	Federal Aviation Reauthorization Act
October 1998	—	Presidential Reaffirmation
February 2001	—	E.O. 13203
June 2002	—	OPM Memorandum

Governmentwide Policies

The contemporary federal policy framework arose in the early
months of the Kennedy administration. A task force headed by then-Sec-
retary of Labor Arthur Goldberg recommended granting federal
employees, postal and nonpostal, the right to unionize and bargain collectively. President Kennedy acceded to this advice and issued Executive
Order (E.O.) 10988 in January 1962. In doing so, he lent indirect presidential approval to emerging efforts to protect state and local employees
through similar state-level enactments (Burton 1979).

E.O. 10988 declared that "participation of employees in the formula-
tion and implementation of personnel policies affecting them contributes
to the effective conduct of public business." It stated that "Employees of
the Federal Government shall have, and shall be protected in the exercise
of, the right, freely and without penalty of reprisal, to form, join and assist
any employee organization or to refrain from any such activity." It provided
for the informal, formal, and exclusive recognition of union representatives,

granting exclusively recognized unions the right to meet and confer "with respect to personnel policy and practices and matters affecting working conditions, so far as may be appropriate subject to law and policy requirements." At the same time, President Kennedy accepted the advice of the Goldberg task force that public employment and private employment were sufficiently different to warrant limiting the power of government employee unions. The task force stated that "The benefits to be obtained for employees by employee organizations, while real and substantial, are limited. No valid purpose will be served by exaggerating them" (Goldberg 1961, cited in U.S. Congress 1979:1192). As a result, E.O. 10988 banned strikes, excluded wages and benefits from negotiability, stipulated management rights, and forbade union-security arrangements.

Despite these limitations, E.O. 10988 greatly facilitated the expansion of federal sector union representation. Between 1964 and 1970, the percentage of nonpostal federal employees belonging to exclusively recognized bargaining units rose from 12 percent to 48 percent (Table 1). Simply put, in the span of just six years, union representation quadrupled.

TABLE 1
Federal Employee Union Recognition,
Selected Years, 1964–2001

Year	Number of employees in recognized units	Percentage of civilian nonpostal federal service in units
1964	230,543	12
1966	434,890	21
1970	916,381	48
1975	1,200,336	59
1981	1,234,256	61
1985	1,244,266	60
1991	1,250,777	60
1992	1,262,859	59
1997	1,098,072	59
1999	1,050,423	60
2001	1,043,479	61

Source: U.S. Office of Personnel Management 2002.

The second governmentwide policy emerged in the form of another executive order, E.O. 11491, issued by President Nixon in October 1969. E.O. 11491 disbanded the informal and formal types of recognition preceding exclusive representation. It created a three-person Federal Labor Relations Council to administer and interpret the order, formed a Federal

Service Impasses Panel to consider negotiation impasses, and allowed the parties to negotiate grievance procedures culminating in binding arbitration. Otherwise, the order retained the strictures of its revoked predecessor, E.O. 10988.

Union representation continued to grow in the 1970s, albeit at a much-reduced pace. In fact, the aggregate nonpostal level of recognition reached its contemporary peak of 60 percent in 1978. During this decade, however, pressures emerged to provide a statutory basis for federal labor-management relations and to expand the rights of federal-employee unions, especially with respect to the scope of bargaining and impasse resolution. A September 30, 1977, report of the Federal Personnel Management Project canvassed the options in the labor-management relations area as part of a comprehensive effort to study reform of the civil service system, a centerpiece of the administration of then-President Carter (U.S. Congress 1979).

After considerable behind-the-scenes negotiations, President Carter agreed to include a section in his civil service reform bill to provide a statutory basis for union rights in the federal service. No longer would the bargaining powers of unions depend on the whim of a president. Beyond this, however, little changed. For the most part, Title VII of the Civil Service Reform Act of 1978 (i.e., the Federal Service Labor-Management Relations Statute) codified E.O. 11491.

Therefore, federal sector unions continued to operate in the comparatively restrictive legal environment that had been in place for the prior 16 years (1962–1978). Unions had a very limited scope of bargaining, no right to strike, no right to the arbitration of impasses (without management assent), no union-security protections, and a fearsome management rights clause emblazoned in statute. Within this framework, labor-management relations acquired an almost surreal, ultra-legal character. The parties bargained adversarially over the utmost trivia, such as where to locate a water fountain at a work site.

A confluence of events, not the least of which was the election of Clinton and Gore in 1992, led to a fourth governmentwide initiative, once again in the form of a presidential order. Specifically, President Clinton issued E.O. 12871 on October 1, 1993. The order created the National Partnership Council and mandated agency heads to establish labor-management partnerships to address ways to improve agency operations. In essence, E.O. 12871 superimposed an expanded venue of joint decision making, intended to be collaborative, on top of the existing collective-bargaining framework. A de facto expansion of the scope of bargaining had occurred, though it lacked enforceability and could not alter statutorily determined conditions of work. Showing the vagaries of presidential orders, Clinton's E.O. 12871 was revoked within a month after President Bush took office (E.O. 13203). The February 17, 2001, order tersely stated, "Executive Order 12871...is revoked. Among other things, therefore, the National Partnership Council is immediately dissolved." Supposedly, this revocation did not constitute an abandonment of labor-management cooperation. The current director of the OPM stated in a memorandum to agency and department heads dated June 21, 2002: "When the President signed Executive Order 13203...,[he] was motivated by his conviction that partnership is not something that should be mandated for every agency in every situation. But while agencies are no longer *required* to form partnerships with their unions, they are strongly encouraged to establish cooperative labor-management relations."

Sector-Specific Policies

Congress has enacted two policies that effectively partition two spheres of federal operations for separate treatment. First, on the heels of an illicit strike by 152,000 postal workers in the summer of 1970, Congress passed the Postal Reorganization Act (PRA). It created the U.S. Postal Service, an independent executive-branch entity. In so doing, Congress permitted collective bargaining on wages and working conditions, a significant change from bargaining in the federal service proper. If the negotiating parties were unable to reach an agreement within 180 days after negotiations began, the PRA provided for binding arbitration. It placed the U.S. Postal Service under the jurisdiction of the National Labor Relations Board (NLRB).

Second, in 1996, Congress passed the Federal Aviation Reauthorization Act (FARA). The FARA, combined with legislation adopted the year before, empowered the administrator of the Federal Aviation Administration (FAA) to establish a personnel system that met the unique needs of the agency. The system included a provision granting broad powers to "negotiate with the exclusive bargaining representatives of employees...and consult with other employees of the Administration." The FARA also provided that if the parties could not reach an agreement, they would avail themselves of the services of the Federal Mediation and Conciliation Service (FMCS). If the FMCS could not mediate a resolution, the disagreement would be submitted to Congress for action. Thus, unlike the PRA, the FARA created a dual system of labor-management relations within an executive-branch department, the Department of Transportation, which houses the FAA.

In short, both the PRA and the FARA show the willingness of Congress and the White House to isolate particular federal sectors for separate labor relations treatment. At the very least, this willingness underscores the ability of certain unions to exert political influence at the right time in the right place (Walters 1999).

A Defining Event: PATCO

The 1981 PATCO strike has received considerable attention. Its overall labor relations significance has probably been exaggerated. However, it did vividly illustrate three points that apply to the federal service at large. First, the strike demonstrated the fundamental weakness of federal-employee unions when confronted with a politically determined executive. Not even a union of employees as strategically situated as air traffic controllers stood a chance under the circumstances, especially when the union committed such an inept miscalculation. The strike was patently illegal. PATCO garnered no meaningful sympathy from brethren unions for so blatantly defying the law, and it enjoyed even less support among the public. Legally and operationally, a prepared and resolved executive crushed PATCO. The lesson was clear for all other federal-employee unions.

Second, PATCO showed just how politicized federal sector labor-management relations can become. The air traffic controllers challenged executive authority, threatened to disrupt economically vital public services, and attempted to intimidate Congress into preempting the executive in what had clearly become extra-legal negotiations between PATCO and Transportation. Such defiance and hubris could not be tolerated without signaling a fundamental incapacity to govern. The upshot is that whenever labor-management relations confront political authority or the public interest, they become issues of much broader philosophical and political import. They threaten to upset the distribution of authority and power across competing interests. Anyone with a stake in this distribution (e.g., an interest in the powers extended to unions) will line up on one side of the debate or another.

Finally, PATCO underscored the raw tensions in the federal service. Adversarialism permeated federal labor-management relations. The parties often distrusted each other and saw their differences much more clearly than their common interests. The absence of marketplace discipline made it possible for them to engage in all sorts of tactics to thwart each other's will. While PATCO tried the illegal, other federal-employee unions became masters of the *ultra*-legal. As a result, needed organizational change came with great difficulty if at all. Adversarialism complicated and magnified a brewing crisis in the public service. Enter reinvention center stage.

Reinventing Government

The United States entered the 1990s with three deficits plaguing government, especially at the federal level. Federal budget deficits had mushroomed to nearly $300 billion annually, jacking up the public debt at a politically unacceptable pace. A parade of blue-ribbon commissions and other government-led investigations had uncovered plentiful waste, fraud, and abuse in the administration of federal agencies and programs. In addition, public confidence in government's innate capacity to perform had plummeted. Calls to privatize, contract out, and downsize government grew politically louder.

In the midst of these prevailing winds, an alternative less severe than radical amputation of government services emerged in the form of reinvention. Popularized in the bestseller by David Osborne and Ted Gaebler (1992), *Reinventing Government: How the Entrepreneurial Spirit Is Transforming the Public Sector,* reinvention called for the infusion of best business practices into government. Popular opinion held that the problem lay not in what government was doing but in how it was doing it. A transformation aimed at inculcating an entrepreneurial spirit into public service was needed to set things right, not a radical retrenchment.

Reinvention, in concept and practice, rests upon certain assumptions and principles that have direct and indirect implications for labor-management relations. Reinventing government embraces government and public service. As Osborne and Gaebler (1992:xxii) assert, "Our purpose is not to criticize government, as so many have, but to renew it." In its report to President Clinton, the National Performance Review (1993:ii) echoed this underpinning: "The National Performance Review focused primarily on *how* government *should work,* not on what it should do." But reinvention was not devoid of values. As deLeon and Denhardt (2000:90) commented: "The reinvention movement takes this idea one step further, arguing that government should not only adopt the *techniques* of business administration, but it should also adopt the *values* of business." To a large extent, the values focused on who government should serve and how its performance should be measured.

More specifically, reinvention rested on a set of assumptions and principles that focused on attaining three political objectives (see Figure 2). The objectives involve simultaneously ridding government of the three chronic deficits: budget, performance, and public confidence (see, e.g., Kettl 1994, 1998; Kettl and DiIulio 1995). In this regard, reinvention is bound to pose paradoxes and contradictions. How does one improve performance while cutting costs (to reduce the deficit)? How does one improve public confidence if it means improving performance in a way that dissatisfies some customers (e.g., tax collections)? Yet, by focusing on the how rather than the what and why, reinvention enjoyed an almost unimpeachable political currency.

What made reinvention so administratively plausible was that it accepted the current role of the federal government as a given. It did not require examining whether or not government should have certain policies, nor did it necessitate a critical review of the propriety of transferring federal functions to the states and localities. By accepting these as givens, reinvention did not materially threaten the existing line-up of interest-group power, *except in the area of labor-management relations*.

The political assumptions behind reinvention made its managerial corpus even more attractive. Who can argue against increased efficiency, market-driven responsiveness, a focus on results, and decentralized processes of operation to promote responsiveness and innovation? These are values or norms that prescribe success. Operationally, they translate into certain requirements that resonate well with a disgruntled taxpaying public. Efficiencies imply reduced expenditures and personnel, which further reduce the costs of government. Market-driven responsiveness foretells greater customer satisfaction. As deLeon and Denhardt (2000: 91) observe, "Closely related to reinvention's emphasis on the market model is its emphasis on customer-driven government." The practical operationalization of certain managerial principles lent itself naturally to the identification of metrics that comported with the overarching political objectives: (1) a shrinking headcount, (2) reduced expenditures, and (3) greater customer or user satisfaction as measured by surveys.

But the glue that held the principles and operational elements together was employee empowerment (Kettl 1994). If employees were not appropriately empowered, their motivation to perform better and more efficiently would diminish. Customer responsiveness would suffer commensurately. Gaining cost savings through improved operations would prove more elusive. Personnel cutbacks would still be possible, but at what cost in performance and service?

FIGURE 2

Managerial and Political Perspectives on Reinvention

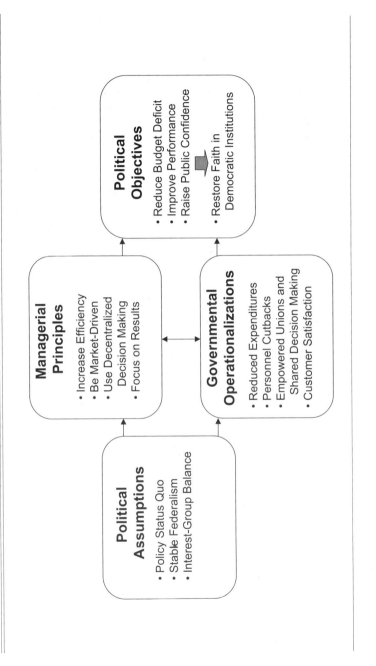

Kettl (1994:vii) highlighted the conceptual and practical centrality of empowerment to reinvention as envisaged by the National Performance Review (NPR):

> Finally glue: The NPR builds on a philosophy of "empowering" government workers to make better decisions. It argues for a more "entrepreneurial" philosophy, with a competition pre-scription replacing monopoly-based command-and-control management. In short, the NPR seeks to shift power from Congress to the bureaucracy and within the bureaucracy, from top to bottom levels.

In government, where comparatively high percentages of the workforce are represented by unions, empowerment is code for empowering unions: "The keystone of the NPR's people strategy lay in building bridges to public-employee unions" (Kettl 1994:13). Tapping into the experiences derived from unionized businesses, this meant fostering labor-manage-ment cooperation: "Building a partnership with the unions thus became the centerpiece of the NPR's relationship with government employ-ees...." (Kettl 1994:13).

Thus, reinvention envisaged empowering federal-employee unions. In this regard, it threatened to upset the policy status quo and the bal-ance of power accorded to business and labor in the political process. If there was to be a particularly controversial element of reinvention, labor-management partnership would predictably be it. Because of its managerial and political connotations, a mechanism had to be found to make partnership feasible. The presidential order provided the mecha-nism by which partnership could be made a vital part of reinvention, without having to obtain congressional approval. And, most certainly, no one expected Congress, even when Democratically controlled, to assent to the diminution of its effective powers.

Partnership and Reinvention

The theoretical and practical basis for making partnership the glue of reinvention rests on the notion that a positive labor-management relations climate can directly and indirectly improve organizational performance (Levine 1995). A growing body of empirical research and anecdotal evi-dence supports this contention (Kochan and Osterman 1994; Rubinstein 2000; Cooke 1989, 1994). The argument invokes several theoretical per-spectives, including exit voice, social capital, communications networks, employee involvement, negotiations, union discipline, and strategic choice (see Masters, Albright, and Eplion 2003). Sheppard, Lewicki, and Minton (1992:156) present the case simply: "There is a strong, clear link between the attributes of a good voice system and a healthy organization.... Increasingly, participation is a cornerstone in efforts to introduce new technology."

Conceptual Framework

Cooke (1989) elaborates on the potential relationships among partnership, unions, and organizational performance. First, a positive overall labor-management climate "is expected to have a direct bearing on company performance" (Cooke 1989:303). In this respect, unions strengthen the voice of employees by motivating increased employee input to the organization. By offering job security through grievance procedures, unions also increase the willingness of employees to venture a contribution. This argument is very consistent with the exit-voice hypothesis developed and applied by Hirschman (1970) and Freeman and Medoff (1984).

Second, a more-positive labor-management climate will encourage unions to intensify their collaborative endeavors. As Cooke (1989:302) observes: "Intensity of collaborative activities directly affects performance; it also has indirect effects, since one key objective of collaboration is to improve labor-management relations, which, in turn, affects performance." One of the factors, parenthetically, which influences such intensity is the institutional strength of the union.

The NPR, created in March 1993 by President Clinton to conduct a six-month study on how "to make the entire federal government both less expensive and more efficient" (NPR 1993:1), was quickly persuaded to go the collaboration route. It heard the accolades of labor-management cooperation from numerous companies that showed how transforming their labor relations had made them more competitive. The NPR (1993:87) echoed these testimonials in setting the stage for a partnership initiative:

> Corporate executives from unionized firms declare this truth from experience. No move to reorganize for quality can succeed without the full and equal participation of workers and their unions. Indeed, a unionized workplace can provide a leg up because forums already exist for labor and management exchange. The primary barrier that unions and employers must surmount is the adversarial relationship that binds them to noncooperation.

From these perspectives, a sound basis emerged for trying to promote collaboration in the federal sector (see Figure 3). The fundamental thesis was that collaboration or partnership would transform an adversarial into a positive labor-management climate, which, in turn, would improve federal agency performance, to the betterment of taxpayers and customers. Such a labor-management transformation was essential because of the widely known and substantively documented adversarial character of federal sector labor-management relations (U.S. General Accounting Office 1991; NPR 1993). The NPR (1993:87–88) cited the findings of the 1991 GAO report in pushing its collaboration initiative:

> The current context for federal labor-management relations, title VII of the 1978 Civil Service Reform Act, presents such a barrier. In 1991, the GAO concluded after an exhaustive survey of union leaders, government managers, federal employees and neutral experts, that the federal labor-management program "is not going well." GAO characterized the existing bargaining processes as too adversarial, bogged down by litigation over minute details, plagued by slow and lengthy dispute resolution, and weakened by poor management. One expert interviewed by GAO summed up the prevailing view: "We have never had so many people and agencies spend so much time, blood, sweat, and tears on so little. I am saying I think it is an awful waste of time and money on very little results." Indeed, the cost of handling unfair labor practice disputes using this system runs into tens of millions of dollars every year.

The stage was thus nicely set for labor-management partnership. The NPR (1993:88) articulated the logic depicted in Figure 3: "We can only transform government if we transform the adversarial relationship that dominates federal union-management interaction into a partnership for reinvention and change." The question, therefore, became how to make partnership happen. The issue was very much more than an operational or logistical matter. It was a political concern. Competing views, reflecting deep-rooted philosophical disagreements, existed on how much to empower unions. And then there was the overriding matter of what was politically feasible. A Democratically controlled Congress and White House, as was present in 1993–1994, did not guarantee pro-union legislation in the area of federal sector labor-management relations. Empowering federal-employee unions competed with congressional dominance and prerogative. It also threatened to upset the broader balance of labor and corporate interests.

FIGURE 3
Conceptual Model

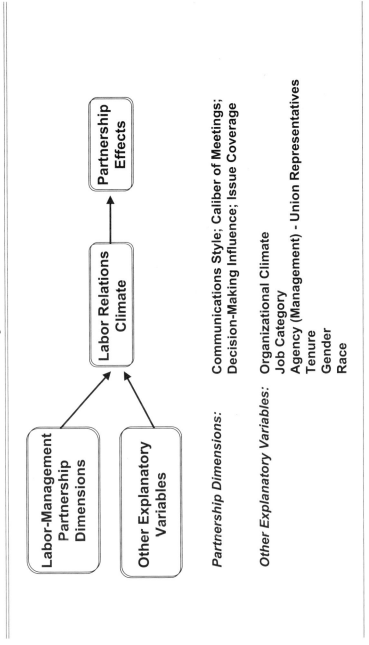

NPR and Union Perspectives

The NPR received solicited and unsolicited advice from the federal-employee unions, principally the American Federation of Government Employees (AFGE), National Federation of Federal Employees (NFFE), and National Treasury Employees Union (NTEU). Behind the scenes, these unions lobbied the NPR and Vice-President Gore, who chaired the review. They had three principal objectives, two of which went beyond partnership per se (AFGE, NTEU, and NFFE 1993). First, the unions sought a partnership framework, which could be implemented conveniently through a presidential order as long as it did not contemplate changing the FSLMRS (see Table 2). The focus of partnership would be promoting high-performance organizations. As the unions declared in a publicly issued report, *Total Quality Partner-ship—A Vision for the Future* (AFGE, NTEU, and NFFE 1993:5): "The executive order would charge the partners with joint responsibility for the creation of high performance and mission oriented workplaces." The unions also envisaged a governmentwide, *super* labor-management partnership to guide the partnering initiative.

Second, the unions wanted the scope of bargaining expanded. They viewed the FSLMRS, especially through its expansive management rights clause, as a barrier to real partnership. From their perspective, it was not sufficient to superimpose a partnership venue on the restrictive collective-bargaining framework. Limitations on the scope of bargaining needed to be relaxed:

> The provisions of the current Federal Service Labor-Manage-ment Relations Statute (5 USC Chapter 71) present significant barriers to labor-management partnership. Under current law, Federal employers and their employees cannot bargain to agreement on such matters as work practices and methods, position classification, technology, work assignments, and other issues which are of vital concern to both parties. This stands in stark contrast to the private sector where labor-management partners have achieved many of their successes in transforming their organizations by negotiating in these very areas (AFGE, NTEU, and NFFE 1993:5).

Finally, the unions pressed for a statutory allowance of union-secu-rity arrangements. In the federal sector, while unions such as AFGE, NFFE, and NTEU had nominally high rates of representation (see Table 3), a majority of the employees represented chose not to join the

TABLE 2
E.O. 12871: A Political Compromise

Policy dimension	Union recommendations	NPR recommendations	E.O. 12871 provisions
National Partnership Council	Create NPC by E.O. to promote partnership	Create NPC to champion partnership	Created 11-person NPC to support creation of partnerships
Governmentwide partnerships	Mandate partnership by E.O. to create high-performance agencies	Direct establishment of labor-management partnership as an executive-branch goal	Ordered agency and department heads to create labor-management partnerships
Scope of bargaining	Eliminate current restrictions on bargaining in management rights clause and mandate bargaining over "permissive items"	NPC will propose statutory changes, if needed	Ordered NPC to make recommendations regarding statutory changes
Union security	Eliminate ban on union security and permit "service" or "fair share" fee systems	NPC will propose statutory changes, if needed	Ordered NPC to make recommendations regarding statutory changes

TABLE 3
The Three Major Federal-Employee Unions,
1991–2001, Recognition Status

Union	1991 No. of units	1991 No. of employees	1997 No. of units	1997 No. of employees	1999 No. of units	1999 No. of employees	2001 No. of units	2001 No. of employees
AFGE	962	642,315	949	596,206	1,012	578,048	1,002	582,753
NTEU	48	151,736	54	136,577	62	135,906	64	139,302
NFFE	370	146,113	353	123,660	303	104,472	243	68,535

union (Masters and Atkin 1989, 1990; Masters and Albright 1993). The federal government was—and is—the nation's largest open-shop employer. Faced with sizable representational duties but comparatively modest dues-paying memberships, these federal-employee unions often experienced serious resource constraints. In this regard, they feared that partnership would stretch them beyond tolerable limits: "It is obvious that the union management partnership will place increased demands on union leadership and finances" (AFGE, NTEU, and NFFE 1993:8). The unions thus advocated amending the FSLMRS to permit "service" or "fair share" fee systems.

In its September 1993 report, *From Red Tape to Results: Creating a Government that Works Better and Costs Less,* the NPR met the unions about halfway. It gave a partnership order and established a *super* partnership council, named the National Partnership Council. When it came to proposed statutory changes, though, political realities—combined with the need for managerial flexibility that reinvention loudly implied—became inescapable. The NPR (1993:88) deferred considerations to what was to be a management-controlled NPC: "The National Partnership Council will propose the statutory changes needed to make labor-management partnership a reality." Before President Clinton issued his partnership order, the unions pushed for whatever liberalization in bargaining rights per se could be established by presidential decree, thus avoiding congressional scrutiny. As we shall see, they did get one such provision in President Clinton's executive order.

Executive Order 12871

E.O. 12871 expressed the purpose of partnership, created and charged the NPC, instructed agency and department heads to establish partnerships, and expanded the scope of bargaining. The order stated that "The involvement of Federal Government employees and their union representatives is essential to achieving the National Performance Review's Government reform objective." To oversee the partnership initiative, it created an 11-person (7 management, 4 union) NPC and invested it with the following responsibilities:

- To promote partnerships throughout the executive branch,
- To issue guidance on partnerships,
- To monitor and evaluate partnerships,
- To work with the President's Management Council to achieve the NPR's reforms, and

- To propose by January 1, 1994, statutory changes necessary to fulfill the objectives of the order.

The substantive jurisdiction of the NPC was left unspecified but was
presumed to encompass matters relevant to improving agency performance. In mandating agency and department heads to establish labor-
management partnerships "at appropriate levels," Executive Order
12871 articulated a more-specific purview to "involve employees and
their union representatives to identify problems and craft solutions to
better serve the agency's customers and mission." Without question, this
was a broad jurisdiction, but one that was not coupled with the delegation of decision-making or enforcement powers. Such authority would
have to occur on an ad hoc basis at the discretion of agency management
and, to the extent management desired, their union counterparts.

Finally, E.O. 12871 ordered agency heads to "negotiate over subjects
set forth in U.S.C. 7106(b)(1) [of the FSLMRS], and instruct subordinate officials to do the same." These subjects were so-called permissive
items. Under the FSLMRS, agencies could negotiate them if they so
elected; it was purely a matter of managerial discretion. Permissive items
included "the numbers, types, and grades of employees or positions
assigned to any organizational subdivision, work project, or tour of duty,
or on the technology, methods, and means of performing work." President Clinton *elected* for agencies to negotiate these matters, which did
not require a change in the statute. Nor, parenthetically, did it touch
management rights, per se.

The NPC got to work immediately. It created several working groups
to review and propose needed statutory changes. Disagreement between
union and management representatives erupted immediately, especially
over matters involving statutory changes in the scope of bargaining and
union security. The NPC was unable to agree on proposals on these
salient issues. Even if it had been able to do so, the various options proposed may never have curried sufficient favor to pass Congress. What
hopes the unions had about legislatively expanding their bargaining and
union-security rights were dashed when the Republicans swept Congress
in the historic 1994 elections. As Ban (1995:139) has written:

> Before the 1994 elections some union officials were optimistic
> about the eventual possibility of legislative action, while others
> recognized it would take a major effort to change congressional
> perceptions [even with Democrats in the majority]. Republican
> control of Congress changed the political environment dramati-
> cally.

Wisely, the NPC did not dwell on the futile pursuit of a consensus on legislative change. Instead, it directed its energies to providing assistance and guidance to agency managers and their union counterparts to promote partnership. Partly through its efforts, but also because of a supplicant eagerness to comply with a presidential decree, labor-management partnerships proliferated rapidly across the executive branch. As the NPC said in its October 1996 report to the president (NPC 1996:1):

> Since the Executive Order was issued, partnerships have continued to grow throughout the executive branch. There are well over one million bargaining unit employees in the federal government. Seventy percent of bargaining unit employees (up from 55% in 1994) are represented by partnership councils. Seventy-two percent (up from 53% in 1994) are covered by partnership agreements.

The U.S. Office of Personnel Management (1998) conducted its last update on the extent of partnership on December 7, 1998. It found that 67 percent of the federal civilian, nonpostal workforce were covered by labor-management partnership councils, even though only 34 percent of the existing bargaining units had councils. Where councils existed, they were typically negotiated into the labor-management contract. This arrangement effectively gave the council a legal status separate from the presidential order. Partnership became a contractual obligation.

What Do Partnerships Do?

We collected survey, interview, and archival data as part of a comprehensive study to evaluate partnerships commissioned by the NPC and OPM. Eight federal agencies of diverse size, mission, and impact opted to participate in the study. These agencies, in turn, identified 54 local and regional partnerships for us to study, plus six agencywide partnerships. The eight agencies encompassed more than 310,000 bargaining-unit employees. The specific sites studied employed about 70,000 persons, including bargaining-unit and non-unit employees.

As part of the study, we surveyed the approximately 650 union and management representatives on the 60 labor-management partnership councils selected. The survey instrument included items on the operations of partnerships, partnership effectiveness, labor-management relations climate, and perceived impacts of partnership on various indicators of agency performance. The questionnaires were administered under elaborate arrangements made with agency sites to ensure confidentiality and anonymity. No council participant received more than one survey, even though some served on multiple councils (local, regional, or agencywide). Questionnaires were administered in late 1999 and winterspring 2000 (for the most part) at the election of the agency sites, which had widely varied schedules. A description of the sample is available in Masters (2001).

Partnership Effectiveness

We asked several questions about the council participants' perceptions of the effectiveness of their partnerships, from a process perspective. Specifically, we asked about the extent to which they believe their council is collaborative and that the parties genuinely listen to each other (the communications-style index). We asked about their council's decision-making influence: (1) whether councils make formal recommendations; (2) if council's recommendations are taken seriously; and (3) if council is an important decision-making body (decision making–influence index). Finally, we asked about the quality of partnership council meeting: (1) do councils meet often enough; (2) are council meetings generally productive; (3) do councils address issues relevant to agency business and mission; and (4) do councils work informally in between meetings to solve problems (meeting-quality index).

The survey results for these three indices are reported in Figure 4. They show that, on average, the council participants tend to agree that their partnerships are collaborative and meaningful, that their councils are at least somewhat important decision-making bodies, and that their meetings are productive and frequent enough. Note that these indices exhibit relatively high reliability coefficients.

Labor Relations Climate

We also asked several items to tap the participants' assessments of the labor-management relations climate in their agency work sites and the degree to which the labor-management situation had changed since partnership was introduced. In particular, we used a previously validated seven-item scale to measure labor-management "harmony" (see Dastmalchian, Blyton, and Adamson 1989). The items in this scale were adapted for the federal sector. We also asked about perceptions of the extent of cooperativeness between labor and management in precouncil days. We asked about how much the labor-management situation had improved or deteriorated in a follow-up question. The harmony index, cooperativeness, and improvement responses are reported in Figure 5.

FIGURE 4

Partnership Effectiveness

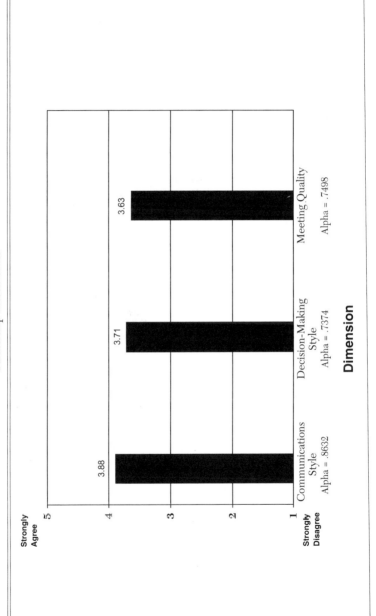

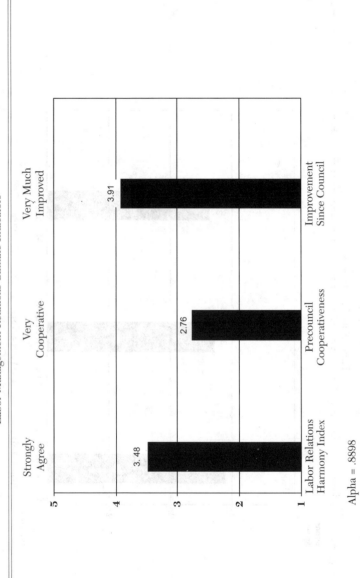

FIGURE 5
Labor-Management Relations Climate Indicators

Alpha = .8898

The harmony index comes in the middle of the neutral-to-agree zone, suggesting that there is only mild agreement overall that the labor relations climate is cooperative. This lukewarm view of things is probably attributable in part to the relatively low point of cooperation exhibited before partnership. The average response to the question about the extent of precouncil cooperativeness was somewhere in the uncooperative-to-neutral zone. In the main, participants did not see much cooperation before partnerships were mandated. They tended to believe, however, that the labor-management relationship had improved at least some since partnership. This sentiment, we hasten to add, was widely shared among the council participants we interviewed, on both the labor and management sides.

Partnership Impacts

Union and management partnership council representatives were asked to indicate the extent to which they agreed that their partnerships had an impact on several areas of organizational performance. The areas included cost savings, internal customer satisfaction, external customer satisfaction, employee productivity, employee morale, labor-management relations, labor-management communications, cultural change, and reinvention itself. We recognize that perceptions do not constitute true measures of impact, but, unfortunately, the agencies uniformly lacked concrete measures of most of these items, especially at a level that could be associated with partnership council activity. Council representatives' perceptions may have had an impact on the degree of commitment they were willing to make to partnership. If they perceived that their councils were not having a particularly effective impact, then they might have had reservations about committing the time and energy needed to make cooperation work. They might have questioned the task significance of what they were doing on a partnership council. This is particularly plausible given that partnerships were essentially add-on activities: council participants were not excused from their federal government duties and responsibilities. Not once in the literally hundreds of interviews we conducted did we encounter anyone whose assignment and expected performance had been lessened because of service on a partnership council. Finding time for partnership was a pervasive concern.

In Figure 6 we report the participants' average responses to nine items pertaining to organization performance. The responses ranged from 3.03 to 3.85, or in the neutral-to-agree zone. Clearly, the strongest level

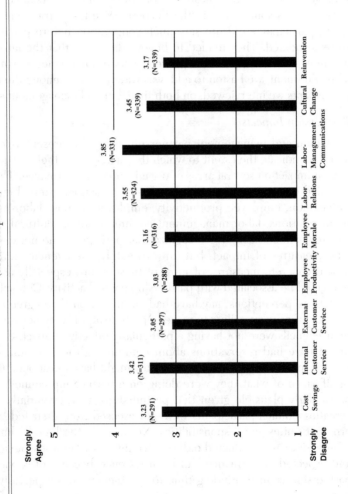

FIGURE 6
Partnership Impact Perceptions
(Mean Responses)

of agreement was expressed on labor relations and labor-management communications items. The next highest expression of agreement came on the item of cultural change, which one would expect to be highly correlated with transforming labor-management relations. After that came internal customer satisfaction, which would pertain to employees and others whose work depended on what the agency did. When it came to the "harder" items of organizational performance, such as cost savings, employee productivity, and external customer satisfaction, the average perceived impact was close to the neutral response. We should mention that the focus of cost savings associated with reinvention came heavily in the form of reducing headcount. The NPR recommended that the president reduce federal personnel by over 250,000, to shrink federal employment to the lowest levels since the early 1960s (Light 1999). The Clinton-Gore administration did make extensive personnel reductions, especially among Department of Defense civilians, and therein among blue-collar workers.

We should note that one of the questions our council-participant interviewees had the most difficulty with was identifying precise impacts or significant achievements made by their councils. The most common response was improved labor-management communications and reduced labor-management conflict (e.g., fewer grievances and other formal actions). Both of these, in the conceptual framework of reinvention, would be antecedents of more mission-related indicators of agency performance, such as programmatic savings and improved productivity, as well as external customer satisfaction.

One area, however, where several partnerships were able to have a positive impact was that of helping their agencies adjust to and implement the seemingly endless reorganization and restructuring missives they received. Whether it was responding to A-76 proposals to contract out or totally revamping an agency's operational structure, these councils worked diligently to rationalize personnel reassignments and site closures and consolidations. In a few cases, the partnerships were actually able to be proactive in leading the organizational-change process and suggesting ways to minimize the personnel disruptions that might hinder restructuring initiatives.

Governmentwide Indicators of Labor-Management Conflict

The survey results and interviews revealed that there was general agreement that partnership was improving the labor-management relations climate and reducing formal complaints that reflect conflict, such as grievances filed, grievance arbitrations, unfair labor practice charges, and bargaining impasses. Several partnerships reported that they had been able to take up many of the items typically negotiated and to create a process that streamlined and shortened the formal negotiations, at considerable cost savings to their agencies. In a few instances, councils had succeeded in making formal contract negotiations superfluous. Unfortunately, federal agencies do not systematically track formal grievances, arbitrations, and filings with the FLRA.

Nonetheless, it is useful to look at the aggregate data collected by the FLRA. In Table 4, we report the frequency of unfair labor practice charges, bargaining impasse filings, appeals of negotiability cases, and appeals of arbitration cases that came before the FLRA over the 1990-to-2000 period. As can be seen, the frequency of unfair labor practice cases fell from a peak of nearly 8,900 in 1992 to fewer than 6,000 by 1997. Bargaining impasse filings also fell, as did appeals of negotiability and arbitration cases.

Obviously, one cannot ascribe the generally downward trend to partnership per se. However, it is important to note that the partnership initiative accelerated the FLRA's move from a litigation model to a collaborative approach to cases. It created the Collaboration and Alternative Dispute Resolution (CADR) program in 1996 to encourage the parties to resolve problems before they got to the FLRA or, if they did get to the FLRA, to resolve them before a formal hearing or decision was required. In its report commemorating its 20th anniversary, the U.S. FLRA (1999:9–10) noted:

> During the first years of the FLRA's operations, its administration of the statute was patterned after the National Labor Relations Board (NLRB)....Under this model, the General Counsel's early focus was on the exercise of statutory prosecutorial functions and the use of litigation....Starting in the late 1980's, the FLRA began modifying existing programs and developing new initiatives aimed at fostering improved labor relations by assisting parties to resolve their own difficulties through interest-based approaches....Executive Branch initiatives in 1993-94 led to further expansion of these activities....In 1996, the three FLRA components joined together to establish the Collaboration and Alternative Dispute (CADR) Program, the first unified Agency-wide program dedicated to assisting parties with resolving disputes on their own terms, at the earliest time, through the use of interest-based problem solving.

TABLE 4
Key Government Labor-Management
Relations Indicators (by year)

Indicators	Frequency										
	1990	1991	1992	1993	1994	1995	1996	1997	1998	1999	2000
Unfair labor practice charges filed with the Office of the General Counsel	7,097	7,327	8,848	8,674	7,446	6,252	6,263	5,323	5,702	5,686	5,638
Bargaining impasses: impasses to the Federal Service Impasses Panel	280	293	253	247	278	170	163	148	175	169	167
Negotiability cases: appeals to the authority	127	128	115	95	43	66	79	58	62	56	65
Arbitration cases: appeals (exceptions) to the authority	209	203	188	180	161	104	117	133	108	125	140

Union Institutional Strength

The last area we look at in terms of partnership impacts is that of union institutional strength. In this regard, the key indicator in the federal sector is union membership, especially in light of the open-shop nature of the federal employment. The unions did not go into partnership blindly. They hoped that their support for reinvention would result in improvements in their institutional position. This is one of the reasons why they eagerly sought some type of union-security legislation, only to have their hopes vanquished by political indifference and ideological opposition (once the Republicans won the Congress in 1994). Parenthetically, the unions knew that reinvention and partnership were double-edged swords. In practice, reinvention stressed "costs less" as much as, if not more than, "performs better." This translated into continual pressures to downsize. During the Clinton years, the downsizing resulted in the shrinkage and outright collapse of numerous bargaining units, especially in the Department of Defense. In addition, not everyone was thrilled about partnering. Some viewed it as tantamount to surrender. One of the most common fears expressed by union representatives was that their members would think that they had "sold out to" or "gone to bed with" management. Proponents of this view believed that it was necessary to protect their adversarial flank on the collective bargaining front.

We provide a snapshot of the unions' membership picture, comparing 1991 to 2001, in Table 5. As can be seen, each union suffered a noticeable drop in representation, which substantially reflected the downsizing implemented as part of reinvention in the case of the AFGE and the NTEU. Both these unions saw their memberships climb, however (each worked hard on organizing in the 1990s), and thus their effective free-riding rates dropped, reflecting an improvement in their institutional strength or position. The situation at the NFFE, however, is in a league all by itself. The union's representational numbers were more than halved in 10 years, due to unit raids and agency reductions. At the same time, its membership dropped to a pathetic 7,528, yielding a phenomenal 90 percent free-riding rate. For all intents and purposes, the NFFE ceased to be a viable concern. To survive, it had no choice but to affiliate with a larger union. It did so in the late 1990s, joining the International Association of Machinists (IAM).

From these data, one can conclude that partnerships have had modest impacts on the unions' positions. The top three unions have lost representation position, in significant part due to the downsizing that accompanied reinvention. However, both the AFGE and the NTEU

Union Institutional Strength

The last area we look at in terms of partnership impacts is that of union institutional strength. In this regard, the key indicator in the federal sector is union membership, especially in light of the open-shop nature of the federal employment. The unions did not go into partnership blindly. They hoped that their support for reinvention would result in improvements in their institutional position. This is one of the reasons why they eagerly sought some type of union-security legislation, only to have their hopes vanquished by political indifference and ideological opposition (once the Republicans won the Congress in 1994). Parenthetically, the unions knew that reinvention and partnership were double-edged swords. In practice, reinvention stressed "costs less" as much as, if not more than, "performs better." This translated into continual pressures to downsize. During the Clinton years, the downsizing resulted in the shrinkage and outright collapse of numerous bargaining units, especially in the Department of Defense. In addition, not everyone was thrilled about partnering. Some viewed it as tantamount to surrender. One of the most common fears expressed by union representatives was that their members would think that they had "sold out to" or "gone to bed with" management. Proponents of this view believed that it was necessary to protect their adversarial flank on the collective bargaining front.

We provide a snapshot of the unions' membership picture, comparing 1991 to 2001, in Table 5. As can be seen, each union suffered a noticeable drop in representation, which substantially reflected the downsizing implemented as part of reinvention in the case of the AFGE and the NTEU. Both these unions saw their memberships climb, however (each worked hard on organizing in the 1990s), and thus their effective free-riding rates dropped, reflecting an improvement in their institutional strength or position. The situation at the NFFE, however, is in a league all by itself. The union's representational numbers were more than halved in 10 years, due to unit raids and agency reductions. At the same time, its membership dropped to a pathetic 7,528, yielding a phenomenal 90 percent free-riding rate. For all intents and purposes, the NFFE ceased to be a viable concern. To survive, it had no choice but to affiliate with a larger union. It did so in the late 1990s, joining the International Association of Machinists (IAM).

From these data, one can conclude that partnerships have had modest impacts on the unions' positions. The top three unions have lost representation position, in significant part due to the downsizing that accompanied reinvention. However, both the AFGE and the NTEU

TABLE 5

Selected Indicators of Union Strength, 1991 and 2001

Union	Year	Representation	Change	Membership	Change	Free-riding ratio
AFGE	1991	642,315		151,000		.76
	2001	582,753	–9%	198,453	+31%	.66
NFFE	1991	146,113		19,451		.87
	2001	68,535	+53%	7,528	–61%	.89
NTEU	1991	151,736		60,269		.60
	2001	139,302	–8%	74,306	+23%	.47

Sources: U.S. Office of Personnel Management 2000, 2002; Gifford 1992; union LM-2 forms.

gained members, and by nontrivial amounts during an era of shrinkage. While partnership may not have caused this, it did not hinder it.

Barriers to High-Performing Partnership

When the agencies were asked to select partnerships for study they were requested to choose partnerships that differed in terms of their effectiveness, from the high to the low end of the continuum. Indeed, the partnership councils varied widely, based on data from interviews and records of meetings and activities they were able to produce. About a half-dozen of these partnerships fell into the high-performance range, though only two were unequivocally so. Another half-dozen were clearly in the low-performing end; in fact, they were dysfunctional. In the process of interviewing council participants and doing background interviews among those involved in developing and implementing partnership policy and practice, we gleaned several features that distinguish high-performing partnerships from their polar counterparts. We were also able to pinpoint the principal barriers to achieving high performance (see Figure 7).

Specifically, the distinctive features of high-performing partnerships are that they are (1) strategic and proactive in outlook; (2) institutionalized, not personality dependent; and (3) focused on achieving the business mission of the agency and competent to lend meaningful advice and guidance. In short, high-performing partnerships anticipated change and were ready to cope with it when it came. They had undergone training and built an infrastructure within the agency and union side to promote partnership. A change in union or agency personnel would not cause the

FIGURE 7
Barriers to High-Performance Partnerships

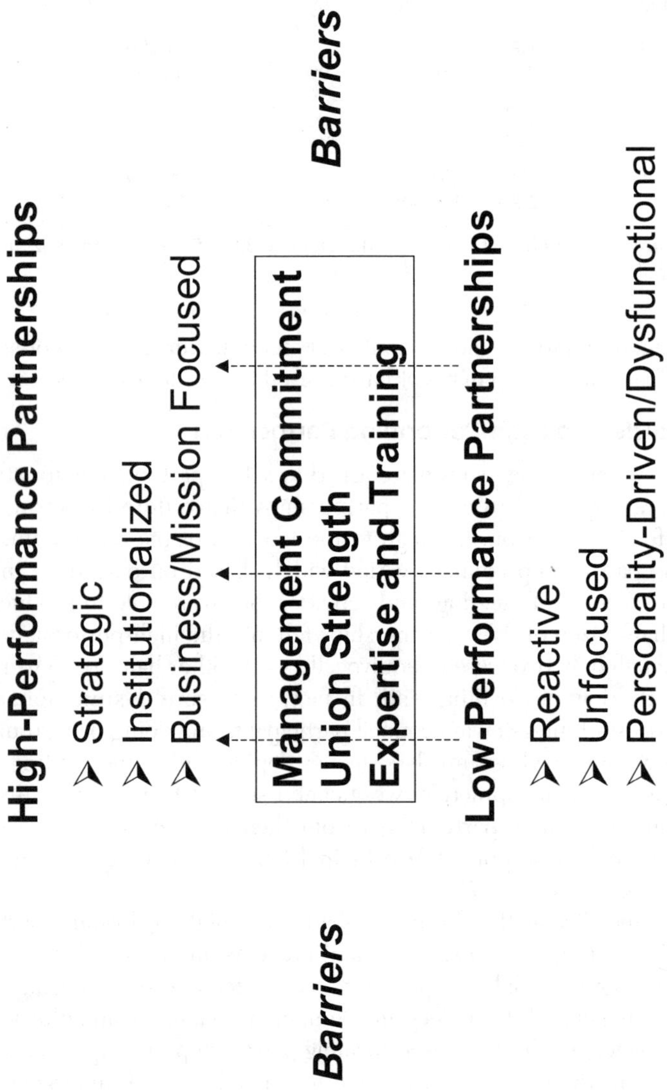

partnership to crumble, unless the change reflected a decided ideological shift away from collaboration toward confrontation. Finally, the partnerships had a much broader interest than personnel or labor relations
matters. They focused on mission and were competent to do so. Where
they lacked expertise, they were able to acquire it.

In marked contrast, the low-performing partnerships were reactive,
unfocused, and personality driven. They had difficulty setting up meetings, determining an agenda (any agenda, let alone a meaningful one),
staying focused on one or two clear goals, and keeping personalities
from causing disruptive behaviors; hidden and petty agendas, or vendet-
tas, pervaded these partnership councils. If there were not an order
mandating them, they would certainly have disappeared. So little interest in or capacity to make them work effectively existed that these partnerships, absent a mandate, might have vanished without any burial.

What factors contribute to such extremes? Invariably, they are systemic. Three in particular emerged as critical. First, high-performing
partnerships enjoyed genuine management commitment, from the very
top (including, where necessary, political appointees). This commitment
translated into the allocation of resources (principally staff) to support
councils and the appointment of quality managers to councils. The union
side picked up this commitment—or its absence—almost instantly.

Second, and almost as important, the union representatives needed
to have a strong union base behind them. Managers had to *know* that
the representatives spoke for the majority of employees in their unions.
If there were few dues-payers in the unit, management was much less
inclined to engage the partnership except in a reactive, postdecisional
mode. If the union was well represented and chose leaders who were
both responsible and competent, it was in a much stronger position to
garner the management commitment so essential to making partnership
work. Management commitment and union strength worked hand-in-
glove in behalf of partnership.

Finally, it was necessary that both sides have the expertise to act on
matters affecting the agency per se. Union representatives who possessed or had access to expertise about strategic planning, business planning, finance, accounting, and the agency's overall budgetary situation
had a definite leg up on their less-informed counterparts. For real partnership to occur, both management and labor had to have access to
information, knowledge, and analytical capability. If management had a
monopoly on these matters, it had reservations about the wisdom of
involving unions in decisions. A psychology of condescension emerged

and often provoked anger on the other side. Parenthetically, numerous
parties also reported benefiting from *joint* training in interest-based
problem solving, negotiating, and conflict resolution.

New Directions and Next Moves

Predicting the future is obviously hazardous. But if past is prologue,
we can appreciate where things are heading, at least over the next five to
ten years. President Bush's management philosophy and rescission of E.O.
12871 are noteworthy in this regard. Bush's Management Agenda does
not mention partnership (see Figure 8). It is literally devoid of mention of
labor-management relations. We might surmise unions are a cipher, a
topic antithetical to the paramount need for managerial flexibility.

FIGURE 8
Bush-Cheney's Management Agenda
vis-à-vis Clinton-Gore's Reinvention

Dimension	Clinton-Gore	Bush-Cheney	Compatibility
Purpose	Reinvent	Reform	High
Principles	Putting customers first	Citizen-oriented	High
	Cutting red tape	Results-oriented	High
	Cutting back to basics	Market-based	High
	Empowering employees	?	?
Labor-management relations	Partnership-shared decision making	Managerial discretion or freedom	Low

Sources: NPR 1993; U.S. Office of Management and Budget 2001.

In revoking E.O. 12871, President Bush took the advice of a Heritage Foundation report, *Taking Charge of Federal Personnel*, issued
shortly before he took office. The January 10, 2001, report (Nesterczuk,
Devine, and Moffit 2001) adopted a political-administration as opposed
to public-administration model. The political model "emphasizes political responsibility—providing presidential leadership to committed top
political officials and then holding them and their subordinates personally accountable for achievement of the President's election-endorsed
and value-defined program" (Nesterczuk, Devine, and Moffit 2001:5).
This model calls for standing up against the "permanent government,"

whose lifelong members include members of Congress and congressional staff, the civil service bureaucracy, and federal-employee unions. In this model, unions stand in the way of politically driven action. Unsurprisingly, the Heritage report urged revoking E.O. 12871:

> President Clinton's effort to "reinvent government" resulted in significant changes, but the net effect has been to undermine strong political management and cabinet government. In order to make promised reductions in staffing, he formed an alliance with federal unions. He issued Executive Order 12871 which established "labor-management partnerships" that elevated federal unions to equality with agency management.

> The new President will need to revoke this executive order and demonstrate from the outset that his approach to reform emphasizes political accountability to the taxpayers. (Nesterczuk, Devine, and Moffit 2001:i)

President Bush not only revoked E.O. 12871, but also ordered the revocation of "any order, rules, regulations, guidelines, or policies implementing or enforcing Executive Order 12871 of October 1, 1993"(Bush 2001). The message was unambiguous: neither the White House nor the Director of the Office of Personnel Management nor the heads of executive agencies were obligated or expected to partner with unions. When combined with the president's interest in promoting the "freedom to manage," it becomes even clearer that the approach to labor-management relations advocated by this administration is at best laissez-faire.

In reality, however, it is the "at best" that rings loud. The tragic events of September 11, 2001, have occasioned two policy developments that foretell the direction of labor-management relations in the federal service (for the foreseeable future). Specifically, in creating the Transportation Security Administration (TSA) and the DHS, the administration has pushed for maximum managerial flexibility. What this means in practice is that the administration wants the unfettered option of declaring certain groups of federal employees ineligible for the protections of the FSLMRS to unionize and bargain collectively.

More specifically, the statute creating the DHS states that any human resource system should "(1) be flexible; (2) be contemporary." Employees in the new DHS are protected by the FSLMRS unless the president determines that "(A) the mission and responsibilities of the agency (or subdivision) materially change; and (B) a majority of the employees have as their primary duty intelligence, counterintelligence, or investigative work directly related to terrorism investigation" (Homeland Security Act of 2002, Public Law 107–296). The new secretary of the DHS may waive protections under the FSLMRS based on these criteria. If this were to be done, the secretary would be required to meet and consult with the union representatives of affected employees. The secretary is also required to establish an ongoing procedure to involve employee representatives in the design of the labor relations and human resources system at DHS.

What does all this mean and portend? It means a highly decentralized approach to dealing with unions. Collaboration or partnership is entirely a matter up to agency and department heads. If unions can convince them that it is in their self-interest to partner, then collaboration may prevail, but without explicit policy support from the White House, OPM, or OMB. The new DHS includes language that is supportive of collaboration but leaves the details up to the new secretary. The DHS statute says that the "Secretary and the [OPM] Director shall—(i) develop a method for each employee representative to participate in any further planning or development which might become necessary" (Homeland Security Act of 2002, Public Law 107–296).

From this vantage point, one might surmise that unions in the federal sector will suffer. Tobias (2003:3) has asserted that collaboration is essential to future union growth in the federal sector: "Unions will have great difficulty organizing the emerging federal work force if unions can't participate with managers and employees in creating challenging work and rewarding successful achievements." In a collaborative frame, the former president of the NTEU goes on to say, "Federal unions may assume the partnership role they have long sought, with attendant increases in the number and share of employees unions represent" (Tobias 2003:4).

To us, the labor relations direction this administration prefers is a closed question. With the TSA and the DHS, plus the rescission order, the president has made unambiguous moves to reverse the course taken by his predecessor. We envisage a labor relations climate more focused on traditional collective bargaining, with associated adversarialism and avoidance.

At the same time, we are unconvinced that this will shrink the demand for union representation. The effect could be just the opposite. In a climate where management pursues flexibility, employees may choose union representation as a necessary check. Thus, density and membership could rise, except where legal protections are removed, as is possible in the new DHS.

Discussion

Federal sector labor-management relations stand at the crossroads. The choice to compete or collaborate will be made in the new DHS. In making this choice, the parties are well advised to review the extensive experience of partnership during the Clinton-Gore administration. Several meaningful lessons were learned.

First, partnership can improve labor-management communications. Second, it can also contribute to the enhancement of the labor relations climate. Third, partnership has the potential to improve agency performance. Fourth, management commitment and commensurate union strength are essential to realizing the potential of collaboration.

Although the labor-management relations model that prevails in the federal sector is a political decision, it should recognize the potential benefits of partnering. The Homeland Security Act of 2002 requires the secretary of DHS to develop an ongoing mechanism for union involvement in the design of the labor-management relations and human resources system. Secretary Ridge should attempt to capture the best of partnership in such a process.

Note

[1] Unfortunately, per an agreement the participating agencies made with the U.S. Office of Personnel Management, we are not permitted to identify or describe them. The agencies that did participate did so voluntarily in arrangements made with OPM. We had no input or control over who participated.

References

American Federation of Government Employees, National Treasury Employees Union, and National Federation of Federal Employees (AFGE, NTEU, and NFFE). 1993. *Total Quality Partnership—A Vision of the Future.* Washington, DC: AFGE, NFFE, and NTEU.

Ballard, Tanya. 2001. "OPM Rescinds Guidance on Labor-Management Partnerships." *Government Executive Magazine.* March 1. <http://www.govexec.com>.

Ban, Carolyn. 1995. "Unions, Management, and the NPR." In Donald F. Kettl and John J. DiIulio, eds., *Inside the Reinvention Machine: Appraising Governmental Reform.* Washington, DC: Brookings Institution, pp. 131–51.

Belman, Dale, Morley Gunderson, and Douglas Hyatt, eds. 1996. *Public Sector Employment in a Time of Transition.* Madison, WI: Industrial Relations Research Association.

Burton, John F., Jr. 1979. "The Extent of Collective Bargaining in the Public Sector." In Benjamin Aaron, Joseph R. Grodin, and James L. Stern, eds., *Public-Sector Bargaining.* Washington, DC: Bureau of National Affairs, pp. 1–43.

Bush, George W. 2001. Executive Order 13203. "Revocation of Executive Order and Presidential Memorandum Concerning Labor-Management Partnership." The White House. February 17.

GOING PUBLIC

Civil Service Reform Act of 1978. 5 U.S.C. Chapter 21, Public Law 95-454. October 13.

Clinton, William J. 1993. Executive Order 12871. "Labor-Management Partnerships." The White House. October 1.

Cooke, William N. 1989. "Improving Productivity and Quality Through Collaboration." *Industrial Relations,* Vol. 28, no. 2 (Spring), pp. 299–319.

_____.1994. "Employee Participation Programs, Group-Based Incentives, and Company Performance: A Union-Nonunion Comparison." *Industrial and Labor Relations Review,* Vol. 47, no. 4 (July), pp. 594–619.

Cummings, Jeanne, and Carlos Tejada. 2002. "Taft-Hartley Could Bloody Labor and Bush," *Wall Street Journal,* October 11, p. A4.

Dastmalchian, Ali, Paul Blyton, and Raymond Adamson. 1989. "Industrial Relations Climate: Testing a Construct." *Journal of Occupational Psychology,* Vol. 62, pp. 21–32.

deLeon, Linda, and Robert B. Denhardt. 2000. "The Political Theory of Reinvention." *Public Administration Review,* Vol. 60, no. 2 (March/April), pp. 89–97.

Doeringer, Peter B., Linda Kaboolian, Michael Watkins, and Audrey Watson. 1996. "Beyond the Merit Model: New Directions at the Federal Workplace." In Dale Belman, Morley Gunderson, and Douglas Hyatt, eds., *Public Sector Employment in a Time of Transition.* Madison, WI: Industrial Relations Research Association, pp. 163–200.

Federal Aviation Reauthorization Act of 1996. 49 U.S.C. Chapter 401, Public Law 101-264. October 9.

Federal Service Labor-Management Relations Statute of 1978. 5 U.S.C. Chapter 71, Public Law 95-454. October 13.

Freeman, Richard, and James Medoff. 1984. *What Do Unions Do?* New York: Basic Books.

Gifford, Courtney O. 1992. *Directory of U.S. Labor Organizations.* 1992–1993 ed. Washington, DC: Bureau of National Affairs.

Goldberg, Arthur. 1961. "Report of the President's Task Force on Employee-Management Relations in the Federal Service." In U.S. Congress. House Committee on Post Office and Civil Service. 1979. *Legislative History of Labor-Management Relations Statute, Title VII of the Civil Service Reform Act of 1978.* November 19. Washington, DC: GPO.

Harnage, Bobby L. 2002. "Personnel Issues in Establishing the New Department." Statement before the House Select Committee on Homeland Security. July 17. <http://www.afge.org>.

Hart, Wilson. 1961. *Collective Bargaining in the Federal Civil Service.* New York: Harper and Brothers.

Hirschman, A. O. 1970. *Exit, Voice, and Loyalty: Responses to Decline in Firms, Organizations, and States.* Cambridge, MA: Harvard University Press.

Homeland Security Act of 2002. 5 U.S.C. Chapter 71, Public Law 107-296. November 25.

Hurd, Richard W., and Jill K. Kriesky. 1986. "Communications: The Rise and Demise of PATCO Reconstructed." *Industrial and Labor Relations Review,* Vol. 40, no. 1 (October), pp. 115–27.

Kearney, Richard C., and Steven W. Hays. 1994. "Labor-Management Relations and Decision-Making: Toward a New Paradigm." *Public Administration Review,* Vol. 54, no. 1 (January/February), pp. 44–51.

Kennedy, John F. 1962. Executive Order 10988. "Employee-Management Cooperation in the Federal Service." The White House. January 17.

Kettl, Donald F. 1994. *Reinventing Government? Appraising the National Performance Review.* Washington, DC: Brookings Institution.

———. 1998. *Reinventing Government: A Fifth-Year Report Card.* Washington, DC:
Brookings Institution.

Kettl, Donald F., and John J. DiIulio, Jr., eds. 1995. *Inside the Reinvention Machine:
Appraising Governmental Reform.* Washington, DC: Brookings Institution.

Kochan, Thomas A., and Paul Osterman. 1994. *The Mutual Gains Enterprise: Forging a Winning Partnership Among Labor, Management, and Government.* Boston, MA: Harvard Business School Press.

Levine, David L. 1995. *Reinventing the Workplace: How Business and Employees
Can Both Win.* Washington, DC: Brookings Institution.

Light, Paul C. 1999. *The True Size of Government.* Washington, DC: Brookings
Institution Press.

Masters, Marick F. 2001. *A Final Report to the National Partnership on Evaluating
Progress and Improvements in Agencies' Organizational Performance Resulting
from Labor-Management Partnerships.* Unpublished manuscript, University of
Pittsburgh.

Masters, Marick F., and Robert R. Albright. 1993. "Federal-Employee Unions and
Workforce 2000." *International Journal of Public Administration,* Vol. 16, no. 6
(June), pp. 781–92.

Masters, Marick F., Robert Albright, and David Eplion. 2003. "What Did Partnerships Do? Perceptions of the Federal Experience." Unpublished manuscript,
University of Pittsburgh.

Masters, Marick F., and Robert Atkin. 1989. "Bargaining Representation and Union
Membership in the Federal Sector: A Free Rider's Paradise." *Public Personnel
Management,* Vol. 18, no. 3 (Fall), pp. 311–24.

Masters, Marick F., and Robert S. Atkin. 1990. "Public Policy, Bargaining Structure,
and Free-Riding in the Federal Sector." *Journal of Collective Negotiations in the
Public Sector,* Vol. 19, no. 2, pp. 97–112.

National Partnership Council. 1996. *A New Vision for Labor-Management Relations:
A Report to the President on Progress in Labor Management Partnerships.* October. Washington, DC: OPM.

National Performance Review. 1993. *From Red Tape to Results: Creating a Government That Works Better and Costs Less.* Washington, DC: NPR.

Nesbitt, Murray B. 1976. *Labor Relations in the Federal Government Service.* Washington, DC: Bureau of National Affairs.

Nesterczuk, George, Donald J. Devine, and Robert E. Moffit. 2001. *Taking Charge
of Federal Personnel.* Backgrounder No. 1404. January 10. Washington, DC:
The Heritage Foundation.

Nixon, Richard M. 1969. Executive Order 11491. The White House. October 29.

Northrup, Herbert R., and Amie D. Thornton. 1988. *The Federal Government as
Employer: The Federal Labor Relations Authority and the PATCO Challenge.*
Labor Relations and Public Policy Series, No. 32. Philadelphia, PA: University of
Pennsylvania, The Wharton School, Industrial Research Unit.

Osborne, David, and Ted Gaebler. 1992. *Reinventing Government: How the Entrepreneurial Spirit Is Transforming the Public Sector.* New York: Plume.

Postal Reorganization Act of 1970. 5 U.S.C. Chapter 71, Public Law 91-375. August 12.

Rubinstein, Saul A. 2000. "The Impact of Co-Management on Quality Performance: The Case of the Saturn Corporation." *Industrial and Labor Relations Review,* Vol. 53, no. 2 (January), pp. 197–218.

Sheppard, Blair H., Roy L. Lewicki, and John W. Minton. 1992. *Organizational Justice: The Search for Fairness in the Workplace.* New York: Lexington Books.

Suntrup, Edward L., and Darold T. Barnum. 1997. "Reinventing the Federal Government: Forging New Labor-Management Partnerships for the 1990s." In Bruce Nissen, ed., *Unions and Workplace Reorganization.* Detroit: Wayne State University Press, pp. 145–58.

Tobias, Robert. 2003. "The Future of Federal Sector Labor-Management Relations Hinges on Whether the Parties—Congress, Administration, and Unions—Make Decisions to Maximize Their Mutual Interests." *Journal of Labor Research,* forthcoming.

U.S. Congress. House Committee on Post Office and Civil Service. 1979. *Legislative History of Labor-Management Relations Statute, Title VII of the Civil Service Reform Act of 1978.* November 19. 96th Congress, 1st session. Washington, DC: GPO.

U.S. Department of Labor. Office of Personnel Management. 2002. Organization Annual Report. LM-2. Washington, DC: DOL.

U.S. Federal Labor Relations Authority. 1999. *The FLRA at 20 Years.* Washington, DC: FLRA.

U.S. General Accounting Office. 1991. *Federal Labor Relations: A Program in Need of Reform.* Washington, DC: General Accounting Office.

U.S. Office of Management and Budget. 2001. *The President's Management Agenda.* Washington, DC: OMB.

U.S. Office of Personnel Management. 1991, 1992, 1997, 2000, 2002. *Union Recognition in the Federal Government.* Washington, DC: OPM.

———. 1998. *National Partnership Council Update.* December 7. Washington, DC: OPM.

Verma, Anil, and Joel Cutcher-Gershenfeld. 1996. "Workplace Innovations and Systems Change." In Dale Belman, Morley Gunderson, and Douglas Hyatt, eds., *Public Sector Employment in a Time of Transition.* Madison, WI: Industrial Relations Research Association, pp. 201–42.

Walters, Jonathan. 1999. "The Powers of Pay." *Government Executive Magazine,* January 1. <http://www.govexec.com>.

Chapter 7

Can Unions Be Transformational Agents in Public Sector Workplace Redesign?

JEFFREY H. KEEFE
Rutgers University

During the past two decades, the majority of private and public sector employers in the United States have undertaken some form of workplace transformation that encourages employee involvement and participation. Among those efforts, the most effective—as measured by productivity and quality outcomes—are those undertaken in unionized workplaces (Kelley and Harrison 1992; Black and Lynch 2001). Nevertheless, the record of success for most of these transformational programs remains highly uneven and is typically limited. Cappelli and Neumark (2001) reported that high-performance work practices in the private sector are associated with higher compensation costs that may not be offset by productivity improvements, thus dampening employer interest in these programs. Employee reports show mixed results, significantly worse in the public sector. According to Freeman (1996), although an estimated 60 percent of unionized public sector employees participated in employee involvement efforts, compared to 55 percent in the private sector, only one in six believed employee involvement efforts were very effective, compared to one in three in the private sector. Union leaders indicated disappointment with their participation in transformation efforts, as well. In an AFL-CIO–sponsored survey, 82 percent of union leaders evaluated the results of their cooperative efforts as either fair or poor (Levine 1997).

The diffusion of workplace transformation efforts remains a source of considerable debate. Studies of the incidence of these practices rely on surveys of private sector experience with results highly dependent on the questions investigated and the universe sampled. The most common transformation practices are offline employee meetings held for the

211

purposes of information sharing, problem solving, or quality improvement. In the most comprehensive analysis to date, Blasi and Kruse (2001), using the U.S. Census Bureau's National Employer Surveys for 1994 and 1997, reported that 80 percent of private sector work sites with more than 20 employees had such offline meetings in 1994 and 74 percent had them in 1997. They also found that among private sector workers, approximately 52 percent participated in such meetings in 1994 and 55 percent in 1997, indicating broad-based diffusion of these participatory meeting practices. They also investigated the depth of these changes by examining the bundling of practices into what is often described as high-performance work systems. (Such bundling is considered necessary to institutionalize productivity- and quality-enhancement processes.) Blasi and Kruse (2001) reported that only 1 percent of U.S. private sector establishments had adopted a bundle of practices associated with high-performance work systems.

Thus, private sector studies suggest that the diffusion of offline employee participation is widespread, but that practices associated with more fundamental workplace change are not. There is breadth without depth. The evidence also indicates that the diffusion process may have plateaued in the private sector during the mid-1990s (Blasi and Kruse 2001; Osterman 1999). However, union involvement appears to be associated with the success of those efforts that are more ambitious.

Although recent interest in these programs originated in the private sector, employee involvement meetings have become widely diffused throughout both the private and public sectors (Freeman 1996). This is true even though the labor-management relations environment in the public sector is distinctly different from that in the private sector. In contrast with the private sector, for example, public sector union membership has grown during the last 30 years whereas private sector union membership has declined by 50 percent, falling from eighteen million to nine million members. In the public sector, 28 states and the federal government provide legal frameworks for collective negotiations, creating a decentralized system of labor-management relations. In contrast, the private sector is overseen by a single, two-tiered national system of labor relations, embodied in the Taft-Hartley Amendments of the National Labor Relations Act (NLRA). Most public sector laws provide much more stringent restrictions on the use of concerted self-help activity and on the scope of bargaining, particularly over conditions of employment. This may make joint transformation practices more attractive to unions in the public sector.

Through their political involvement, public sector unions participate in the selection of political leaders, who serve in a capacity similar to private sector executives. Politicians more favorably disposed to unions may consider transformation efforts a more positive and effective alternative to privatization. Nonetheless, the challenge in workplace change efforts in the public sector is to reform a very special bureaucracy, the civil service. This bureaucracy may impede organizational performance and stifle flexibility, but it also insulates employees and agencies from political corruption, nepotism, and antilabor politicians. A final factor making work change efforts more complex in the public sector is that the workforce comprises many more professionals and managerial employees who not only are supervised by management, but who may themselves supervise union member–employees.

Nevertheless, while recognizing these differences, I believe that the more intensely studied private sector experience may provide some insights into the challenges facing public sector union leaders engaged in workplace change efforts. The impetus for these programs in both sectors often arises from crisis. In the private sector, the deteriorating competitive position of a firm or facility, which jeopardizes union-represented jobs, frequently stimulates union participation. The impetus for public sector union participation often arises either from a budgetary crisis that threatens layoffs or the privatization of public services.

The Evolution of Union Involvement in Participative Programs

A series of automobile industry studies have tracked the evolution of employee-participation programs and their ability to influence plant performance. Katz, Kochan, and Gobeille (1983) found that quality-of-work-life (QWL) programs were associated with modest improvements in product quality but not in productivity in their survey of 18 General Motors (GM) plants during the 1970s. More-intensive QWL programs produced results no greater than those associated with less-intensive programs. Katz, Kochan, and Weber (1985) studied 25 GM plants during the oil crisis of 1978–1980. They concluded that QWL had no effect on efficiency and a somewhat negative effect on quality. Katz, Kochan, and Keefe (1987) studied the performance changes of 53 GM plants between 1979 and 1986, using more rigorous methods than the earlier studies. They found that both worker and union participation in *technology* decisions was significantly associated with a reduction in the ratio of supervisors to workers, a reduction in labor hours for car assembly, and improvements in product quality. Corporatewide employee involvement and team initiatives, however, had no measurable effects on productivity, quality, or supervisory ratios.

The results of that study underscore the importance of local-union and local-management participation in the design and implementation of participative programs. There, both employee involvement and team systems were programs created through corporate and international union collective bargaining that plants and local unions were expected to implement, often under considerable pressure and the promise of rewards from above. There were no officially sanctioned programs for participation in technology decisions, however. Union and worker participation on technology questions originated at the local level. This locally initiated participation improved operating performance substantially—as measured by the corporation's plant-level productivity and quality data—whereas the official programs had no measurable performance effect (Keefe and Katz 1990). This result reinforces Cook's (1990) survey findings regarding the importance of local union leadership's involvement as possibly the most critical factor for program success.

The auto industry studies suggest that both managements and unions were continually learning how to improve performance through participation. The research based on 1970s data found no effect on productivity and mixed results on quality. The research using data from the early and mid-1980s found no impact from the corporatewide programs, but positive outcomes from locally initiated cooperation on technology issues. The most recent data show that the more comprehensive the joint activity, the larger the economic benefit from participation. The Dunlop Commission (1994) concluded, based on its review of this research, that if participation remains limited in scope and isolated in specific shop-floor programs, it will not have a significant impact on firm performance. Further evidence of the benefits of union participation is provided by the GM-UAW partnership at Saturn, the ultimate experiment in labor-management relations to date. The major source of Saturn's success (improved coordination and quality) arises from greater levels of lateral communication facilitated by the union comanagers (Rubinstein 2000).

Participation programs not only affect productivity and quality directly, but they may also have indirect effects by influencing the tenor of labor-management relations. Worker-participation programs have generally been associated with reductions in grievance rates (Ronchi 1981; Havlovic 1991). Lower levels of grievance activity have been found to improve product quality and plant productivity (Katz, Kochan, and Gobeille 1983; Katz, Kochan, and Weber 1985; Nosworthy and Zabala 1985; Cutcher-Gershenfeld 1991). Productivity in union steel mills having an average number of grievances was 1.2 percent lower than that in mills with no grievances, for example, according to Ichniowski (1986).

Another factor that may result in quality improvements and increased productivity is improving employee attitudes through participation. Nosworthy and Zabala (1985) estimated that between 1959 and 1976 a 10 percent annual improvement in worker attitudes and behavior would have translated into a 3–5 percent reduction in the annual unit costs of production in U.S. automobile manufacturing. Central to improving worker attitudes is constructing positive employee-supervisory relations. In a study that found a positive independent effect on employee-supervisory relations for workplaces that had active teams, Cook (1990) concluded that the single most important factor in improving employee-supervisory relations was union leader involvement in joint labor-management steering committees.

The Importance of Unions in the Success of Participation Programs

A growing number of studies have found that local union involvement in workplace transformation programs has significantly improved labor productivity, product quality, labor-management relations, and outcomes that are important to employees, such as employment security. Eaton and Voos (1992) found that unionized workplaces were more likely to be engaged in substantive participation processes, such as teams and employee-involvement committees, than nonunion workplaces. These joint substantive efforts were expected to yield productivity improvements. Levine and Tyson (1990:197–98) reached a similar conclusion, finding that substantive participation usually had a positive effect on productivity. They identified several characteristics of a firm's industrial relations, each one strongly associated with unionization, that were likely to influence how employee participation positively affected productivity over time.

Other studies have found that participation may work best when it takes the form of union-management joint action, as opposed to unilateral management imposition of teamwork (Bluestone and Bluestone 1992:184–85). A national survey of manufacturing managers found that the involvement of union leaders in participative programs significantly improved firm performance in quality, productivity, and the quality of supervisory and employee relations (Cook 1990). Consistent with this perspective, unionized companies with joint committees were found to have significantly higher productivity than nonunion companies with such committees (Kelley and Harrison 1992). Unionized firms with jointly administered employee-participation programs achieved quality improvements that were greater than those achieved by nonunion firms, although the difference was not statistically significant (Cook 1992). Union support for, and involvement in, workplace programs also increased the amount of innovation underway in unionized plants (Kochan, McKersie, and Chalykoff 1986). Managers in unionized firms reported that participation, gain sharing, and joint labor-management committees each significantly contributed to improved performance on productivity, quality, unit labor costs, and profitability (Voos 1987). Union support has also been shown to add credibility to the process and to be critical to program survival and institutionalization (Eaton 1994).

In a 1987 study that examined 86 local unions to determine the role of union influence over participation programs, Eaton (1990) found that local unions affected both the participative process and its outcomes through a variety of channels. The most surprising result of her study indicated that bargaining power was not a significant correlate of union control and influence. Seeking concessions from management on program direction or content did not necessarily translate into influence or control. Significant predictors of union influence included the bargaining structure, the union's resources, the international union's policy, and whether the goal of the program was to save jobs. Her most important finding, however, was that unions were not necessarily constrained by the power environment from exercising influence over the program. This may mean that relatively weak unions can still exercise some control over program outcomes and processes.

Why Do Unions Matter in Workplace Transformation?

Research suggests that unions contribute to the success of workplace transformation programs in a number of ways. First, unions bring the workforce's collective voice into the process (Eaton and Voos 1992). As democratic institutions, local unions aggregate members' preferences through a political process, clarifying and debating alternatives (Freeman and Medoff 1984). The leadership's function is to promote a dialogue by interacting with members and union activists while shaping a new vision of the employment relationship and a new role for the union in the workplace. Through a bottom-up discussion, the local union can build member and union commitment to the transformation process. In the workplace, the union balances program goals and the concerns of both management and workers, and in so doing increases the legitimacy and longevity of the program (Eaton 1994). Tying program outcomes to meaningful goals for each of the stakeholders is important in generating highly motivated participation. Union involvement can ensure that union and worker concerns are actually addressed (Kochan, Katz, and Mower 1984).

Unions also protect represented employees from reprisal through the collectively bargained grievance arbitration procedures, which should reduce employees' concerns about their candid participation (Levine and Tyson 1990). Formal union involvement in workplace transformation aids management in demonstrating its commitment to the process. Management's greatest challenge is continually to reaffirm its credibility and demonstrate its commitment to a participative or quality process (Crosby 1985). By bringing the union into a formal partnership, management signals the importance of workplace transformation for the future success of the organization. Unions provide an institutional mechanism to extend participation to higher levels of the organization, making sure that representational issues that may arise within the workplace can be addressed jointly further up in the managerial hierarchy (Eaton and Voos 1992). Unions reduce status differentials and encourage group cohesiveness, an essential ingredient in promoting effective workplace transformations (Levine and Tyson 1990).

Unions significantly reduce wage differentials within jobs and between workers and managers (Freeman and Medoff 1984). This should facilitate co-equal worker participation without engendering a sense of pay inequity in the process. Unions also seek to overcome status differentials in their efforts to promote member solidarity and a collective identity. Union seniority systems tend to reduce competition among workers. Unionized firms are significantly less likely to rely on merit pay or other individualized pay systems with subjective performance standards that may disrupt participative efforts (one of Deming's 14 points); they are more likely to rely on group-based gain-sharing incentives (Eaton and Voos 1992). Productivity-based gain sharing is more apt to be successful in unionized workplaces (Kaufmann 1991). Unions reduce employee turnover and increase the linkage between employer survival and employee benefits. Unions increase average employee compensation by 20 percent in the private sector (Freeman and Medoff 1984) and 5–10 percent in the public sector (Freeman 1986). Recent efficiency wage studies in economics suggest that these wage differentials can reduce employee shirking and improve productivity and quality because they impose a significant opportunity cost on workers associated with job loss.

Unionized workplaces may already be more productive than nonunion workplaces. In 1978, Charles Brown and James Medoff published the first quantitative analysis of the union-productivity effects; they found a union-productivity differential of 22 percent in U.S. manufacturing industries. A survey of 21 industry-productivity studies found that 15 analyses reported positive union-productivity effects in industries as diverse as construction, cement, hospitals, public schools, metalworking plants, and household furniture. Another 3 industry studies found no union-productivity effects in hospitals, municipal libraries, and banks. One study of sawmills found a negative union-productivity effect and 2 studies of coal found mixed results. After reviewing all these studies, Belman (1992) concluded that unions were associated with higher productivity.

Unionized workplaces have more formal rules and procedures governing daily operations than nonunion workplaces (Freeman 1992). These are often thought to be an obstacle to change. Adler (1993a, 1993b), however, reported that the secret of the success of the GM-Toyota joint venture—New United Motors Manufacturing, Inc., or NUMMI—is worker participation in changing highly detailed rules and procedures that regulate the precise standards of quality achieved in this facility. The UAW workforce is expected to comply with these rules in performing their jobs. Unionized workers, who are more accustomed to following rules (though often frustrated by their inflexibility), may be better suited than nonunion workers to participate in a quality process based on rule making and conformance to standards. Further evidence for this proposition is supplied by union-productivity studies by Clark (1980) and Zigarelli (1994) that found that the union productivity effects were associated with rule changes and tighter coupling of administrative procedures associated with unionization. Slichter, Healy, and Livernash (1960) decided that the single most-important impact of collective bargaining on management was to require management to manage by policy, which in their analysis significantly improved firm performance. Each of these studies indicated that unionization improved management's administrative performance, a factor that may also be helpful to workplace transformation efforts and of central concern to public sector unions and their members.

Unions are the only legally sanctioned form of employee participation that can deal with substantive issues of concern to employees. The

NLRA specifically forbids employer-dominated labor organizations including employee-representation plans that deal with wages, hours, working conditions, or grievances. This prohibition was upheld by the National Labor Relations Board in the highly publicized *Electromation* case, which probably transfers directly to public sector settings (Dilts 1993). In unionized settings, employers must bargain with the union about participation programs that involve mandatory subjects of bargaining. Since most state public sector labor laws are modeled after the NLRA, these prohibitions against employer-dominated labor organizations and the duty to bargain with the union should apply in the public sector (Ball 1996). Current research also suggests that if programs fail to address important topics, such as those that are considered mandatory bargaining subjects, they are less likely to survive. Moreover, employers who unilaterally implement participative programs could find themselves charged with unfair labor practices and required to cease and desist in these efforts. Thus, public sector management needs to involve local union leadership in any successful transformation process.

Local Union Leadership and Union Effectiveness

Union leadership is fundamentally political leadership that depends upon effectively representing and satisfying constituent demands. Hammer and Currall (1988) advanced a stakeholder model of local union leadership that included three dimensions of leadership effectiveness, each from the perspective of one of three constituent groups: the local union members, the employer, and the national union. These three groups place specific demands on the local leadership that reflect their own practical needs and political concerns, and they evaluate the local leadership based on the extent to which the local can satisfy their respective requirements (Hammer and Currall 1988).

The first dimension of effectiveness they call local union strength, which is the ability of the local union leadership to satisfy membership demands. Survey research shows that American workers have tended to focus on better wages, health and pension benefits, and job security as their most important union goals (Strauss and Gallagher 1991). In general, members were more satisfied with union performance on traditional bread-and-butter issues than on quality-of-work-life issues (Kochan, Katz, and Mower 1984). Members were least satisfied with union administration or internal union-member relations. Yet Fiorito, Gallagher, and Fukami (1988) found that membership satisfaction was highly dependent on positive perceptions of good internal union relationships.

The second dimension of union leadership effectiveness in Hammer and Currall's (1988) model is the extent to which the employer's requirements are met. Employers are viewed as the driving force and dominant actors in the transformation of the American industrial relations system (Kochan, Katz, and McKersie 1986). Employers responding to a more competitive environment place new demands on local leaders that go beyond negotiating contracts and handling grievances. The leaders are pressured to abandon the traditional industrial relations model with its job-control unionism and adopt a model that enhances flexibility through worker participation, decentralized bargaining with local autonomy, and broad job classifications. Employers also often seek a constructive and stable labor-management relationship, which facilitates competitive unit labor costs, product quality, customer service, and flexible staffing.

The third dimension of union leadership effectiveness addresses the concerns of the national union. Its primary goal is to strengthen the union, or at least not to weaken it with concession bargaining and substandard local agreements that deviate substantially from other agreements in the industry. A study of NEA locals in Pennsylvania found that when the union president was seen as active, efficient, concerned, and involved in both internal and external union affairs, the local organization was seen as stronger and healthier by national union representatives (Hammer and Wazeter 1993).

The union's internal processes also influence leadership effectiveness. On balance, democracy increases local union effectiveness in representing members' interests (Strauss 1991). Democratic participation in local unions is greatly influenced by the activist core of union stewards and committee members who serve both as intermediary between the union leadership and the rank and file and also as countervailing force preventing the union leadership from becoming autocratic. In many unions the steward-member relationship is the key for democracy.

Consequently, I add a critical fourth dimension of union leadership effectiveness to Hammer and Currall's model, the development of shop stewards and other union activists. Shop stewards play a key role in union-management relations as the rank-and-file leaders in the workplace. No other level of action leadership possesses such intimate, direct contact with the members (Barling, Fullagar, and Kelloway 1992:125). Stewards fulfill the critical function of handling members' grievances and daily conflicts with supervisors and one another. As socialization agents, grievance processors, problem solvers, and communicators, shop stewards have the ability to influence members' attitudes toward, and involvement in, the union (Barling, Fullagar, and Kelloway 1992:145). In addition, union leaders often rely on stewards as their chief source of information about members' attitudes (Strauss 1991), and political challenges to the local union leadership are most likely to come from the shop stewards.

In transformational workplaces, effective local union participation requires local leaders to be able to persuade the stewards of the need for change. Stewards not only exert influence over the rank and file, but they are most likely to serve on joint labor-management committees representing the unions' interests in the transformation process. Local leaders must rely on their own abilities to persuade stewards to adopt an expanded role in leading workplace change. (In this sense, union leadership has been identified as the very essence of leadership. Unlike managers who have formal authority, union leaders must persuade, since their limited power resources are highly dependent on constituent support [Barling, Fullagar, and Kelloway 1992:126]). Stewards can greatly affect a local union's relationship with supervisors and managers, either undermining or augmenting workplace transformation efforts. In general, union stewards have been found to have positive attitudes toward worker-participation programs (Kochan, Katz, and Mower 1984).

Union Ambivalence about Participation Programs

Union participation in transforming work organizations has nevertheless encountered concerns and obstacles from both workers and union activists. Workers are reluctant to support union participation in change efforts because they fear diminution of their working conditions without any real benefit to themselves, the union, or their organization's performance. They fear, for example, that participative programs will produce more stressful work (Parker and Slaughter 1988) or greater management control (Barker 1993). Nonetheless, employee interest in participation programs is now fairly well established. Freeman (1996) reported that interest in participative programs might be even higher among public sector than private sector employees. Survey responses, starting with Kochan, Katz, and Mower's (1984) study, have shown a high level of interest among workers in the issues most central to participation processes. Research has consistently found that employee participation can serve as a stress moderator (Quick, Quick, Nelson, and Hurrell 1997), and Appelbaum, Bailey, Berg, and Kalleberg (2000) found no evidence that the high-performance work systems they studied were associated with higher levels of worker stress.

Nevertheless, when some workers accustomed to job-control union-ism contemplate the prospect of high-performance teams, they react militantly, often ridiculing management and their peers and denouncing any union leader who advocates such changes. They anticipate a loss of their unique identities, their freedom and autonomy, and their well-defined rights and responsibilities. They fear that without the traditional sources of protection provided by their job descriptions and their con-tracts, they will become prey to every capricious whim of their bosses (Zuboff 1988:404).

In addition, participative programs have become stigmatized as an important instrument in employers' union-avoidance strategies (Lawler 1990). The purpose of these strategies is to improve employee satisfac-tion with their employers through participative programs, thereby reduc-ing the likelihood that a union can successfully organize. Such programs are not necessarily designed to improve operating performance, though; their goal is union prevention. The highly publicized *Electromation* (1992: 996) case reemphasized the importance of this strategy. Shortly after the NLRB ordered management to disband its employee-representation plan there, the Teamsters easily won a union-certification election. Not surprisingly, Kochan, McKersie, and Chalykoff (1986), using Conference Board data from 1977 and 1983, found that workplace innovation was less likely in unionized plants, even when the same corporation's union-avoidance strategy relied on participation programs in their new non-unionized facilities. To overcome suspicion, therefore, employers often need to demonstrate a commitment to the union before participative programs can be undertaken jointly.

A segment of organized labor also views participative programs as a device to undermine independent labor organizations. According to this perspective, the purpose of these programs is to allow management slowly to transform unions into employer-dominated labor organiza-tions. Over the past two decades, considerable controversy has brewed about the influence of employee-participation programs on unions, specifically, whether these programs erode member support for their unions. The majority of the reported evidence indicates, however, that on balance local unions were rated as being more effective by their members who were involved in worker-participation processes than by those who were not (Kochan, Katz, and Mower 1984:123). Participative programs had positive outcomes for the union when the union was a joint sponsor of the program (Verma 1989). Participation was also asso-ciated with higher levels of union loyalty (Eaton, Gordon, and Keefe

1992). Grievance-system effectiveness was the single most important predictor of members' attitudes toward their unions, however. Members who perceived the grievance system as effective had greater loyalty and responsibility to the union, were more satisfied with the union, and believed the participation program would not harm the union. In summary, there is no evidence to support the critics' argument that the presence of a participative program undermines workers' support for their union provided that the union maintains its primary role as advocate of union-member interests.

In recent years, new sets of concerns have emerged about participating in workplace transformation efforts among union leaders favorably disposed to these change efforts. First, many union leaders believe management is not prepared to make fundamental changes. They see managers and supervisors as the greatest barrier to these management-initiated efforts (Klein 1988). Successful change efforts produce some real losses in authority and employment security for lower-level managers and supervisors, creating strong incentives for them to undermine the process. These perverse incentives are frequently not addressed in the change-management process. As a result, these programs stall at their initial stages, and union leaders who stake their credibility on selling their members on the importance of the workplace transformation have their integrity undermined when the transformation process stalls.

In many of these programs management salvages its efforts by institutionalizing the least-threatening elements of the transformation effort, the occasional offline work-group meetings for information sharing and problem solving. Many union leaders view these meetings as a positive step toward good management practices, but as substantially less than the fundamental transformation promised by the change-management consultants. Before embarking on a joint transformation effort, union leaders and political executives must assess and challenge management's credibility, determination, and commitment. While unions can improve the likelihood of success, they cannot overcome a lack of commitment by management.

Union leaders who seek to maintain credibility with their members are reluctant to support the change-management hyperbole and quasi-religious fervor often associated with these programs. Many would prefer that management make a careful and sober self-assessment of what change efforts it is willing to support. If these efforts will be limited to occasional offline meetings and joint labor-management discussions, many union leaders would prefer that the process proceed on an informal basis, with neither consultants nor overstatements about fundamental change. They would prefer to be kept informed about the changes under-way and to see clear guidelines for managers to avoid mandatory bargain-ing subjects and to refrain from anti-union remarks. In return, many union leaders would be willing to support management's efforts to improve management. From their view, these offline discussions are an essential part of good management, involving employees and demonstrat-ing respect for their ideas and contributions.

A second set of union concerns emerges around the scarcity of union-leadership resources and the appropriate roles for union leaders. Perl-man (1929) offered two insights into the dilemmas facing contemporary local union leaders. First, the most distinctive feature of American labor is its never-ending battle to stay organized. Union leaders must devote their scarce leadership resources to organizing, socializing, mobilizing, and building the commitment of their activists and members. They must train activists in the methods of constructive conflict to advance a labor agenda. Second, American workers will cheerfully submit to an almost military union discipline in their struggle against the employer; but they mistrust, obstruct, and turn out union leaders who have become shop-floor bosses under any scheme of worker control.

Union leaders, no matter how committed they are to workplace transformation, cannot become surrogate managers and survive their union's election process. At the most fundamental level, union leaders are expected to represent the members' interest by engaging in conflict with management. Since most members are conflict adverse, they need leaders who are willing to engage in conflict on their behalf, whether with a supervisor or with the larger employer organization. This explains why our research found that members who believed the grievance sys-tem was effective had greater loyalty and responsibility to the union, were more satisfied with the union, and believed participative programs would not harm their union (Eaton, Gordon, and Keefe 1992). Union leaders need to maintain their primary role as advocate of union-mem-ber interests, which often means maintaining a strong grievance proce-dure and being a visible and vocal advocate of the members' interests and concerns to management. This may entail engaging in public con-flict over and around the participation management program itself, when needed. While both parties may be committed to the success of the program, their agreement springs from different interests and requires periodic symbolic reenactment.

While union leaders have a strong interest in solving mismanagement, unions often lack the resources to devote their leadership talents to this endeavor. Mismanagement not only impairs organizational performance, thereby undermining members' job security, it inevitably produces conflict among employee–members over unequal or disparate treatment by management (Hodson 1996, 2001).

To support these efforts, local union leaders need to resolve their scarce–leadership resource and role-violation problems. To that end unions have collectively bargained new resources for these programs. National unions sponsoring these change efforts have negotiated union-appointed joint-program coordinators with an equal number of members appointed by union and management. While insulating the local political leadership, this approach is replete with problems. Local union leaders often hope that their labor-appointed joint coordinators will assist them in organizing their members and in solving their role-violation problems. But unions have encountered loyalty problems and issues arising from the ambiguous roles of these joint coordinators. Because they spend most of their time with their management partners filling quasi-management roles, their loyalty to the union is suspect. In 1986, for example, CWA-appointed QWL coordinators crossed CWA picket lines at AT&T to report to work during a strike, effectively ending the QWL program at AT&T by demonstrating to everyone that they, the union coordinators, had become agents of management within the union rather than agents of the union within management.

Local union leadership must also be concerned about how their participation in, or support for, workplace change efforts affects their members and local union politics. There are debates about how participation may polarize the membership, particularly if resources are flowing to one relatively elite group while others are left out. Activists in the local may also divide philosophically on the participation question. Finally, if there are jobs created for union joint coordinators, the patronage issue needs to be explicitly addressed. Patronage has been used effectively to stabilize the incumbent union leadership. For example, since the 1980s, the GM-UAW contracts have provided for the appointment of joint coordinators by the international union. By the early 1990s, there were as many appointed local and regional joint-coordinator positions as elected local officers and committeemen. The dissidents protested and complained of favoritism in the appointment process. They learned that if the local leadership was loyal to the international officers, they got to participate in the selection of the local's joint coordinators. This provided the loyalists with patronage jobs to reward key supporters and neutralize potential challengers with appointed positions. This patronage system provided local leaders with a strong incentive to support the international union's policies and programs. Dissident local leaders reported coming under pressure from their own activists and supporters who wanted the appointed jobs and from their opponents who could promise these jobs to their supporters, if elected. Eventually, these patronage appointments solidified the support for the international and stabilized the local unions, even in the face of massive employment losses.

On the other hand, disputes over patronage can also destabilize local leadership. Central to the defeat of the original local UAW president at Saturn, for example, were charges of patronage in how he allocated the 400 UAW comanager jobs at Saturn. While these joint coordinator positions represent a political innovation that distances the political leadership from management, they do not fully solve the scarce–leadership resources and role-violation problems that confront local union leaders when they embark on transformational efforts.

Finally, as a result of traumatic plant-closing experiences in manufacturing, skepticism pervades union ranks about corporate intentions for these programs. Based upon my own experiences, discussions, and observations of older manufacturing plants, some joint union-management programs have been cynically but successfully used by corporations as an end-game strategy in closing facilities that require a skilled and experienced workforce for their continued operation. In these scenarios corporate planners decide to relocate production, triggering a multiyear implementation process. In the older, home facility, the union, managers, and workers are told that—because of their high wage and benefit costs and low productivity—they are losing out to the competition. As a result, concessions are negotiated and a joint productivity program is undertaken. Productivity and performance improve and costs are reduced, but in the end it is not enough, and the facility closes—with a highly profitable end game for the corporation. By promoting and relying on false hopes, the facility successfully retains its highly productive workforce until it closes, making a seamless transition for the company. But for the workers, the union, and the local community their good faith efforts cannot, and were never going to be able to, prevent a devastating loss. These end-game programs have generated skepticism about the misuse of these processes.

Nonetheless, union concerns about the potentially negative effects of participative programs have not impeded the diffusion of such programs in unionized workplaces. Recent surveys suggest that since the late 1980s, roughly half of both unionized and nonunionized firms in the private sector have established formalized participation programs (U.S. GAO 1987; Delaney, Lewin, and Ichniowski 1989; Cook 1990, 1992; Osterman 1994, 1999). Unionized firms were at least as likely to have adopted new flexible practices as nonunion firms (Eaton and Voos 1992; Osterman 1994). The practices adopted, however, were quite varied: no one pattern emerged. The research provides no support for the notion of a linear movement away from Taylorist and mass-production models of work organization (Appelbaum and Batt 1994:68).

The Research on Local Union Leadership

While the research suggests that local union leadership support and involvement yield positive returns to participation programs, we know relatively little about the dimensions of this local leadership activity. In the United States, there is no research literature on what constitutes effective local-union leadership. The few studies published on American local unions (e.g., Cook 1963; Sayles and Strauss 1953) focused on the internal political environment of local leaders and not on the dimensions of leadership or leadership skills (Hammer and Currall 1988).

Transformational Leadership

In the 1980s, as U.S. companies restructured in order to survive in the face of increasing economic competition from foreign companies, leadership scholars began to focus on the role of leaders in the transformation and revitalization of organizations (Yukl 1989). In 1978, the political scientist James MacGregor Burns advanced the theory of transformational leadership, which has served as the basis for a major leadership research program. Transformational leadership refers to the process of influencing major changes in the attitudes and assumptions of organization members and building commitment for the organization's mission, objectives, and strategies. Transformational leaders empower subordinates to participate in the process of transforming the organization. Burns contrasted transformational leadership with transactional leadership under which followers are motivated by appeals to their self-interest and laissez faire leadership styles.

Since union leaders are political leaders, often without transactional resources, their circumstances require that they master transformational leadership skills. In fact, they tend to score high on transformational leadership attributes, although only one published study has systematically applied the transformational leadership model to unions. Fullagar, McCoy, and Shull (1992) studied how transformational leadership developed commitment to the union among apprentices who were new union members. Transformational leadership characteristics were strong predictors of the apprentices' subsequent union commitment and union attitudes. The authors found that both leader charisma and individual consideration facilitated the socialization of new union members and helped develop positive union attitudes. Barling, Fullagar, and Kelloway (1992) and Clark (2000) believe that effective union leaders place greater emphasis on the use of transformational leadership to gain strong personal identification with the goals and objectives of the union, and to encourage members to transcend their own self-interests and become more active and ideologically identified with organized labor. Unions rely more on transformational leadership than their managerial counterparts. This may partially explain why union involvement is critical for the success of workplace transformation efforts.

Challenges of Successful Transformations: Roles of Leaders

During the last two decades, over 60 percent of unionized public sector employees have participated in some form of employee-involvement program, and a majority of public sector employers have undertaken some form of workplace transformation process that encourages employee participation. The most effective are those undertaken in unionized workplaces. The research literature demonstrates that union participation in major transformation efforts improves the likelihood of their success.

Public sector union membership has been growing during the last 30 years. Most public sector laws provide stringent restrictions on the scope of bargaining, however, particularly over conditions of employment. This narrow scope of bargaining may make joint labor-management transformation practices particularly attractive to public sector unions. On the other hand, the challenge for public sector workplace change is to reform a very special bureaucracy, the civil service. The civil service bureaucracy may impede management flexibility, but it often provides some meaningful protections to employees.

Unions can contribute to the success of workplace transformation programs in a number of ways. In particular, unions bring the workforce's collective voice into the process. As democratic institutions, local unions aggregate members' preferences through a political process, clarifying and debating alternatives. Unions also protect represented employees from reprisal through the collectively bargained grievance arbitration procedures.

Union leadership is fundamentally political leadership that depends on representing and satisfying constituent demands. Union leaders tend to score high on the transformational leadership attributes that are often identified as necessary in workplace-change programs. This may partially explain why union involvement is critical for the success of workplace transformation efforts. Unions by law are democratic institutions. Local union leadership must be able to persuade stewards and activists that they need to adopt an expanded role in leading workplace change. Stewards greatly affect a local union's relationship with supervisors and managers, either undermining or augmenting workplace transformation efforts. In general, union stewards have positive attitudes toward worker-participation programs.

Union leadership resources are scarce, and members have a strong sense of the appropriate roles for their leaders to play. Role violators are often punished. Union leaders are expected to represent their members' interests and maintain their primary role as advocates, maintaining a strong grievance procedure and being visible and vocal advocates of the members' interests and concerns to management. This may entail engaging in public conflict over the participation-management program itself, when needed. No matter how committed they are to workplace transformation, union leaders cannot become surrogate managers and still survive their union's election process.

Many union leaders believe management is not prepared to make fundamental changes. In fact, managers and supervisors are sometimes the greatest barrier to these management-initiated change efforts. If successful, these change efforts can result in losses of authority and employment security for lower-level managers and supervisors, thereby creating strong incentives for them to undermine the process. These perverse incentives must be addressed before any substantial change effort is launched, or the program will likely be sabotaged and fail in its initial stages.

Management in many of these failed programs often salvages its efforts by institutionalizing the least-threatening elements of the transformation effort, like the occasional offline work group meetings for information sharing and problem solving. Although many union leaders view these meetings as a positive step toward good management practices, they represent substantially less than the fundamental transformation often promised. It is crucial for union leaders and agency managers to assess and challenge management's credibility, determination, and commitment before embarking on a joint transformation effort. While unions may improve the likelihood of success, they cannot overcome a lack of commitment by management.

Union leaders who want to support major workplace change efforts also need to resolve the problems of scarce leadership resources and role violations. If these change efforts involve them in the management of the organization, requiring a considerable investment of time and energy in meetings, planning, and discussions, and if they lose sight of their representational responsibilities, they will lose the trust and support of their members and their value to the change process. Thus they may face considerable peril from participating in joint union-management change efforts.

Union leaders who seek to maintain credibility with their members are often reluctant to support the change-management's quasi-religious fervor and overstatements. They would prefer that management make a careful self-assessment of what change efforts it is willing to support and merely proceed on an informal basis if its support is likely to be limited to occasional offline meetings and some joint labor-management discussions. It is important to these union leaders for any potential change programs to have clear guidelines for managers to avoid mandatory bargaining subjects, to refrain from anti-union remarks, and to share information and progress reports. With such guidelines in place, these leaders would be willing to support management's efforts to improve management, realizing that offline discussions can be beneficial as an essential part of good management, involving employees and demonstrating respect for their ideas and contributions. By improving the labor relations climate and employee attitudes, even modest participation programs can result in increased productivity and quality.

References

Adler, Paul. 1993a. "The 'Learning Bureaucracy': New United Motors Manufacturing, Inc." In Barry Staw and Larry Cummings, eds., *Research in Organizational Behavior,* Vol. 15. Greenwich, CN: JAI Press, pp. 111–94.
———. 1993b. "Time and Motion Regained." *Harvard Business Review,* Vol. 71, no. 1 (January-February), pp. 97–108.
Appelbaum, Eileen, Thomas Bailey, Peter Berg, and Arne Kalleberg. 2000. *Manufacturing Advantage: Why High Performance Systems Pay Off.* Ithaca, NY: ILR Imprint, Cornell University Press.
Appelbaum, Eileen, and Rose Batt. 1994. *The New American Workplace.* Ithaca, NY: ILR Press.

Ball, Carolyn. 1996. "Is Labor-Management Cooperation Possible in the Public Sector Without a Change in Law?" *Journal of Collective Negotiations in the Public Sectors*, Vol. 25, no. 1, pp. 23–30.

Barker, James R. 1993. "Tightening the Iron Cage: Concertive Control in Self-Managing Teams." *Administrative Science Quarterly*, Vol. 38, no. 3 (September), pp. 408–37.

Barling, Julian, Clive Fullagar, and E. Kevin Kelloway. 1992. *The Union and Its Members*. New York: Oxford University Press.

Belman, Dale. 1992. "Unions, the Quality of Labor Relations, and Firm Performance." In Lawrence Mishel and Paula Voos, eds., *Unions and Economic Competitiveness*. Armonk, NY: M. E. Sharpe, pp. 41–108.

Black, Sandra E., and Lisa M. Lynch. 2001. "How to Compete: The Impact of Workplace Practices and Information Technology on Productivity." *Review of Economics and Statistics*, Vol. 83, no. 3 (August), pp. 434–45.

Blasi, Joseph, and Douglas Kruse. 2001. "High Performance Work Practices at Century's End: Incidence, Diffusion, Industry Group Differences and the Economic Environment." Working Paper, Rutgers University.

Bluestone, Barry, and Irving Bluestone. 1992. *Negotiating the Future: A Labor Perspective on American Business*. New York: Basic Books.

Brown, Charles, and James Medoff. 1978. "Trade Unions in the Production Process." *Journal of Political Economy*, Vol. 86, no. 3 (June), pp. 355–78.

Burns, James McGregor. 1978. *Leadership*. New York: Harper and Row.

Cappelli, Peter, and David Neumark. 2001. "Do 'High Performance' Work Practices Improve Establishment-Level Outcomes?" *Industrial and Labor Relations Review*, Vol. 54, no. 4 (July), pp. 737–75.

Clark, Kim B. 1980. "The Impact of Unionization on Productivity: A Case Study." *Industrial and Labor Relations Review*, Vol. 33, no. 4 (July), pp. 451–69.

Clark, Paul. 2000. *Building More Effective Unions*. Ithaca, NY: ILR Imprint, Cornell University Press.

Cook, Alice. 1963. *Union Democracy: Practice and Ideal*. Ithaca, NY: ILR Press.

Cook, William. 1990. *Labor-Management Cooperation: New Partnerships or Going in Circles?* Kalamazoo, MI: Upjohn Institute.

————. 1992. "Product Quality Improvement Through Employee Participation: The Effects of Unionization and Joint Union-Management Administration." *Industrial and Labor Relations Review*, Vol. 46, no. 1 (October), pp. 119–34.

Crosby, Philip B. 1985. *Quality Without Tears*. New York: Plume Publishing.

Cutcher-Gershenfeld, Joel. 1991. "The Impact on Economic Performance of a Transformation of Workplace Relations." *Industrial and Labor Relations Review*, Vol. 44, no. 2 (January), pp. 241–60.

Delaney, John, David Lewin, and Casey Ichniowski. 1989. "Human Resource Policies and Practice in American Firms." BLMR 137. Washington, DC: U.S. DOL, Bureau of Labor-Management Relations.

Dilts, D. 1993. "Labor-Management Cooperation in the Public Sector." *Journal of Collective Negotiations in the Public Sector*, Vol. 22, no. 4, pp. 305–11.

Dunlop Commission. 1994. *Fact Finding Report: Commission on the Future of Worker-Management Relations*. May. Washington, DC: U.S. DOL and U.S. DOC.

Eaton, Adrienne. 1990. "The Extent and Determinants of Local Union Control of Participative Programs." *Industrial and Labor Relations Review*, Vol. 43, no. 5 (July), pp. 604–20.

————. 1994. "Factors Contributing to the Survival of Employee Participation Programs in Unionized Settings." *Industrial and Labor Relations Review,* Vol. 47, no. 3 (April), pp. 371–89.

Eaton, Adrienne, Michael Gordon, and Jeffrey Keefe. 1992. "The Impact of Quality of Work Life Programs and Grievance System Effectiveness on Union Commitment." *Industrial and Labor Relations Review,* Vol. 45, no. 3 (April), pp. 591–604.

Eaton, Adrienne, and Paula Voos. 1992. "Unions and Contemporary Innovations in Work Organization, Compensation, and Employee Participation." In Lawrence Mishel and Paula Voos, eds., *Unions and Economic Competitiveness.* Armonk, NY: M. E. Sharpe, pp. 173–216.

Electromation, Inc., 309 NLRB 990 (1992), *enforced,* 35 F.3d 1148 (7th Cir. 1994).

Fiorito, Jack, Daniel Gallagher, and Cynthia Fukami. 1988. "Satisfaction with Union Representation." *Industrial and Labor Relations Review,* Vol. 41, no. 2 (January), pp. 294–307.

Freeman, Richard. 1986. "Unionism Comes to the Public Sector." *Journal of Economic Literature,* Vol. 24, no.1 (March), pp. 41–86.

————. 1992. "Is Declining Unionization in the U.S. Good, Bad or Irrelevant?" In Lawrence Mishel and Paula Voos, eds., *Unions and Economic Competitiveness.* Armonk, NY: M. E. Sharpe, pp. 143–69.

————. 1996. "Through Public Sector Eyes: Employee Attitudes toward Public Sector Labor Relations in the U.S." In Dale Belman, Morley Gunderson, and Douglas Hyatt, eds., *Public Sector Employment in a Time of Transition.* Madison, WI: IRRA Research Volume, pp. 59–83.

Freeman, Richard, and James Medoff. 1984. *What Do Unions Do?* New York: Basic Books.

Fullagar, Clive, D. McCoy, and C. Shull. 1992. "The Socialization of Union Loyalty." *Journal of Organizational Behavior,* Vol. 13, no. 1 (January), pp. 12–26.

Hammer, Tove Helland, and Steven Currall. 1988. "Leadership Effectiveness in Local Unions: The Role of Union Officers in a Changing Industrial Relations Environment." Unpublished manuscript, Cornell University.

Hammer, Tove Helland, and David Wazeter. 1993. "Dimensions of Union Effectiveness." *Industrial and Labor Relations Review,* Vol. 46, no. 2 (January), pp. 302–19.

Havlovic, Stephen. 1991. "Quality of Work Life and Human Resource Outcomes." *Industrial Relations,* Vol. 30, no. 3 (Fall), pp. 469–79.

Hodson, Randy. 1996. "Dignity in the Workplace under Participative Management: Alienation and Freedom Revisited." *American Sociological Review,* Vol. 61, no. 4 (October), pp. 719–38.

————. 2001. *Dignity at Work.* New York: Cambridge University Press.

Ichniowski, Casey. 1986. "The Effects of Grievance Activity on Productivity." *Industrial and Labor Relations Review,* Vol. 40, no. 1 (October), pp. 75–89.

Katz, Harry, Thomas Kochan, and Kenneth Gobeille. 1983. "Industrial Relations Performance, Economic Performance, and Quality of Working Life Efforts." *Industrial and Labor Relations Review,* Vol. 37, no. 1 (October), pp. 3–17.

Katz, Harry, Thomas Kochan, and Jeffrey Keefe. 1987. "Industrial Relations and Productivity in the U.S. Automobile Industry." *Brookings Papers on Economic Activity.* Special Issue on Microeconomics. Vol. 1987, no. 3, pp. 685–715.

Katz, Harry, Thomas Kochan, and Mark Weber. 1985. "Assessing the Effects of Industrial Relations and Quality of Work Life Efforts on Organizational Effectiveness." *Academy of Management Journal,* Vol. 28, no. 3 (September), pp. 509–26.

Kaufmann, Roger. 1991. "The Effects of IMPROSHARE on Productivity." *Industrial and Labor Relations Review,* Vol. 45, no. 2 (January), pp. 311–22.

Keefe, Jeffrey, and Harry Katz. 1990. "Job Classifications and Plant Performance." *Industrial Relations,* Vol. 29, no. 1 (Winter), pp. 111–18.

Kelley, Mary Ellen, and Bennett Harrison. 1992. "Unions, Technology, and Labor-Management Cooperation." In Lawrence Mishel and Paula Voos, eds., *Unions and Economic Competitiveness.* Armonk, NY: M. E. Sharpe, pp. 247–86.

Klein, Janice A. 1988. "The Changing Role of First-Line Supervisors and Middle-Managers." U.S. Department of Labor, Bureau of Labor-Management Relations and Cooperative Programs. Report No. 126. Washington, DC: DOL.

Kochan, Thomas, Harry Katz, and Robert McKersie. 1986. *The Transformation of American Industrial Relations.* New York: Basic Books.

Kochan, Thomas, Harry Katz, and Nancy Mower. 1984. *Worker Participation and American Unions: Threat or Opportunity?* Kalamazoo, MI: W. E. Upjohn Institute.

Kochan, Thomas, Robert McKersie, and John Chalykoff. 1986. "The Effects of Corporate Strategy and Workplace Innovations on Union Representation." *Industrial and Labor Relations Review,* Vol. 39, no. 4 (July), pp. 487–501.

Lawler, John J. 1990. *Unionization and Deunionization: Strategy, Tactics, and Outcomes.* Columbia: University of South Carolina Press.

Levine, David, and Laura D'Andrea Tyson. 1990. "Participation, Productivity, and the Firm's Environment." In Alan Blinder, ed., *Paying for Productivity.* Washington, DC: Brookings Institution, pp. 183–237.

Levine, Marvin, 1997. "The Union Role in Labor-Management Cooperation." *Journal of Collective Negotiations in the Public Sector,* Vol. 26, no. 3, pp. 203–22.

Nosworthy, J. R., and Craig Zabala. 1985. "Work Attitudes, Worker Behavior, and Productivity in the U.S. Automobile Industry." *Industrial and Labor Relations Review,* Vol. 38, no. 4 (July), pp. 544–57.

Osterman, Paul. 1994. "How Common Is Workplace Transformation and Who Adopts It?" *Industrial and Labor Relations Review,* Vol. 47, no. 2 (January), pp. 173–88.

———. 1999. *Securing Prosperity: The American Labor Market, How It Has Changed, and What to Do About It.* Princeton, NJ: Princeton University Press.

Parker, Mike, and Jane Slaughter. 1988. *Choosing Sides: Unions and the Team Concept.* Boston: South End Press.

Perlman, Selig. 1929. *A Theory of the Labor Movement.* Philadelphia, PA: Porcupine Press.

Quick, James Campbell, Jonathan D. Quick, Debra Nelson, and Joseph J. Hurrell. 1997. *Preventive Stress Management in Organizations.* Washington, DC: American Psychological Association.

Ronchi, Don. 1981. "Quality of Working Life Movement." *Employee Relations,* Vol. 3, no. 3, pp. 2–6.

Rubinstein, Saul. 2000. "The Impact of Co-Management on Quality Performance: The Case of the Saturn Corporation." *Industrial and Labor Relations Review,* Vol. 53, no. 2 (January), pp. 197–218.

Sayles, Leonard, and George Strauss. 1953. *The Local Union*. 2d ed. 1967. New York: Harper and Row.

Slichter, Sumner, James Healy, and E. Robert Livernash. 1960. *The Impact of Collective Bargaining on Management*. Washington, DC: Brookings Institution.

Strauss, George. 1991. "Union Democracy." In George Strauss, Daniel Gallagher, and Jack Fiorito, eds., *State of the Unions*. Madison, WI: Industrial Relations Research Association, pp. 201–36.

Strauss, George, and Daniel Gallagher. 1991. "Union Membership Attitudes and Participation." In George Strauss, Daniel Gallagher, and Jack Fiorito, eds., *State of the Unions*. Madison, WI: Industrial Relations Research Association, pp. 139–74.

U.S. General Accounting Office (GAO). 1987. *Survey of Corporate Employee Involvement Efforts*. Washington, DC: GAO.

Verma, Anil. 1989. "Joint Participation Programs: Self-Help or Suicide for Labor?" *Industrial Relations*, Vol. 28, no. 3 (Fall), pp. 401–10.

Voos, Paula. 1987. "Managerial Perceptions of the Economic Impact of Labor Relations Programs." *Industrial and Labor Relations Review*, Vol. 40, no. 2 (January), pp. 195–208.

Yukl, Gary. 1989. *Leadership in Organizations*. 2d ed. Englewood Cliffs, NJ: Prentice-Hall.

Zigarelli, Michael. 1994. "Unionization and School Effectiveness." Diss., Rutgers University.

Zuboff, Shoshana. 1988. *In the Age of the Smart Machine: The Future of Work and Power*. New York: Basic Books.

CHAPTER 8

The Modern Guild: The Prospects for Organizing around Quality in Public Education

CHARLES KERCHNER
Claremont Graduate University

Some years ago my wife and I happened upon a silversmith's shop in a small town in Ireland. We were greeted by a radio tuned to an Irish-language station and then by the proprietor, a fiery nationalist who spoke of Cromwell's men and "blood flowing down the streets and splattering against this very shop" as if it had happened yesterday. He spoke just as passionately about his silver: beautiful pieces, many with contemporary interpretations of ancient Celtic designs. As he brought out one particularly striking piece, he turned it so that the marks on its base were visible. "Never buy without these," he said. "This one is my mark; it shows the pride I take in my work. The middle one is the government mark; it shows that the silver is pure. The last one is the guild hallmark; it shows that I am a member and that other artisans recognize the piece's quality."

The three marks on the silver goblet's base provide a basis for discussing contemporary unionism among public school teachers in the United States: personal ability and pride, government regulation, and a collective judgment about quality. Quality is the problem of today for American public schools. American unionism has historically been pragmatic, focused on the problems of the day. So now producing quality has become union work.

Producing quality is not a question of returning to some golden age; public schools are better in many ways than they ever were (Lint and Dunbar 1990) More students graduate from high school and more go to college than was ever the case, and this is happening in the face of a huge immigration bulge and increasing economic inequity and class segregation. But both the academic standards and the country's workforce needs have shifted substantially in the last 30 years. Now both perseverance in elementary and high school and achievement are required for a job that will allow a graduate to support a family above the poverty level.

For decades, high schools operated on a sliding scale of quality expectations. High standards existed for those students headed toward four-year colleges, particularly selective ones. Lower standards were tolerated for others (Toch 1991). The new aspiration of high standards for all, as opposed to a few, changes everything (Grant and Murray 1996). Even though there are debates about how best to teach reading and math and differences over which of the many school reform programs are best, there is overwhelming evidence that good teaching counts heavily in producing good student outcomes. Moreover, the evidence strongly suggests that simply using a prescriptive "reform package" can go only so far in helping a school move forward. Scripted teaching and coherence created by a program imported into the organization can be effective in awakening a school that is flat on its back. But the more a school advances toward universal high standards, the more teaching is required to move from enacting routines developed by others and toward highly skilled work involving innovation, passion, and adaptivity.

The current question for teacher unions is whether they will continue to enforce and amplify the existing relationships and industrial division of labor or whether they will organize around the principles of craft, artistic, or professional workplaces. In a larger sense, the question is whether teacher unions can lead in creating a new institution of public education rather than continue to rally around anger caused by the flaws in the current system.

The recent history of reforms leaves the question in the balance. It is easy to point to interesting examples of reforms, and it is possible to find clusters of reforms that begin to reinforce one another, building what organizational designers call a virtuous circle, a series of self-reinforcing reforms. It is equally easy to note the very slow spread of reforms and their treatment by the national and state union organizations as optional activities, tolerated but not particularly encouraged. Barriers to change can be found in the culture of teachers and school administrators and in current organizational arrangements, but most of all in the patterning effect of contemporary labor law and policy, a topic addressed in the second half of this chapter.

The Guilds and Contemporary Teacher Unions

Guilds grew within a system of artisanal production in which the worker was responsible for production from beginning to end, as the first column in Table 1 shows. A guild worker performed all the phases of production requiring skill and had considerable latitude for how work was to be performed as well as for creativity and innovation, subject to the specifications of a client. This system of production dominated the economy of northern Europe from the late Middle Ages to about 1800, when it was eclipsed by the growth of industrial production.

Teaching has always had elements of artisanal work, and some teacher union locals in the United States have begun to organize around its characteristics. They have started to focus on what has been called the "other half of teaching," the substance of their work as opposed to the conditions under which it takes place. They have begun to define and enact standards for teaching quality, and they are claiming their place as school reformers. While most of the innovation has taken place at the local level, both the American Federation of Teachers (AFT) and the National Education Association (NEA) have officially put them-selves in the quality education business. Both have endorsed peer review, training standards for teachers, and teacher work schedules that treat professional development as part of a teacher's job, not an add-on option. Although often referred to as "professional unionism," the prac-tices that represent these frontiers of teacher unionism reflect the val-ues and traditions of craft and artistic work, as well as the traditional professions (Kerchner and Mitchell 1988). On the frontiers of teacher organization, unions are involved in induction, training, quality assur-ance, and shaping the rewards and incentives for work, much as did the ancient guilds.

Shape of the Worker Organization

Guilds operated as a network of individual producers. The network reached deeply into the lives of its members, in some cases exercising authority over such questions as marriage and standards of personal conduct. There was a training hierarchy of apprentices, journey work-ers, and masters, of course, but masters stood shoulder-to-shoulder in the guild, participating in selecting overmasters, making guild rules, and enforcing guild decisions (Walker 1973).

The literature on postindustrial organizational forms idealizes guilds, which seem a perfect counterpart to new, network-style organizations (Fox 1974a, 1974b; Piore and Sabel 1984; Lawler 1992). Guilds are com-patible with teamwork, a flexible workforce, and the general disintegra-tion of large, vertical organizational forms. But the idealizing of guild forms in education runs up against the reality that for the foreseeable

TABLE 1

Function and Structure of Historic, Current, and Potential Artisan
Organizing Mechanisms

System Characteristic	Historic Guild	Industrial Union	Modern Guild
Union represents worker interest in	Whole production process	Economic and working conditions	Whole production process
Shape of work organization	Network to network organization	Dual hierarchy: labor and management	Participative hierarchy:
	Individual producers	Problems flow upward, decisions downward	Resources and decision making flow downward
			Teachers develop collegial practice, voice in school operations
Union gains power by	Market monopoly	Collective bargaining	Collective bargaining
	Civic legitimacy	Lobbying	Lobbying
		Electoral politics	Joint operations
			Electoral politics
Union operates through			
• standard setting	Exclusive control, subject to limits of practicality	No formal role	Educational standards agreement
• induction	Controls access to apprenticeships	No formal role	Negotiated contract or subsidiary agreements
• professional development	Operates journey worker system	No formal role	
• worker and work quality assurance	Examination prior to acceptance as a master, Hallmark system	No formal role	Joint labor-management oversight
• rewards and incentives	Access to middle class, "a comfortable burgher existence"	Negotiating benefits and salaries weighted by education and years of service	Negotiating amendments to the standard salary schedule

future most teachers will work in large, institutionalized public bureaucracies. They will be employees rather than independent contractors,
and much of their economic security will continue to be tied to their
jobs.

By the time teachers organized in the 1960s and 1970s, the artisanal
organization of society had passed, and so had the era of craft unionism.
Well before teacher collective bargaining spread across the country,
public schools followed a pattern of industrial organization (Tyack 1974;
Tyack and Hansot 1982). The logic of industrial organization created a
clear division between work creation and control, on the one hand, and
task execution, on the other. Under industrial bureaucracy, which was
codified into industrial labor relations, managers asserted control over
the content and design of teaching. In labor relations terms, these were
management rights and not mandatory subjects of bargaining. Frequently, law and custom excluded the content of teaching from the bargaining process or other labor-management agreements altogether.
Strictly interpreted, industrial organization would hold teachers responsible only for the faithful reproduction of lesson plans and classroom
routines developed elsewhere. Invention, creativity, and spontaneity
would not be required or expected and sometimes not even tolerated.
Teacher unions are employer-based, and state labor laws typically try to
restrict their involvement to the economic and work-rule conditions
under which teaching takes place.

Teacher unions developed a hierarchy of their own to interact with
school managers. Building representatives or stewards were part of a
local hierarchy containing both an elected governing board and an executive. Locals combined into states and states into national organizations.
The rules of combination varied substantially, with AFT unions retaining more authority in local organizations and the NEA building more
powerful state organizations, with locals interconnected through a web
of professional staff and regional service centers. Despite these structural differences, though, both unions operate on a dual-hierarchy
model, with the union hierarchy specifically built to match that of management. Problems flow upward, and, despite the union's democratic
form, authority generally flows downward.

Teacher unionism brought workplace democracy to schools but did
not challenge public schooling's bureaucratic structure. If anything,
school administration became more explicitly managerial as terms such
as *management team* or *instructional cabinet* entered the vocabulary of
educators. Particularly in high schools, positions of authority such as

department heads, which were formerly occupied by teachers, became administrative positions. By and large, patriarchal or matriarchal management faded as school leadership became subject to the strictures of contractual work rules and due-process requirements. These strengthened the bureaucracy rather than tearing it down.

Whereas the medieval guilds operated close to the product and production process, teacher unions operated through three processes that worked largely outside the process of teaching: collective bargaining, lobbying, and electoral politics. The AFT, whose membership was concentrated in central cities, became very powerful in local politics, particularly in New York City, Detroit, Philadelphia, Miami, and Pittsburgh, where presidents held office for decades. The NEA built powerful statewide organizations, and in states such as Michigan, New Jersey, and California, they were considered the most powerful political organization in the state. In many they were the largest electoral contributor (Lieberman 1997).

Public school teaching has been relatively isolated work in recent years. Teachers gained control over their work through the separation of their classrooms from the eyes of others, including both school administrators and other teachers. Despite heavy borrowing from the scientific management movement, classrooms never were factories. Furthermore, despite bell schedules and thick policy documents, there is more than a little truth to the teacher refrain that "I'm in charge when the classroom door is closed." In the industrial sense, schools have always been incomplete bureaucracies.

Still, formally, schools are industrial organizations. Industrial unionism in education has operated under the legal fiction that it is possible to cleave between workers' legitimate collective economic and working-condition interests and client service provision, which was made a managerial prerogative. Of course, such a division is impossible. Schools are utterly dependent on teachers not acting like industrial workers, and school organizations are almost always incapable of operating on a literal command-and-control basis. Thus the recent interest in the guild form has arisen.

The promise of the modern guild is to infuse contemporary public bureaucracies with a network form of worker organization and the conspicuous ownership of work that typified ancient guilds. The issue, of course, is whether bureaucracy and network forms can operate at the same time and place. The evidence from the frontiers of teacher unionism is that they can, but that the process of change is difficult and not assured of success.

The modern guild form of teacher union envisages a participative hierarchy under which both union and management keep their hierarchical structures, which may be altered over time. Collective bargaining expands to include education-quality issues. A network structure of labor-management problem-solving committees operates in the school district. Decisions and resources flow downward to individual schools, and teachers gain a more substantive voice in how schools are run.

Union Power and Its Limits

Historically, guilds gained power by controlling the market. They determined who could become a guild producer, and they regulated outputs while seeking quality production. They were not primarily profit maximizers; instead, they sought stability through creating a small number of masters who did not infringe on one another's business. They rejected capitalistic entrepreneurship for the purpose of mass exports and fought against the influx of unskilled labor, the force that would eventually be their undoing once machine production overwhelmed handcraft. Guilds also protected their membership from poverty in case of business problems or illness (Epstein 1991:166–67). To regulate their membership, they imposed fines on producers of substandard goods and on members who hurt their neighboring guild-members' businesses by hiring too many journeymen (cheap labor) or who sold ready-made goods in storefront shops (Shorter 1973:7). In medieval Europe, they represented their members in the marketplace through political power by gaining a seat on the town council (Shorter 1973:6). Thus, guilds held power through both market influence (as a monopoly in many cases) and becoming part of the local ruling order. Guildhalls still dot European town centers as markers of the status and importance of these ancient unions. Even though the guild system led to abuses, it existed in reasonable ecology for centuries and provided an emerging middle class a social counterweight to the aristocracy. Guild members found joy and creativity in their labor, did work for its own sake or because God willed it, and sacrificed individual advantage for the good of the community (Shorter 1973.10–11).

To be sure, the guild system was one of market control, but there were severe limits on the ability of a guild to engage in price gouging or to create shortages of needed goods. Community pressure rose to ease the restrictions on trade and, if they were not heeded, the community found breeches of the community-enforced monopoly justified (Walker 1973:48).

Like the guilds, industrial unions gained power by taking wages out of competition: successfully organizing the majority of an industry's producers meant that workers in one firm made about what those in any other made. The firms could still compete, but not by driving wages down. So long as the industry itself faced little competition from nonunion suppliers, the system improved worker wages and corporate profits simultaneously.

For most of the last century, public schools operated in a similarly protected labor market. Most public schools effectively operated as monopolies in their local areas. Private and religious schools existed throughout the country, but in most locations, public schools held a monopoly over public funds and enrolled the vast majority of students. They were civic institutions, in some ways paralleling the medieval guilds in their position in the local society. And, like the guilds, they were subject to local market controls, particularly the willingness of local property owners to tax themselves. In fact, the unions often moderated their wage demands somewhat when a local tax increase would be required.

How Unions Operate

The stark difference between the medieval guilds and contemporary teacher unions lies not in relative economic power but in the concentration of attention on conditions of work rather than on the content of work itself. Where historic guilds integrated economic concerns for members with control over the production process and protection of its quality, the legally sanctioned role of teacher unions is highly constricted. There is no legally required role for teacher unions in standard setting, induction, professional development, or quality assurance. Yet on the frontiers of teacher unionism, teacher unions are dealing with work content and quality issues, just as have some industrial unions (Rubinstein, Bennet, and Kochan 1993; Rubinstein 2000).

Developing and Enforcing Quality Standards

Medieval guilds embedded standard setting in the work process and in training new members. They controlled the product market. Individuals may have produced oaken barrels or wrought-iron hinges, but they entered into trade under the watchful eyes of the guild. Standards of production were generally maintained not through product testing but through observation of the apprentice work process and the reputation of masters. Poorly trained journeymen would reflect badly on the reputation of the master who had trained them. Many guilds established a system of trademarks through which the quality (or lack thereof) of a member's work would be readily traceable (Epstein 1991:126). Individuals in any area with a reasonable number of items trademarked by a master would know the quality of his work, even if the master lived hundreds of miles away.

Like the medieval guilds, modern prototypes rest on the bedrock of standards. Without standards, teaching will always be subject to scripted teaching programs and the division between the conception of work and its execution. If there are no standards, it is impossible for the union to negotiate a role in developing them, enforcing them, or training teachers to meet them. Only if educational standards are known, and the pedagogy for reaching them is available, can teachers reclaim the artisanal definitions of their job. Standards also make coordination and self-organization easier. They reduce the amount of time and the complexity of interactions between collaborators and make it possible for teachers to interact about education-quality issues without depending on an administrator.

Teacher unions have engaged what is known as the standards movement in two ways. First, they have weighed into the political debate over standards and have worked to convince their skeptical members that standards are both important and good for teachers. Forces on the political left and the political right have opposed curriculum standards. Local control advocates, mostly conservative, fear intrusion of the national government into local schools. The religious right fears the intrusion of values they do not support. Teacher and curriculum innovators oppose standards that will constrain their ability to create a more inquiry-based curriculum. So unions face a difficult situation. Their members like the autonomy of having few external checks on their work, the closed-door phenomenon, but standards advocates, including union members, argue that having known and knowable standards is the only way teachers can gain control of the quality process.

At the national level, the AFT has made standards the key to its quality-schools strategy. Its argument has been that judging school progress is impossible without explicit standards and that school reform without reference to student achievement is impossible. The pressure for standards comes simultaneously with increased use of external tests to measure achievement and to rank schools publicly. In many states, these tests have taken on a high-stakes characteristic, determining whether students graduate from secondary school, for example, or whether they are eligible for admission to colleges and universities. The

NEA supports standards in general but has been more hostile to high-stakes consequences for students and teachers.

The second way teacher unions have engaged in the standards movement is by developing the means to put standards in action. Perhaps the best current example can be found in New York City, where the United Federation of Teachers (UFT) has created a curriculum guide for integrating standards into the classroom. Although published state and city standards had already provided detailed lists of what students should know at each grade level, the UFT-developed standards guide provides detailed building blocks and is what UFT President Randi Weingarten calls a how-to guide (Goodnough 2002). The UFT has invested two million dollars in the curriculum guides, with 70 teachers working on the process over a period of three years. Eventually, the UFT plans to produce a guide for every grade and subject (UFT 2002). The union's newspaper editorialized, "As the UFT sees it, curriculum development is union work" (UFT 2002). Not everyone agrees. A principal told the *New York Times* that the union involvement was "a wolf in sheep's clothing," simply a disguised infiltration into management prerogatives (Goodnough 2002).

Induction

Medieval guilds controlled entrance into the field; contemporary teacher unions do not. Public school teachers generally get their jobs by obtaining prescribed college degrees and state-issued credentials and then passing through a school district hiring process. No job rights move from one employer to another, as is the case in some craft unions. Nevertheless, the leading edge of teacher union practices reveals involvement in recruiting and induction.

In fact, it is not unusual for teacher unions to participate in recruitment activities and have an unofficial hand in hiring. This occurs most frequently during eras of good feeling between labor and management. For example, David Lebow, president of the Montebello Teachers Association, currently participates with his district in all job fairs and other recruitment venues. At the union's urging, the district's human resources department has developed fast-track hiring procedures that allow them to make offers to attractive candidates more quickly than other districts. As a result, Lebow notes, school began that year with faculties of fully credentialed teachers, a rarity in Southern California where working-class school districts frequently have 30–40 percent of their faculties working on emergency credentials (interview with David Lebow, August 2002).

In some locations, unions have taken a strong role in teacher education prior to employment, through cooperative programs with universities. Such programs exist in Minneapolis, Cincinnati, Columbus, Miami–Dade County, San Francisco, New York City, Los Angeles, and other cities. In addition to providing initial certification for new teachers, many of the union-sponsored programs are also linked to socialization and training after employment.

Socialization and Training

Traditional guilds had three goals. The first was to control training as a way of ensuring worker competence and high standards of product quality. Guilds established and enforced the contractual relations between apprentices and journey workers and their masters, oversaw disputes, and established systems to pass skills on to others. Prospective masters began their training as apprentices, undertaking tasks with little complex responsibility. They graduated to the rank of journeymen and traveled to acquire skills. Recognizing within themselves a self-destructive tendency toward provincialism and technological stagnation, the guilds insisted that journeymen travel about, seeing how leather hides or ivory combs were produced in places far from their hometowns. Upon returning, these journeymen ideally infused new skills and energy into the system (Shorter 1973:7–8). At the end of their training period, journey workers would create an exhibit—a masterwork—as a means of demonstrating their skill and claiming their place as a master.

Almost all teacher unions also involve themselves in some kind of professional teacher development, some modest and some substantial and highly integrated with the district. Interestingly, it is often the union rather than the school district that provides the continuity to keep a professional-development project alive. If handled well, the union connection to professional development can create a powerful systemic effect connecting professional development to training and induction, assessment of schools and teachers, the curriculum, and the salary schedule. The Minneapolis and New York City public schools offer particularly good examples of long term working relationships that have focused increasingly on student standards and achievement.

The Minneapolis process illustrates effects of gradually building and deepening the relationship between management and labor. Begun in 1984 with a joint Labor-Management Task Force on Teacher Professionalism, the process spawned a mentor teacher program and, five years later, a new teacher-evaluation process. The professional development program, which is administered by a joint district-union panel, links professional education to the method by which teachers gain tenure, teachers' pay, and teacher support and evaluation.

The Minneapolis Public Schools and the Minneapolis Federation of Teachers have also created a residency: a one-year program that provides for a reduced teaching load and increased professional development for newly licensed teachers. Matched with experienced teachers, residents participate in study groups, conduct action research, observe master teachers, and build their professional practice skills by working toward achievement of specified standards of effective teaching. The standards are part of the collective bargaining contract (Koppich 2002).

In New York City, the UFT and the school system collaborate in creating staff development that is embedded in the schools and the teachers' workdays. More than 220 teacher–specialists serve as staff in professional-development teacher centers in schools. Through the centers, these teachers deliver classroom coaching and mentoring and direct assistance with such school-adopted interventions as Success for All. A substantial number of the teacher–specialists have received intensive workshop training to move new educational standards from rhetoric to reality.

Embedded staff development has been spurred by the increased attention being given to standards and accountability. Some 97 New York City schools had been on the state chancellor's list of schools on academic probation. Both the union and the district needed a way to intervene in these schools and in others in danger of placement on the probation list. One major response, according to UFT staff members, was a paradigm shift within the union to focus on outcomes and instruction. Another was to endorse providing high-quality professional development in the schools and to operate a program to do so. Community School District 2, which includes a widely diverse economic swath in central Manhattan, has a particularly well-developed embedded staff development program (Elmore and Burney 1997). There, interestingly, union staff teachers appear to be treating professional development as an entitlement under the contract rather than as a mandated duty.

Another new approach comes from the Chicago Teachers Union, which has started the nation's first union-run graduate program in teacher leadership (Rossi 2002). Deborah Lynch, the union president, explained their plan: "We are focusing on preparing and supporting superior teachers for the many leadership roles in schools that even the best administrators cannot do alone" (Rossi 2002). Teachers will be prepared as mentors, bringing new teaching techniques to schools and assuming leadership on local school councils and professional advisory committees. When coupled with changes in the salary schedule, the graduate program also opens new avenues of advancement for teachers for whom completion of the program will mean a $6,000 salary increase, as well as a stronger role in school-level leadership.

Teacher Quality Assurance

Under industrial unionism, teacher quality is management's prerogative and its problem. For a modern guild, however, it is an essential union function. Through either direct action or negotiation, the labor organization seizes a place for itself in hiring and evaluating teachers. Then it legitimates its position in law and practice through policy and legislation. The most vivid examples of this can be found in the spread of peer-review legislation and the birth of the National Board for Professional Teaching Standards, which has created a certification process and a board-certified label for experienced teachers.

Peer Review. Peer review demonstrates how teachers can create knowledge of their own practice. In the 50 or so school districts that have enacted it, peer review brings higher standards to teaching. It changes the conception of teaching by recognizing the importance of engagement and commitment, as well as skill and technique. It recognizes a legitimate role for teachers in establishing and enforcing standards for their own occupation.

For unions, it represents both a radical departure from established industrial norms and a rediscovery of traditional craft and guild union functions. Under peer review, the union's role balances protection of individual teachers with a protection of teaching. As Albert Fondy, president of the Pittsburgh Federation of Teachers, explained, "a union is not conceived with the primary mission of protecting the least competent of its members" (Kerchner and Koppich 1993:48).

Peer review started in 1981 when the Toledo, Ohio, schools and the Toledo Federation of Teachers added a one-sentence clause to their contract, by which teachers agreed to police the ranks of their veterans in return for the right to review new teachers at work. Since then, peer review has spread among progressive districts. Both the AFT and NEA now support it, the NEA having changed its position in a historic policy shift in 1997. Interest in peer review has increased in the wake of the NEA's policy change. In May 1998, a peer-review conference sponsored by the Columbus, Ohio, local drew more than 500 participants from 30 states (Bradley 1998). Among the districts with active peer-review programs are Seattle, Washington; Columbus, Ohio; Rochester, New York; Pittsburgh, Pennsylvania; Minneapolis, Minnesota; Hammond, Indiana; and Poway, California. In 1999, the California legislature authorized peer review statewide and provided economic incentives for those districts and unions that adopted it.

National Board Certification. Because education is a prerogative of the states, each state maintains machinery for initial teacher licensing. Up until 1986 the country had never had a national system of board certification of experienced teachers, similar to board certification in the medical specialties. That year, with endorsement from U.S. presidents from both parties, the National School Boards Association, virtually every professional and academic society, and the NEA and AFT, the National Board for Professional Teaching Standards (NBPTS) was founded to create rigorous, practice-based examinations for experienced teachers. Examinations on some 22 subject specialties have been developed and are now being offered. These examinations recognize the contextual character of teaching and thus largely involve artifacts from a teacher's own classes, including portfolios of lessons and student work, videotapes of the teacher in action, self-assessment, and peer evaluation. The National Board, which is supported by both public and private funds, has 63 members, the majority of whom are teachers.

The number of board-certified teachers is still small: about 23,000 out of a teaching workforce of over two million (NBPTS 2002). However, each year brings a significant increase in the number of teachers responding to incentives to undergo the two-year examination process. Both national teacher unions have supported legislation to encourage teachers to become certified, and many local unions have bargained salary incentives for board certification. Numerous states and localities—often with private foundation support—have adopted fee supports, created salary supplements, allowed license portability, or made provision for board certification to count toward license renewal or continuing education units. Collective bargaining allows schools to link monetary incentives to board certification. In New York City, for example, a board-certified teacher qualifies for a salary differential of approximately $3,700; in Cincinnati, $1,000; in Rochester, New York, $1,500. Some cities, like Minneapolis and Hammond, Indiana, advance board-certified teachers in their regular salary schedules. In Chicago, the union has raised foundation support to fund professional development and all fees of an unspecified number of candidates for board certification.

Board certification is important in its own right, but the influence of the board's methodology—teacher evaluation based on demonstrated practice rather than university credit hours alone—is already having an influence in other domains. The same set of ideas that created National Board assessments is beginning to be applied to novice teachers. Districts and unions are beginning to consider using the types of evaluative mechanisms and standards developed by the National Board for their internal teacher evaluations. The methodology of board certification and the process of peer-review evaluation and renewal are beginning to support one another.

Incentives and Rewards

Guilds provided powerful incentives for prospective members. They were the gatekeepers to occupations that generally provided above-subsistence incomes and a full measure of social status. As a result, guild membership, like craft-union membership in the recent past, became a prized family possession passed from father to son.

As industrial unions, the AFT and NEA provided a different incentive structure, one tied to the pay-and-benefit structure negotiated by the union, the retirement system, the conditions of work protected by the work-rules agreements, and the accrued property right protected by seniority provisions. Jobs did not become family property as they did with ancient guilds, and the unions did relatively little to determine whether a school was capable of attracting and keeping a high-quality teaching staff. Nevertheless, unionization produced good economic returns for teachers: although estimates vary, most have found an 8 to 12 percent wage effect from unionization (Kerchner 1986; Stone 2000).

The Salary Schedule. What is called the standard single salary schedule is one of the most ubiquitous organizational characteristics of public schools. Both in the 37 states where teachers are allowed to bargain contracts and in the 13 where they are not, teachers are paid according to the amount of education they have and the number of years they serve in the district (Odden and Kelley 1997). Although the credit or blame for the lack of linkage between pay and performance frequently goes to the unions, the salary schedule's origins can actually be traced to civil service and its universal application to the post–World War II enrollment boom.

School districts had to be able to attract women by paying them as much as male teachers, who had previously been paid more.

The salary schedule contains powerful incentives. Starting salaries are intended to attract teachers, and during times of teacher shortage both unions and managements advocate emphasizing the lower steps of the salary schedule. Additional education is rewarded; in fact in many states, teacher-certification laws require it. As a result, teachers are a highly degreed group.

The shape of teacher compensation also rewards long tenure. Where public school salaries tend to be lower than those in private sector jobs with similar educational requirements, pensions and benefits—particularly health care plans—tend to be somewhat higher. Pensions are not portable, however, and pay off substantially only at retirement. Thus, a teacher past about the tenth year in a district is effectively fitted with golden handcuffs.

The salary schedule also reveals an industrial division of labor, which has become more pronounced since the onset of bargained salary schedules. Teaching has become more identified with direct instruction and less with interacting with students in informal settings and role modeling. Aides have taken over supervision duties, and after-school activities are paid so poorly that many teachers have declined to undertake them. To be sure, teachers still direct bands, coach sports, and oversee student clubs, but they do so in spite of the economic incentives, not because of them.

Alternative Compensation Systems. The salary schedule was established to reward expertise in the form of more education and experience and to remove pay rates from favoritism. It also made a logical connection between compensation and quality. Teachers who had more education and more experience were thought to be better prepared and to have more finely honed skills. Within the last decade, however, there has been a concerted effort to target teacher compensation more specifically. First, many school districts now provide monetary incentives for teachers who have highly desirable skills or who teach in an area of chronic shortage, particularly bilingual teachers, those who teach special education, and math or science teachers. Second, there is substantial interest in specifying the knowledge and skill that will be recognized in the salary schedule. Most of this interest has been spawned by the work of Allan Odden and colleagues, who popularized the idea (Odden and Kelley 1997). Third, highly tentative efforts are being made to tie teacher compensation directly to the achievement of students.

Departures from the standard salary schedule have remained on the "undiscussable" list for most unions and, indeed, for most schools. Against the advice of its leadership, the NEA convention in 2000 adopted a strong resolution against any form of merit pay either to attract or reward teachers: "The Association opposes providing additional compensation to attract and/or retain education employees in hard-to-recruit positions....The Association also believes that performance pay, such as merit pay, or any other system of compensation based on evaluation of an education employee's performance, are inappropriate" (Editorial 2000: A34).

A few unions have adopted alternatives anyway. In Cincinnati, Ohio, the school district and the Cincinnati Federation of Teachers (an AFT affiliate) adopted a salary schedule tied to five career, skill, and responsibility levels, which has proven extremely controversial. Its implementation has been slow, following a pilot run in 1999–2000 (Blair 2000).

In a more radical departure, the Denver Public Schools and the Denver Classroom Teachers' Association (an NEA affiliate) captured attention by agreeing to a pilot program that tied a small amount of salary for all teachers in participating schools to student performance. Each teacher in the 16 pilot schools was to receive $500 for participating and up to $1,000 more if the majority of a teacher's students improved (Janofsky 1999). Almost all qualified for the extra $1,000.

Evaluations of the project pointed to its complexity: that changing the salary schedule deals with more than how and how much a teacher is being paid and what incentives are used. The questions being raised had to do much more with the school district infrastructure and organization than it did with how teachers should be paid. For example, evaluators found that the district's data system was not sophisticated enough to provide teachers with timely information on student achievement and that the student-assessment system was not sophisticated enough to provide multiple measures of achievement. Teachers, in particular, criticized the standardized testing system as too narrowly focused and too inaccurate.

Test scores were generally higher in the pilot-program schools than in a control group, but it was hard to link the effect of pay to student performance. The presence of high teacher objectives, whether or not those objectives were met, appeared to be more influential. At the same time, the pilot program seemed not to devastate working relations between teachers; on the contrary, teachers seemed to cooperate more (Community Assistance and Training Center 2001).

The district and union decided to continue the pilot study and both to design a new compensation system and to attend to the district infrastructure issues before the school board and teachers vote on a new system in 2004. Superintendent Jerry Wartgow noted, "In the final analysis, teachers will not vote on pay for performance as we've known it for the past three years, but on an entirely new salary system. We need a more flexible system of rewards to provide incentive and recognition to those teachers who put in more effort and make a greater contribution" (PFPDT 2002:1).

More than anything, the Denver efforts show how complex incentive systems are. Rewards do not always serve as incentives or change behavior (Mitchell, Ortiz, and Mitchell 1987). Incentives are aimed at different behaviors: some encourage people to become teachers; others promote teaching well. Incentives are not always attached to pay; in fact, in teaching relatively few are. Furthermore, an individual reward for performance merit pay in teaching exists alongside a strong intrinsic reward: the feeling of accomplishment for having taught well. Helping students achieve is probably the most frequently cited and strongest teacher motivator (Conley 1991; Little and McLaughlin 1993; Lortie 1975; McLaughlin and Yee 1988; Rosenholtz 1989; Smylie 1994).

In sum, the examples of contemporary teacher union reforms provide a sketch of a modern guild in operation. Increasingly, unions are realizing that their role is to negotiate on behalf of teaching as well as teachers. As Albert Shanker noted, "it is as much the duty of the union to preserve public education as it is to negotiate a good contract" (AFT 1998:3).

The examples from leading unions also illustrate the ways in which labor-management relations shape the identity of teaching as an occupation. If, collectively, teachers are content with jobs that follow industrial-era scripts—if they are content to work specified hours, follow a prescribed curriculum, and follow detailed behavioral rules—then they can get by with industrial-era labor relations in which the union's exclusive concerns are wages and work rules. But if teachers aspire to craft, artistic, or professional jobs, they must also have different expectations of their unions, because unions mediate most of the fiscal and psychological contracts between teachers and school districts. In terms of educational policy, deciding what kind of teachers we want also decides what we want unions to do.

Labor Law and Policy to Support a Modern Guild

The Irish silversmith's goblet provides a useful guide to shaping public policy in support of a modern guild for public school teaching. The master's personal hallmark speaks of pride in work and an accountability system attached to the product. The guild's hallmark speaks of its engagement in the production system. The government's hallmark speaks of its legal oversight.

Teachers do not have the equivalent of the silversmith's hallmark, but they do deeply imprint students. It is relatively easy to find traces of individual teacher influence. Stories of successful teachers have created a genre of books and film, perhaps best exemplified by *Stand and Deliver,* the movie about Jamie Escalante, who taught calculus at Garfield High School in East Los Angeles and whose students performed so well on Advanced Placement examinations that the test makers thought they had cheated. In the Escalante genre, teachers are highly talented, seen as mavericks, engaged in their work to the point that it damages their health, and controversial with colleagues and school administrators. Most of all, they are remembered by students who testify to the teachers' life-changing effects. Movie, text, and scholarly ethnographic studies repeat this theme (Johnson 1990; Lortie 1975; Waller 1932). Even test score data are beginning to show an individual teacher effect. Studies of Tennessee data show that the effects of a superlative teacher, or a bad one, can be seen in student progress for the next two or three years (Sanders 1998).

Teachers, and not just the storied ones, clearly bring passion and pride to their work. Most work far beyond the contractually required hours planning lessons and grading papers at home, volunteering for uncompensated activities, investing their own funds in their further education, and buying basic instructional materials that their school districts seem unable to supply. But teachers are also well-socialized to an industrial mind-set, reluctant to open their classroom space to the scrutiny of colleagues, and frequently willing to consider school or district problems part of "management's work." Furthermore, they do not consider it the job of their unions to solve problems in school operations. After reading a book on union reform a 30-year veteran teacher wrote, "I do not want to pay union dues to an organization that does anything but help me in defense of my job, income, benefits. Do you understand?" (personal communication, April 4, 2002).

Much has been made of the recalcitrance of unions to consider changing to accommodate alternative ways of delivering schooling. Indeed, there is delicious irony in the fact that teacher unions, which organized in opposition to the authority system of public education, should be the fiercest defenders of that system. But, for the most part, union leaders are reflecting their members' views. Unlike many policy activists, teachers do not believe that public education is facing a large institutional transformation or that schooling needs to change in major ways. Younger teachers are more likely than veterans to see a need for change, but they rarely associate their union with such activity. There appears to be a growing gap between what unions do and what novices want. Polls conducted by the unions themselves suggest a low level of union identification among younger teachers, who have a strong desire for the union to help them teach better and particularly to help them survive the first, difficult years. In addition, most teachers are deeply imprinted with a culture of individualism and find it difficult to "re-create for [themselves] the moral universe of a [guild-based] society in which the success of the community came before the advantage of the individuals within it" (Shorter 1973:11).

Unlike the silversmith's guild, public education is not marked with a union label. Teachers rarely wear union insignia at work, and the union logo rarely appears in schools, except on the union bulletin board. Yet, just as teachers imprint students, unions imprint education and, in many ways, unions are ideally positioned to act as engines of reform in public education. In the turbulent world of urban public schools, where a superintendent's tenure averages less than three years, the teacher union is often the most stable of the organizational and political players. Union presidents or executive directors tend to have long tenure in office. Contracts have a continuity that bridges superintendency, and the political structure of unions is frequently capable of being reactivated when new issues arise.

However, just as one can observe and enumerate examples of union organizing around educational quality and student achievement, any observer would be forced to note that teacher union organizing outside of its industrial origins has not spread rapidly. Both of the national unions exhibit tentativeness about how departures from industrial unionism should proceed. In the late 1980s, the AFT promoted site-based management and school decentralization as the keystones of organizational reform only to abandon the effort in favor of a strong emphasis on standards and coherent reform strategies. When Bob Chase became president of the NEA in 1996, he proclaimed a "New Unionism" that was supposed to ignite a bubbling pot of locally initiated reforms, but the evidence illustrates the difficulties of moving forward. Factions of the NEA found Chase's ideas treasonable. The leaders of Wisconsin's largest affiliates wrote: "Your remarks are not only appalling, they ignore the fundamental strength of a union....We are union and we are proud; we stand in solidarity to defend against those who are attempting to destroy us" (Fuller, Mitchell, and Hartmann 2000:114–15).

Opposition has had its effect. An examination of the NEA web site in fall 2002 showed references to the New Unionism only in inconspicuous places and in material that was at least two years old (see the NEA web site: www.nea.org). AFT and NEA locals associated with the Teacher Union Reform Network (TURN) have undertaken many of the boldest reforms, including those described in this chapter, but TURN comprises fewer than 25 locals, and its ideas have not spread rapidly.

Part of the slowness of the spread of reform can be attributed to ideology, part to politics, and part to capacity. Julia Koppich, who has run a union capacity-building project, reports that unions were internally organized around traditional operations, such as the processing of grievances, rather than the emerging tasks of assuring quality. Moreover, the staff and leadership were frequently out of touch with the membership (personal conversation with Julia Koppich, November 1, 2002). Much of the reforms of the 1980s and early 1990s involved unions taking what is called joint custody of reform (Kerchner and Koppich 1993). In many cases, these efforts stretched the unions beyond their capacity to deliver. The capacity question is not simply a matter of staff; it is a matter of what the staff knows how to do. Most union staff gained their positions because they were good organizers or good advocates, not because they were especially skilled at day-to-day operations. These people are generally better at rocking boats than steering them. Organizing—a core union skill—requires motivating people to action, usually for a short period of time for a political campaign, a strike, a representation election, or some other episodic event. Unions are less well organized for the steady work of education, creating and spreading a curriculum, professional development, or the actual operation of schools.

Ideologically, both teacher and administrator cultures endorse the status quo, and efforts to depart from it are viewed with suspicion. In addition, although often opponents at the bargaining table, union staff and school administrators are frequently united in their embrace of the hierarchical management logically paired with industrial unionism. By word and deed, most school administrators believe that a union's voice needs to be made as quiet as possible and the scope of negotiations restricted to teachers' economic interests. Although the American Association of School Administrators has sponsored some efforts in "joint team" training, administrators do not generally think of unions as partners in educational reform. A majority of union staff probably feels the same. It is not uncommon to hear staff members say, in effect: we just want to represent teachers; we've no interest in running the district. We've got plenty to do just keeping an eye on those principals who won't live by the contract. That is a big enough job in itself.

Normative beliefs translate into political positions. For example, peer review, which union leadership has taken substantial risks to establish and develop, is seen by some as backward movement for public policy. Consider Myron Lieberman's (1997) commentary that calls professionalization "a step backward" in public policy:

> In some respects, the basic issue in peer review appears to be whether it is possible to reconcile the concept of a union, legally and practically responsible for promoting the interests of its members, with the concept of a professional organization. This depends on how we define "professional organization." If it is defined as an organization to protect the public, as NEA publications imply, we must bear in mind that "professional" organizations eventually become as self-serving as unions. (p. 44)

Thus, as a result of both internal and external opposition, union reform appears to have little of the momentum that characterized the growth of collective bargaining in the 1960s and 1970s. Without a driving force behind it, guild-like changes are unlikely to spread very rapidly. Therefore, for those advocating change, it is important to consider the role of public policy and particularly the role of labor law in driving change.

Advocating labor-law change is not without hazard. Public policy is always a blunt instrument and often as not the expectations of a policy's initiators are dashed on the rocks of reality. The drafters of the National Labor Relations Act (NLRA), for example, had in mind a far different labor relations system than that which developed over the last 60 years. The world created in Senator Wagner's head was in many ways a world grounded in the democratic philosophies of John Dewey and such institutional economists as John Commons. The resulting society was supposed to be more cooperative and democratic in its workplaces and organizations because organized labor would be a legitimate, powerful, and essential institution in the larger society. Instead, we got a much more fractious and adversarial system than the founders intended.

Yet, nothing is more powerful than labor law as a force to transform public education. The patterning effect of labor law can be seen in the rapid adoption of collective bargaining practices in only a few years during the 1960s and 1970s. Teacher unions moved rapidly into a position of power and influence, and teachers proved more than capable of both voice and militancy. While the effects of adopting collective bargaining on the education process itself are still debated, the power of unions to change teaching and schools has become obvious. To bring about elements of guild-like organization, labor law will again need to send strong policy signals.

Make the Frontiers Safe and Legal

It has been easy to find examples of unions and school managements that inhabit the labor relations frontiers. Virtually all of them have taken steps beyond traditional relationships within existing labor laws. If both labor and management want to establish a new relationship, and if each is willing to fight the traditionalists within their camp, then a new relationship is possible. But there is no legal incentive to push forward or to leave the comfort of industrial relations.

For public policy to support changes in teacher labor relations, labor law will have to make what are now the frontiers of educational labor relations safe for permanent settlement. Unionists should not have to wonder whether participating in joint labor-management committees or making substantive decisions are likely to be interpreted as supervisory work, thus rendering teachers ineligible for collective bargaining rights. The NLRA posits a fundamental dividing line between labor and management because legislative history and court decisions interpreting the law have asserted that collective bargaining by managerial employees would create intolerable, divided loyalties (Rabban 1991).

The 1980 U.S. Supreme Court decision in *National Labor Relations Board v. Yeshiva University* reinforced the separation of workers and managers in higher education, as did the more recent case involving nurses (*National Labor Relations Board v. Health Care & Retirement Corporation of America* 1994). Faculty members at Yeshiva were denied collective bargaining rights because their faculty senate and its committees made substantive decisions at their university. They were considered "supervisors" under the law and ineligible for bargaining rights. The 1947 Taft-Hartley amendments to the NLRA specifically excluded supervisors from coverage, specifying [in section 2(11)] that supervisors are those who have the authority to hire, transfer, suspend, lay off, recall, promote, discharge, assign, reward, or discipline other employees. Although this federal legal doctrine has never been applied to a state case governing public school teachers, it stands as a symbolic barrier, a monument that the law did not intend workers and management to share decisional power. "In the end, the *Yeshiva* case is troubling because it is at war with the idea of consensus between professional employees and their administrators...." (Schlossberg and Fetter 1986:15).

Thus, consensus and joint labor-management committees are legally suspicious. Although Senator Robert Wagner espoused cooperation among workers, the law for which he is remembered, and the state statutes derived from it, nearly universally place barriers in the way of a close working relationship between unions and management. The framers of the law were concerned with so-called company unions, organizations that looked like unions but were dominated by management and formed to forestall worker organization by independent unions. Section 8(a)(2) of the NLRA provides that it shall be an unfair labor practice for an employer to "dominate or interfere with the formation or administration of any labor organization or contribute financial or other support to it." Under the statute, employee organizations (Section 2(5)) included virtually any kind of employee representation committee or organization that deals with wages or working conditions.

Peer review challenges both the ideology and the practice of current labor relations in rather obvious ways. The courts have held that by achieving the status of exclusive representative for a group of employees, a union also takes on a duty to "exercise fairly the power conferred upon it in behalf of all those for whom it acts, without hostile discrimination among them" (*Steele v. Louisville & National R. Co.* 1944:202–03).

This duty is felt in several circumstances, but the one most associated with peer review is the representation requirement when employees are disciplined or discharged. The courts have held that a union has discretion in deciding how far to press a grievance brought by a member in these cases, so long as it does not discriminate against or among groups of members (Morris 1971). In other words, not every grievance needs be carried to arbitration or into the courts. But in peer-review cases, the union approves of and participates in a process in which members judge other members, and unions have generally agreed that they will not challenge the substance of peer-review rulings. So, while the existing peer-review experiments have produced no successful legal challenges from teachers who were judged to be incompetent, the status of unions remains unclear. A statute that anticipated workers' serving in a professional peer-review situation should therefore be honored.

Peer review also challenges sections of education statutes that reserve the managers' right to evaluate employees. Principals in Rochester, New York, unsuccessfully challenged the teacher union's introduction of peer review on this ground. To get around this potential problem, in districts in California that have adopted peer review, administrators sign the final recommendations, thus complying with the letter of the law. A recent analysis of peer review by union attorneys makes suggestions for contractual language that would assure that teachers serving either on peer-review panels or as supervising teachers would not compromise their status as bargaining-unit members (AFT–NEA 1998). But the law does not send a clear message that these guild-like activities are what unions and management need to do; rather, these activities seem to be what they can get away with, if they want.

For a modern guild to come about, it would be necessary to encourage joint labor-management enterprises like professional practice committees and jointly sponsored professional development schools, such as the one in Cincinnati, without violating the employer assistance or domination prohibition. Such a position is very different from that advocated by the supporters of the TEAM Act (Teamwork for Employees and Management Act), which was defeated in Congress in 1996. The TEAM Act would have amended section 8(a)(2) of the National Labor Relations Act to allow employers to form or assist nonunion organizations to address issues of productivity and efficiency. I believe that discussions about productivity and quality should operate through the union rather than around it. School managers already have the ability to undertake the kinds of relationships described in the TEAM Act. The fact that so few have done so suggests that a public policy intervention is necessary to activate large numbers of teachers to work together to create better schools.

I believe that development of a legal structure more conducive to the implementation of professional values requires changes in the concept of company domination. Collegial committees or joint operations *need* support from employers. Teachers *need to* be able to form committees that advise and actually make policy, and school authorities need to be able to assist those committees with staff support and budgets without violating the labor statute.

I agree with David Rabban's suggestion that "the definition of company domination that best promotes professional values should be limited to actual employer interference with the independent decision making of employee committees, whether or not this interference derives from anti-union animus. Unless committees of professional employees are able to reach their own conclusions, they cannot provide the employer with the expert advice that justifies their existence" (Rabban 1990: 755).

Addressing the labor law issues necessary to make guild-like teacher unions legally safe provides symbol and substance for changes in labor-management relations, but not incentives. Yet state statutes under which teachers bargain have not been much of a barrier to innovative practices in places where people wanted to undertake them. Virtually all practices described in this chapter have taken place without changing laws. (One exception is that Ohio changed its statute specifically to allow union participation in peer-review programs.) Most of the existing labor reforms have taken place within existing statutory restrictions, simply because both labor and management wanted changes to come about and the statutes and case law were sufficiently permissive that union efforts to organize around quality and management promotion of, or agreement with, these efforts have not prompted legal challenge. When there has been a challenge, the courts have ruled in favor of the innovative practice. The principals union in Rochester, New York, for example, sued the district and teachers' union over their negotiated peer-review and teacher career-ladder program. The suit was dismissed and never came to trial.

What the process needs now is an incentive.

Negotiating What Matters Most

Public policy conveys expectations by requiring behavioral change. In the case of teacher collective bargaining, statutes could not require that school administrators and board members believe in workplace democracy or a legitimate economic voice for teachers, but it did require them to bargain with the teacher union. Over time some of those relationships became productive while others became toxic, but the process of bargaining remained a requirement. If public policy is to encourage guild-like unions, then labor law needs to prod both unions and employers into substantive interaction about what matters most: educational quality, broadly considered.

Julia Koppich and I are working toward developing a prototype labor law that would create incentives for negotiating educational quality. We are far from having the details worked out, but we believe the labor relations system must

- Oblige unions and management to assume joint custody of reform. Teachers' unions and school district management must be bound by a common interest. Both must feel responsible, and be held responsible, for the outcomes of education improvement efforts.

- Result in contracts in which improving student achievement is central. To make improving achievement a principal purpose of negotiated agreements, districts and unions must be obligated to agree on a set of measurable student-learning goals around which other elements of the contract are structured.

- Remove all statutory restrictions on the topics of labor-management negotiations. If the primary purpose of labor-management agreements is improving student achievement, districts and unions must be free, indeed must be obliged, to discuss all subjects relating to this interest (Koppich and Kerchner 2003).

The process of devising a labor policy and outlining a labor statute is far from finished. There are a number of possible ways forward. One is to specify previously permissive or forbidden subjects of bargaining as mandatory subjects. The California Teachers Association advocated such legal requirements, and a bill that would have required them was introduced in the California legislature in 2002, where it died under threat of gubernatorial veto (Skelton 2002). Another approach is to create a mandatory duty to consult on a broad range of items (see Malin, this volume). My approach would be to require an agreement about student-achievement goals and how to produce them, allowing the parties to negotiate what they wish in order to meet the goals they have set for themselves.

Conclusion: What Kind of Teachers Do You Want?

Labor law is capable of shaping not only the conditions under which teachers work but also the content of their work. For decades, scholars have asserted that substantive change in American public education would not take place until teachers gained some of the powers associated with traditional professions. But even the traditional professions are becoming much more the subjects of hierarchical management and their workplace judgments confined by standards of practice and corporate management. Thus, looking at the guild form of unionism as one tied to individual practice or a producer's cooperative misses the workplace reality of virtually all teachers and most employed professionals.

However, inserting a substantial adaptation from the guild form into public bureaucracies offers a real possibility that teacher unionism can be the vehicle for substantive change in public school organization and operation. Clearly, examples exist of attempts to create and use teacher unions to induct, train, and socialize teachers and to hold them accountable. Merely outlined earlier in this chapter, they are described in more detail in earlier publications (Kerchner and Koppich 1993; Kerchner, Koppich, and Weeres 1997; Kerchner and Koppich 2000; Kerchner 2001). Developing guild-like labor relations is clearly possible. Some teachers, their unions, and their employers are willing to place their hallmarks on public education, as the Irish silversmith did. The question of the design and function of the government's hallmark remains unclear. Without it, guild-like teacher unionism becomes a laudable but optional exercise. With the right policy intervention, government asserts its interest in what matters most.

References

AFT. 1998. "Redesigning Low Performing Schools: It's Union Work." Paper presented at the American Federation of Teachers, Convention Resolution. Washington, DC, July 19.

AFT–NEA. 1998. *Peer Assistance and Review: An AFT/NEA Handbook.* Washington, DC: AFT–NEA.

Blair, Julie. 2000. "Cincinnati Teachers to Be Judged, Paid on Performance." *Education Week,* September 27, p. 1.

———. 2002. "Minneapolis Labor Leaders Mold A Different Kind of Union." *Education Week,* January 30, p. 1.

Bradley, Ann. 1998. "Peer-Review Programs Catch Hold As Unions, Districts Work Together." *Education Week,* June 3, p. 1.

Community Assistance and Training Center. 2001. *Pathway to Results: Pay for Performance in Denver.* Boston: Community Assistance and Training Center.

Conley, Sharon C. 1991. "Review of Research on Teacher Participation in School Decision Making." In Gerald Grant, ed., *Review of Research in Education.* Washington, DC: American Educational Research Association, pp. 225–66.

Editorial. 2000. "Without Merit." *Wall Street Journal,* July 10, p. A-34.

Editorial. 2002. "UFT Curriculum Guides Point the Way." *New York Teacher.* <http://www.uft.org/?fid=196&tf=1137&nart=648> [October 8, 2002].

Elmore, Richard F., and Deanna Burney. 1997. "School Variation and Systemic Instructional Improvement in Community School District #2, New York City." Unpublished manuscript, Harvard University.

Epstein, Steven A. 1991. *Wage Labor and Guilds in Medieval Europe.* Chapel Hill: University of North Carolina Press.

Fox, Alan. 1974a. *Beyond Contract: Work, Power, and Trust Relations.* London: Faber and Faber.

———. 1974b. "Discretion, Status, and Rewards in Work." In Alan Fox, *Beyond Contract: Work, Power and Trust Relations.* London: Faber and Faber, pp. 13–65.

Fuller, Howard L., George A. Mitchell, and Michael E. Hartmann. 2000. "Collective Bargaining in Milwaukee Public Schools." In Tom Loveless, ed., *Conflicting Missions: Teachers Unions and Educational Reform.* Washington, DC: Brookings Institution Press, pp. 110–49.

Goodnough, Abby. 2002. "Teachers' Union Publishes Guide for Classroom, and Stirs Debate." *New York Times*, Sept. 13. <http://www.nytimes.com/2002/09/13/education/13CURR.html> [October 8, 2002].

Grant, Gerald, and Christine Murray. 1996. "The Second Academic Revolution." In Robert L. Crowson, William Lowe Boyd, and Hanne B. Mawhinney, eds., *The Politics of Education and the New Institutionalism: Reinventing the American School*. New York: Falmer Press, pp. 93–100.

Janofsky, Michael. 1999. "For Denver Teachers, a Pay-for-Performance Plan." *New York Times*, Sept. 10, p. A19.

Johnson, Susan Moore. 1990. *Teachers at Work: Achieving Success in Our Schools*. New York: Basic Books.

Kerchner, Charles T. 1986. "Union Made Teaching: The Effects of Labor Relations on Teaching Work." In Ernst Rothkopf, ed., *Review of Research in Education*. Washington, DC: American Educational Research Association, pp. 317–52.

Kerchner, Charles Taylor. 2001. "The Struggle for the Knowledge-Based Workplace." *International Journal of Educational Management*, Vol. 15, no. 5, pp. 220–38.

Kerchner, Charles Taylor, and Julia E. Koppich. 1993. *A Union of Professionals: Labor Relations and Educational Reform*. New York: Teacher's College Press.

———. 2000. "Organizing Around Quality: The Frontiers of Teacher Unionism." In Tom Loveless, ed., *Conflicting Missions? Teachers Unions and Educational Reform*. Washington, DC: Brookings Institution, pp. 281–316.

Kerchner, Charles Taylor, Julia E. Koppich, and Joseph G. Weeres. 1997. *United Mind Workers: Unions and Teaching in the Knowledge Society*. San Francisco: Jossey-Bass.

Kerchner, Charles T., and Douglas E. Mitchell. 1988. *The Changing Idea of a Teachers' Union*. Stanford Series in Education and Public Policy. New York and London: Falmer Press.

Koppich, Julia E. 2002. "Distributing the Pie: Allocating Resources Through Labor-Management Agreements." Unpublished manuscript, Julia Koppich and Associates, San Francisco.

Koppich, Julia E., and Charles Taylor Kerchner. 2003. "Negotiating What Matters Most." *Education Week*, Vol. 56, February 12, pp. 56, 41.

Lawler, Edward, III. 1992. *The Ultimate Advantage: Creating the High-Involvement Organization*. San Francisco: Jossey-Bass.

Lieberman, Myron. 1997. *The Teacher Unions: How the NEA and AFT Sabotage Reform and Hold Students, Parents, Teachers, and Taxpayers Hostage to Reform*. New York: Free Press.

Lint, Robert L., and Stephen B. Dunbar. 1990. "The Nation's Report Card Goes Home: Good News and Bad about Trends in Achievement." *Phi Delta Kappan*, Vol. 72, no. 2, pp. 127–33.

Little, Judith W., and Milbray W. McLaughlin. 1993. *Teachers' Work: Individuals, Colleagues, and Contexts*. New York: Teachers College Press.

Lortie, Dan C. 1975. *Schoolteacher: A Sociological Study*. Chicago: University of Chicago Press.

McLaughlin, John M. 1994. "Education as a Growth Industry: Suggestions for State Boards of Education." St. Cloud, MN: St. Cloud State University.

McLaughlin, Milbrey W., and Sylvia Mei-Ling Yee. 1988. "School as a Place to Have a Career." In Ann Lieberman, ed., *Building a Professional Culture in Schools.* New York: Teachers College Press, pp. 23–44.

Mitchell, Douglas E., Flora Ida Ortiz, and Tedi K. Mitchell. 1987. *Work Orientation and Job Performance: The Cultural Basis of Teaching Rewards and Incentives.* Albany, NY: State University of New York.

Morris, Charles J., ed. 1971. *The Developing Labor Law.* Washington, DC: Bureau of National Affairs.

National Labor Relations Board v. Health Care and Retirement Corporation (HRC), 511 U.S. 571. 1994.

National Labor Relations Board v. Yeshiva University, 444 U.S. 672. 1980.

NBPTS. 2002. "America's Classrooms Gain More Than 7,800 National Board Certified Teachers in 2002." Washington, DC: National Board for Professional Teaching Standards. <http://www.nbpts.org/news/latest.cfm> [April 30, 2003].

Odden, Allan, and Carolyn Kelley. 1997. *Paying Teachers for What They Know and Do: New and Smarter Compensation Strategies to Improve Schools.* Thousand Oaks, CA: Corwin Press.

PFPDT (Pay for Performance Design Team). 2002. "Wartgow, Wissink Discuss Teacher Salaries and Careers." *Focus on Results,* August, pp. 1, 4.

Piore, Michael J., and Charles F. Sabel. 1984. *The Second Industrial Divide: Possibilities for Prosperity.* New York: Basic Books.

Rabban, David M. 1990. "Can American Labor Law Accommodate Collective Bargaining by Professional Employees?" *Yale Law Journal,* Vol. 99, no. 4, pp. 689–758.

———. 1991. "Is Unionization Compatible with Professionalism?" *Industrial and Labor Relations Review,* Vol. 45, no. 1 (October), pp. 97–112.

Rosenholtz, Susan J. 1989. *Teachers' Workplace: The Social Organization of Schools.* White Plains, NY: Longman.

Rossi, Rosalind. 2002. "Teachers Union Launches Unique Graduate School." *Chicago Sun-Times,* March 29. <http://www.suntimes.com/output/news/cst-nwsctu29.html> [October 2, 2002].

Rubinstein, Saul A. 2000. "The Impact of Co-Management on Quality Performance: The Case of the Saturn Corporation." *Industrial and Labor Relations Review,* Vol. 53, no. 2 (January), pp. 197–218.

Rubinstein, Saul, Michael Bennett, and Thomas Kochan. 1993. "The Saturn Partnership: Co-Management and the Reinvention of the Local Union." In Bruce E. Kleiner and Morris M. Kaufman, eds., *Employee Representation: Alternatives and Future Directions.* Madison, WI: Industrial Relations Research Association, pp. 339–70.

Sanders, William L. 1998. "Value-Added Assessment." *School Administrator,* Vol. 55, no. 11, pp. 24–27.

Schlossberg, Stephen I., and Steven M. Fetter. 1986. *U.S. Labor Law and the Future of Labor-Management Cooperation.* Washington, DC: GPO.

Shorter, Edward, ed. 1973. *Work and Community in the West.* New York: Harper and Row.

Skelton, George. 2002. "Making Textbooks a Bargaining Tool for Teachers Is a Tough Sell." *Los Angeles Times,* April 15. <http://www.latimes.com/local/la-00002854apr15.column> [April 16, 2002].

Smylie, M. 1994. "Redesigning Teacher's Work: Connections to the Classroom." In L. Darling-Hammond, ed., *Review of Research in Education,* Vol. 20. Washington, DC: American Educational Research Association, pp. 129–79.

Steele v. Louisville & Nashville R. Co., 323 U.S. 192. 1944.

Stone, Joe A. 2002. "Collective Bargaining and Public Schools." In Tom Loveless, ed., *Conflicting Missions? Teachers Unions and Educational Reform.* Washington, DC: Brookings Institution, pp. 47–68.

Toch, Tom. 1991. *In the Name of Excellence.* New York: Oxford University Press.

Tyack, David B. 1974. *The One Best System: A History of American Urban Education.* Cambridge, MA: Harvard University Press.

Tyack, David, and Elisabeth Hansot. 1982. *Managers of Virtue: Public School Leadership in America, 1820–1980.* New York: Basic Books.

UFT. 2002. "UFT Releases Historic Curriculum Resources Guides." *New York Teacher,* September 24. <http://www.uft.org/?fid=200&tf=1140&nart=638> [October 8, 2002].

Walker, Mack. 1973. "Hometowns and Guilds in Early Modern Germany." In Edward Shorter, ed., *Work and Community in the West.* New York: Harper and Row, pp. 34–53.

Waller, Willard. 1932. *The Sociology of Teaching.* New York: Longman.

CHAPTER 9

Public Sector Labor Law Doctrine and Labor-Management Cooperation

MARTIN H. MALIN
Chicago-Kent College of Law

Introduction

The 1996 report of the Secretary of Labor's Task Force on Excellence in State and Local Governments (U.S. DOL 1996) chronicled the advantages of labor-management cooperation in the public sector. As the task force found, labor-management cooperation leads to improvements in the delivery of public services, increased cost effectiveness, improved quality of work life, and reduced labor-management conflict. The task force also identified numerous barriers to labor-management cooperation, however. Those barriers included an "over-reliance on legalisms and formalities" (U.S. DOL 1996:65). The task force specifically singled out conflict and doctrine concerning the scope of bargaining in the public sector as contributing to this particular barrier:

> Because it affects the capacity of an agency or jurisdiction to improve service, the clearest need is for workers, managers and union leaders to be able to discuss the full range of issues affecting the service they are working to improve. In a traditional labor-management relationship characterized by formal or legalistic approaches, such discussion often is precluded by concerns over setting precedents that might lead to giving up prerogatives. (p. 65)

This chapter explores the relationship between current public sector labor law doctrine and labor-management cooperation. In investigating this relationship, it finds that current doctrine employs a balancing approach to the scope of bargaining in the public sector that results in a narrow scope and encourages issue-by-issue litigation over whether the parties will discuss a matter at all. The negative effects of current doctrine are reinforced by a legislative tendency to react to actual and perceived deficiencies in public services by narrowing the scope of bargaining even

267

further. Consequently, to the extent that labor-management cooperation exists, it does so in spite of, rather than because of, the law. As a result, the more cooperative and successful a relationship becomes, the less relevant the law becomes.

The chapter examines the rationales behind the formalistic approach to, and narrow scope of, collective bargaining in the public sector. It identifies several reasons that are flawed: blind adoption of private sector precedents, an overly narrow view of the union's role at the bargaining table, and concern that public sector collective bargaining is undemocratic. It then focuses on a legitimate concern underlying the narrow scope of bargaining: the impact of public sector impasse resolution procedures.

The chapter analyzes a fundamental flaw in public sector labor law doctrine: the view that the law can only compel full collective bargaining over a subject or leave it to complete unilateral employer determination. It suggests alternative models to be explored that can render the law more relevant to the practice of labor-management cooperation.

The Current State of Affairs

More than ten years ago, a report to the U.S. Department of Labor identified the narrow scope of bargaining in the public sector as a barrier to successful labor-management cooperation programs (Moberly 1989). Unfortunately, the relationship between public sector labor law doctrine concerning the scope of bargaining and labor-management cooperation has not improved. The scope of bargaining remains narrow and, as a result, when labor-management cooperation occurs it does so in spite of, rather than because of, the legal doctrine.

Legal Doctrine and the Scope of Bargaining

Public sector labor relations statutes take diverse approaches to defining what subjects must be negotiated by a public employer with its employees' exclusive bargaining representative. Many copy the language of the National Labor Relations Act (NLRA)[1] and require bargaining on wages, hours, and terms and conditions of employment.[2] Others expressly define those subjects over which collective bargaining is required by listing a range of topics that is narrower than the NLRA's.[3] Statutes of both types often contain broadly worded management rights provisions not found in the NLRA.[4] Even where a statute lacks express management rights language, a court may imply its own concept of inherent managerial prerogatives.[5]

The problem that labor boards and courts have had to confront is how to deal with two potentially extremely broad concepts. At some level, every public sector decision affects conditions of employment and at some level every decision affects public policy or managerial authority. Even bargaining about such basic matters as wages affects the allocation of scarce public resources and, thereby, affects the determination of public policy. The Court of Appeals of Maryland aptly described the situation: "[V]irtually every managerial decision in some way relates to 'salaries, wages, hours, and other working conditions,' and is therefore arguably negotiable. At the same time, virtually every such decision also involves educational policy considerations and is therefore arguably nonnegotiable" (*Montgomery County Education Association v. Board of Education* 1987:986).

The most common response to this problem has been to balance the interests of employees in bargaining an issue against the impact of the issue on managerial prerogatives and public policy. This balancing test has taken various forms, none of which have been conducive to labor-management cooperation.

One form of the balancing test is, in effect, a presumption against collective bargaining. For example, in *Corpus Christi Fire Fighters Association v. City of Corpus Christi* (1999:728), the Court of Appeals of Texas opined that bargaining is required on a subject "only if it has a greater effect on working conditions than on management prerogatives." It held that grooming standards for firefighters and changes to rules governing the evaluation of employees who drove city vehicles were not mandatorily bargainable.

Similarly, the California Supreme Court, in holding that the decision to eliminate a bargaining unit position and reassign its duties was a mandatory subject of bargaining, opined, "If an action is taken pursuant to a fundamental managerial or policy decision, it is within the scope of representation only if the employer's need for unencumbered decision making in managing its operations is outweighed by the benefit to employer-employee relations of bargaining about the action in question" (*Building Material and Construction Teamsters v. Farrell* 1986:660).

In Pennsylvania, the presence of an express management rights provision has been determinative in setting presumptions. The general Pennsylvania public employee labor relations statute contains an express management rights provision. This led the Pennsylvania Supreme Court to hold that a subject is mandatorily bargainable if "the impact of the issue on the interest of the employe in wages, hours and terms and conditions of employment outweighs its probable effect on the basic policy of the system as a whole" (*Pennsylvania Labor Relations Board v. State College Area School District* 1975:268). On the other hand, the Pennsylvania statute governing police and firefighter collective bargaining does not contain a management rights provision and Pennsylvania courts have interpreted it to require bargaining unless "the managerial policy . . . substantially outweigh[s] any impact an issue will have on the performance of the duties of the police or fire employees" (*Fraternal Order of Police v. Pennsylvania Labor Relations Board* 1999:1190).

Most jurisdictions, however, have not expressly declared a presumption either in favor of bargaining or against it. Instead, they have opined that whether an item is a mandatory subject of bargaining will turn on whether its impact on working conditions or its impact on public policy predominates.[6] These jurisdictions candidly confess that such subject-by-subject balancing does not lend itself to predictability or consistency.[7] Typically, the courts leave such determinations to the labor relations board to make in the first instance.[8]

A survey of the results of such ad hoc balancing across jurisdictions makes it clear that whether a subject primarily affects working conditions or managerial policy is in the eyes of whoever is reading the scale. Conflicting results have been reached on numerous subjects, including class size,[9] school calendar,[10] drug testing,[11] smoking,[12] and subcontracting.[13] Sometimes, the same observer of the scale has drawn fine lines between mandatory and nonmandatory subjects. For example, the California Court of Appeal has held that drug testing of a firefighter was a mandatory subject of bargaining but suggested that the balance between employer prerogative and employee interests would be struck differently upon a showing that the order to drug test was motivated primarily by concerns of public safety (*Holliday v. City of Modesto* 1991:212–13). The Florida Supreme Court has held that a city need not negotiate drug testing of police officers where there is reason to suspect drug involvement but suggested that a general random drug testing program would require bargaining (*Fraternal Order of Police v. City of Miami* 1992:35).

The employer's motivation is also significant in determining whether a subject must be bargained in New York. In *Levitt v. Board of Collective Bargaining* (1992), the City of New York unilaterally instituted a requirement that all applicants for employment and for promotion disclose any debts they owed to the city and either pay those debts or agree to have payments deducted from their wages as a condition of employment or promotion. The court held that the directive was a mandatory subject of bargaining because its primary motive was to raise revenue. The court suggested that if the directive had been concerned with reputation and character as a qualification for employment or promotion, bargaining would not have been required.

Legal hair splitting is also quite evident in Oregon. The Oregon Court of Appeals has held that firefighter manning is not a mandatory subject of bargaining but the number of firefighters who will respond to a fire call is (*International Association of Fire Fighters v. City of Salem* 1984). Teachers in Oregon fare no better than firefighters in seeking certainty regarding what they have a right to negotiate. The Oregon court has distinguished between the length of the school day, which it views as a nonnegotiable matter of educational policy, and the number of teacher-student contact hours, which must be negotiated (*Gresham Grade Teachers Association v. Gresham Grade School* 1981). It also has distinguished between the school calendar, which need not be negotiated, and vacation periods and the definition of work year for salary purposes, for which bargaining is required (*East County Bargaining Council v. Centennial School District* 1984). Similarly, the Minnesota Court of Appeals has ruled that the establishment of a ride-along policy under which college student interns and Explorer scouts accompany police officers in their squad cars is not a mandatory subject of bargaining but such decisions as the shifts on which they ride and procedures for handling emergencies are (*City of West St. Paul v. Law Enforcement Labor Services* 1991).

The consequences of such case-by-case, jurisdiction-by-jurisdiction application of the balancing test, particularly when combined with the fine splitting of hairs apparent in some jurisdictions, has produced a surreal type of legal realist approach to the scope of bargaining in the public sector. Under this approach, there are no settled rules of general applicability that guide the parties' conduct. Instead, the law becomes what the labor board or court declares it to be in any particular case and the precedential effects of the declaration beyond that particular case are minimal. This approach encourages issue-by-issue litigation over bargaining rights and managerial prerogatives and discourages cooperative discussion of issues of mutual concern. It engenders the type of legal formalism identified by the Secretary of Labor's Task Force (U.S. DOL 1996:65) as a significant barrier to labor-management cooperation.

The negative impact on labor-management cooperation of the ad hoc balancing test's incentive to litigate might be mitigated if the test produced a relatively broad scope of bargaining. As then Professor, now Judge, Harry Edwards observed three decades ago (1973:916):

> The collective bargaining process is in part a therapeutic process and it should permit the parties to address fully all problems which affect the bargaining relationship. If the employer is opposed to a given union demand, he can discuss the problem raised, and then, if appropriate, he can persist in rejecting it. This is a more satisfactory approach in terms of encouraging stable and harmonious labor relations, than to have the employer refuse to discuss an issue in the first instance because it is legally nonnegotiable.

Thirty years ago, Edwards predicted an increasingly broad scope of bargaining in all jurisdictions (1973:916–19). Sixteen years later, Robert Moberly (1989) found that the narrow scope of bargaining in the public sector posed a major barrier to labor-management cooperation.

This narrow scope of bargaining in the public sector results in issues on which employees should have meaningful input being left to unilateral employer determination. For example, in the Florida police drug testing case, the record reflected that two of the officers who were ordered to submit to drug tests had made a number of arrests in a high drug area of the city. The order to be drug tested came as a result of an anonymous telephone tip that they had been seen purchasing marijuana. They submitted under protest and tested negative (*Fraternal Order of Police v. City of Miami* 1992:32). The facts thus raised two legitimate concerns: (1) that the city be able to rid the force of police officers using or trafficking in illegal drugs and (2) that the city and its officers be able to deal with anonymous tips aimed at harassing officers who were a threat to drug dealers and other law breakers. Both issues directly affected the city's ability to deliver high-quality law enforcement services. The resolution of both issues could have benefited from input by police officers through their exclusive bargaining representative. The court, however, saw the issue solely as one of management's prerogative to drug test officers suspected of illegal drug use.

Similarly, in *Racine Education Association v. Wisconsin Employment Relations Commission (WERC)* (1997), the court upheld a decision by the WERC allowing the Racine Unified School District to implement unilaterally a pilot program with a year-round school calendar because it was not a mandatory subject of bargaining. The conclusion that the decision to move to a year-round calendar was a matter of educational policy thus had the ironic result of cutting out the representative of the school district's teachers from participation in a decision concerning what would best improve the delivery of educational services.

The ad hoc balancing of employee interests in negotiating a subject against the impact of negotiations on managerial prerogatives encourages parties to litigate negotiability rather than engage in meaningful dialogue designed to resolve problems of common interest and focus on quality service delivery. The narrow scope of bargaining that application of the balancing test has produced in most jurisdictions has cut the exclusive bargaining representative completely out of meaningful voice in resolving issues, leaving determinations to unilateral employer fiat. Two additional developments have aggravated these barriers to labor-management cooperation.

First, there has been a tendency for legislatures to react to real or perceived service deficiencies by further restricting the scope of bargaining. For example, in Ohio, the legislature reacted to perceived inefficiencies in state university professors' workload by prohibiting bargaining on that subject.[14] Similarly, in Illinois, a major component of the 1995 Chicago School Reform legislation amended the Illinois Educational Labor Relations Act to prohibit decision and impact bargaining on the following subjects: charter school proposals and leaves of absence to work for a charter school, subcontracting, layoffs and reductions in force, class size, class staffing and assignment, class schedules, academic calendar, hours and places of instruction, pupil assessment policies, use and staffing of pilot programs, and use of technology and staffing to provide technology. The amendment applied only to the city of Chicago.[15]

Second, there has been a tendency where labor and management have cooperated in spite of the law to deny enforcement to the fruits of that cooperation. In some instances, for example, courts have denied enforcement to collectively bargained agreements, reasoning that the agreements infringed on the absolute authority of the employer.[16]

In Chicago, despite the legislative prohibition on bargaining numerous subjects that traditionally were negotiated, the Chicago Teachers Union and the Chicago Board of Education reached understandings on these subjects and the board promulgated them unilaterally as board policy. The collective bargaining agreement provided for grievances to be filed and arbitrated over alleged violations of board policy. Nevertheless, the Illinois Educational Labor Relations Board and the Illinois courts have held that the prohibition on bargaining extends to, and prohibits arbitration of, alleged violations of board policy. This has resulted in case-by-case adjudication of whether grievances alleging violations of board policy are arbitrable.[17]

Labor-management cooperation ultimately corrected the situation. On April 16, 2003, the Illinois General Assembly amended the Illinois Education Labor Relations Act to make the decisions which had been prohibited subjects of bargaining permissive subjects and the impact of the decisions mandatory subjects (Public Act 93-0003 (April 16, 2003)). The amendment had the support of the Chicago Board of Education and the Chicago Teachers Union. This amendment should end the litigation over arbitrability.

The successful cooperative effort to change the statute in Chicago is rare. The natural reaction of unions when courts and labor boards deny enforcement to negotiated agreements is to ask, Why bother cooperating if the fruits of the cooperation are legally meaningless? At a minimum, denial of enforcement undermines certainty in bargaining. Enforcement denials also appear to occur on an ad hoc basis and frequently leave the parties with little guidance in determining whether a particular agreement will raise an enforcement challenge (see Befort 1985:1266–67).

Another denial of legal enforcement to a cooperative initiative occurred in the federal government, which has the narrowest scope of bargaining of all systems. President Clinton (1993) ordered executive agencies to negotiate permissive subjects of bargaining. His executive order was rendered essentially unenforceable, however, when the Federal Labor Relations Authority (FLRA) held that the order did not constitute an election to negotiate and, therefore, the FLRA lacked jurisdiction to enforce it through the unfair labor practice procedures of the Federal Service Labor Management Relations Act (*U.S. Department of Commerce, Patent and Trademark Office* 1998).

Cooperation in Spite of the Law

Public sector labor law doctrine has emphasized a competition between employee rights to bargain and employer prerogatives that has raised several barriers to labor-management cooperation. Where significant labor-management cooperation exists, it generally has developed independently of the law. Nowhere was this phenomenon more evident than in the federal government during the Clinton administration.

Initially, collective bargaining by federal government employees was dependent for its legal status on Executive Order 10988, issued by President Kennedy in 1962, and Executive Order 11491, issued by President Nixon in 1969. A key criticism of the executive order system was that it left collective bargaining rights to the grace of the president. The Civil Service Reform Act of 1978 was intended to respond to this criticism by creating a statutory basis for federal employee collective bargaining rights and by establishing an independent regulatory agency to administer the statute.

Beginning with his discharge of striking air traffic controllers, President Reagan ushered a period of highly adversarial labor relations into the federal sector. A desire to deal with the unhealthy state of federal sector labor relations led to the issuance of Executive Order 12871 by President Clinton on October 1, 1993. Among other things, Executive Order 12871 established the National Partnership Council and called for the creation of labor-management partnerships throughout the Executive Branch. The goal of such partnerships was to "champion change in Federal government agencies to transform them into organizations capable of delivering the highest quality services to the American people" (President Clinton 1993:655).

Because the scope of bargaining under the Federal Service Labor Management Relations Act is so narrow, partnerships became the mechanism by which unions and management handled most significant issues. Clinton administration Office of Personnel Management (OPM) Director Janice Lachance (1998:418) characterized the state of federal sector labor relations as follows: "Partnership is the high wire act and collective bargaining is the safety net."

It is easy to see why collective bargaining under the statute declined in importance and relevance in the federal sector during the Clinton administration. In 1997, the National Partnership Council reported a trend among partnerships to focus on what the council characterized as "nontraditional issues," including reorganizations, quality issues, improvements in customer service, re-engineering and streamlining work, impact of new technology, reductions in force, budget and staffing levels, privatization, and procurement (National Partnership Council 1997).

Players besides OPM Director Lachance noted the decreasing relevance of statutory procedures in federal sector labor relations. For example, the February 1999 National Partnership Council meeting featured the U.S. Forest Service Partnership Council. National Federation of Federal Employees representative Mike Buttons (1999) reported:

> Our issue resolution rate is high. When the Council has resolved an issue, the labor-management obligations associated with it at the national level are completed. Because of many issues resolved in Partnership, very few are now addressed in formal negotiations.

Similarly, then FLRA General Counsel Joseph Swerdzewski (1998) characterized the FLRA's decision declining to enforce Executive Order 12871's requirement that agencies bargain over permissive subjects as no big deal. He advised, "The bottom line from where we sit today, only six months after the decision, it does not seem to have had a major impact on slowing or stopping or otherwise interfering with the partnership process." He explained why: "The law doesn't drive how people deal with each other."

In the final days of the Clinton administration, OPM (2001) issued a report that, among other things, catalogued the successes produced by labor-management partnerships. Specific examples listed in the report included:

- Partnering between the Internal Revenue Service (IRS) and National Treasury Employees Union (NTEU) to modernize and restructure the IRS, resulting in measurable improvements in customer service and job satisfaction.

- Partnership between American Federation of Government Employees (AFGE) Local 3973 and Defense Contract Management Command's Raytheon Missile Systems facility resulted in overwhelming improvement in customer service ratings as workload increased 100 percent and the workforce downsized, with $900,000 saved from the reduction in labor-management litigation.

- The U.S. Mint and AFGE Mint Council engaged in joint strategic planning, resulting in the U.S. Mint's consistent ranking near the top in the American Customer Satisfaction Index and its production of record numbers of coins and return of record profits to taxpayers.

- The Social Security Administration (SSA) and AFGE partnership reengineered practices related to SSA's toll-free number, resulting in SSA outscoring all other organizations for 800 number customer satisfaction in 1995, and in a 1999 customer satisfaction rating of 88 percent.

- Partnerships between the James A. Haley Veterans' Hospital and AFGE Local 547, the Florida Nurses Association, and the Tampa Professional Nurses Unit reduced delivery time for critical medication from 92 minutes to 20 minutes, cut turnaround time for x-ray reports from 8 days to 1 day, and reduced processing time for pension and compensation exams from 31 days to 18 days.

- An NTEU–Customs Service partnership designed a seven-step strategy to increase seizures of illegal drugs. During the six-month life of the joint action plan, narcotics seizures increased by 42 percent and drug currency seizures increased by 74 percent.

- Partnership between the Defense Distribution Depot in San Joaquin and AFGE Local 1546 saved $950,000 per year by reducing workplace accidents by 20 percent and ergonomic injuries by 40 percent, reduced overtime expenses from $9.8 million to $1.4 million, and reduced production costs from $25.42 per unit to $23.48 per unit.

In many respects, federal sector labor relations came full circle during the Clinton administration. Labor-management relations began dependent on executive orders for their existence. Criticism of reliance on executive orders led to the enactment of the Federal Service Labor Management Relations Act, as part of the Civil Service Reform Act of 1978. During the Clinton administration, however, the most significant developments in federal sector labor relations occurred through partnerships, which again relied on an executive order as the basis for their existence. The success of federal sector labor relations was measured by the degree to which the law had become irrelevant.

The first two years of the administration of George W. Bush have demonstrated the tenuous nature of labor-management cooperative programs when they are based on something other than a statute. The day after OPM issued its report detailing the successes of labor-management partnerships, the Heritage Foundation issued a report with a competing view of management of the federal workplace (Nesterczuk, Devine, and Moffitt 2001). The Heritage Foundation called on President Bush to make revocation of Executive Order 12871 his first act in the area of management of government. The report argued that labor-management partnerships were a major impediment to the Bush administration's ability to implement its political and policy agenda. The report branded career civil servants as the "permanent government," a segment that it opined must be controlled and limited to using its expertise to implement policies set by the president and his political appointees. It called on the Office of Presidential Personnel to "make appointment decisions based on loyalty first and expertise second, and argued that the whole government apparatus must be managed from this perspective" (Nesterczuk, Devine, and Moffitt 2001: "Lesson # 4").

The Heritage Foundation report criticized Executive Order 12871 for "reduc[ing] the leverage any President can exert to ensure that his policy agenda is accepted and faithfully implemented by the agencies.

Without the central management tools to encourage and reward constructive behavior, the President's agenda will be subordinated to internal organizational priorities" (Nesterczuk, Devine, and Moffitt 2001: "Strategy # 7"). Thus, the Heritage Foundation called for a return to a command-and-control approach to personnel management, with the command and control exercised by political appointees selected for their loyalty to the president rather than their technical expertise.

President Bush acted quickly on the Heritage Foundation's recommendations. On February 17, 2001, he issued Executive Order 13203, which revoked Executive Order 12871, dissolved the National Partnership Council, and directed the heads of all executive agencies to "promptly move to rescind any orders, rules, regulations, guidelines, or policies implementing or enforcing Executive Order 12871 . . ." (President Bush 2001:761).

Despite the revocation of Executive Order 12871, several labor relations professionals expressed initial confidence that labor-management cooperation would continue in federal executive agencies.[18] However, actions such as the issuance of Executive Order 13252 on January 7, 2002, stripping certain employees of the Department of Justice of their collective bargaining rights on national security grounds; issuance of a memo on June 6, 2002, amending Executive Order 13180 so that air traffic control was no longer characterized as an "inherently governmental function"; and the bitter debate over collective bargaining rights of employees transferred to the newly created Department of Homeland Security have led to a revival of bitter adversarial rhetoric not seen since the Reagan administration (see Bologna 2002:928). As Masters and Albright suggest elsewhere in this volume, partnership in the federal government is now up to agency and department heads. The administration has emphasized flexibility, which it sees as antithetical to union representation. This may force unions to revert to adversarial bargaining and litigation or risk becoming irrelevant.

Methods to the Madness

The legal formalism engendered by the dominant public sector approach to determining the scope of bargaining (the use of an ad hoc balancing test) has developed into a significant barrier to labor-management cooperation. This development cries out for an analysis of the rationale behind the balancing approach and the resulting narrow scope of bargaining in the public sector. An analysis of case law from a variety of jurisdictions reveals four factors that have contributed to this state of affairs.

Analogy to the Private Sector

Many jurisdictions have simply borrowed the law governing the scope of negotiations from the private sector. There are numerous cases where courts rely on precedent established under the NLRA.[19] This phenomenon is not surprising. It dates to the earliest years of public sector collective bargaining legislation. The first state to enact a public employee collective bargaining statute was Wisconsin. The statute placed responsibility for administration of the act with the Wisconsin Employment Relations Board (WERB), the agency that had been administering the Wisconsin Employment Peace Act in the private sector for many years. It was only natural for the WERB to adapt private sector concepts to the new public sector statute. Similarly, in other jurisdictions, many, if not most, public sector practitioners come from private sector backgrounds. It is also natural for them to look to private sector legal concepts. This tendency is reinforced by statutory language in many public sector labor relations acts that mirrors the NLRA.

Jurisdictions that look to NLRA precedent derive a balancing test from the Supreme Court's decision in *First National Maintenance Corporation v. National Labor Relations Board* (1980).[20] In *First National Maintenance*, the Court held that an employer was not required to bargain its decision to terminate a contract with a particular customer even though that decision had a negative impact on employee job security. The Court observed that in determining whether a decision was a mandatory subject of bargaining, it is necessary to balance the employer's need for unencumbered managerial control against the benefits that could flow from bargaining about the decision. Reliance on *First National Maintenance* led the California Supreme Court to adopt a balancing text with a presumption against collective bargaining. That court indicated that a matter which is a "fundamental managerial or policy decision" is negotiable "only if the employer's need for unencumbered decision making in managing its operations is outweighed by the benefit to employer-employee relations of bargaining . . ." (*Building, Material and Construction Teamsters v. Farrell* 1986:653).

Narrow Views of the Union's Role

In *First National Maintenance*, the Court took a very narrow and negative view of the union's role at the bargaining table. The Court considered that the union's primary aim in bargaining the decision would be to delay the inevitable. It opined that the employer had to be freed from the delays and uncertainties of the bargaining process to run the business effectively (*First National Maintenance* 1980:683). Indeed, at one time, the NLRB interpreted *First National Maintenance* to require bargaining only where a decision turned on labor costs (*Otis Elevator Company* 1984). In other words, the only positive role the NLRB regarded a union as playing at the bargaining table was to offer concessions in wages and benefits.

The narrow view of what the union may bring to the table that was developed in the private sector has led to a similarly narrow view of the scope of bargaining in the public sector. For example, the Florida Court of Appeal relied on the narrow and negative view of the union's role expressed in *First National Maintenance* in holding that drug testing of police officers is not a mandatory subject of bargaining. After reciting a parade of horribles that would result from having drug-impaired police officers, the court opined:

> To label the drug testing issue as a mandatory subject of collective bargaining could hamper the City's and the citizenry's unquestioned right to a drug-free police force, thereby permitting to exist "a powerful tool for achieving delay, a power that might be used to thwart management's intentions in a manner unrelated to any feasible solution the union might propose."[21]

Unfortunately, beyond noting the similarity in statutory language, most courts do not probe the degree to which public and private sector concerns are analogous and the degree to which adoption of private sector precedents is appropriate. There is good reason to discount the utility of *First National Maintenance* and its progeny as a guide for determining the scope of bargaining in the public sector. As the Connecticut Superior Court has aptly observed:

> The test employed in [the NLRA] in determining what is encompassed in the terms "wages, hours and other conditions of employment" finds them to cease to be mandatory bargaining subjects at the point where union proposals cross the border and infringe on the "core of entrepreneurial control." Governmental bodies are not entrepreneurial. Private business and industry's focus and management depends (*sic*) on decisions from a person who organizes, operates, and assumes the risk for business ventures aimed at earning a profit. In contrast, decisions of governmental units are circumscribed by a constitution and a body of laws which dictate the purpose, manner, organization, and form of operation of that branch of

our government. Such units exist to fulfill some already out-lined constitutional and statutory purpose, not some profit making choice of purpose dictated by a private entrepreneur (*State v. Connecticut Board of Labor Relations* 1993:*3).

Recognition of the public nature of public sector collective bargaining does not automatically translate into a broader scope of bargaining, however. Several jurisdictions have seized upon the public nature of public sector collective bargaining to justify a narrow balancing test in negotiability determinations.

Perceived Tensions between Collective Bargaining and Democracy

A number of writers have contended that public sector collective bargaining is inherently antidemocratic. They suggest that all issues discussed at the bargaining table are political issues that should be decided in the regular political process. They consider it inappropriate to give unions, which they regard as one of many interest groups, an avenue of access to public decision makers that is not available to other interest groups.[22] Similar concerns have been used by some jurisdictions to narrow the scope of bargaining.

The South Dakota Supreme Court's decision in *Aberdeen Education Association v. Board of Education* (1974) provides an extreme example. The court expressed concern that collective negotiations not impinge on the ability of "the whole people to speak by means of laws enacted by their representatives" (*Aberdeen Education* 1974:841) and held a number of items, including teacher preparation periods, the scheduling of teacher conferences, and the availability of aides to perform nonteaching duties such as playground supervision, to be outside the scope of bargainable subjects.

Similarly, the Maryland Court of Appeals has held that school calendar and employee reclassifications are prohibited subjects of bargaining:

Local [school] boards are state agencies, and, as such, are responsible to other appropriate state officials and to the public at large. Unlike private sector employers, local boards must respond to the community's needs. Public school employees are but one of many groups in the community attempting to shape educational policy by exerting influence on local boards. To the extent that school employees can force boards to submit educational policy to an arbitrator, the employees can distort the democratic process by increasing their influence at the expense of these other groups.[23]

Concerns that public sector collective bargaining undermines democratic government are misplaced. When matters are not subject to collective bargaining, they are determined unilaterally by the employer after input from various interest groups. Labeling a matter a mandatory subject of collective bargaining does not eliminate the access of other interest groups to the public decision maker. The duty to bargain requires negotiation but does not compel the employer to reach agreement with the union. Public officials remain accountable to the public for the agreements they reach, or fail to reach, with their employees' unions (see Befort 1985:1261).

It is true that collective bargaining gives unions an avenue of access to public officials not available to other interest groups. In this regard, however, unions are not unique. Other groups have other avenues of access uniquely available to them. Moreover, in many instances there is a need for public employees to have a special avenue of access. Public employees are vastly outnumbered by members of the general public in their capacity as users and consumers of employees' services. As users and consumers the public desires more and better services at lower costs. Labor costs are the largest part of most public-entity budgets. Consequently, unions seeking wage increases and other concessions that would raise labor costs are at a disadvantage vis-à-vis every other interest group in the budget-setting process. That disadvantage justifies providing them with collective bargaining as a special avenue of access (see Summers 1974).

Although requiring bargaining on any particular subject is not per se incompatible with democratic accountability of public officials, one aspect of the bargaining process does raise legitimate concerns in this regard. When bargaining is required, negotiations must proceed either to agreement or through statutorily mandated impasse resolution procedures.

The Impact of Impasse Procedures

It has become trite to say that state governments are laboratories for experimenting with different approaches to public problems. However, the laboratory analogy is particularly true where collective bargaining impasse resolution is concerned. Different jurisdictions employ various models that rely on strikes and other economic pressure, nonbinding fact-finding, or interest arbitration to resolve bargaining impasses.[24]

The type of impasse procedures provided in the labor relations statute has played a role in determining the scope of bargaining. For example, in *In the Matter of New Jersey Transit Bus Operations, Inc.*

(1991), the New Jersey Supreme Court observed that the state statute governing public transit collective bargaining provided for impasses to be resolved through arbitration. The court contrasted this statute to the general public sector collective bargaining statute, which provided only for nonbinding fact-finding. The court concluded that by establishing a binding impasse procedure for transit employees, the legislature manifested its intent to place unions representing transit employees on a more equal footing with transit employers than the legislature was willing to provide for public employees in general. It concluded that, consistent with this intent, the scope of bargaining in public transit would be broader than the scope of bargaining in the general public sector.

More often, however, the presence of interest arbitration has the effect of narrowing the scope of bargaining. The Iowa Supreme Court has observed on several occasions that in determining whether a proposal concerns a mandatory subject of bargaining, it is determining whether it will subject impasses over the proposal to arbitration.[25] Sometimes the effect of the availability of interest arbitration is in the background as the negotiability issue arises only after the parties have actually negotiated and been unable to reach agreement. In such circumstances, the negotiability ruling determines whether the employer is obligated to arbitrate or to comply with an arbitration award.[26]

Interest arbitration differs from the private sector model of collective bargaining in several ways. The most obvious is that it substitutes adjudication for economic (and in the public sector, political) power to resolve impasses. Just as important, under the private sector NLRA model of collective bargaining, an employer is free to press an issue by acting unilaterally once impasse has been reached. In public sector interest arbitration jurisdictions, however, employers generally are prohibited from making unilateral changes with respect to mandatory subjects of bargaining; they must await the outcome of the arbitration, instead.[27]

The presence of interest arbitration as an impasse procedure justifies a narrow scope of bargaining in the public sector. Interest arbitration allows public officials to escape political accountability for their decisions. Public employers may avoid reaching agreement with the union on politically sensitive issues and avoid accountability by blaming the arbitrator for whatever award is imposed.[28]

More importantly, the nature of interest arbitration makes it a forum poorly suited for resolving certain issues. The interest arbitration process is inherently conservative. Parties are in interest arbitration because their collective bargaining process has broken down. Interest arbitrators have the impossible task of crafting the contract that the parties would have agreed to if their bargaining process had been successful. In doing so, arbitrators look to how the issues in dispute have been resolved in comparable communities. They do so because there is no better proxy for what the parties would have agreed to, had their bargaining process not broken down. Consequently, comparability is often the most important factor in interest arbitration.[29]

Reliance on comparability works well for settling disputes over many terms and conditions of employment on which the parties are unable to reach agreement. There are other subjects, however, for which the criteria used in interest arbitration to impose a settlement on the parties may not be appropriate.

Consider, for example, class size. If class size is regarded as a matter of teacher workload, comparability analysis works very well. There will be disputes over the criteria for defining comparable communities. Some may emphasize population, size, property tax base, and geographic location while others may urge examination of levels of student achievement as measured by standardized test scores and similar factors. However, once decisions are reached regarding the factors that render communities comparable for this purpose, the workload in comparable communities will work as a starting point in determining the workload the parties would have agreed to, if their bargaining process had succeeded.

Class size is not only a matter of teacher workload, however. Communities with identical demographics, property valuations and tax rates, student scores on standardized tests, teacher salaries, per-pupil expenditures, and other criteria arguably relevant to determining comparability may reasonably differ on whether investment in smaller class size, increased pull-out programs for students, or improved technology is likely to produce the best educational outcomes. At the middle and high school levels, there may be a trade-off between block scheduling and smaller class size. In such circumstances, comparability does not provide a useful guideline for hypothesizing the outcome that the parties would have reached if their bargaining process had been successful. One should not assume that merely because two other communities opted to invest in smaller class size, the community in which the bargaining impasse was reached would have agreed to follow suit, rather than invest in technology or employ block scheduling.

Other factors commonly relied on in interest arbitration are also not likely to be helpful in resolving an impasse over subjects like class size.

Ability to pay is not likely to be helpful, for example, if the competing proposals have similar costs. These problems may be aggravated, depending on the type of interest arbitration employed. For example, in jurisdictions using final-offer package arbitration,[30] an arbitrator faced with an issue not amenable to resolution through traditional interest arbitration criteria likely will focus on other issues in dispute that are amenable to resolution in deciding which party's final offer to award.

Interest arbitration is not the only impasse resolution method employed in the public sector. Many jurisdictions rely on nonbinding fact-finding.[31] Fact-finding tends to run along a continuum from a supermediator model to a pure adjudicator model.[32] A fact finder who functions primarily in a mediatory capacity uses the power to issue findings of fact and recommendations for settlement to pressure the parties into reaching agreement. Often the agreement becomes the fact finder's recommendations, which the parties then accept. In such cases, the fact finder may provide political cover for the negotiators and reduce the employer's accountability to the public. On the other hand, a fact finder who tends toward a pure adjudicator's role will encounter the same problems in trying to resolve certain issues as an interest arbitrator.[33]

A Way Out?

The incompatibility between a broad scope of bargaining and interest arbitration or fact-finding suggests a major flaw in the dominant public sector labor law doctrine. Jurisdictions have routinely and blindly followed the NLRA model by dividing matters into mandatory and nonmandatory subjects of bargaining. This either-or approach leaves no alternative other than to subject a matter to the full effects of a duty to bargain, including a duty to submit the matter to interest arbitration or fact-finding, or to leave the matter to complete unilateral control by the employer. When bargaining on a subject is not mandatory, the employer has complete power to exclude the union from the decision-making process. It has no duty to provide the union with information relevant to the issue.[34] Indeed, it may bypass the union when seeking employee input on a subject.

For example, in *Corpus Christi Fire Fighters* (1999:728), the fire chief formed an employee committee to create a questionnaire to survey firefighters concerning grooming standards. The chief did not involve the union in the process. The court found no unfair labor practice because it determined that the subject was not one of mandatory bargaining.

The blind adoption of the NLRA model has made the stakes in the classification of a subject so high that it encourages litigation rather than cooperation. Employers feel compelled to litigate to protect what they regard as their ultimate decision-making authority from intervention by a third-party arbitrator or fact finder. Unions feel compelled to litigate because they view it as their only vehicle to compel employers to listen to their voices on particular issues. Consequently, instead of addressing specific problems and searching for common ground, the parties are diverted to a battle over legal formalities.

Regardless of the advisability of this model for the private sector, there is no rational justification for it in the public sector. Decisions by private employers are entrepreneurial in nature, focused on the employer–property owner's decision making concerning the nature and direction of the business. Decisions by public employers, however, are political in nature, focused on the nature and types of public services to be provided. Collaboration with the employees' exclusive bargaining representative focuses the discussion on quality: the quality of service delivery and the quality of work life. A focus on the legal character of an issue becomes relevant only if the union seeks to force a resolution through statutory impasse procedures. Consequently, jurisdictions should experiment with an alternative that is somewhere between a duty to bargain that includes submission to all impasse resolution procedures and unilateral employer determination.

Public sector labor law doctrine is ripe for the recognition of an intermediate duty to consult. Such a duty would include a prohibition on bypassing the exclusive representative and a duty to provide the exclusive representative with relevant information. It would mandate discussion of subjects on which bargaining is not required but would not subject disputes on such matters to interest arbitration or other impasse procedures.

Minnesota has adopted a model of a duty to consult for some of its employees. In so doing, the Minnesota legislature emphasized the role of such a duty in promoting labor-management cooperation:

> The legislature recognizes that professional employees possess knowledge, expertise, and dedication which is (*sic*) helpful and necessary to the operation and quality of public services and which may assist public employers in developing their policies. It is, therefore, the policy of this state to encourage close cooperation between public employers and professional

employees by providing for discussions and the mutual exchange of ideas regarding all matters that are not terms and conditions of employment.[35]

The Minnesota statute requires that employers meet and confer with representatives of their professional employees to discuss policies and other matters relating to employment which are not mandatory subjects of bargaining.[36] It requires that such meet-and-confer sessions take place at least once every four months.[37] It prohibits the employer from meeting and conferring with any employee or group of employees in a bargaining unit, except through their exclusive bargaining representative.[38] The U.S. Supreme Court has upheld the constitutionality of this latter provision (*Minnesota State Board v. Knight* 1984).

A duty to consult, or to meet and confer, is not the same as a duty to bargain. As the Minnesota Supreme Court has recognized, an employer can thwart the intent behind the duty by merely going through the motions of consultation (see *Minneapolis Federation of Teachers v. Minneapolis Special School District* 1977:805). This is because it is impossible to force two parties to cooperate; it is only possible to encourage them.

A duty to consult, however, will encourage cooperation. It will reduce the incentive to seek refuge in formalistic legal categories of bargaining rights and employer prerogatives. Employers will be able to give employees a voice through their exclusive bargaining representatives without fear that by so doing they could end up defending their decisions in interest arbitration or fact-finding. Unions will be assured that employers may not bypass them and deal directly with employees and may not withhold information from them that is relevant to particular issues. Under a duty-to-consult model, the parties will not be able to refuse to discuss a subject. Regardless of whether such discussions are labeled bargaining or meeting and conferring, they may lead to agreement in many instances and to a narrowing and better understanding of differences in others.

Litigation over whether such discussions, once held, were legally negotiations or consultations will be confined primarily to instances where the union seeks to advance the subject to the formal impasse resolution procedures. Thus, recognition of a duty to consult will defer the battle over the formal legal classification of an issue as a subject of bargaining or a subject of consultation, from the initial raising of the issue, where the legal classification dispute serves as a barrier to labor-management cooperation, to the impasse resolution stage, where the legal classification substantively matters. In between, the parties may find considerable common ground or the union, feeling that its voice has been heard even though it did not get everything it wanted, may decide not to press the matter further.

Of course, as the experience in the federal sector during the Clinton administration demonstrates, there is no legal impediment to the employer inviting employee voice through the exclusive bargaining representative into a broader area of decision making. As Executive Order 13203 demonstrated, however, such invitations are subject to withdrawal at any time in the absence of a statutory foundation.

A statutory duty to consult is superior to reliance on the parties to cooperate on their own for another reason. Traditional labor law doctrine concerning the duty to bargain sets clearly defined boundaries and roles for union and management. Labor-management cooperation blurs these lines (see OPM 2001: § V(1)). Parties understandably will be hesitant and feel vulnerable when moving outside traditional bargaining roles. Yet major commitments by both sides are necessary to develop the trust that is critical for labor-management cooperative programs to succeed (see OPM 2001: § V(2)). Providing a statutory basis for a duty to consult may increase the parties' confidence in making the necessary investments.

Jurisdictions should not automatically adopt the Minnesota statute verbatim. One of the great advantages of public sector labor relations law is the ability of jurisdictions to experiment with different methods of implementing a particular concept. There are many issues, particularly those involved in the enforcement of the duty to consult and the point at which the employer may act unilaterally, that should be worked out through such experimentation. However, development of a duty to consult can reverse the role of public sector labor law doctrine from an inhibitor of and barrier to labor-management cooperation to a promoter of cooperation.

Conclusion

Labor-management cooperation has many positive effects on public sector labor relations. Legal doctrine, therefore, should encourage it. Unfortunately, current public sector labor law doctrine serves as a barrier to labor-management cooperation. Under current doctrine, courts and labor boards engage in an ad hoc balancing of employee interests in bargaining against employer prerogatives. This approach encourages litigation rather than cooperation. Where cooperative efforts succeed, they do so in spite of, rather than because of, the law.

A crucial flaw in current public sector labor law doctrine is its importing of the NLRA's dichotomy between mandatory and non-mandatory subjects of bargaining. Such a dichotomy forces courts and labor boards to subject matters to the full range of public sector impasse procedures, including interest arbitration and fact-finding, or to leave the matter to complete unilateral employer control.

Jurisdictions should experiment with a duty to consult that will fall midway between a duty to bargain and unilateral employer control. Recognition of such a duty would reduce the incentive to litigate by requiring parties to discuss matters even though they may disagree over whether such discussions are bargaining or consultation. In so doing, a duty to consult will encourage labor-management cooperation in the public sector.

Acknowledgements

The author gratefully acknowledges helpful comments from Rafael Gely, excellent research assistance from John DiJohn, and financial support from the Marshall-Ewell Research Fund at Chicago-Kent College of Law.

Notes

[1] 29 U.S.C. §§ 158(a)(5) and 158(b)(3) impose a duty to bargain on employers and unions. 29 U.S.C. § 158(d) defines the duty as the obligation to bargain in good faith with respect to "wages, hours and other terms and conditions of employment."

[2] See, e.g., Ill. Comp. Stat. § 315/7; 26 Me. Rev. Stat. Ann. § 979-D(1); Mich. Comp. L. Ann. § 423.215; Pa. Stat. Ann. tit. 43, § 1101.701.

[3] See, e.g., Ia. Code § 20.9; Kans. Stat. Ann. § 75-4327(b).

[4] See, e.g., Ia. Code § 20.7; Ill. Comp. Stat. § 315/4; Pa. Stat. Ann. tit. 43, § 1101.702.

[5] See, e.g., *Fraternal Order of Police, Lodge No. 5 v. Pennsylvania Lab. Rel. Bd.*, 727 A.2d 1187 (Pa. Cmwlth. Ct. 1999) (distinguishing police and firefighter labor relations statute that lacks a management rights provision from general public employee statute that contains one but concluding that establishment of civilian review board to investigate complaints of police misconduct was not mandatorily bargainable because matters of managerial policy substantially outweighed impact on employee job performance); but see *State v. Maine Lab. Rel. Bd.*, 413 A.2d 510 (Me. 1980) (holding that decision to open state liquor stores on a state holiday was a mandatory subject of bargaining, relying, in part, on absence of management rights provision in state labor relations statute).

[6] See, e.g., *West Hartford Educ. Ass'n v. DeCourcy*, 295 A.2d 526 (Conn. 1972); *Fraternal Order of Police, Miami Lodge 20 v. City of Miami*, 609 So.2d 31 (Fla. 1992); *Montgomery County Educ. Ass'n v. Board of Educ.*, 534 A.2d 980 (Md. 1987); *City of Lynn v. Labor Rel. Comm'n*, 681 N.E.2d 1234 (Mass. App. 1997); *Springfield Educ. Ass'n v. Springfield Sch. Dist. No. 19*, 621 P.2d 547 (Or. 1980); *West Bend Educ. Ass'n v. Wisc. Empl. Rel. Comm'n*, 357 N.W.2d 534 (Wisc. 1984).

[7] See, e.g., *City of Lynn v. Labor Rel. Comm'n*, 681 N.E.2d 1234, 1237 (Mass. App. 1997)("[A]ny attempt to define with precision and certainty the subjects about which bargaining is mandated . . . is doomed to failure.").

[8] See, e.g., *Central City Educ. Ass'n v. Illinois Educ. Lab. Rel. Bd.*, 599 N.E.2d 892 (Ill. 1992).

[9] Compare *West Hartford Educ. Ass'n v. DeCourcy*, 295 A.2d 526 (Conn. 1972); *Boston Teachers Union v. School Committee*, 350 N.E.2d 707 (Mass. 1976) with *Hillsborough Classroom Teachers Ass'n v. School Bd.*, 423 So. 2d 969 (Fla. App. 1982); *NEA-Topeka v. Unified Sch. Dist. 501*, 592 P.2d 93 (Kans. 1979); *City of Biddeford v. Biddeford Teachers Ass'n*, 304 A.2d 387 (Me. 1973); *Seward Educ. Ass'n v. School Dist.*, 199 N.W.2d 752 (Neb. 1972); *Dunnellen Bd. of Educ. v. Dunnellen Educ. Ass'n*, 311 A.2d 737 (N.J. 1973); *Teachers Ass'n v. Helsby*, 315 N.E.2d 775 (N.Y. 1974).

[10] Compare *State v. Board of Lab. Rel.*, 1993 WL 7261 (Conn. Super. Jan. 8, 1993) with *Montgomery County Educ. Ass'n v. Board of Educ.*, 534 A.2d 980 (Md. 1987).

[11] Compare *Holiday v. City of Modesto*, 280 Cal. Rptr. 206 (Cal. App. 1991); *County of Cook v. Licensed Practical Nurses Ass'n*, 671 N.E.2d 787 (Ill. App. 1996) with *Fraternal Order of Police, Miami Lodge 20 v. City of Miami*, 609 So.2d 31 (Fla. 1992).

[12] Compare *Newark Valley Central Sch. Dist. v. Public Emp. Rel. Bd.*, 632 N.E.2d 443 (N.Y. 1994) with *AFSCME Local 1186 v. State Bd. of Lab. Rel.*, 620 A.2d 766 (Conn. 1993).

[13] Compare *Appeal of Hillsboro-Deering Sch. Dist.*, 737 A.2d 1098 (N.H. 1999) with *Amalgamated Transit Union, Local 1593 v. Hillsborough Area Regional Transit Auth.*, 742 So. 2d 380 (Fla. App. 1999); *City of Belvidere v. State Lab. Rel. Bd.*, 692 N.E.2d 295 (Ill. 1998); *Local 195, IFPTE v. State*, 443 A.2d 187 (N.J. 1982).

[14] See *Central State Univ. v. AAUP*, 526 U.S. 124 (1999)(upholding the constitutionality of the statute codified at Ohio Rev. Code § 3345).

[15] 115 Ill. Comp. Stat. 5/4.5.

[16] See, e.g., *Board of Educ. v. Round Valley Teachers Ass'n*, 914 P.2d 193 (Cal. 1996)(holding unenforceable provision of contract requiring 30 days' notice and statement of reasons for non-renewal of probationary teacher's contract); *Chicago School Reform Bd. of Trustees v. Illinois Educ. Lab. Rel. Bd.*, 721 N.E.2d 676 (Ill. App. 1999)(holding unenforceable collective bargaining agreement provisions governing dismissal of non–tenure eligible full-time–basis substitute teachers); see generally Hodges 1990.

[17] See, e.g., *Chicago Teachers Union v. Illinois Educ. Lab. Rel. Bd.*, 778 N.E.2d 1232 (Ill. App. Ct. 2002); *Chicago School Reform Bd. of Trustees v. Illinois Educ. Lab. Rel. Bd.*, 741 N.E.2d 989 (Ill. App. Ct. 2000), *vacated and remanded*, 754 N.E.2d 1281 (Ill. 2001); *Chicago Bd. of Educ.*, 15 Pub. Emp. Rptr. Ill. ¶ 1077 (Ill. Educ. Lab. Rel. Bd. 1999); 15 Pub. Emp. Rptr. Ill. ¶ 1038 (Ill. Educ. Lab. Rel. Bd. 1999); 15 Pub. Emp. Rptr. Ill. ¶ 1037 (Ill. Educ. Lab. Rel. Bd. 1999); 15 Pub. Emp. Rptr. Ill. ¶ 1036 (Ill. Educ. Lab. Rel. Bd. 1999).

[18] See "HHS Rescinds Permissive Bargaining Election" (2001:842); "Order Will Not End Cooperation Efforts" (2001:251).

[19] See, e.g., *Building Material & Construction Teamsters' Union, Local 216 v. Farrell*, 715 P.2d 648 (Cal. 1986); *Fire Fighters Union Local 1186 v. City of Vallejo*, 526 P.2d 971 (Cal. 1974); *San Francisco Fire Fighters Local 798 v. Board of Supervisors*, 5 Cal. Rptr. 2d 176 (Cal. App. 1992); *Holliday v. City of Modesto*, 280 Cal. Rptr. 206 (Cal. App. 1991); *Long Beach Police Officer Ass'n v. City of Long Beach*, 203 Cal. Rptr. 494 (Cal. App. 1984); *Solano County Employees' Ass'n v. County of Solano*, 186 Cal. Rptr. 147 (Cal. App. 1982); *AFSCME Local 1186 v. State Bd. of Lab. Rel.*, 620 A.2d 766 (Conn. 1993); *Greater Bridgeport Transit Dist. v. State Bd. of Lab. Rel.*, 653 A.2d 229 (Conn. Super. 1993); *State v. State Bd. of Lab. Rel.*, 1993 WL 7261 (Conn. Super. Jan. 8, 1993); *Central City Educ. Ass'n v. Ill. Educ. Lab. Rel. Bd.*, 599 N.W.2d 892 (Il. 1992); *State v. Maine Lab. Rel. Bd.*, 413 A.2d 510 (Me. 1980).

[20] 452 U.S. 666 (1980); see, e.g., *Building Material & Construction Teamsters' Union, Local 216 v. Farrell*, 715 P.2d 648 (Cal. 1986)(relying on *First National Maintenance* for balancing test); *Central City Educ. Ass'n v. Ill. Educ. Lab. Rel. Bd.*, 599 N.W.2d 892 (Ill. 1992)(same).

[21] *City of Miami v. F.O.P., Miami Lodge 20*, 571 So. 2d 1309, 1326 (Fla. App. 1989), *aff'd*, 609 So. 2d 31 (Fla. 1992)(quoting *First National Maintenance*, 452 U.S. at 683).

[22] See, e.g., Corbett (1979:255–57); Kilberg (1970:192–95); Summers (1980:5).

[23] *Montgomery County Educ. Ass'n v. Board of Educ.*, 534 A.2d 980, 987 (Md. 1987)(citation omitted); see also *Appeal of City of Concord*, 651 A.2d 944, 946 (N.H. 1994)(expressing similar concerns).

[24] For an overview of the different models see Malin (1993:316–35).

[25] See, e.g., *State v. Public Emp. Rel. Bd.*, 508 N.W.2d 668 (Iowa 1993); *Charles City Educ. Ass'n v. Public Emp. Rel. Bd.*, 291 N.W.2d 663 (Iowa 1980); *Charles City Community Sch. Dist. v. Public Emp. Rel. Bd.*, 275 N.W.2d 766 (Iowa 1979).

[26] *City of Danbury v. International Ass'n of Fire Fighters, Local 801*, 603 A.2d 393 (Conn. 1992); *Jackson Fire Fighters Ass'n v. City of Jackson*, 575 N.W.2d 823 (Mich. App. 1998).

[27] See *Green County*, Dec. No. 20308-B (Wisc. Emp. Rel. Bd. 1984), reprinted in Edwards, Clark, and Craver (1991:502), and cases cited at note 16 therein.

[28] The effects of this ability to avoid accountability are mitigated in those jurisdictions that allow the employer's governing body to reject the interest arbitration award, usually by a super-majority vote. See, e.g., Ill. Comp. Stat. § 315/14(n).

[29] See Currie and McConnell (1991:713–14); Laner and Manning (1984:856–59).

[30] See, e.g., Wisc. Stat. § 111.77.

[31] At least in the State of Washington, an employer that repeatedly breaches its duty to bargain in good faith may find itself compelled to arbitrate, even though the statute provides only for fact-finding. See *Municipality of Metro. Seattle v. Public Emp. Rel. Comm'n*, 826 P.2d 158 (Wash. 1992).

[32] For a discussion of the competing models, see, e.g., Gerhart and Drotning (1980:108–12); Jackson (1988:28–38).

[33] A small minority of jurisdictions recognize public employees' right to strike. Reliance on a right to strike as the ultimate tool for impasse resolution is less likely to distort the democratic process than reliance on fact-finding or interest arbitration. Not all rights to strike, however, are created equal. Several jurisdictions require exhaustion of a fact-finding process prior to a strike, resulting in significant reliance on fact-finding as the primary vehicle for resolving bargaining impasses. Even where prestrike fact-finding is not required, the employer may be precluded from acting unilaterally at impasse. Compare *Philadelphia Housing Auth. v. Labor Rel. Bd.*, 620 A.2d 594 (Pa. Cmnwlth. 1993)(holding that employer may not act unilaterally unless union strikes) with *Kewanee Community Unit Sch. Dist. No. 229*, 4 Pub. Emp. Rptr. Ill. (LRP Publications) ¶ 1136 (Ill. Educ. Lab. Rel. Bd. 1988)(following NLRA model).

[34] See, e.g., *Village of Franklin Park v. State Lab. Rel. Bd.*, 638 N.E.2d 1144, 1148 (Ill. App. 1994)(relying on NLRA precedent).

[35] Minn. Stat. § 179A.08.

[36] Minn. Stat. § 179A.07(3).

[37] Minn. Stat. § 179A.08(2).

[38] Minn. Stat. § 179A.07(4).

References

Aberdeen Education Association v. Board of Education, 215 N.W.2d 837 (S.D. 1974).

Befort, Stephen F. 1985. "Public Sector Bargaining: Fiscal Crisis and Unilateral Change." *Minnesota Law Review*, Vol. 69, pp. 1221–75.

Bologna, Michael. 2002. "Unions Accuse Bush of Touting Security as Federal Sector Union Busting Strategy." *Government Employment Relations Reporter* (BNA), September 24, p. 928.

Building Material & Construction Teamsters' Union v. Farrell, 715 P.2d 648 (Cal. 1986).

Bush, George W. 2001. Executive Order 13203 (February 17, 2001), 3 C.F.R. 761 (published in C.F.R. in 2002).

———. 2002a. Executive Order 13252 (January 7, 2002), 3 C.F.R. 195 (published in C.F.R. in 2003).

———. 2002b. Memo amending Executive Order 13180 (June 6, 2002). <http://www.whitehouse.gov/news/releases/2002/06/20020606-5.html>. [May 15, 2003.]

Buttons, Mike. 1999. Transcript of National Partnership Council Meeting, February 10, 1999. <http://www.opm.gov/npc/HTML/FEBTRANS.HTM> [June 2, 1999].

City of West St. Paul v. Law Enforcement Labor Services, Inc., 466 N.W.2d 27 (Minn. App. 1991).

Clinton, William J. 1993. Executive Order 12871. (October 1, 1993), 3 C.F.R. 655–57 (published in C.F.R. in 1994).

Corbett, William L. 1979. "Determining the Scope of Public Sector Collective Bargaining: A New Look Via a Balancing Formula." *Montana Law Review,* Vol. 40, pp. 231–85.

Corpus Christi Fire Fighters Association v. City of Corpus Christi, 10 S.W.3d 723 (Tex. App. 1999).

Currie, Janet, and Sheena McConnell. 1991. "Collective Bargaining in the Public Sector: The Effect of Legal Structure on Dispute Costs and Wages." *American Economic Review,* Vol. 81, pp. 693–718.

East County Bargaining Council v. Centennial School District, 685 P.2d 452 (Or. App. 1984).

Edwards, Harry T. 1973. "The Emerging Duty to Bargain in the Public Sector." *Michigan Law Review,* Vol. 71, pp. 885–934.

Edwards, Harry T., R. Theodore Clark, Jr., and Charles B. Craver. 1991. *Labor Relations Law in the Public Sector: Cases and Materials.* 4th ed. Charlottesville, VA: Michie.

First National Maintenance Corporation v. NLRB, 452 U.S. 666 (1980).

Fraternal Order of Police, Lodge No. 5 v. Pennsylvania Labor Relations Board, 727 A.2d 1187 (Pa. Cmwlth. Ct. 1999).

Fraternal Order of Police, Miami Lodge 20 v. City of Miami, 609 So.2d 31 (Fla. 1992).

Gerhart, Paul F., and John F. Drotning. 1980. *A Six State Study of Impasse Procedures in the Public Sector.* Final Report 108-12 (MSA DRA 80/04). Labor-Management Services Administration, Division of Research and Analysis, U.S. Department of Labor. Washington, DC: DOL.

Gresham Grade Teachers Association v. Gresham Grade School District No. 4, 630 P.2d 1304 (Or. App. 1981).

"HHS Rescinds Permissive Bargaining Election: Cooperation to Continue, Memorandum Says." 2001. *Government Employment Relations Reporter* (BNA), July 31, p. 842.

Hodges, Ann C. 1990. "The Steelworkers Trilogy in the Public Sector." *Chicago-Kent Law Review,* Vol. 66, pp. 631–83.

Holliday v. City of Modesto, 280 Cal. Rptr. 206 (Cal. App. 1991).

International Association of Fire Fighters, Local 314 v. City of Salem, 684 P.2d 605 (Or. App. 1984).

In the Matter of New Jersey Transit Bus Operations, Inc., 592 A.2d 547 (N.J. 1991).

Jackson, Richard L. 1988. *Fact-Finding under the School Boards and Teachers Collective Negotiations Act of Ontario.* Toronto: Education Relations Commission, Queen's Printer for Ontario, pp. 28–38.

Kennedy, John F. 1962. Executive Order 10988. (January 17, 1962), 3 C.F.R. 521–28 (1959–1963 compilation, published in C.F.R. in 1964).

Kilberg, William J. 1970. "Appropriate Subjects for Bargaining in Local Government Labor Relations." *Maryland Law Review,* Vol. 30, pp. 179–98.

Lachance, Janice. 1998. "OPM Director Lachance Addresses Future of Federal Workforce." *Government Employment Relations Reporter* (BNA), April 13, p. 418.

Laner, Richard, and Julia W. Manning. 1984. "Interest Arbitration: A New Terminal Impasse Procedure for Illinois Public Sector Employees." *Chicago-Kent Law Review*, Vol. 60, pp. 839–62.

Levitt v. Board of Collective Bargaining, 589 N.E.2d 1 (N.Y. 1992).

Malin, Martin H. 1993. "Public Employees' Right to Strike: Law and Experience." *University of Michigan Journal of Law Referees*, Vol. 26, pp. 313–401.

Minneapolis Federation of Teachers v. Minneapolis Special School District, 258 N.W.2d 801 (Minn. 1977).

Minnesota State Board v. Knight, 465 U.S. 271 (1984).

Moberly, Robert B. 1989. "Legal Impediments of Labor-Management Cooperation in State and Local Government." In *U.S. Labor Law and the Future of Labor-Management Cooperation*. Final Report 5 to the Department of Labor, Bureau of Labor Management Relations and Cooperative Programs, BLMR 134 (June).

Montgomery County Educ. Ass'n v. Board of Educ., 534 A.2d 980 (Md. Ct. App. 1987).

National Labor Relations Act (NLRA), 29 U.S.C. §§ 151–168. 2000.

National Partnership Council. 1997. *Report to the President on Progress in Labor-Management Partnerships* (December 31, 1997). <http://www.opm.gov/npc/97report> [June 2, 1999].

Nesterczuk, George, Donald J. Devine, and Robert E. Moffit. 2001. *Taking Charge of Federal Personnel*. Heritage Foundation Backgrounder No. 1404 (January 10). <http://www.heritage.org/Research/GovernmentReform/BG1404.cfm> [November 27, 2002].

Nixon, Richard M. 1969. Executive Order 11491. (October 29, 1969), 3 C.F.R 191–205, (1969 compilation, published in C.F.R. in 1970).

OPM. 2001. U.S. Office of Personnel Management. Labor-Management Partnership. *A Report to the President* (January 9, 2001). <http://www.opm.gov/lmr/report/index.htm> [November 27, 2002].

"Order Will Not End Cooperation Efforts, Manager, Union Officials Say at Meeting." 2001. *Government Employment Relations Reporter* (BNA), Feb. 27, p. 251.

Otis Elevator Co., 269 N.L.R.B. 891 (1984).

Pennsylvania Labor Relations Board v. State College Area School District, 337 A.2d 262 (Pa. 1975).

Racine Education Association v. Wisconsin Employment Relations Commission, 571 N.W.2d 887 (Wisc. App. 1997).

State v. Connecticut Board of Labor Relations, 1993 WL 7245 (Conn. Super. January 8, 1993).

Summers, Clyde W. 1974. "Public Employee Bargaining: A Political Perspective." *Yale Law Journal*, Vol. 83, pp. 1156–1260.

Summers, Robert S. 1980. "Public Sector Collective Bargaining Substantially Diminishes Democracy." *Government Union Review* (Winter), pp. 5–22.

Swerdzewski, Joseph. 1998. Transcript of National Partnership Council Meeting, November 10. <http://www.opm.gov/npc/HTML/NOV98.HTML> [June 2, 1999].

U.S. Department of Commerce, Patent and Trademark Office, 54 F.L.R.A. 360 (1998).

U.S. Department of Labor. Secretary of Labor. Task Force on Excellence in State and Local Government Through Labor-Management Cooperation. 1996. *Working Together for Public Service*. Washington, DC: GPO.

CHAPTER 10

Wearing Two Hats: The Unionization of Public Sector Supervisors

ADRIENNE E. EATON AND PAULA B. VOOS
Rutgers University

Introduction

Of the many differences between public and private sector collective bargaining, one of those potentially most important, but often ignored, is the unionization of supervisors and other managers. Private sector supervisors and managers lack representation rights.[1] In contrast, public sector supervisors and other lower- to middle-level managers have the right to engage in collective bargaining in more than a dozen states, including many of the most highly populated. In these states, supervisors have exercised those rights in large numbers.

Curiously, supervisory collective bargaining has not entered the discussion regarding the restructuring of work and labor relations in the public sector—even though work restructuring has raised issues about representation rights in the private sector.[2] The report of the U.S. Secretary of Labor's Task Force on Excellence in State and Local Government (U.S. DOL 1996), for example, seems to assume that supervisors sit on the managerial side of collective bargaining. Its discussion of experimentation with self-managed teams, flattened managerial hierarchies, and mid-level manager obstruction of cooperative programs does not explore the implications of managerial representation (p. 77 of the report, for example). Nor does it identify the potential advantages of having supervision collectively represented in cooperative efforts—even though non-representation of supervisors' interests in cooperative efforts has been identified as a problem for such programs in the private sector (Voos, Eaton, and Belman 1993).

This chapter takes a new look at public sector supervisory unionization. We approach the question of supervisory unionism with the assumption that employees deserve collective bargaining rights unless there are strong public policy reasons to withdraw them. We recognize that there are major issues in the structuring of those rights (such as whether it is

best for units or unions to differ between supervisors and their subordinates). Thus, the empirical focus of this chapter is whether or not collective bargaining by supervisors creates serious problems for the functioning
of the labor relations system or, more broadly and importantly, affects
how well governmental units perform their missions. Unlike prior research on the impact of supervisory unions, which predates the current
discussion of work structuring in the public sector, we explore, albeit
somewhat superficially, whether supervisors' organizing hurts or helps
cooperative restructuring efforts. Our research involved interviews with
public sector managers and union representatives in New Jersey, one of
the states that has given both first-level supervisors and moderately high-
level managers collective bargaining rights.

Review of Prior Research

Research on the question of public sector supervisory unionism has
tended to focus on the interrelated constructs of loyalty, identity, and
organizational commitment. This reflects both the legislative and judicial
justifications for the exclusion of supervisors in the private sector. The
logic of exclusion is rooted in the supposed need of the employer for the
undivided loyalty of supervisors or other managerial employees. Union
membership is assumed to take away, or at best divide, that loyalty.

Most prior studies have focused on supervisors in local government.
Hayford (1975) surveyed local government employees in Iowa, breaking
them into four groups: rank-and-file employees, nonbonafide supervisors, bonafide supervisors, and upper-level agency managers. Bonafide
supervisors identified more closely with upper-level management on the
definition of the supervisor's role. Interestingly, nonbonafide supervisors
reported the least identification with management. Wheeler and
Kochan (1977) looked at differences in fire department officers' identification with management, based on both union status and bargaining
structure. Officers were surveyed on their agreement with their chief or
rank and file on six issues. Overall, officers tended to agree with the
rank and file on pay and benefits and manning issues but with their
chief on enforcement of rules and discipline. Union representation or
nonrepresentation and whether the officer involved was in the same
unit as the rank and file were unimportant.

Murrman (1978) examined the relationship between unionization
and supervisor identification with management within another uniformed service, police. While there was no relationship for sergeants,
unionized lieutenants had lower identification with management.[3] A

more recent study (Piskulich 1995) examined supervisory unionism in a medium-size city in Michigan. In this city all but two city employees, the city manager and the assistant city manager, were in one of two unions (one for supervisors and one for "executives"). The study looked at both labor relations processes (management's preparation for collective bargaining and contract administration) and broader managerial issues, like the budgeting process and "day-to-day working relationships." Piskulich found that the unionized managers "consider themselves management" and have an instrumental rather than ideological attachment to union membership. Piskulich concluded, "No threats [to effective management] associated with contract administration, fragmentation, and loyalty were reported or noted" (p. 280). The lack of problems was, in part, explained by particular practices that helped managers handle their dual roles. First, separate bargaining units were viewed as "reinforc[ing] the divide with the rank and file." Second, the bargaining process and preparation for it were divided into money and operational issues so that managers could give input into the bargaining on operational issues (work rules) wearing their managerial hats. Third, "weekly meetings of the manager's cabinet help[ed] bind department heads to team and organization."

Scott and Seers (1987) examined organizational commitment and agreement with management on specific bargaining issues among supervisors employed by the state of Alabama in two state residential facilities. Half of the sample in the study were union members. Union members were significantly more likely than nonmembers to differ with management on 11 of 13 bargaining issues. Bonafide and less-than-bonafide supervisors had similar views on bargaining issues, although supervisors with bonafide authority expressed significantly greater organizational commitment. Union membership had no impact. The authors concluded that "there is little basis for automatically denying bargaining rights to public sector supervisors." They also concluded "that the tendency in the public sector to bestow supervisory titles and status without comparable level of authority is...counterproductive" (p. 129).

In contrast to these studies of attitudes, Wheeler's studies of firefighters have attempted to focus on the "bottom line" by looking at the impact of union status and bargaining unit structure on individual and departmental performance. Wheeler and Kochan (1977) asked chiefs and officers whether unionization made the officers' jobs easier or harder. The majority of officers and chiefs reported that it made no difference on all or most job dimensions. The majority of chiefs also reported, however, that unionization did make discipline and grievance handling more difficult. Moreover, unionization was possibly related to performance problems for line officers above the rank of captain, but the evidence on that was mixed.[4] Officer surveys demonstrated a strong desire for both union membership and single bargaining units for all.

Wheeler (1983) looked at the impact of officer unionization on fire department effectiveness. A 10-item index of fire department effectiveness was developed, including items that the author argued "reflect the public interest." These include work quality, efficiency, anticipating problems, and adaptability to change. Regression results indicated no significant relationship between union status and performance. However, there was a significant and negative bivariate correlation between effectiveness and bargaining units that included officers above the rank of captain together with the rank and file.

Overall, prior research has identified little negative impact from the unionization of supervisors. Problems seem more likely to arise with the highest-level supervisors, with issues most closely related to collective bargaining and discipline, and when supervisors, especially high-level supervisors, are in the same bargaining units as their subordinates. Piskulich's (1995) work indicates that even problems in labor relations processes are not inevitable and that management practices can ameliorate potential problems. At the same time, some of the research points to other sources of problems in public sector management, particularly the tendency to misidentify or mistitle jobs as supervisory when in fact they involve little to no real authority.

Law and Practice in New Jersey

The statute governing public sector labor relations in the state, the New Jersey Employer-Employee Relations Act (NJSA 34:13) was originally passed in 1968 and amended in 1974 (the law is also known as Chapter 303). Coverage was broad from the beginning and remains so. Employees are defined as any public employee "except elected officials, members of boards and commissions, managerial executives and confidential employees" (NJSA 34:13A-3(d)). The term managerial executive is defined in this way:

> "Managerial executives" of a public employer means persons who formulate management policies and practices, and persons who are charged with the responsibility of directing the effectuation of such management policies and practices, except that in any school district this term shall include only the superintendent

or other chief administrator, and the assistant superintendent of the district. (Chap. 123, Sect 2; NJSA 34:13A-3(f))

Public Employee Relations Commission (PERC) and New Jersey State Supreme Court decisions have further elucidated the meaning of this language.[5] Neither the court nor PERC has challenged the logic of the divided-loyalty exclusion; rather, they have contended that the public sector context alters the level of authority in which that division becomes a problem.

In addition to basic coverage, the law provides guidance regarding appropriate bargaining units. Supervisors, defined as those "having the power to hire, discharge, discipline, or to effectively recommend the same," were explicitly given the right to representation; however, their representation was limited by the requirement that it be by a different labor organization and that they be placed in separate units from their subordinates (NJSA 34:13; *Turnpike Authority v. AFSCME Council 73* 1997, p. 345). In an early decision (*Board of Education v. Wilton* 1971), the state Supreme Court found that different levels of supervisors must be placed into different bargaining units.

In practice this broad, inclusive statute has made for unionization and participation in negotiations for a wide range of public employees. Recent estimates for the public sector in New Jersey put the rate of coverage by a union or employee association at 64 percent for state workers and 71 percent for local public employees (AFL-CIO Public Employee Department 1997, using 1994–1996 CPS data). For some sectors or occupations (e.g., teachers and nonvolunteer fire departments), coverage approaches 100 percent.

In state government outside the prisons and state institutions, there are four major bargaining units, all represented by locals of the Communications Workers of America (CWA): Administrative and Clerical (approximately 8,500 persons), Professional (12,000), Primary Level Supervisor (12,000), and Higher Level Supervisor (2,400). The eight separate CWA locals to which these workers belong are organized, not by bargaining unit, but geographically or by department. In some state departments, like Community Affairs, Education, Environmental Protection, Labor, or Transportation, a single union represents the vast majority of workers in the agency, supervisory or not.[6] It is not clear that separate units, and separate contracts, matter much in practice—pattern bargaining is strong for all state workers and the four separate contracts contain only minute differences.

In state institutions and in the turnpike authority, different unions represent different levels of state workers. In the state institutions for the developmentally disabled and psychiatric patients, for instance, CWA-represented supervisors (primary and higher-level) oversee CWA members in professional, administrative, and clerical titles. But they also supervise American Federation of State, County, and Municipal Employees (AFSCME) members who constitute the large direct-care workforce.[7]

State government managers who are legally excluded from collective bargaining are not, in fact, unorganized. Prior to layoffs early in 2002, there were about 3,000 managers in state government who were not eligible for union representation, out of a total workforce of about 65,000 persons. About 800 of these 3,000 managers belonged to the Public Sector Managers Association (PSMA). This association was formed in 1991 when managerial pay compression began to surface as a major issue. Compression resulted from a decision in the mid-1980s to detach managerial pay changes from their traditional patterning after the negotiated union pay increases. Although PSMA has no bargaining rights, it does have dues checkoff and it represents managers' interests in the political process and before administrative decision-making bodies.

Practice is also diverse in local government. It appears to be more unusual there for supervisors and the workers they supervise to be in the same union; where they are in the same international, they are typically in separate locals.[8] Volunteer fire companies are common in the state, but in larger municipalities with public firefighters, there are typically separate units and locals for the rank and file and different levels of officers. In public schools, teachers are typically represented by the New Jersey Education Association, but school principals are in a different union, as are higher-level educators.

In this broad coverage of public sector supervisors above the first level, New Jersey resembles 10 other states.[9] Fifteen other states and the District of Columbia provide rights for first-level supervisors only or provide coverage for particular types of supervisors (e.g., police and fire alone).[10] Coverage has major consequences for the extent of organization in a state. States with broad coverage feature high union density in both state (60 percent) and local (65 percent) government (see Table 1). This likely translates into union power and a strong union culture in the public sector. Our study explores more-specific impacts within New Jersey state government.

TABLE 1

Public Sector Union Density

Type of Supervisor Coverage	No. of States in Category	Average % of Local Government Employees Unionized	Average % of State Government Employees Unionized
Representation rights for supervisors above first level	11	65	60
Mixed practices or rights for first-level supervisors only	16	50	37
Representation rights for some public sector workers, but not supervisors	8	47	32
New Jersey		71	64

Source: Union density estimates are from CPS 1994–96 data; they are contained in AFL-CIO, Public Employee Department (1997); for information on state laws, see Bureau of National Affairs, *Labor Relations Reporter: State Labor Laws*, various issues. Given well-known problems with the CPS union-membership question, these estimates are biased toward zero.

Research Methods

To explore the impact of supervisory unionism, we conducted interviews regarding what problems had been observed with the operation of this system, either on the managerial or union side. Those interviewed worked in two contexts in state government, the first being a Trenton-based department with a regulatory mission employing many professionals, technical experts, and clericals. The second context covered state institutions for the developmentally disabled, mental patients, and troubled juveniles. The first situation involved a local that represented all employees; the second involved two different unions, one representing supervisory and the other nonsupervisory employees.

The positions of the interview subjects are listed in the appendix. They include union representatives from the major unions representing state employees, outside of education and uniformed services: CWA and AFSCME. Some of the union representatives also had experience in, or responsibility for, local government. For the employer, we interviewed labor relations and human resource managers as well as several nonrepresented line managers, ranging from low-level section chiefs to high-level assistant commissioners (some of whom were civil service workers and some essentially political appointees). Our questions focused on identifying actual or potential conflicts of interests or other problems that arise with the unionization of supervisors. We probed the managers about each of several specific types of conflicts. Because of the paucity of formal labor-management cooperation in the state in both the public and private sector (for the private sector, see Keefe, Eaton, and Begin 1989; Eaton and Keefe 1996), we were restricted for the most part to asking interview subjects about informal and occasional union-management cooperation efforts rather than large formal programs or full-scale restructuring initiatives. Managers had a great deal to say about such efforts but could only speculate about the possible functioning of greater cooperation initiatives in the context of organized supervisors.

Findings

Issues for Management

"Managerial" Decisions: Expenditures, Policy, and Mission. We asked public sector managers about possible conflicts of interest around both mundane "managerial" decisions like purchasing and core decisions about policy and mission.[11] In general, questions about union influence on these matters tended to be greeted with incomprehension or humor for two reasons. One is because the authority of managers (represented or not) in state government is quite seriously circumscribed, and the other is because most public sector workers who are represented by unions are not particularly motivated by pro-union ideology on a day-to-day basis.[12]

Likewise, in the implementation of policy—such as the application of a particular piece of regulation—respondents were all sure that favoritism was a nonexistent issue. Instead, according to one manager, lower-level managers are sometimes pressured in the application of regulations by legislators. In such a case, union representation actually helps buffer these managers from pressure and protects them from political considerations in their decision making.

Work Stoppages. The clearest set of problems for management occurred around work stoppages and the provision of minimally necessary public services. Strikes are essentially illegal in the New Jersey public sector,[13] but they nonetheless occur occasionally. When supervisors are represented, there are fewer nonunion personnel to deliver services during a work stoppage. Yet only a minority of the nonrepresented managers viewed a potential walkout that included supervisors as problematic. The biggest concerns arose in the state institutions where operations are "24-7" and patient care cannot be discontinued. Trenton-based department managers were, in general, less concerned, although one manager who worked in state government during the last actual work stoppage (in 1979) viewed the resulting situation as an important downside to supervisory representation.

A majority of state managers said that occasional union job actions were not a big problem because they are rare, known about in advance, and typically very short. Furthermore, they said that nonsupervisory personnel (e.g., computer professionals) were often just as necessary for emergency operation as supervisors. Moreover, systems of accommodation under which unionized supervisors sometimes cross other employees' picket lines seem to have emerged in local government to minimize the problems of providing essential services during work stoppages.[14]

Work stoppages are so rare that they should not be viewed as a reason to ban representation for supervisors. One possible way of further minimizing potential problems would be to extend interest arbitration to public sector employees who are deemed "essential." The state of Minnesota has done precisely that: only some supervisors are counted in the ranks of essential employees there. An alternative would be to extend binding interest arbitration to all public sector employees in New Jersey from its current limited use in the area of public safety.[15]

Discipline. It has been claimed that unionized supervisors are less likely to discipline subordinates, especially when those subordinates are in the same labor organization, and that this creates problems for management.[16]

Virtually everyone we spoke to recognized that this was a potential issue, but opinion was split as to whether or not it was truly a problem. Most of the line managers we interviewed claimed to have seen no evidence that unionization of supervisors in fact made supervisors more reluctant to issue discipline. They pointed to the fact that discipline does take place. As one manager put it, "People can wear two hats": supervisors can simultaneously be conscientious managers (disciplining employees when necessary) and loyal union members.

A minority (3 managers out of 12) reported that there was too little discipline in state agencies and that supervisors were very reluctant to discipline employees. One believed this was primarily a civil service problem, rather than a union problem, and advocated the elimination of civil service protections for state employees so that discipline and discharge could occur more easily. One thought that the state unions did encourage "systems of accommodation," under which routine poor performance and small problems were not dealt with until they became big problems. He believed that intervention often came too late, when the situation was quite serious. But even he acknowledged that this situation was probably as much a result of the culture of the agency as of unionization: supervisors and higher-level managers in this department came up through the ranks and remained close to their co-workers, socializing regularly and sometimes participating in the same community and interest organizations. In addition, many of these supervisors were technical experts and not professionally trained managers. Finally, under the civil service system, considerable work was required by a manager for success in the discipline process, and this made all managers, union or not, reluctant to initiate discipline. All this suggested to us that insofar as there are problems with discipline in state government, they probably are not due to supervisory unionization—only one supervisor even thought that unionization contributed to a lack of appropriate discipline.

All those we interviewed agreed that supervisors in the institutions who were represented by CWA were avid in their discipline of subordinate employees who were AFSCME members. But it was not evident that the institutions, with their much higher rates of discipline and grievances, had the "correct use" of discipline. Several interviewees regarded the institutions as having a highly hierarchical culture ("a plantation mentality") in which discipline and grievances were high because of the intense nature of the work and the close supervision that took place.

At this point we cannot say what amount of formal disciplinary activity is too low, too high, or just right for state employees. We found little evidence that represented supervisors systematically fail to initiate discipline when it is appropriate. However, if management believes that supervisors are unduly reluctant to discipline employees, it needs to take primary responsibility for developing procedures for supporting supervisors who undertake this burdensome task, whether or not the supervisor is union-represented, is part of the civil service, or is neither. Unions that represent supervisors might constructively be involved in such a management-led initiative.

Benefits from Managerial Representation. Some managers claimed that benefits to the employer from managerial representation included less turnover and better morale stemming from more-regularized and less-disruptive establishment of pay increases and greater perceived equity and predictability in treatment of the workforce. This perspective was predicated on perceived problems with the nonunion alternative: salary compression has historically been a problem for state managers in New Jersey and unionization has helped remedy that. Furthermore, some claimed that being in the union made them better supervisors, with greater knowledge of the contract and the appropriate procedures for discipline. Related to this generally positive view of supervisory unionism, most, but not all, of the managers we talked to thought the line between represented supervisors and nonrepresented managers should be drawn higher, reducing the problems of pay compression that have arisen in the state for managers who are not now represented.[17]

More recently, with the downturn in New Jersey state revenues, there have been layoffs focused on nonrepresented managers, some of whom were political appointees and some of whom were professionals caught in a system in which they lacked union protection. Had these persons been union-represented and had they had sufficient seniority, they would have had "bumping rights" into lower-level jobs in the bargaining unit for positions for which they were qualified. Given this context, the advantages of union representation for supervisors in a system in which other employees are represented become obvious to all managers. From a societal perspective, such representation (and rights in times of layoffs) is attractive insofar as it helps retain highly skilled and highly capable employees in state government who have been promoted to supervisory ranks.

Issues for Labor Organizations

Supervisors and nonsupervisors are formally in different bargaining units in the state of New Jersey, but they often find themselves in the same local union, particularly in state government. What are the resulting issues for labor organizations, and what actions have they taken to minimize possible problems? The primary issues arise with regard to grievances when one union member disciplines another. Other issues around contract negotiations and work stoppages seem to be less problematic. Nonetheless, we found that New Jersey unions had figured out ways to handle the issues that arose to the satisfaction of a majority of their members.

Discipline and Grievances against Discipline. Most grievances involve a single member and, thus, only one union representative. Some cases, however, can entangle members at different levels in the organization. A grievance against a supervisor–member, for instance, could result in discipline for the supervisor by higher-level management, if management believes that the grievance developed because of poor practices on the part of the supervisor.[18] In that situation, the union might be called on to represent the supervisor–member in its own disciplinary procedure. All the unions we talked to resolved this difficulty by assigning different staff people to represent the different members, just as they had different shop stewards in different units (so that supervisors could go to other supervisors with their concerns and nonsupervisors could go to nonsupervisors).

Yet there were still differences in the practices unions used to deal with this situation, differences that appear related to different philosophies of representation. These philosophies seem sometimes to have been developed by individuals rather than organizations. When we met with the full staff in one local, it appeared that they had not previously discussed the different approaches they were using. Unions should consider developing an organizational approach to these issues rather than leaving it up to individual staff members.

Some union staff indicated that, because any advice given might be used to discipline another union member, they told supervisors in these situations to talk to management. They felt it was not the union's job to assist in making them better supervisors. Other union staff indicated that their response would depend on the situation. If there was a good steward to support it, they would push the supervisor to engage in problem solving; if not, they would push the supervisor to "do discipline right." Despite these differences, however, employer representatives from the agency represented by this union local reported that there was a great deal of informal problem solving around disciplinary issues.

In a second CWA local in state government, a "wall" has been erected between the two union staff people involved and information is not supposed to be shared. This second local emphasizes that a grievance is against a contract violation, not against an individual manager who may or may not be a member. Nonetheless, some supervisor–members in this local still call the union for help in handling problems with subordinates.

We also found a wide variety of philosophies around these issues in other local unions, ranging from those who insist that supervisors issuing discipline do so as managers and hence should not be assisted by the union, to those who try to minimize formal discipline through member-to-member techniques designed to resolve workplace problems.[19] While the unionization of supervisors raises issues for local unions, these problems may be dealt with in a variety of fashions, the preferred "solution" reflecting the labor relations and management philosophy of the persons involved. (We regard the problem-solving approach as particularly helpful and consonant with labor-management cooperation intended to improve public service, but we respect the fact that formal discipline systems are needed to deal with some employee problems.) Whatever one's philosophy of discipline, however, it became apparent from talking to the union staff that New Jersey state supervisor–members need better training in the solution of workplace problems, personnel issues, and the discipline of subordinates.

Contract Negotiations. In New Jersey state government, there is very open and public conflict in most bargaining rounds between CWA and AFSCME, in part reflecting the different distribution of members in the two organizations (there are more supervisors in CWA). While there is some informal communication between the two unions, they sit at different tables. Different economic packages suit the memberships of the two unions better, and each attempts to reach agreement with the state first so that its settlement is imposed on the other union (under the pattern bargaining practice of the state). It is not clear whether labor organizations that represent both supervisors and nonsupervisors tend to negotiate contracts favorable to the nonsupervisory group (who are a majority of members) or to supervisors, or professionals, or both (who are often union activists).[20] The tensions within unions around economic issues at times of contract renewal are not really different for supervisors and nonsupervisors than for skilled workers and laborers, or other groups of employees with divergent economic interests. Unions can and do make compromises that resolve these tensions.

Impact on Cooperation and Restructuring Efforts

What, if any, is the role of unionization of supervisors in labor-management cooperation? Although in general there has been little in the way of formal cooperation or partnership in the public sector in New Jersey, there are some exceptions. In the judicial system, labor-management committees at both a state and work-site level were created when the state began its takeover of the county courts (U.S. DOL 1996:148). These committees helped standardize what had been widely variant human resource practices, including such basics as pay and job descriptions. Although the effort waned with a change in top management

(chief justice of the New Jersey Supreme Court), many of the committees have continued to meet.

These committees often include representatives from supervisory
and nonsupervisory units. Unionized supervisors are reported to speak
freely and to assert their interests, leading to a more realistic and honest
discussion of particular issues where their needs or views differ from
those of nonsupervisory workforce, such as on performance appraisals,
for example. One union representative explicitly contrasted the contributions to these efforts of supervisor–members to the inhibited voice of
nonrepresented managers serving on a joint health and safety committee in another state agency. That representative argued that cooperative
discourse is improved when all voices are heard and that it is important
for managers and supervisors to feel free to make comments without
inhibition. These observations provide mild support for the notion that
the representation of supervisors can improve the functioning of cooperative efforts. It is also valuable for even higher-level nonrepresented
supervisors to be involved in cooperative efforts, of course.

At the same time, it does seem likely that the unionization of supervisors could make work restructuring and the flattening of managerial
hierarchies familiar in the private sector somewhat difficult. For
instance, not long ago, the state department of personnel was considering a major effort to reduce and restructure job titles. The department
tabled this in 2001 after the passage of a bill requiring union negotiations over the creation of new titles. Such negotiations would be
extremely complicated and difficult. The fact that supervisors are represented most likely increases the complexity but it does not create it. As
with any issue, bargaining involving multiple interests is difficult but
should produce improved outcomes with wide legitimacy. In January
2002, a new governor, elected with strong labor support, took office in
the midst of a large budget shortfall. It is certainly arguable that his ability to cope with the state's budget problems is severely constrained by
the potential political consequences of laying off unionized state workers. As mentioned earlier, layoffs thus far have taken place only among
the already-thin ranks of nonrepresented managers.

Concluding Observations

In the course of this research, we interviewed many individuals knowl-
edgeable about the actual consequences of the unionization of supervisors
in New Jersey state government. Despite continuous probing, our interviews found few problems that arose in the day-to-day performance of

managers. Rather, our interviews showed that if problems arose, they did so in the highly unusual context of a work stoppage or around the nonroutine issue of discipline. With discipline, the problems encountered did not seem to be major and did not seem to be due primarily to the unionization of supervisors. Although more concerns were raised about the representation of supervisors and subordinates by the same local union than about representation per se, we cannot conclude that this has created major problems. There was broad acceptance of the idea that with appropriate accommodations by management and the union organizations involved, supervisors could both receive representation in their role as employees and continue to act on the job in a managerial capacity. People can wear two hats. People can be loyal to the mission of the agency (and act as supervisors to further that mission), while they are also union members.

At the same time, we found the matter of supervisory representation rights to be a lens that revealed a number of bigger issues for management in the public sector. It is likely these arise not only for the state of New Jersey, but also for other public employers. Pay compression was a big problem in the system we studied—a problem that had led to demand for representation by higher and higher levels of public sector managers. A related issue involved the limited ability of high-performing employees to garner continued gains in compensation over a lifetime career in state service. The primary way to create promotion opportunities for employees who have "topped out" in a given pay grade is to create jobs with a supervisory element. As a result, and consistent with other research, it seems likely that many more employees are classified as supervisory on paper than actually have much authority (see note 17 for an example). Given this reality, it is not surprising that no one we talked to wished to eliminate representation rights for supervisors: even the most anti-union thought only that such rights should not be extended further "up the ladder" or insisted that a separate union local should in fact be required as a representative for supervisors. Any move to reclassify nonbonafide supervisors would need to grapple simultaneously with the compensation issues. Such reclassification was paired with attention to the compensation issues, for example, when the state assumed responsibility for its county court systems (an effort in which labor-management committees played an important role).

Another issue that emerged in the course of interviews included problems stemming from the absence of finality in a negotiations system that is lacking either binding interest arbitration or the right to strike, and the resulting need to deal with occasional, albeit infrequent, work stoppages. It would be better to fix the underlying problem with this system for all state employees than to use the very infrequent work stoppages that result from the existing system as an excuse for denying representation rights to supervisors.

Arguably, the lack of formal union-management cooperation initiatives in this governmental system is another problem. There was no evidence that supervisory unionism was the cause of this situation. If anything, the unionization of supervisors appears to facilitate informal cooperation and problem solving in the workplace. The unions we studied assist frontline workers and their supervisors in problem solving around day-to-day issues and foster a sense of common mission. In this they resemble many "self-managed" unionized private sector workplaces. Furthermore, these public sector unions face many of the same questions about their role in managing, particularly in discipline, that private sector unions involved in managerial decision making face (Kaminski 1999; Rubinstein 2001). What is less clear is in whose interest this collaboration takes place. Formal partnering requires private sector unions involved in management to consider the interests of the business while representing the needs of members. The extent to which the collaboration made possible by broad unionization of public sector workers in New Jersey balances the public interest or is tilted toward employee interests remains an open and important question. In any case, New Jersey would appear ripe for more formal labor-management cooperation initiatives.

Workplace problems and discipline raised issues beyond the role of the unions. There were a variety of differing opinions about the appropriate use of the formal disciplinary system in resolving occasional problems with subordinate employees. Clearly, research on performance management in the public sector is highly desirable. Moreover, whatever training systems now exist for public sector supervisors in the optimal performance of their managerial roles, it seemed clear to us that state managers want additional help with these issues from their employer and from their labor organizations. Unions that represent supervisors need to think more systematically about what role they should play in assisting their members in this regard.

We find that supervisors, like the growing number of union leaders and members participating in managing their enterprises in the private sector, can wear two hats. This suggests that the fundamental theoretical approach to representation that emphasizes loyalty is conceptually inadequate. A better approach to determining who should have bargaining rights would be premised on the ability of individuals and institutions to manage multiple social roles and balance multiple conflicting interests. We hope that this study and other empirical studies of how systems in which supervisors are represented actually work can provide a fresh perspective on these issues.

Appendix:
Titles of Interview Subjects:[21]

Assistant commissioners, state agency (2)
Assistant division director, state agency
Bureau chiefs, state agency (2)
CEO, state developmental center
Director, human resources, state agency
Director, labor relations, state agency
Division directors, state agency (3)
Former chair of Public Employee Relations Committee
Former director, AFSCME Council
Local union presidents (CWA) (2)
President (and Bureau Chief), Public Sector Managers Association
Professional staff member, Office of Employee Relations, governor's office, state of New Jersey
Retired faculty, Industrial Relations and Human Resources Department, Rutgers University (2)
Union staff representative (AFSCME)
Union staff representatives (CWA) (7)

Notes

[1] The 1947 Taft-Hartley amendments to the National Labor Relations Act (NLRA) excluded supervisory employees from the protections of the Act. In 1974, the Supreme Court extended this exclusion to all managerial employees in the Bell Aerospace case (*NLRB v. Bell Aerospace*). Later Supreme Court decisions further enlarged the excluded groups by defining private sector professors making curriculum and other policy decisions as managers (*NLRB v. Yeshiva University* 1980) and nurses "directing less skilled employees" as supervisors (*NLRB v. Health Care and Retirement Corp.* 1994; *NLRB v. Kentucky River Community Care* 2001).

[2] For instance, under the logic of the *Yeshiva* case, workers could lose representation rights as restructuring and self-management accords them more decision-making authority (Germana 1991:421–22).

[3] The research design left open the question of causation: it is likely that lieutenants who were more alienated from management sought union representation in the first place.

[4] There were also few reported problems with union representation for lieutenants. There were, however, negative correlations between the assessments of performance by chiefs and union status for line officers above the rank of captain. The largest negative correlations came in the categories of labor relations performance, rather than more general managerial performance. The same questions in the officer

data, which the authors argued for various methodological reasons were likely to be more reliable, produced few significant correlations.

[5] For a thorough discussion of many of the issues, see the New Jersey Supreme Court case *Turnpike Authority v. AFSCME Council 73* 1997.

[6] This situation, which appears to contradict the legal requirement of separate organizations or units for supervisors, apparently falls within the loophole provided in the statute that allows supervisors and nonsupervisors in the same organization if "established practice, prior agreement, or special circumstances, dictate" (Section 7).

[7] In the prisons, guards are represented by the Patrolmen's Benevolent Association (PBA), with different supervisory levels in different units, whereas CWA represents clericals, professionals, and two levels of supervisors, again in different units. In the Turnpike Authority, the higher-level supervisory unit is now represented by AFSCME, and the International Federation of Professional and Technical Engineers (IFPTE) represents others.

[8] There are 567 municipalities and 21 counties in the state of New Jersey. Virtually all possible legal arrangements (and perhaps some that aren't) are present in these jurisdictions. For instance, in the capital city of Trenton, AFSCME represents both blue-collar workers and their supervisors, although in different locals. In Middlesex County, AFSCME represents blue-collar workers and their "working foremen" in the same local. Independent unions often represent supervisors in local government, including law enforcement. The Middlesex County Board of Social Services, for instance, has two bargaining units, an agencywide unit represented by CWA and a supervisory unit represented by an independent (Middlesex County Welfare Administrators Organization).

[9] Alaska, Connecticut, Florida, Hawaii, Maine, Massachusetts, Michigan, Minnesota, New York, and Washington.

[10] Rhode Island, Wisconsin, Nevada, California, Maryland, Pennsylvania, New Hampshire, Vermont, Delaware, Nebraska, Oklahoma, North Dakota, South Dakota, Missouri, Tennessee, and the District of Columbia. While we made every attempt to be inclusive, additional states may provide rights for specific groups of supervisors.

[11] These issues also arise out of the private sector record (U.S. Senate 1947:4; U.S. House 1947). In *NLRB v. Bell Aerospace* (1974:270), for instance, the employer expressed concerns over the conflicts of interest that would arise if buyers were unionized. The allegation was that a unionized purchasing agent might favor a union supplier over a nonunion supplier. Spinning out this logic, one could argue that a public agency's regulatory decisions could be influenced positively or negatively by pro-union bias of unionized supervisors, if, for instance, the company to be regulated was itself unionized.

[12] The state's system for making "large" capital expenditures (e.g., computers) is so full of checks and balances that managers have little real control over the source of purchase. Smaller purchases of supplies, like paper, are made centrally. It would be quite difficult to direct such state business improperly. Hiring of professional services is somewhat more complicated, but even here, where the possibilities are greater, the managers we interviewed cited no examples of improper, "union-biased" choices.

[13] The existence of a right to strike is contested by unionists in the state. The prohibition of strikes is not statutory but arises from the state constitution. Therefore, a public employer must go to court to get an injunction against a strike, which it can always get. Before this action is taken, however, the strike is technically not illegal, and, in fact, employers do not always seek such injunctions.

[14] One union staff person claimed that when nonsupervisory employees strike, his local determines whether or not supervisor–members need to cross picket lines to provide an emergency level of municipal services. If so, they simultaneously explain the situation to the union and employees on strike and arrange for some symbolic act of solidarity (such as picketing by a few supervisors while off-duty). If supervisors are not needed, the local encourages members to exercise their individual right of conscience to honor a picket line. This union representative claimed that this system of accommodation was widespread in local government and worked well.

[15] At the time of this writing, a bill extending interest arbitration broadly to the public sector in New Jersey has been introduced in the legislature.

[16] It should be noted that supervisors in state government, primary and higher level, are merely recommending discipline to higher-level labor relations specialists. The supervisors do build the discipline case, however, and their recommendations are often accepted.

[17] In recent years, the line between represented and nonrepresented managers has been contested repeatedly by CWA. For instance, CWA recently petitioned for and won representation rights for the lowest level of nonrepresented managers, known as section chiefs, in the Departments of Environmental Protection and Transportation. This case demonstrates an important dynamic in public sector pay systems. The section chief title was created historically in order to give higher-level professionals more pay in a compensation system in which the pay for a position strongly reflects managerial responsibility. In fact, though, the section chiefs have very little managerial authority. In the long run, this compensation strategy has backfired because since the mid-1980s managerial pay increases have systematically been lower than bargaining-unit pay increases.

[18] This situation is not all that different from other types of grievances in the private or public sector that pit one member against another, such as access to overtime or promotions. These occurrences may be uncomfortable for the union, but they are not typically debilitating.

[19] For instance, in a second CWA local, there was no wall erected when cases involved multiple members at different levels; staff members were reported to communicate, but typically in a competitive way· "They both wanted to win!" A third local union, in this case functioning in local government, handled things differently. Here there was a heavy emphasis on solving problems between or among members before they got to actual discipline. If this was not possible, and formal discipline resulted, the staff members representing the two union members would discuss the case. This local union had an emphasis on "problem solving" and contended that formal disciplinary systems were often less successful in working out problems, and improving employee performance, than its own member-to-member techniques.

[20] One person pointed out to us that this is why it is a good thing for supervisors and nonsupervisors to have the legal right to separate bargaining units—if either group became convinced its interests were not being served by the current representative, it could decertify and then gain independent representation.

[21] Most interview subjects were promised confidentiality. Thus, we have chosen to report titles with no identifying information.

References

AFL-CIO. Public Employee Department. 1997. *Public Employees Bargain for Excellence: A Compendium of State Public Sector Labor Relations Laws.* Washington, DC: AFL-CIO.

Board of Education of West Orange v. Wilton. 57 N.J. 404 (1971).

Bureau of National Affairs. Various years. *Labor Relations Reporter: State Labor Laws.* Washington, DC.

Eaton, Adrienne E., and Jeffrey Keefe. 1996. "The Incidence of Participative Programs in the Private Sector in New Jersey." Paper presented at the Industrial Relations Research Association Annual Meeting, San Francisco, January 5–7.

Germana, Ben. 1991. "Protecting Managerial Employees under the National Labor Relations Act." *Columbia Law Review,* Vol. 91, no. 2 (March), pp. 405–29.

Hayford, Stephen L. 1975. "An Empirical Investigation of the Public Sector Supervisory Bargaining Rights Issue." *Labor Law Journal,* Vol. 26, no. 10 (October), pp. 641–53.

Kaminksi, Michelle. 1999. "New Forms of Work Organization and Their Impact on the Grievance Procedure." In Adrienne E. Eaton and Jeffrey Keefe, eds., *Employment Dispute Resolution and Worker Rights in the Changing Workplace.* Madison, WI: Industrial Relations Research Association, pp. 219–46.

Keefe, Jeffrey, Adrienne E. Eaton, and James Begin. 1989. "Has Labor-Management Cooperation Come to New Jersey?" In J. R. Chelius, ed., *The Economy of New Jersey, Human Resources.* Vol. 2. Trenton, NJ: The Make New Jersey Work Roundtable, pp. 81–94.

Murrman, Kent F. 1978. "Police Supervisor Collective Bargaining Representation and Identification with Management." *Journal of Collective Negotiations in the Public Sector,* Vol. 7, no. 2, pp. 179–89.

NLRB v. Bell Aerospace Company, Division of Textron, Inc., 416 U.S. 267, 85 LRRM 2945 (1974).

NLRB v. Health Care and Retirement Corp., 146 LRRM 2321 (1994).

NLRB v. Kentucky River Community Care, 121 U.S. 1861 (2001).

NLRB v. Yeshiva University, 103 LRRM 2526 (1980).

Piskulich, J. P. 1995. "Hearts and Minds: A Case Study of Executive and Supervisor Unions in Local Government." *Journal of Collective Negotiations in the Public Sector,* Vol. 24, no. 4, pp. 271–83.

Rubinstein, Saul. 2001. "The Local Union Revisited: New Voices from the Front Lines." *Industrial Relations,* Vol. 40, no. 3 (July), pp. 405–35.

Scott, Clyde, and Anson Seers. 1987. "The Loyalty of Public Sector Supervisors: The Effects of Unionization and Administrative Authority." *Journal of Collective Negotiations in the Public Sector,* Vol. 16, no. 2, pp. 117–31.

Turnpike Authority v. AFSCME Council 73, 150 N.J. 331 (1997).

U.S. House. 1947. *Labor-Management Relations Act, 1947.* 80th Cong., 1st sess., April 11, 1947. H. Report 245: pp. 1–71.

U.S. Department of Labor. Secretary of Labor. 1996. Task Force on Excellence in State and Local Government. 1996. *Working Together for Public Service.* Washington, DC: GPO, May.

U.S. Senate. 1947. *Federal Labor Relations Act of 1947.* 80th Cong., 1st sess., April 17, 1947. S. Report 105: pp. 1–41.

Voos, Paula B., Adrienne E. Eaton, and Dale Belman. 1993. "Reforming Labor Law to Remove Barriers to High Performance Work Organizations." *Proceedings of the IRRA Spring Meetings* (Seattle, WA, April 29–May 1, 1993). Madison, WI: Industrial Relations Research Association, pp. 469–77.

Wheeler, Hoyt N. 1983. "Supervisor Unionization and the Effectiveness of Fire Departments." *Journal of Collective Negotiations in the Public Sector,* Vol. 12, no. 3, pp. 167–76.

Wheeler, Hoyt N., and Thomas A. Kochan. 1977. "Unions and Public Sector Supervisors: The Case of Firefighters." *Monthly Labor Review,* Vol. 100, no. 12 (December), pp. 44–48.

ABOUT THE CONTRIBUTORS

Robert R. Albright is associate professor at the Lally School of Management of Rensselaer Polytechnic Institute. He received his Ph.D. in human resource management and labor relations from the University of Pittsburgh's Graduate School of Business in 1994. The American Council of Education named him a Fellow for the 1999–2000 school year. Albright coauthored *The Complete Guide to Conflict Resolution in the Workplace* (AMACOM, 2002) with Marick Masters. One focus of his teaching is on strategy and organizational behavior courses given to MBA and Executive MBA participants.

Lorenzo Bordogna is professor of economic sociology at the University of Milan, Faculty of Political Science. Among his recent publications are "Italy: Articulating Tripartite National Dialogue with Company Bargaining" (In Ghellab and Vaughan-Whitehead, *Sectoral Social Dialogue in Future EU Member States*, ILO, 2003), "Decline or Transformation? Change in Industrial Conflict and Its Challenges" (*Transfer*, 2002, with G. P. Cella), and "Between the 'Black Hole' and Innovative Labor Relations and HRM Practices in Small Size Enterprises" (European IIRA Congress, 2001, with R. Pedersini).

Jonathan Brock is an associate professor at the University of Washington's Evans School of Public Affairs. He was the founding chair of the Cascade Center executive education and the Electronic Hallway case-writing program. Brock has served three U.S. secretaries of labor, most recently as executive director of Secretary Reich's Task Force on Excellence in State and Local Government Through Labor-Management Cooperation. He was prime author of the task force's consensus report, which received the Abner Award from the Society of Professionals in Dispute Resolution. Among his publications in personnel and labor relations are *Managing People in Public Agencies* and *Bargaining Beyond Impasse*.

John F. Burton, Jr. is a professor in the School of Management and Labor Relations at Rutgers University. He was president of the Industrial Relations Research Association (IRRA) in 2002 and was IRRA Editor in 1990–94. He earned a B.S. in industrial and labor relations from Cornell University and both an LL.B. and a Ph.D. in economics from the University of Michigan. He has been on the faculty at

Cornell University, the University of Chicago, and Yale University. His research interests include workers' compensation, occupational safety and health, and public sector collective bargaining.

Adrienne E. Eaton is a professor of labor studies and employment relations at Rutgers University. She earned her Ph.D. at the University of Wisconsin. Her research, which focuses on both traditional and "new" forms of labor-management relationships, has been published in the major industrial relations journals and as chapters in numerous books. Her most recent research examines neutrality and card check agreements from a variety of perspectives. She co-edited *Employment Dispute Resolution and Worker Rights in the Changing Workplace,* the 1999 Industrial Relations Research Association research volume, with Jeffrey Keefe.

Stephen Goldsmith, who was Mayor of Indianapolis from 1992 to 1999, is a professor of the practice of public management and faculty director for the Innovations in American Government Program at Harvard's John F. Kennedy School of Government. Currently, Goldsmith serves as Chair for Civic Innovation at the Manhattan Institute and as Chair of the Corporation for National and Community Service. While serving two terms as Mayor of Indianapolis, his efforts to create labor-management relationships earned him and the city's union leadership an Innovation in American Government award (in 1995).

Jeffrey H. Keefe is assistant professor of labor and employment relations at Rutgers University. His research on work reorganization, unions, labor-management relations, and advanced information technology has appeared in leading scholarly journals, such as *Industrial Relations, Industrial and Labor Relations Review,* and *Brookings Papers on Economic Activity,* as well as in numerous books. He is currently engaged in a multiyear study of work and employment relations in the telecommunications industry, which has been funded by the Sloan Foundation.

Charles Kerchner is the Hollis P. Allen Professor of Education at the Claremont Graduate University. An author of many books and articles on teacher unionization, his works include *The Changing Idea of a Teachers' Union* (Falmer Press, 1988) with Douglas Mitchell, *United Mind Workers: Unions and Teaching in the Knowledge Society* (Jossey-Bass, 1997) with Julia Koppich and Joseph Weeres, and *A Union of Professionals* (Teacher's College Press, 1993) with Koppich. He is currently researching a book on labor law for teachers.

David B. Lipsky is professor of industrial and labor relations and director of the Institute on Conflict Resolution at Cornell University.

From 1988 until 1997 he served as dean of the School of Industrial and Labor Relations at Cornell. Lipsky has published extensively on negotiation, conflict resolution, and collective bargaining and has served as a mediator, factfinder, or arbitrator in numerous public sector labor disputes. Among his publications are *Emerging Systems of Managing Workplace Conflict*, with Ronald L. Seeber and Richard D. Fincher (2003), *Negotiations and Change: From the Workplace to Society*, with Thomas A. Kochan (2003), and *The Appropriate Resolution of Corporate Disputes: A Report on the Growing Use of ADR by U.S. Corporations*, with Ronald L. Seeber (1998).

Martin H. Malin is professor of law and director of the Institute for Law and the Workplace, Chicago-Kent College of Law, Illinois Institute of Technology. He has written extensively in labor and employment law, particularly public sector labor law. He is coauthor of *Public Sector Employment* (West Group, forthcoming) and author of *Individual Rights Within the Union* (BNA, 1988). From 1984 to 1986, as a consultant to the Illinois public sector labor boards, he drafted the regulations implementing the Illinois public sector collective bargaining statutes. His honors include memberships in the Labor Law Group, National Academy of Arbitrators, and College of Labor and Employment Lawyers.

Marick F. Masters is a professor of business administration and of public and international affairs at the University of Pittsburgh, where he directs the newly formed Center on Conflict Resolution and Negotiation. He has published numerous articles and two books: *Unions at the Crossroads* (Quorum, 1997) and *The Complete Guide to Conflict Resolution in the Workplace* (AMACOM, 2002). He recently completed a comprehensive study on labor-management partnerships in the federal government for the U.S. Office of Personnel Management on behalf of former President Clinton's National Partnership Council.

Sonia Ospina is an associate professor of public management and policy and director of Management Specialization at New York University's Wagner Graduate School of Public Service. Her areas of interest are organizational and management theory; leadership in public contexts; public management reform, governance, and collaborative problem-solving both in the United States and in Latin America; diversity in public service; and human resource management. Ospina is the author of *Illusions of Opportunity: Employee Expectations and Workplace Inequality* (Cornell University Press, 1996) and of numerous articles published in academic journals and books edited in Spanish and English. She was the director of the doctoral program at the Wagner School between 1998 and 2001.

Terry Thomason was the director of the Schmidt Labor Research Center and an associate professor at the University of Rhode Island when he died at the age of 51 in April 2002. He received undergraduate and master's degrees from the University of Alabama and a Ph.D. in industrial and labor relations from Cornell University. He was a faculty member at McGill University from 1988 to 1999. His research interests included workers' compensation, collective bargaining in the private and public sectors, and health and safety. Thomason contributed several chapters to IRRA volumes and co-edited the 1998 IRRA research volume, *New Approaches to Disability in the Workplace*.

Robert M. Tobias is a professor of public administration at American University, where he heads the Institute for the Study of Public Policy Implementation. Tobias was appointed by the President and confirmed by the Senate to be a member of the Internal Revenue Service Oversight Board. For 31 years prior to his work at American University, Tobias was with the National Treasury Employees Union, where he served as president from 1983 to 1999. In that position he worked to establish collaborative labor-management relationships with the goal of creating a workplace that is more satisfying and productive and delivers better service to the public.

Paula B. Voos currently chairs the Labor Studies and Employment Relations Department at Rutgers University and is president of the Industrial Relations Research Association. Voos has published numerous research articles on the economics of collective bargaining, labor law, and the representation of supervisory employees in the public sector. She edited *Contemporary Collective Bargaining* (IRRA, 1994) and co-edited *Unions and Economic Competitiveness*, with Larry Mishel (M.E. Sharpe, 1992). In 1993–94, Voos served on the Commission on the Future of Worker Management Relations as an appointee of President Clinton.

Allon Yaroni is a doctoral candidate and an adjunct faculty member at the Robert F. Wagner Graduate School of Public Service, New York University. Yaroni specializes in urban affairs and public policy. He team-teaches public policy and microeconomics in the master's program there. Before joining the Wagner School, he served as assistant to the chief scientist (Prime Minister's Office, Israel) and held a research position at the Israel Democracy Institute. Yaroni holds a master's of philosophy degree from New York University and a master's degree in public policy and a bachelor's degree in economics and statistics from Tel-Aviv University in Israel.

Sustaining Members

Sustaining Members provide a one-time contribution of $5,000 to $10,000

AFL-CIO
The Alliance for Employee Growth and Development
Boeing Quality Through Training Program
Ford Motor Company
General Electric Foundation
National Association of Manufacturers
National Education Association
UAW-Ford National Education, Training and Development Center
United Steelworkers of America

Annual Members 2003 *

AFL-CIO
American Federation of Teachers
Carlson School of Management, University of Minnesota-
Twin Cities, Industrial Relations Center
Center for Human Resources, The Wharton School-
University of Pennsylvania
Centre for Industrial Relations-University of Toronto
Communications Workers of America
Department of Labor Studies & Industrial Relations-Penn State University
Division of Labor Studies-Indiana University
George Meany Center for Labor Studies
Institute of Labor & Industrial Relations-University of Illinois
at Urbana-Champaign
Lucent Technologies
National Education Association
New York Nurses Association
Rollins College, The Hamilton Holt School
School of Management and Labor Relations-Rutgers University
Sloan School of Management-Massachusetts Institute of Technology
Society for Human Resources Management
St. Joseph's University

Annual organizational memberships are available at the following levels:
Benefactor, *$5,000 or more- - - - - - - - 6 employee members*
Supporter, *$1,000 to $4,999 - - - - - - - 6 employee members*
Annual or Major University, *$500- - 2 employee members*
Educational or Non-Profit, *$250 - - - 2 employee members*